The Assassination of
ROBERT F. KENNEDY

WILLIAM W. TURNER
JONN G. CHRISTIAN

Random House New York

The Assassination of
ROBERT F. KENNEDY

A Searching Look at the Conspiracy and Cover-up 1968-1978

Library of Congress Cataloging in Publication Data
Christian, Jonn
The assassination of Robert F. Kennedy.
1.   Kennedy, Robert F., 1925-1968—Assassina-
tion.   I.   Turner, William W., joint author.
II.   Title.
E840.8.K4C5   364.1'524   77-90234
ISBN 0-394-40273-1

Manufactured in the United States of America
9 8 7 6 5 4 3 2
First Edition

This book is respectfully and affectionately dedicated to William W. Harper, one of the world's premier criminalists, and a man whose personal and professional sacrifices should one day be acknowledged by a grateful American public

Acknowledgments

IT WOULD TAKE A BOOK IN ITSELF TO NAME EVERYONE TO WHOM WE became indebted over the years as *The Assassination of Robert F. Kennedy* evolved from an investigative project to a finished volume. But we would especially like to thank Vincent T. Bugliosi, Robert J. Joling and Allard K. Lowenstein, eminent lawyers all, whose forensic skills and determined probing are chronicled herein. Also Jocelyn Brando, Robert Vaughn, Dianne Hull and Paul Le Mat, Hollywood citizen-actors whose moral support and encouragement were indispensable over the long haul.

The tedious task of transforming our investigative file into a manuscript was aided immeasurably by John A. "Jack" Thomas, a young man willing to open his mind and dedicate himself to the project, and English-born Lorraine Y. S. Cradock, who undertook more responsibility than most native citizens might have in turbulent times. We are also grateful to Fremont Bodine "Peter" Hitchcock, a friend whose unfortunate and premature death kept him from knowing that his contribution has borne fruit, and to the late Sara Jane Churchill De Witt, her son Jack and her daughter Mrs. Bill (Bettie) Anderson for their unlimited understanding and encouragement; and to Ms. Jackie Henken, a young woman concerned and caring enough to get involved in the most important of ways. And it would hardly be an exaggeration to say there would be no book without the commitment and forbearance of our families, who proved through often hectic phases of this project that love is indeed boundless.

Nor can a book see the light of print without a publisher, for which we are appreciative of Random House and its editorial director Jason Epstein for their vision and resolve in taking it on. We are likewise indebted to our working editor Susan Bolotin for her inexhaustible patience in nurturing it through the production process. To say that *The Assassination of Robert F. Kennedy* is not the easiest book they have been involved with is to say that the sun rises in the east, and we suspect, now that the tribulations are over, that they do care.

Contents

Introduction

AS <u>HELTER SKELTER</u> SO LUCIDLY DEPICTED THE PROSECUTION'S USE
of direct and circumstantial evidence against the Manson Family,
and *The Godfather* provided a clear window to the inside machina-
tions of organized crime, *The Assassination of Robert F. Kennedy*
stands as a unique study on the subject of contemporary political
murder in America. It might well be classified by historians as the
Helter Skelter–Godfather of assassination books.

The story at hand concerns itself with what I consider to be
the single most important issue of our time: the assassinations of
our finest leaders over the past decade and a half. The central
theme here is the conspiracy and cover-up surrounding the assassination of Senator Robert Kennedy, with evidential tributaries leading in the direction of the murders of President John F. Kennedy
and Dr. Martin Luther King, Jr., as well as the attempt on the
life of Governor George C. Wallace. The implications are staggering.

This thoroughly researched and meticulously documented book
is the end result of its authors' relentless pursuit of the actual facts
in these cases, which in my opinion has produced the most impres-
sive investigative file ever privately assembled. In effect, it is a
formidable grand jury presentation in book form. And the information presented herein surely warrants the immediate re-examination
of the entire assassination issue at the highest levels of the United
States government.

I wholly concur with the authors of this book that we, the
American public, deserve resolution of the disturbing unanswered
questions in these murders at the earliest moment, or we face the
distinct possibility that further attempts on the lives of more political

leaders could occur at any time. I'm convinced that most thinking Americans sense this too; and I'm certain that the readers of this book will soon join the swelling numbers of us demanding that justice be done, for the future of our nation is truly the responsibility of each of us.

DR. ROBERT J. JOLING

Dr. Joling is a former president of the American Academy of Forensic Sciences (1975-76); Vice President, International Association of Forensic Sciences. Member: British Academy of Forensic Sciences; the American Bar Association; Association of Trial Lawyers of America; American College of Legal Medicine; American Arbitration Association. Graduate, Juris Doctoris, Marquette University Law School, 1951. Admissions to Practice: Supreme Court of the United States; United States Tax Court; District Courts of Arizona and Wisconsin; Wisconsin Supreme Court. He is a law partner in Joling & Rizzo, Kenosha, Wisconsin.

Prologue

CALIFORNIA WAS MAKE-OR-BREAK FOR SENATOR ROBERT F. KEN-
nedy in his quest for the 1968 Democratic presidential nomination.
On May 28 he lost the Oregon primary to Senator Eugene
McCarthy, and a setback the following week in the nation's most
populous state would probably ruin his chances. On the other hand,
a victory would gain him 174 delegate votes and much-needed
momentum for the showdown at the national convention in Chicago.
It would virtually eliminate McCarthy, leaving only Hubert H.
Humphrey in his way. A symbol of the old politics with the albatross
of Lyndon Johnson's escalated war in Vietnam hanging from his
neck, the Vice President was not a good bet to withstand the tides
of renewal surging through the party. Most observers thought that
RFK would ride the tide past Humphrey and defeat the Republicans'
likely candidate, Richard M. Nixon.

Kennedy came to California for a home-stretch drive so frenetic
that on election eve he was on the brink of collapse. He had to
cancel a San Diego appearance that night, but the next morning he
was back on his feet, buoyed by a just-completed poll showing him
safely ahead of McCarthy. After a day of last-minute campaigning,
he went to the Malibu home of movie director John Frankenheimer
for a quiet supper party that included Roman Polanski and his
fated wife Sharon Tate. After supper Frankenheimer drove him to
the Ambassador Hotel, where he would watch the election returns
on television in the Royal Suite.

By midnight he was ready to claim victory. He checked himself
in a full-length mirror before leading his entourage down a service
elevator to the Embassy Room on the ground floor. The ballroom

was jammed with campaign workers and supporters, and a thunderous cheer went up as the candidate came into view. Speaking into a bundle of microphones on the small stage, he gave a brief speech. "Mayor Yorty has just sent me a message that we have been here too long already," he cracked, drawing laughs from the audience (Sam Yorty was a right-wing Democrat who had supported Nixon against RFK's brother in the 1960 election). RFK wound up by flashing the V sign and exhorting, "On to Chicago! Let's win there!"

Kennedy intended to meet with the press in their headquarters in the adjacent Colonial Room. Ordinarily, he would have crossed the ballroom floor and exited through the main door, but the crush of people was so great that a last-minute decision was made to route him through a service pantry. A maître d' gripped his right wrist tightly and led him through the gold curtain behind the stage and into the pantry. His progress was slow as he greeted admiring kitchen workers.

Suddenly a gunman sprang at him, snarling, "Kennedy, you son of a bitch!" He fired two rapid shots. Kennedy reeled backwards, flinging his right arm in front of his face for protection. People grabbed for the gunman.

Kennedy landed on his back, his arms splayed outward as in a crucifixion, a halo of blood widening around his head. Within inches of his right hand was a clip-on bow tie he had apparently snatched from someone close-by as he sagged from the impact of three bullets in his body and head.

Up in San Francisco we—the authors of this book—were stunned by the news. William Turner had run for the U.S. Congress in the same Democratic primary, with Jonn Christian as his campaign manager. As the chief plank in our platform we had advocated the establishment of a joint Senate-House committee to reinvestigate the 1963 assassination of President John F. Kennedy. Now the final line of our campaign brochure seemed horrifyingly prescient: "To do less not only is indecent but might cost us the life of a future President of John Kennedy's instincts."

Robert Kennedy died slightly more than a day later. When the plane carrying his body back to New York landed at Kennedy International Airport, NBC television correspondent Sander Vanocur, who had covered the RFK campaign, came down the ramp to face his own network's cameras. Forcing back tears, he reported that during the flight Edward Kennedy had remonstrated bitterly about the "faceless men" who had been charged with the slayings of his brothers and Dr. Martin Luther King, Jr. First Lee Harvey Oswald, then James Earl Ray, and now Sirhan Sirhan. Always faceless men with no apparent motive. "There has to be more to it," Ted Kennedy had told Vanocur.

But Ted Kennedy's words, uttered in a private moment and never to be repeated by him in public, were lost in the rush as the campaign instantly went into reverse. What had begun as a great national groundswell of revulsion against the war, so strong that it swept an incumbent President out of the running, became a nightmare of reaction and irrelevancy. There were pious outcries in Congress for tougher gun laws, breast-beating in the media about how America's violent society had spawned another deranged assassin, and demands for a law-and-order crackdown.

It was almost anticlimactic when Hubert Humphrey finagled the Democratic nomination at the violence-wracked convention and tried to pull the shattered party together. He was no match for Richard Nixon, who cynically called himself the "peace with honor" candidate and boasted of a "secret plan" for ending the conflict (which would drag on for four more years). So the nation had another "accidental President" catapulted to power by a "lone nut" assassin.

The conclusion that Sirhan Sirhan had acted alone and unaided was duly arrived at by the Los Angeles Police Department, which had primary investigative jurisdiction. The FBI, which conducted a parallel inquiry under the civil rights laws, concurred. And most of the American people accepted the theory, since the case seemed as open and shut as the shooting of Oswald by Jack Ruby in front of millions of television viewers.

Committed though we were to reopening the John Kennedy case, we did not immediately dispute the official verdict. We had no way of knowing, in the days that followed RFK's death, what we were later to learn about the case.

Scarcely a month after the assassination, through a curious set of circumstances, we came upon a self-ordained evangelist who told about a chance encounter with Sirhan the day before the shooting.

It was a bizarre story, and it set us off on our own investigation that has continued to this day. What we discovered led us to disbelieve the preacher's story, then search for what was behind it. For he in fact had told it not merely to us but to the Los Angeles police, filing his report only hours after the shooting.

Our efforts came to a climax in the summer of 1975 when a little-noticed trial shed stark new light on a crime that altered the course of American history.

The Assassination of
ROBERT F.
KENNEDY

1

The Evangelist and the Cowboy

IT HAD BEGUN AS A SOMEWHAT ROUTINE CIVIL TRIAL, ONE OF hundreds each year in Los Angeles Superior Court that drone on to uneventful verdicts. It opened on July 2, 1975, in Department 32, Judge Jack A. Crickard presiding. The plaintiff was Jerry Owen, a hallelujah evangelist who bills himself as "The Walking Bible" because of a professed ability to quote all 31,173 verses of the Holy Book, punctuation marks and all.

The primary defendant was television station KCOP, an independent channel in the City of Angels. In 1969 Jerry Owen had contracted with KCOP for air time each Sunday for a year for a religious program called *The Walking Bible,* but after three broadcasts the station abruptly canceled the program. In 1970, after months of bitter wrangling, Owen filed a breach-of-contract and defamation-of-character suit against KCOP seeking $1.4 million in damages. In response to an interrogatory question posed in 1974, Owen stated that he had been libelously accused by then-president of KCOP John Hopkins of being "a thief, burned down six churches, was a convict, undesirable, a crook, a fraud, etc., [a] no good, sent to prison for arson, and not a minister of the Gospel, was involved in [Senator Robert F.] Kennedy's death."*

A secondary defendant was Ohrbach's department store, a fixture on the Wilshire Boulevard "Miracle Mile." On June 17, 1969, in the midst of his short-lived television series, Owen was arrested in the store for shoplifting three shirts. He was convicted and fined $250, but when the City Attorney's office unaccountably failed to contest his appeal, the conviction was vacated. Owen assumed that the "thief" in Hopkins' purported statement referred to the shoplifting incident.

In preparing for the trial, the defense team had assembled a hefty background file on the plaintiff. He was born Oliver Brindley Owen on April 13, 1913, in Ashland, Ohio, the son of a Baptist minister who subsequently migrated to California. In his youth Owen took to the boxing ring, and by the early 1930s was a sparring partner—"a punching bag," as he puts it—for Max Baer, who became heavyweight champion in 1934. The amiable behemoth paid Owen $100 a week and took him around the country. "If not for him, I'd be pickin' cotton in Bakersfield," Owen once wisecracked to a reporter. Baer gave his protégé a diamond initial ring with an inscription inside: "To Curly from Max Baer."†

During this period "Curly" Owen was a Hollywood fringe character, playing bit roles in such movies as Mae West's *Diamond Lil* and *Prison Cell Break* with George Raft. He enjoyed rubbing elbows with celebrities, and according to several persons who knew

---

* Defendant's Exhibit #132, filed for identification in Los Angeles County Superior Court on October 10, 1974. (In another interrogatory, Owen's handwritten responses read that he had been falsely accused of being "a T shirt steeler [*sic*], a theif [*sic*], [a] church burnner [*sic*], Hypocrite and Impostor, Involved with assination [*sic*] of Kennedy.")

† Ely (Nevada) *Times* (April 26, 1974).

him, dropped names like Humphrey Bogart, Loretta Young and Bob Hope.* After Baer lost his crown to Jimmy Braddock in 1935, Owen enrolled at the University of Southern California to play freshman football.

But his budding gridiron career ended in 1937 when, in a flash of inspiration, he became "acquainted with a man named Jesus." As his own promotional brochure described it, Owen "found a prayer room by a little church, and for the next seven days he didn't leave this little room, but read the Bible through from Genesis to Revelation, without eating, drinking or shaving. It was as though he were spellbound by the majesty of the scriptures as they opened up to him for the first time in his life! He read-read-read until sleep blurred his vision. He did not speak to anyone, but just read the Bible through." Miraculously, Owen found that he had total recall of the Bible and "the verses tumbled out for him to read to the people." Ordaining himself, he embarked on an evangelistic career.

Soon thereafter, Owen's name began appearing on police blotters from coast to coast. In 1939 he was hauled into court in San Francisco to answer grand-theft charges brought by an elderly member of his congregation who complained he had bilked her out of $2,700. "He told me that God had directed him to come to me in his hour of need," she testified. "I gave him the money. He said, 'This is between the Almighty God and you and me. Above all, don't tell your husband.'" As a newspaper account described the scene: "The packed courtroom was sympathetic when the Rev. Mr. Owen's 20-year-old wife, Beverly, nearing motherhood, cried and was led from the courtroom. But at other times in the hearing some of the spectators were openly hostile to the evangelist. Those, he proclaimed, were former sheep who had been turned against him by rival preachers jealous of the growth of his Gospel Center."†

On February 17, 1945, Owen was arrested by the Portland, Oregon, police vice squad in a downtown hotel and charged with "disorderly conduct involving morals." Said Owen of the woman in the case: "She has been just like a sister to me. She's a good kid and has gotten off on the wrong foot. When I got off the train she

* In his "Walking Bible" brochure—sent on request to KCOP viewers— Owen features himself in a publicity photo with Baer and Hope.

† San Francisco *Examiner* (May 17, 1939).

told me she was in trouble and wanted me to go to her hotel room and wait until her boyfriend could come so I could talk it over with them."

"You don't expect us to believe that, do you?" the judge rejoined, leveling a sentence of a $50 fine and thirty days in jail (Owen posted an appeal bond and the case was continued indefinitely). Again he blamed his predicament on rival preachers out to defame him.*

In 1945 a Los Angeles woman filed a complaint seeking support of a minor child and to establish that he was the father, but it was never brought to trial.† In 1947 a girl whom he had met four years earlier when he ran his "Open Door Church" in Des Moines, Iowa, followed suit. According to a police report, "The child was born in November, 1947, and Owen forwarded $420 for hospital expenses. [The girl] later received word that Owen . . . would not be able to marry her."‡

A glimpse of the flamboyant preacher in action was given in a Terre Haute newspaper when he pitched his tent in Indiana in 1948. As two thousand people packed the tent and spotlights bathed the platform, "A big man, well over six feet, tall and of athletic build, wearing a sporty-looking gray suit, a rather flashy four-in-hand tie and bareheaded (his curly hair was cut rather short) appeared at the side of the platform. An excited hum swept the tent. 'That's him . . . that's Jerry Owen,' those who knew him whispered to those who had come for the first time." As ushers hawked programs for fifty cents, Owen bounded onto the platform and began an intimate monologue with the sky: " 'Bless these good people, Dear Jee-sus, and return their offering two-fold in your blessing. Oh, here's a sweet little girl. I bet she's got a great big kiss for old Jerry. Why don't some of you older girls come on down with your $10 and give the preacher man a kiss?' "

As the reporter described the event, Owen shouted, " 'Well, let's get going. The spirit is on me tonight.' " He did a jitterbug

* Portland *Oregonian* (February 18, 1945).

† Los Angeles Superior Court Docket No. D282986, May 29, 1945.

‡ Notarized Los Angeles police report obtained from Los Angeles County Clerk's office, July 7, 1969.

and grabbed the microphone to reel off Bible verses. "Text after text would be shouted, screamed at the audience," the reporter marveled. "The man was wearing himself into a hysterical frenzy that communicated itself to the audience." After scoring the evils of alcohol and tobacco, the preacher told of a faith healing he had accomplished. "Save me Jerry, save me Jerry!" Owen quoted a man on the brink of death as imploring. "I don't want to die!" Owen held his hand and prayed with him for five hours, and the crisis passed. "Isn't he wonderful!" the newspaper reporter overheard an elderly woman say as she daubed at her eyes. "I'll be back again tomorrow."*

In March 1950 Owen got into another scrape with his pray-for-pay competition while holding revival meetings in a Baltimore theater. With a contingent of followers he broke up a service being conducted across town by one Reverend C. Stanley Cook because of "a misstatement made by Brother Cook about me and another man's wife." Owen was convicted of disorderly conduct and fined $55. The newspapers had a field day quoting Max Baer, who happened to be visiting Baltimore, as being surprised that his erstwhile ring mate had turned to preaching. "The first time I heard you quoting from the Bible," Baer twitted Owen in front of reporters, "I couldn't believe it. I didn't think you could memorize 'The Village Blacksmith'—you'd leave him standing under the tree."†

Scarcely two months later the Indianapolis *News* headlined: EVANGELIST FACES CHARGES OF "SEX AND SALVATION" TOUR. The local prosecutor had filed charges against Owen for taking a sixteen-year-old delinquent schoolgirl on a six-state junket, helping her assume aliases to escape authorities and being intimate with her on at least two occasions. However, the federal authorities declined to prosecute under the White Slave Traffic Act because there had been no commercialization, and the state charges were dropped when the girl changed her mind and refused to testify. The girl, an accomplished pianist, disclosed that Owen had her play hymns "in a different manner" at the church services he conducted so that the

* Terre Haute *Standard* (August 15, 1948).
† Baltimore *Sun* (March 8, 1950).

emotions of the worshipers would be aroused. "I believe he was very sincere in his religion and believed in what he preached," she said, "because he wouldn't let me drink or smoke."*

Smoke? Owen's rap sheet under FBI Number 4 261 906 revealed that on March 22, 1964, a warrant was issued in Tucson, Arizona, charging him with "Arson in the first degree with intent to defraud Insurer and Conspiracy" in connection with the 1962 burning of his church building. Although Owen alibied that he was out of town at the time, a witness at his trial, Samuel Butler, testified that the preacher had offered him $1,000 to torch the church. Owen was convicted of arson conspiracy and sentenced to eight to nineteen years in prison, but the conviction was reversed on June 27, 1966, after Butler recanted his testimony in a death-bed statement.

The Tucson church was not the first of Owen's premises to go up in smoke. Los Angeles police records list similar incidents in Castro Valley, California, in 1939; Crystal Lake Park, Oregon, in 1945; Dallas, Texas, in 1946; Mount Washington, Kentucky, in 1947; and Ellicott City, Maryland, in 1951. Owen collected insurance settlements in several of the fires, but in the Maryland blaze his $16,000 claim was rejected because of alleged fraud. "A witness observed Owen moving personal effects out of the house prior to the fire and then return them," the police records state. But the persistent preacher appealed and was eventually awarded $6,500.

BY 1968 OWEN WAS LIVING IN SANTA ANA, THIRTY MILES SOUTH of Los Angeles in Orange County. He styled himself the "Shepherd of the Hills," and circulated around shopping centers giving free pony rides to children who promised to memorize a Bible verse and attend church on Sunday. He traded horses on the side. And he owned a piece of a club fighter named "Irish Rip" O'Reilly.

It was the horses and the boxing game, Owen testified in the KCOP trial, that brought about his chance association with Sirhan Sirhan. On the afternoon of June 3, 1968, the eve of the California primary election, he said that he was driving his pickup truck

---

* Indianapolis *News* (May 18, 1950).

through downtown Los Angeles on his way to purchase some boxing gear for O'Reilly. At a red light he let two hitchhikers climb into the back of the truck. After a dozen or so blocks they got off at another red light and appeared to converse with a man and woman standing on the corner. As Owen got ready to pull away, one of the hitchhikers got in the cab with him and struck up a conversation. Owen described him as a diminutive young man of foreign extraction who remarked that he worked as an exercise boy at a race track. When Owen mentioned that he traded horses as a sideline to his ministry, the young man said that he was in the market for a lead pony (used to walk horses around the track before and after races). After some haggling, he agreed to buy a palomino from Owen for $300.

The young man asked Owen to stop for a few minutes at the rear entrance to the Ambassador Hotel so that he could run in and "see a friend in the kitchen." Owen obliged. When he returned, the young man told Owen that he would meet him that night with the money for the horse. But at the appointed time and place the young man, accompanied by the same two men and the woman he had been seen with that afternoon, said he hadn't been able to raise all of the money. He produced a single $100 bill. The upshot of this intricate story was that Owen was asked to deliver the horse to the same rear entrance to the hotel the following night at eleven, at which time the full amount would be paid. But Owen couldn't make it because he was due to preach a sermon in Oxnard, seventy miles northwest of Los Angeles.

When Owen returned to Los Angeles on the morning after the election, he recognized Sirhan's picture on television as the hitchhiker who was going to buy his horse. At the urging of some friends he went straight to the police and told his story "like a good citizen." He felt that he nearly had been duped into becoming part of a bizarre getaway scheme after Kennedy was shot at the Ambassador Hotel the previous night.

For the first thirteen days of the trial the question of Owen's strange story about picking up Sirhan had been muted as the plaintiff's lawyers completed their case and the defense began its preliminary arguments.

Then, on July 29, KCOP trial attorney Vincent T. Bugliosi

stood and prepared to call his star witness. In 1970 Bugliosi had gained fame as the chief prosecutor of Charles Manson and his killer cult. Leaving the District Attorney's office a year later, he entered private practice and wrote *Helter Skelter*, a best-selling account of the Manson case. Trim and fastidious, the forty-one-year-old Bugliosi was wearing the midnight-blue pin-striped suit and vest with red tie that had become his trademark during the Manson Family trial, one of the longest and most intricate in the annals of American jurisprudence.

The brilliant criminal lawyer had (as we shall see) been summoned to enter the trial at virtually "one minute to midnight."

Bugliosi hooked a thumb to his vest. "The defense calls Mr. Bill Powers," he sang out.

A lanky cowboy strode to the witness stand. Jerry Owen thrust his head forward from powerful shoulders and glared at the surprise witness.

When Owen told his story, he apparently had no inkling that Bill Powers would appear for the defense. In fact, Bugliosi had located the cowboy only two days before, and it was not until the last minute that he had been able to persuade him to testify. What he had to say clashed head-on with Owen's account of the chance encounter with Sirhan.

William Lee Powers was a cowboy straight out of the Marlboro ads, raw-boned with a weather-beaten face cross-hatched with scars from endless wrangles with wild mustangs and sharp-horned steers. He spoke in the drawling, idiom-laced argot of the range. By 1968 he had settled down to running Wild Bill's Stables on the banks of the Santa Ana River in Santa Ana. "I had horses for hire, I boarded horses, and also trained horses and gave riding lessons," he testified after being sworn in.

Yes, he knew Jerry Owen back then, he said. Owen had a place "three or four blocks down the river," and used to come by Wild Bill's Stables quite often. "Did you have many conversations with this Reverend Owen?" Bugliosi asked.

A. Numerous conversations. He come around periodically. I kept some horses for him before. One time I boarded some ponies for him and then I had two horses in there that he wanted broke.

Q. During these conversations you had with him, did he ever talk about his political philosophy?

A. Yes, he talked about—

The answer was cut off by one of Owen's attorneys, Arthur Evry, who leaped to his feet and shouted, "Your Honor! I will object! What is the relevancy of his political philosophy in this action for slander?"

"We are trying to show this man has a possible involvement in the assassination of Senator Kennedy," Bugliosi replied. "If that doesn't have relevancy, I don't know what has!"

Owen alleged in his complaint that he had been libeled and slandered by KCOP officials when they allegedly claimed that he had been involved in the RFK assassination.

Bugliosi was asserting a defense to the charge of libel and slander—that the statements were in fact true. Judge Crickard, however, seemed dumfounded at this sudden escalation of the trial from alleged civil wrongs to the murder of a presidential candidate. Before he could recover, Bugliosi continued on the offensive, "Let's assume for the sake of argument, your Honor, that this Jerry Owen was a right-wing reactionary type, who had a dislike for Senator Kennedy. Is counsel saying this wouldn't have any relevancy to this case?"

"I imagine you could find 15,000,000 people who might fit that same bill," Evry argued. "I don't think that in itself has any relevance to this case."

Bugliosi thought differently. "Mr. Owen, your Honor, by the pleadings, has said that the allegation he was 'involved' in the assassination of Senator Kennedy was untruthful. We are trying to show Owen's background—and counsel is objecting!"

Evry responded that he was only objecting to questions about Owen's "political beliefs and political motives," in effect saying that the question of motive did not bear on the crime. And the judge sustained him. Actually, a hint as to Owen's political leanings was already in the trial record: in his testimony earlier Owen had pedantically commented that "we have to be on the lookout for communists that want all religious programs off television and radio."

Bugliosi turned back to his witness and asked, "Did Mr. Owen ever mention President Kennedy or Senator Kennedy?" Evry objected again, but Crickard overruled him. Powers replied that Owen had in fact talked about the Kennedys at different times. But when Bugliosi asked, "What did he say?," it was Crickard who cut in, questioning the relevancy. Bugliosi argued that he was trying to establish the origins of Owen's involvement in the assassination. "It's not relevant," the judge ruled. "I am sure there are millions of people who talked about the Kennedys and still do, and about the government of the United States. It doesn't seem pertinent to this lawsuit."

It was difficult for Bugliosi to understand why Owen's frame of mind about the Kennedys was not pertinent. Shaking his head in frustration, he walked slowly back to his place at the far end of the counsel table and flipped through some papers. Now he would have to go straight to the point.

"DID YOU EVER HEAR JERRY OWEN USE THE NAME SIRHAN?" Bugliosi asked Powers.

Yes, Powers replied. He had employed a stablehand named Johnny Beckley who was breaking in horses belonging to Owen. "Well, he didn't like the way Johnny was handling the horses and was cowboying around," Powers recounted, "and he said he had other people at the [race] track and stuff that could handle horses in the right manner, and the name Sirhan was mentioned."

Q. By whom?
A. By Mr. Owen.
Q. Are you positive about this? [Bugliosi asked.]
A. I am *very* positive.

How could he be so certain? "Well, because it was an unusual name," Powers replied, "and then shortly after the assassination I heard Sirhan's name again. And Mr. Sirhan was a horseman, too, and that's why I remember."

The preacher and his lawyers stirred in their chairs. Owen's contention that the first time he had met Sirhan before the assassination, entirely by chance, had just been rebutted by a witness testifying under oath in a court of law. This would be the first in a series of dramatic breakthroughs in the case.

Powers testified that Owen began coming to the stables between sixty and ninety days before the assassination. Then, in the month of May, Powers sold Owen a 1951 Chevrolet pickup truck for approximately $350. But the preacher put down only about $50 and never did pay the balance. One afternoon "a very short time" before the assassination—it might have been election eve—Owen rolled up to the stables in a late-model Lincoln Continental and said he'd pay what he owed on the truck. The preacher offered him a $1,000 bill, but Powers didn't have the $700 change. The cowboy was duly impressed, testifying in answer to Bugliosi's question, that in the past, Owen "kind of never had any money" and sometimes had to borrow bales of hay to feed his horses. All at once he was flashing a roll consisting of what Powers estimated to be between twenty-five and thirty $1,000 bills and driving an expensive car in place of his battered family station wagon or the old pickup he had bought from Powers.

Q. Then I take it that it wasn't one of these "Montana bankrolls" with one $1,000 bill on top and one-dollar bills below?
A. No. Being in the horse business, that is what I carry. No, it wasn't one of those.
Q. It is your testimony, then, that there were many $1,000 bills?
A. There was a lot of serious money there, yes.

Powers recalled that there were two other men in the Lincoln that day. In the front passenger seat was "a large colored man" who talked about his days as a boxer. And in the rear was a dark-complexioned young man whom Powers believed he had seen before "in the backyard" of Owen's home. "He was a slender, small person," he said.

Sirhan Sirhan is approximately five feet four inches, 140 pounds, of slender build, with dark complexion. Bugliosi produced an official photograph of Sirhan Sirhan, entered it as an exhibit and displayed it to Powers.

Q. The gentleman seated in the back seat of Owen's Lincoln, did he resemble this man?

A. There is a resemblance, yes. I am not going to say this is him, but there is a likely resemblance, yes.

Q. When you say "a likely resemblance," are you talking about the face or physique, or both?

A. Just overall.

Bugliosi was satisfied with the answer, since an unqualified identification of a person seen only fleetingly would indicate a witness too eager to please.

Q. At the time of this $1,000 incident, was anyone with you?

A. Johnny Beckley and a man by the name of Jack Brundage.

Powers had told Bugliosi, when they conferred prior to the court session, that Beckley, Brundage and a third stablehand, named Denny Jackson, were present when Owen drove up in the Lincoln. Brundage had repaired a taillight on the old pickup for Owen a day or so before. According to Powers, after the assassination all three were fairly certain that it was Sirhan in the back seat. In fact, Beckley was absolutely sure: he even mentioned that he had seen Owen and Sirhan riding horseback together on the levees of the Santa Ana River in the weeks before the assassination. Powers had lost track of Brundage and Jackson,* but he was still in touch with Beckley, who was living in Los Alamitos. The previous day, at Bugliosi's urging, he had phoned his former stablehand to ask him to consider testifying. Instead Beckley left town. "This ain't like Johnny to run off," Powers told Bugliosi. "Maybe he knows more'n he ever told me."†

The plaintiff's lawyers were repeatedly objecting that Powers' testimony was not relevant. In overcoming one such objection,

---

* A year after the trial, Powers located Denny Jackson and arranged for author Christian to talk to him. Jackson confirmed the Sirhan sighting in Owen's Lincoln. "Yeah, I saw that roll of thousand-dollar bills and those strangers in that Lincoln that day," he acknowledged. "I thought it looked kind of funny, him with all that money, fannin' it out like that, showin' off."

† Powers located Beckley three months later—in the most rural part of Missouri. The ex-cowhand said he feared for his life.

Bugliosi argued, "Well, your Honor, we are alleging, in defense, that Mr. Owen possibly was involved in the assassination of Senator Kennedy. Now, if just prior to the assassination he was walking around with $30,000 and he was not the gunman, I don't see how the court can say that is not relevant. We have an eyewitness testifying that this man had about $30,000 on his person and he never had been seen with large amounts of money before. Right before the assassination he is with someone who looks like Sirhan and he is carrying $25,000 or $30,000. It couldn't possibly be more relevant circumstantial evidence."

After some parrying back and forth, Crickard allowed Bugliosi to "go directly to that particular incident." The attorney asked Powers about Owen's late-model Lincoln again, making certain that the record reflected Owen's sudden and unexplained wealth at a crucial time. Then he elicited a more thorough description of the young man in the back seat of the Lincoln. Powers said that he was a "Spanish-type fellow . . . I would say in his twenties, early twenties." Nationality? "Well, I wouldn't think he was American." Did he speak with an accent? "I don't remember that."*

When Evry objected again, the judge sustained him. With that, Bugliosi had to give up his attempt to draw a clear picture of Sirhan in the back seat of Owen's Lincoln on or just before June 3, 1968. And when he tried to get a fuller description of the roll of bills, Crickard himself interrupted, saying, "We have to get to something that bears on this case."

Bugliosi looked exasperated. "Well, we are talking about some things that are pretty important, your Honor, not just to this lawsuit, but to Senator Kennedy's assassination."

"They have to be relevant to this lawsuit or this isn't the place to take them up," Crickard retorted, invoking the undue consumption of time rule. When Bugliosi asked to be heard on the point, the judge curtly responded, "Let's go on to the next point."

But Bugliosi persisted, trying to break out of Crickard's confinement of the issues. He suggested that there was a link between Owen's carrying a large roll of $1,000 bills and the assassination,

---

* A native of Palestine, Sirhan was often mistaken for a Mexican. He spoke English without an accent.

one that would become clearer when tied in with other areas of testimony. "There is no foundational proof for it," Crickard countered. Bugliosi said that he intended to bridge the testimonial gap. "Well, the tie-in will be when I call Mr. Owen back to the witness stand and I ask him where he got the money. Conspiracies are not hatched down in Pershing Square with a megaphone.* These conspiracies are hatched in the shadows. The court is demanding that I put on evidence, either a tape-recorded conversation or a film, showing Mr. Owen saying, 'Let's get Kennedy!' Anything short of this apparently is not admissible in this courtroom."

Crickard seemed irritated and embarrassed. "You are setting up your own standards that are different than the court's," he remonstrated. He repeated his criteria of relevancy and foundational proof.

Bugliosi kept up the challenge: "I can just say in deference to the court, that I personally have handled many murder cases, your Honor, and I am not walking into this courtroom having just been sworn in across the street by the State Bar. I have never in all my experience as a trial lawyer, in handling criminal cases, been told by any court—or seen any opinion by any appellate court—that for someone who allegedly is involved in a murder, his having large sums of money in his possession around the time of the murder has no legal relevance."

Crickard insisted that there had to be an evidentiary tie-in between the money and the other events. "Just the fact that they can exist separately for a million other causes is just as possible, and we don't have the time to go down the million other causes," he said.

It annoyed Bugliosi that the judge was providing an argument for the other side. "We are not 'going down' a million other causes," he protested. "Now, if Mr. Owen wants to get on the witness stand and testify that he got this $30,000 through the stock market, swell; but I think we have the right to put this evidence on. As the world knows, Sirhan was at the assassination scene. The question is: was anyone behind him?"

---

* Pershing Square is the Los Angeles counterpart to London's Hyde Park where "soap-box orators" hold forth.

Evry and his client whispered at their table as Bugliosi continued, "We have someone who is close to Sirhan with a large sum of money. If he can explain how he got that money, fine. But to preclude us from showing that Owen had $30,000, while *with* Sirhan, right before the assassination, on the grounds it is not relevant—the only thing I can say is—what do we have to put on in this court to show it has relevance?"

Evry stood up to offer a concession. "We will offer a stipulation to the fact that Mr. Owen had $30,000. Apparently he is trying to confirm that the plaintiff in this case was, during 1968, raising very substantial sums of money. I am willing to stipulate to that extent." Evry said that he was making the offer to "save a good deal of the court's time."

What Bugliosi did not know (he had just been brought into the case) was that in a deposition taken some time before, Owen had declared that in 1968 he "lived off my wife's tax-free inheritance," having earned only $1,000 from a three-week preaching engagement. But Bugliosi sensed that Evry's concession was no more than a ploy to dispose of the sudden-wealth issue before it could be fully explored, and insisted that the stipulation include a time frame "within a couple of days prior to the assassination." Evry refused, saying Owen had the money "long before the assassination." Bugliosi declined to accept the stipulation.

Q. Have you testified to the truth on the witness stand today, sir?
A. Yes, I have. I have told it just the way it is [Powers answered].
Q. Do you have any hesitancy about your statement being examined by anyone?
A. No, I would take one of those lie detector tests if necessary. What I told is just the way it is.

As we'll see later on, Bugliosi's key witness would have further damaging testimony to offer at this unusual trial.

The judge declared a recess. Owen's lawyers huddled to assess the sudden and dramatic turn in the course of the trial.

The following morning the story in the Los Angeles *Times* was headed: BUGLIOSI CLAIMS CONSPIRACY IN ROBERT KENNEDY SLAYING.

"Choosing the unlikely forum of a civil slander suit," the story began, "veteran prosecutor Vincent T. Bugliosi sought this week to reopen the investigation into possible conspiracy in the June 5, 1968 assassination of Sen. Robert F. Kennedy." The account contained highlights of Powers' testimony, pointing out that it contradicted Owen's story that he had first met Sirhan hitchhiking in Los Angeles the day before the election.

AS JUDGE CRICKARD WOULD OBSERVE TOWARD THE END OF THE trial, Jonn Christian was the "proximate cause" of the Owen versus KCOP litigation. Shortly after the RFK assassination we had by chance come upon Owen's hitchhiker story and learned that Owen had recited it to the Los Angeles police nine hours after the shooting. For reasons that we will explain later, we decided that the story was spurious and began to probe behind it. In 1969 Christian briefed the KCOP management on the curious background of Owen when *The Walking Bible* program went on the air. Hoping to find out where Owen was getting the substantial amounts of money required to pay for the program, Christian urged KCOP not to cancel it.

But KCOP did cancel, and the lawsuit ensued. It was not until virtually the end of the 1975 trial that the station's legal counsel, fearing that Crickard was leaning toward the plaintiff, decided to mount a vigorous "affirmative defense" by attempting to prove that the allegedly slanderous statements attributed to KCOP representatives about Owen's involvement in the assassination were in fact true statements. At this point we arranged for Vince Bugliosi to join the KCOP defense and bring his formidable forensic skills into play.

We had not learned about Bill Powers and what he had witnessed until several months after KCOP terminated *The Walking Bible* program. Powers told us that the police had interviewed him several times shortly after the assassination, but had dealt with him harshly and warned him not to repeat to anyone what he had seen. This was no surprise, since we had found that the Los Angeles police had systematically browbeaten witnesses whose accounts conflicted with the official verdict that there had been no conspiracy.

As the *Times* observed, a civil trial was an unlikely forum to press for the reopening of a political murder case, but by 1975 the unlikely was becoming commonplace. Watergate had jarred Americans into the realization that no dirty trick was impossible, and rekindled skepticism about the assassinations of John and Robert Kennedy and Martin Luther King, Jr.

It was through a mutual interest in reopening the investigation of the death of President Kennedy that the authors first met in 1968. We decided that since assassination was, by definition, a political crime, we would make a political issue of it by running for Congress. And in part because of that campaign, we were eventually introduced to the enigmatic Jerry Owen, "The Walking Bible."

2
Campaign '68

WITH JONN CHRISTIAN AS HIS CAMPAIGN MANAGER, BILL
Turner ran in the Democratic primary in what was then the
6th Congressional District of California, comprising a diagonal
half of San Francisco and practically all of Marin County to
the north across the Golden Gate Bridge. It was the same
Democratic primary that Eugene McCarthy and Robert
Kennedy were hotly contesting at the presidential level. And
this was the first time that the JFK assassination issue, which
had been raised in a plethora of books and articles, became the
principal plank in a campaign for national office.

In January, Turner had appeared on a San Francisco
television program to discuss his own lengthy investigation

into the Dallas tragedy, focusing on elements connected to intelligence agencies, anti-Castro Cuban exiles and organized-crime figures (this was long before the CIA-Mafia alliance to assassinate Fidel Castro was exposed). Christian was in the studio audience, and after the program he introduced himself. Turner's initial impression was that the stocky, bearded man came on too strong and should be kept at arm's length. What the investigation didn't need, he thought, was another "researcher" whose theories were based on guesswork rather than evidence.

But as it turned out, Christian's approach was hardly bluster. He carried solid credentials, having been a radio and television newsman from 1956 to 1966. Born thirty-five years earlier in a farm town not far from Sacramento, Christian first went on the air with a CBS affiliate in his home area. Gravitating to San Francisco, he did free-lance stints before winding up as assignment editor at KGO-TV, the local ABC outlet. His specialty was rooting out "political crooks," which amounted to pioneering in those pre-Watergate days of television news. His first major target was Oakland Mayor John O'Houllihan, suspected of embezzling funds belonging to a client in his private law practice. With camera crews and reporters, Christian chased the elusive mayor across the country. He got his story, and O'Houllihan was soon out of office and in jail. Christian next zeroed in on the tax assessors for San Francisco and Alameda counties, and they ended up convicted of accepting "campaign contributions" that were actually graft. But when he turned to those who had given the bribes and demanded a grand jury investigation, his cameras were shut off by the station management.

Christian's friend and mentor through his investigative-reporting career was one of the legends of the print media, Paul C. Smith, former editor of the San Francisco *Chronicle*. Personal secretary to President Herbert Hoover, confidant of FDR, press secretary to Wendell Willkie and journalistic godfather of Pierre Salinger, Smith had been close to John and Robert Kennedy from the inception of their political careers. After the President was struck down and the Warren Commission blamed Oswald alone, Smith intuitively felt that the truth had not been revealed. "Something's really wrong," he told Christian. "I can't put my finger on it, but this country is going in the wrong direction."*

Christian had reason to recall Smith's disquiet when he became a special consultant to an association of service-station operators who had filed an antitrust suit against a giant trading-stamp company, charging fraud, price manipulation and conspiracy. Although close to $100 million in damages was sought, the case was eventually compromised and settled out of court for less than one percent of that amount. Christian viewed the token settlement as the consequence of a power play begun several years before. Robert Kennedy's Justice Department had filed an antitrust action against the company—Justice attorneys drew on Christian's store of knowledge in the field of corporate buccaneering—but after the President's assassination, Lyndon Johnson's new team at Justice quietly dropped the prosecution. This severely compromised the service-station operators, who were forced to enter their civil suit playing a much weaker hand. If large corporate interests could benefit so decisively from an abrupt change in administration, Christian wondered, could not some cabal among them somehow have arranged for the President's death?

The notion was hardly dispelled by a set of events that began on a quiet Sunday afternoon in April 1967. An erstwhile broadcast colleague named Harv Morgan, who was doing a radio talk show on San Francisco's KCBS station, phoned Christian and asked him to come down to the studio and sit in on an interview with Harold Weisberg, author of a series of self-published books called *Whitewash* that were critical of the Warren Report. Weisberg lived in rural Maryland, so the interview was held via long-distance phone. The show was scheduled for one hour but ran on for four, with listeners calling in such numbers that the switchboard was jammed.

After reading the books, Christian called Weisberg in Maryland to discuss references to FBI bungling and cover-up in its investigation of the assassination. Several days later Christian was contacted by an FBI agent who had worked tangentially on the trading-stamp-

* Smith's autobiography, *Personal File*, is required reading in many journalism classes. Smith died in 1976.

company case. "Meet me at Roland's," the agent said, referring to a saloon where the two had occasionally met for drinks.

"Who do you know in Maryland that might be of extreme interest to certain people within the FBI?" the agent whispered.

"Harold Weisberg," Christian answered. "He's the only one I know in Maryland."

The agent confided that he had heard an "inside rumor" that a phone tap had intercepted Christian's conversation with Weisberg a few days before, and hinted that an order had been issued for Christian's line to be monitored from then on.

At first Christian was stunned, then angered. "To hell with the taps," he fumed. "If the FBI is that concerned about the critics, there must be something to the criticism!"

It was against this backdrop that Christian met Turner. Tall and sandy-haired, forty-one-year-old Turner came across as a nice enough guy but hardly the type of push-and-shove journalist that Christian was accustomed to. But Christian noted that he had a capacity for collecting and storing data. His investigative approach was disarmingly low-key, but it seemed to work.

Turner was a Navy veteran of World War II and a Canisius College graduate whose ice-hockey career had been interrupted by appointment as an FBI special agent in 1951. He participated in a number of well-known FBI cases, including the 1959 kidnap-murder of Colorado brewery magnate Adolph Coors, Jr., and as an inspector's aide he reviewed the Los Angeles division's program against organized crime. He was also specially trained in wire-tapping, bugging and burglary—a "black-bag job" on the Japanese consulate in Seattle was one assignment—and did counterespionage work. He received three personal letters of commendation from J. Edgar Hoover.

But by 1961 Turner's doubts about the aging Director's policies had grown to the point where he poked the tiger from inside the cage by seeking a congressional investigation of the FBI. He urged them to look into the Bureau's questionable tactics, softness on organized crime and the stultifying personality cult surrounding Hoover. At the time, Hoover was at the peak of his power, and he was able to discharge Turner as a "disruptive influence" with hardly a murmur of dissent from members of Congress.

Taking up journalism, Turner wrote for magazines ranging from *Playboy* to *The Nation* and wrote a number of police science articles for the legal press. In 1968 his first books, *The Police Establishment* and *Invisible Witness: The Use and Abuse of the New Technology of Crime Investigation*, were published, and he began work on *Hoover's FBI*.

Turner's involvement with the investigation of John Kennedy's assassination had begun immediately after the shooting when he flew to Dallas on assignment for a national magazine to look into the breakdown in security. As the Warren Commission inquiry progressed, stories appeared in the press that witnesses heard all the shots come from the building where Lee Harvey Oswald was employed. Turner wrote to the Commission, pointing out how deceptive the sounds of gunfire could be. On August 8, 1964, general counsel J. Lee Rankin replied that the Commission had "concluded its deliberations and was in the process of preparing its final report." When the hurried report was issued in time for the fall elections, Turner read it through and decided it was heavily flawed. He turned from skeptic to critic.

THE DECISION THAT TURNER WOULD RUN FOR CONGRESS STEMMED from a February 1968 "ways and means" meeting that Christian arranged at the Pacific Heights mansion of a friend, Fremont Bodine Hitchcock, Jr. "Peter" Hitchcock was a millionaire many times over, a member of the polo-playing Hitchcock family that moved in the most select society circles. He was hardly a Kennedy man (during the 1964 Republican National Convention in San Francisco, the Barry Goldwaters stayed at his home, and in 1968 he contributed substantially to the U.S. Senate campaign of the reactionary Max Rafferty) but he had gone to Harvard with John Kennedy and harbored a kind of perverse admiration for him. The sentiment survived the fact that before their marriage his wife, Joan, carried on an affair with Kennedy, whom she had met through Peter Lawford.*

---

* In 1975, when JFK's extracurricular romances were being dragged through the press, Joan Hitchcock could not resist going public with her

Hitchcock was skeptical about the conclusions of the Warren Report, and invited to the gathering Amory J. "Jack" Cooke, a vice president of the Hearst Corporation married to Phoebe Hearst; newscaster Harv Morgan, now with KGO; and Hitchcock lawyer George T. Davis. Turner presented his findings from Dallas and New Orleans, where he had assisted District Attorney Jim Garrison in his probe. There was unanimous agreement that the Warren Commission had fumbled its assignment.

What to do about it was another problem. Although Jack Cooke thought that the Hearst press might be open-minded, we were dubious. Editor in chief William Randolph Hearst, Jr., possessed an unshakable faith in the institutions of government, whether they concerned the Vietnam war or the Warren Report. Hearst feature writers Jim Bishop and Bob Considine had endorsed the Warren Report virtually before the ink was dry.

When someone suggested that the issue belonged in the hands of Congress, the idea of a political campaign was born. For the first time in his life Peter Hitchcock agreed to contribute to a Democrat, at least to the extent of paying the filing fee. So we sat down and composed a brochure for the Turner campaign.

THE ASSASSINATION OF PRESIDENT KENNEDY BROUGHT IMMEDIATE AND DRASTIC CHANGES IN THE FOREIGN AND DOMESTIC POLICIES OF THIS COUNTRY. WE MUST SOLVE THE PROBLEMS THESE CHANGES CREATED.

The polls show that an overwhelming majority of Americans don't believe the Warren Report. After investigating the case for over three years, I am convinced that the President was the victim of a domestic extremist plot. Whether to allow his murder to remain an unsolved homicide on the books of the Dallas Police Department is the silent issue of this campaign. I intend to bring it into the open by seeking a joint Senate-House investigation.

To do less not only is indecent but might cost us the life of a future President of John Kennedy's instincts.

---

memoirs. See, for example, the San Francisco *Chronicle* (December 27, 1975).

It was California's master politician Jesse Unruh who said "money is the mother's milk of politics," and it quickly became apparent that we were in for a difficult weaning. Due to our late start we lost out on funds that had been committed elsewhere. Besides, interest seemed to be fixed almost exclusively on the close contest between McCarthy and Kennedy. We received a few contributions from persons who were concerned by the assassination issue, most notably Sally Stanford, the legendary ex-madam of San Francisco. "I want to contribute to your campaign," she said after we dropped by to talk about it, "but first I have to go to my vault." With that, she reached down into her ample bosom and withdrew five $100 bills. We immediately named her "vice chairlady" of the campaign.*

But the Democratic regulars whose nods could loosen purse strings were resolutely opposed to reopening the Kennedy case. For one thing, the Warren Commission had been set up by a Democratic President, and Earl Warren was a liberal hero. For another, the Kennedy family themselves were on record as opposing further inquiry. Throughout the campaign we would be braced with the questions "What about the Kennedys? If there was a conspiracy, don't you think that Bobby Kennedy would do something about it?"

"Certainly," we'd reply, "but only if he could positively prove it." When the Warren Report was released, Robert Kennedy had acquiesced in its findings, although adding the enigmatic comment, "I have not read the Report and do not intend to." In fact, RFK had suspicions about his brother's death from the moment it happened. He instinctively felt that his archenemy Jimmy Hoffa might somehow have been responsible, and that members of the Secret Service had been bribed because the protection broke down so badly. He assigned Daniel P. Moynihan, then Assistant Secretary of Labor and a trusted member of the Kennedy inner circle, to investigate. Although Moynihan's report exonerated the Teamsters boss and the Secret Service of any complicity, Kennedy remained

* In 1976 Ms. Stanford was finally elected mayor of suburban Sausalito after being frustrated for years by the city's bluenoses. When the election results were in, the city manager commented, "She'll be the most interesting mayor in the state." But her enemies were ungracious, saying she was just out to upgrade her image. Sneered Sally: "Prestige, my ass!"

curious. In 1967 he sent his former press secretary Edwin O. Guthman, then a Los Angeles *Times* editor, to New Orleans to meet with Jim Garrison, and during the 1968 primary campaign he disappeared for several hours in Oxnard, California, to check privately on a report that a telephone call warning of the assassination originated there on the morning of November 22, 1963.*

When RFK announced that he was going to run for President, we considered it important that he be briefed on the evidence of conspiracy in his brother's death, for his own life might now be in danger. The most promising channel to the candidate was Jesse Unruh, speaker of the California Assembly and Kennedy's campaign chairman in the state, who happened to be a friend of Christian's. At first Unruh resisted any involvement, but Christian persisted into early 1968. Eventually he became receptive to the idea that lightning might strike twice and suggested that Christian be brought into the press relations section of the campaign, where he would have access to Kennedy. In late May Christian received notice to stand by for a summons to Washington headquarters— after RFK was nominated at the convention in July.

Yet in public RFK deflected questions on the assassination or, if pushed, paid lip service to the Warren Report. For example, on the campus of San Fernando Valley State College on March 25 he tried to brush off students' questions on the subject and became visibly annoyed when they persisted. "Your manners overwhelm me," he finally yielded. "Go ahead, go ahead, ask your questions."

"Will you open the archives if elected?" a student shouted in reference to the more than two hundred documents Lyndon Johnson had authorized to be sealed until the year 2039.

"Nobody is more interested than I in knowing who is responsible for the death of President Kennedy," he responded. "I would not reopen the Warren Commission Report. I have seen everything that's in there. I stand by the Warren Commission."†

---

* Curiously enough, Oxnard, then a small town off the beaten track, also figured in Owen's hitchhiker story. As we have seen, he said that he could not meet Sirhan at the Ambassador Hotel on election night because he had to preach in Oxnard.

† London *Times* (March 26, 1968).

Such statements were highly pragmatic, for it would have been damaging to his campaign to publicly express doubts—anything less than absolute proof would have left him open to accusations of irresponsibility and rumor mongering. The practical course to discovering more about the assassination was to control the Justice Department with its vast investigative resources. And the only way to control the Justice Department was to gain the presidency.

ON THE EARLY EVENING OF APRIL 4 A BULLETIN OUT OF MEMPHIS reported that Dr. Martin Luther King, Jr., had been shot and killed by a sniper. The next morning we received a call from George Davis, the attorney we had met at Peter Hitchcock's, asking us to come to his office for a conference. We had high hopes that Davis might be able to get our campaign off dead center. A peppery sixty-two-year-old with flowing silver hair and a staccato manner of speech, Davis was a widely known trial lawyer in California.

After some discussion about the King assassination, Davis pointed to his bookcase and remarked almost casually, "You know, I am the leading authority on hypnosis and the law." Then he dropped a bombshell. The lawyers for Clay L. Shaw, then under indictment in New Orleans for conspiracy in the JFK assassination as a result of DA Jim Garrison's investigation, had asked him to associate in the case. "The main witness against Shaw was hypnotized by the prosecution to help him recall details," Davis explained. The witness, Perry Russo, later testified that he had been present in September 1963 when Shaw and Lee Harvey Oswald talked about a plan to kill the President.

Davis proposed that Turner, who was close to Jim Garrison, arrange a private meeting between himself and Garrison at which the DA would lay out his entire case against Shaw. "If I can be more convinced than I am now about Garrison's case," he said, "I might be of a mind to move into the case and, you know, help him out."

We exchanged glances. The only way Davis could help Garrison by joining the Shaw defense would be to feed back information, which would be a serious breach of the canon of ethics. Whatever he was trying to propose, it didn't sound helpful and we let it pass.* Davis capped the meeting by offering to become our campaign chairman, which we gratefully accepted, since he thought he could raise enough money to get us through the election. But as it turned out, he generated no contributions at all.

Practically bereft of funds for advertising, we sought some way to pull off a press coup. The opportunity came on the languid Sunday of May 5. Sundays are usually slow news days, and this one was no exception. By chance the city editor's desk at the San Francisco *Chronicle* was being manned over the weekend by an old sidekick of Turner's, Charlie Howe. A hard-bitten combat veteran of the Korean War who specialized in military-affairs reporting, Howe possessed an independent streak the newspaper's editors found difficult to manage. Turner dropped in on Howe and took him out for a quick drink. He laid out some photographs on the bar.

Charlie Howe knew he was eying a grabby picture story. The photographs, taken by press photographers at Dealey Plaza within minutes of the JFK shooting, showed three men being led away by shotgun-toting Dallas policemen. They had been picked up behind the celebrated Grassy Knoll, but the Warren Commission had evinced no interest in who they were, why they were detained or what became of them. The scowling man leading the trio had a thin face, jutting jaw, wide mouth, thin lips, a triangular nose and squinty eyes. In juxaposition to him Turner had placed an artist's sketch of the suspect in the Martin Luther King slaying. The sketch bore no resemblance to James Earl Ray, then being sought by the FBI as the "lone gunman" in the King case, but it did appear strikingly similar to the Dealey Plaza suspect.

"I'll run it," Charlie Howe said. "Should be able to give it good play."

The slow-news day helped. On the front page of the *Chronicle* when it hit the streets that evening were a report of scattered

* As far as we know, Davis never did join the Shaw defense. Shaw was acquitted in a 1969 trial. According to Victor Marchetti, at the time an assistant to CIA Director Richard Helms, Shaw had collaborated with the Agency and Helms reciprocated by instructing that every possible aid be given to his defense. Shaw died in 1975.

fighting on the outskirts of Saigon, word that telephone workers had ratified a new contract, and an item out of Washington that the House Un-American Activities Committee advocated the restoration of detention camps to confine black militants. There was also a filler story that Robert Kennedy was optimistic on the eve of the Indiana primary.

But the headline read: STARTLING THEORY: KING KILLER "DOUBLE"! Centered on the front page were the two pictures with the caption "Strange Parallel." The story said: "A former FBI agent yesterday raised the spectre of a link between the assassinations of President Kennedy and Dr. Martin Luther King" with evidence strong enough to "warrant a Congressional investigation." It said that Turner noted that in both assassinations a rifle with telescopic sight "was conveniently left at the crime scene," and that in both there was an abundance of similar physical evidence, including city maps with significant points circled. " 'As you know,' " Turner was quoted, " 'the police use modus operandi files in any crime. Criminals tend to repeat certain things, have certain habits.' "

The story was a shot in the arm for the campaign, and for several days the city was abuzz with "strange parallels" talk. But the coup turned out to be a final lunge. The war chest, which had contained only a paltry $2,000, was empty. Although a private poll showed us neck and neck with our opponent, he doubled his previous expenditure of $17,000 and put on a media blitz. When the votes were tallied on the night of June 4, he had about 41,000 to Turner's 32,000. It was not a bad showing under the circumstances, and certainly indicated that people were responsive to the assassination issue.

Then came the electrifying news from Los Angeles. We stared mutely at the final line of our campaign brochure: " might cost us the life of a future President of John Kennedy's instincts . . ."

3

"The Walking Bible" Talks

ON MONDAY MORNING, JULY I, LESS THAN A MONTH AFTER
the RFK assassination, George Davis phoned Jonn Christian.
"Well, I suppose by now you've read the newspapers," he
began. "I've cracked the Kennedy assassination wide open,
and I need your help and Bill's."

Christian was perplexed. We had both been out of town
over the weekend and hadn't read the papers. "Read yesterday's *Examiner*," the attorney urged with a note of excitement
in his voice, "then get down here as soon as you can."

The story was headed: MINISTER HIDING IN S.F.,
CLAIMS R.F.K. CLUE. Credited to the Associated Press, it
opened:

A clergyman from Southern California is hiding for his life in
the San Francisco area today, claiming that he met the killer of

Sen. Robert F. Kennedy before the assassination, that he has evidence of possible conspirators he saw with him, and that his life and the lives of his entire family have been threatened.

The minister—whose name cannot be revealed at this time for his own security—used San Francisco attorney George T. Davis as his spokesman.

There followed a brief account of how the unnamed clergyman happened to pick up a young hitchhiker in Los Angeles on the day before the assassination whom he later identified as Sirhan. He immediately reported the incident to the Los Angeles police, and shortly thereafter received a telephoned threat. "Keep your mouth shut if you know what's good for you and your family," the anonymous caller warned. A week later the threat was repeated. The clergyman contacted Davis, who appealed unsuccessfully to the Los Angeles police for protection.

According to the article, Davis believed that the clergyman's life was actually in danger and that the police were negligent. "Los Angeles authorities," Davis charged, "have taken the position that there is no conspiracy in this case, so this man's story is not important."

We hurried to Davis' office. He said that the clergyman was one Jerry Owen, who was not only a client but a friend of thirty years' standing. Owen had called him on Friday evening after arriving in the Bay Area, and when Davis couldn't reach us he called the Associated Press because he thought something had to be done without delay. The AP had dispatched reporter Jim White to Davis' ranch near Napa Valley, where Davis had Owen sequestered. The attorney had tried unavailingly to get help from Los Angeles Police Chief Tom Reddin, and had been unable to reach either Attorney General Thomas Lynch or Jesse Unruh.*

Davis thought Owen's story strongly suggested that Sirhan had accomplices—the three men and a girl who had offered Owen

* Reporter White, who happened to be a neighbor of Turner's in suburban Mill Valley, later gave us a copy of the tape recording he made at the Davis ranch. In the background Davis can be heard placing calls to the police and the Attorney General's office.

$100 as down payment on the horse Sirhan was going to buy, and who had instructed him to deliver the animal to the rear of the Ambassador Hotel at eleven o'clock on election night. If the police would not guard Owen, Davis said, there was only one insurance policy: "Break this story wide open all across the country!"

Relying on Davis' judgment, we agreed to help. Christian would offer an exclusive national story to his ex-colleagues at ABC, while Turner would act as investigative adviser on any follow-up to the story. We were not discouraged by the fact that the AP story, which had gone out on the national wire Saturday night, had not been widely picked up. Owen had insisted that his name not be used, which detracted from the story's credibility. And the Los Angeles press had been put off by the police labeling the clergyman as a "nut." By producing Owen in the flesh on nationwide television, the story should pack a wallop. And once it was out, anyone who tried to silence Owen would only be adding credibility to his story.

Davis promised to bring Owen before the cameras at ten-thirty the following morning. When Christian outlined the story to the radio and television people, they reacted enthusiastically. It was important that the interview come off on time in order to feed the network in New York, which was three hours ahead of the West Coast.

BY TEN-THIRTY IN THE MORNING THE ABC CREWS HAD THEIR equipment set up in the reception room of Davis' office suite. The room was shut off from the outside but brightened by a large picture window framing an interior garden of subtropical flora. As the clock ticked, the room became enveloped in small talk. And speculation. Who were the other persons? What kind of conspiracy was there?

Finally, at eleven-twenty, Davis appeared and the crews switched on their floodlights. Davis introduced the two men with him as bodyguards for Owen. Apologizing for the delay, he explained that only minutes before, the Los Angeles authorities had called advising that they were flying to San Francisco to "take charge." Davis said that he had finally made contact with Attorney General Lynch, who had personally phoned Chief Reddin in Los Angeles. The police had personally warned Davis that there was a judge's gag order outstanding that prohibited witnesses from making public statements. There could be no interview.

The broadcast crews complained bitterly, and Christian angrily remonstrated with Davis that the public interest demanded that Sirhan's accomplices be exposed. The authorities had no right to misuse a court order to squelch versions of the case conflicting with their own, he argued. Davis said that he was sorry, but there was nothing he could do. "Anyway, I've already sent Mr. Owen back to my ranch to wait until the authorities arrive tomorrow," he said.

As Christian and the ABC contingent trooped out the door, Davis beckoned to Turner to follow him. "Bill, see what you make of all this," he said as they rode the private elevator up to Davis' inner sanctum. The attorney led the way into a large conference room where, standing at the end of the table, was the object of all the fuss. "Bill, meet Jerry Owen," Davis said. At sixty-two Owen still exuded physical strength. He stood well over six feet and weighed close to 250 pounds, a beefy, florid man with a roundish face dominated by a bulbous nose and darting blue eyes. His hair was graying-dark and kinky, which long ago had given rise to the nickname "Curly." He was dressed in a brown business suit, and he wore wing-tip oxfords. His hands were like hams, and his handshake was crushing. Owen looked every inch the aging prizefighter, which he was.

After Davis left the room to make some phone calls, Owen raised the question of John Kennedy's assassination. Obviously Davis had briefed him on Turner's participation in the Jim Garrison investigation. As Turner spread a number of photographs from his attaché case on the table, Owen looked them over. His finger came to rest on one of Edgar Eugene Bradley of North Hollywood, who six months before had been indicted by a New Orleans grand jury for conspiracy in the JFK assassination (the charges were later dismissed). Bradley was the West Coast representative of Dr. Carl McIntire, the fundamentalist minister who founded the American Council of Christian Churches in opposition to the "modernist" National Council of Churches.

"Do you know Bradley?" Turner asked.

"Yes," said Owen. He explained that he had casually met him a couple of times in Los Angeles, the last in 1964. "I was affiliated with McIntire's church in the late fifties," Owen said, "but got out because those people were too radical for me."

The mention of the right-wing McIntire church, which had roundly condemned Roman Catholicism in general and the Kennedys in particular, prompted Turner to ask Owen to tell his story on tape. The preacher complied. Clutching the microphone in his hands, his eyebrows knitted in concentration, he began a minutely detailed rendition. Noting his intensity, Turner didn't interrupt during the fifty-seven-minute soliloquy. In condensed form, this is what Owen said occurred:

On Monday afternoon, June 3, Owen left his Santa Ana home in his old Chevy pickup truck with a conspicuous chrome horse ornament on the hood. He was dressed in Levi's, cowboy boots and a plaid shirt. He was on his way to Oxnard, where a friend boarded a dozen Shetland ponies and a palomino horse for him. He had a buyer for a Shetland, and he was going to bring one back.

Owen stopped at a Los Angeles sporting-goods store to pick up a robe, shoes and trunks for a heavyweight boxer named O'Reilly who he had an interest in. He was going to drop off the shoes and robe in Hollywood for decorating with shamrocks.

While he stopped at a red light at 7th and Grand, two young men asked if he was going out Wilshire Boulevard toward Hollywood, and without waiting for an answer hopped in the back of the truck. "I looked in the mirror and noticed that the one was kind of a bushy, dark-haired fella and the other was of the same complexion and I thought that they were Mexicans or Hindus or something, kind of on the hippie style."

At a stoplight at Wilshire and Vermont, the pair got out and the taller one began talking to a well-dressed man, about thirty-five and a "dirty blonde" girl, who looked about twenty-one, who were standing on the corner. The pair was wearing "occult" medallions on chains around their necks. The smaller man returned to the truck and asked, "Do you mind if I ride with you on out?"

Turner noticed that Owen was talking very deliberately, and that his tone was turning very confidential.

The horse ornament prompted a discussion of horses. The hitchhiker said "he was an exercise boy at a race track, and talked about how he loved horses, and quickly wanted to know if I had a ranch where he could get a job." As they proceeded out Wilshire, the hitchhiker pointed to Catalina Street and asked, "Would it be all right if we stopped? I have a friend in the kitchen."

Owen swung left on Catalina and stopped in a cul-de-sac at the rear entrance to the Ambassador Hotel. The hitchhiker mentioned that he wanted to buy a lead pony to use at the race track, and "I told him I had a dandy up in Oxnard." After some ten minutes went by, Owen started to leave, thinking the hitchhiker would not return, when "he came on a run. I noticed his tennis shoes on, a sweatshirt."

As they headed toward Hollywood, Owen asked the young man if he was Mexican, and he said no, he was born in Jordan. "Well, that struck up a little conversation because my wife and I are planning to go to Jerusalem."

Owen parked in front of the Hollywood Ranch Market and delivered the boxing paraphernalia to a shop across the street. Upon his return to the truck the hitchhiker "told me that if I could meet him at eleven o'clock on Sunset Boulevard, he would be able to purchase this horse for the sum of three hundred dollars. There was a little talk of two hundred fifty dollars or something, but I told him that I would let it go for three hundred. I'd guarantee the horse, if it didn't work out I would take it back because the horse is a ten-year-old comin' on eleven, and he had been used as a pickup horse and as a pony horse and well broke, but he's a one man's horse."*

* The references to "pickup" and "pony" horse indicated that the Owen animal had been used at thoroughbred race tracks.

Owen made it clear that he needed money, and that the $300 would help him pay some pressing debts.

It was now close to six o'clock. The hitchhiker directed Owen to a bowling alley on Sunset Boulevard and said, "At eleven o'clock tonight I'll meet you here and I'll have the money to pay for the horse." Owen mentioned that he might kill some time by going to the Saints and Sinners Club on Fairfax, which caused the hitchhiker to ask if he was Jewish. "No, I'm not Jewish, I'm Welsh," Owen replied. "Well, I have no use for the Hebes!" the hitchhiker sneered. Owen smiled, "I'll be there at eleven."

Owen went to the Plaza Hotel, where his old friend "Slapsie Maxie" Rosenbloom [an ex-fighter] lived. "Curly," Maxie said, "you gotta be at the Saints and Sinners tonight, it's the last night at Billy Gray's Band Box—they're closin'. This'll be the greatest meeting of all and, with you and Henry Armstrong being the charter members, come on and be there!" Owen balked, "I can't go, Max. I'm dressed like a hayseed." Rosenbloom insisted, "Ah, what's the difference, Curly?" He looked at the truck and horse and laughed at Owen driving that rig right in the heart of Hollywood.

"And I went to Saints and Sinners, and I had O'Reilly the boxer with me, and they introduced him that night." At eleven, Owen pulled up to the bowling alley. Across the street was an older-model off-white Chevy sedan. In the streetlight Owen could see a man resembling the man he had seen that afternoon on the corner of Wilshire and Vermont, and there "was the girl, from the looks of her hair and that." The hitchhiker got out from the car and said, "I am very sorry. Here's a hundred-dollar bill, and I was supposed to have the rest of the money but I don't. But if you'll meet me in the morning about eight o'clock, I assure you that I'll take the horse definitely."

"Well, now look," Owen said, "I've waited and I should be up in Oxnard. But I'll tell you what I'll do if you really mean business and want the horse. I'll stay in this hotel right across the street."

Owen registered in a $4 room with phone but no bath. At close to eight the next morning the telephone rang and a voice he had never heard before wanted to know if he was the man with the truck in the parking lot. Owen went down to the lobby. The man was wearing an "expensive-looking late-style suit. He had on a turtleneck sweater that was kind of an orangish-yellow color with a chain around his neck and a big, round thing that you see 'em all wearing now, and as I looked at him, he had on what appeared to be an expensive pair of alligator shoes. He had a manicure. He had one of those cat's-eye rings on his little finger." The stranger said, "Joe couldn't make it. Take this hundred dollars if you can be down on the street where you left him out yesterday afternoon.* At 11 o'clock tonight. If you can be there with the horse and trailer, he'll definitely take the horse." Joe was the hitchhiker.

Owen peered into the man's car outside and recognized the same girl. "Look," Owen said, "I've waited overnight, I stayed in the hotel and I was told that we would have it definitely at eleven this morning. I have to be in Oxnard tonight to speak at the Calvary Baptist Church there, and I got some business there, and I cannot be down on the street tonight at eleven."

Owen handed the man his card with the legend "SHEPHERD OF THE HILLS, Free Pony Rides For Boys and Girls Who Go To The Church Of Their Choice, Learn a Bible Verse, and Mind Their Parents." On it was his unlisted telephone number at his Santa Ana home. Owen said that he would deliver the horse wherever they wanted when they had the money. He left for Oxnard, where he preached a sermon at the Calvary Baptist Church. He stayed overnight with unnamed parishioners.

The following morning Owen hooked his two-horse trailer to the pickup truck and loaded it with a brown-and-white-spotted mare, a little white stallion and a black gelding. The last two were extras he hoped to sell because he "needed a little extra finances." He drove back to Los Angeles en route home. He had not seen television or heard a radio, and knew nothing about RFK having been shot.

Arriving in Los Angeles around noon, he stopped on the spur of the moment at the Coliseum Hotel to see if an old-time

* The cul-de-sac at the rear of the Ambassador Hotel.

fight manager named Bert Morse still ran the coffee shop there. He was going to talk to Morse about the fight game. "But coming through the bar there is a television. I heard something about the rigmarole, and about the eight shots being fired, but being a minister, I just went through the bar and into the counter area and set down and ordered a lunch."

While eating, Owen got his first word of the RFK shooting. He heard a radio report that the suspect had black, bushy hair and wore tennis shoes. Bert Morse arrived and started talking about his horses, Diamond Dip and Hemet Miss, which raced on local tracks, and about boxing. Then Owen repeated to Morse his story about picking up "a couple of hippies." He said, "Isn't it funny, a guy shows you a hundred-dollar bill?"

All of a sudden a picture flashed on television and Owen thought, Hey, that's the guy that was in my truck!

Then a waitress handed him a copy of the Hollywood *Citizen-News* and there he was. "That's the kid!" So the waitress and Morse and boxing trainer Doug Lewis urged him to report his experience to the police. Owen balked, saying, "It's no use, they've caught him single-handed." And Morse spoke up, "I know, but have you been following this Garrison investigation of the other Kennedy?" Owen retorted, "Naw, I'm in church work and a minister. I don't want to be bothered with it." But the waitress said, "Well, I'll tell you what I'd do if I was you," and everyone agreed with her that Owen should report his story.

Owen drove over to the nearby University Station of the Los Angeles police. The minute the police heard his story they had him "drive in and leave the pickup and trailer in the back, and I heard them say something about taking fingerprints." Owen recited his story with a tape recorder going and a stenographer taking notes. One cop came in the room and said, "He sure knows what he's talking about because it was just released that they found four-hundred dollars in bills on the suspect, and there was nothing about any money on him until then." After telling his story, Owen was allowed to leave. "I went outside and it looked like on the doors and on the side of the truck that there'd been some kind of powder or something.

I didn't see them take any fingerprints, but I heard the detectives say they would."

That was the basic hitchhiker story.* Owen said that about two o'clock the next afternoon he received the first threatening call on his unlisted number at home. "Are you the Shepherd?" the anonymous voice growled. "The man with the horses? Keep your motherfucking mouth shut about this horse deal—or else!"

On Wednesday, June 19, the police called and invited Owen to come down to their Parker Center headquarters. Owen called a retired Methodist minister and old friend named Jonothan Perkins, and asked him to come along. "Perk, come on, let's go down to the police station. I want you to be with me when I go in there, I don't want to go in alone." The aged minister obliged. "Now look, Perk," Owen said as they entered Parker Center, "you believe in prayer. You pray because I've just had a threat."

Owen was ushered into the offices of Special Unit Senator (SUS), a group set up especially to investigate the assassination. He was shown an assortment of mug shots, and picked out one as being the hitchhiker. The detective said he was "not at liberty" to reveal whether it was Sirhan.

That afternoon Owen headed for Phoenix, Arizona, on unexplained business. Two days later he drove through the night to arrive in Santa Ana by early morning. He was asleep when the phone rang with a second threat. "We told you to keep your motherfucking mouth shut," the caller rasped, slamming down the receiver without another word.

On June 26 Owen received another call from SUS asking him to come right down to Parker Center. He begged off, however, insisting that he had to leave for a speaking engagement in Oxnard, after which he was going straight to the San Francisco area. A man identifying himself as Sergeant Sandlin came on the line, saying that he, too, was going to the Bay Area and would like to meet with him there. Owen gave Sandlin the name of George Davis as his contact.

* The complete Owen-Turner interview appears as the first section of the Appendix.

On Friday, June 29, Owen called home from Oakland and was told by his wife that Sandlin was at the Hyatt House in Palo Alto and wanted to get together with him. The preacher made a note of the hotel's number and stuck it in his pocket. Then an old pal, Ben Hardister, a private detective who had volunteered to act as his bodyguard, took him to the Athens Club, where he picked up a newspaper to pass the time. It contained a story headed "Witnesses Disappear" about the Martin Luther King case. "And the report stated that the two witnesses in this case mysteriously disappeared," Owen said. "The woman that owned the rooming house, and one of the tenants there that saw suspect James Earl Ray and could identify him with the gun, or goin' into the bathroom or somethin'." Seeing Ray's picture, Owen said his mind "drifted back to Jack Ruby goin' in and shootin' the fella. Then I have occasionally heard flashes about Jim Garrison and witnesses dyin' or mysteriously disappearing or somethin' happening all of a sudden." Owen's voice seemed to reflect genuine concern.

Owen said that he heard about threats made to prosecuting attorneys in the Sirhan case, and now he, too, was worried about his own predicament. The detectives at the University Station had assured him that his name wouldn't get in the newspapers, but still he wondered. When he had told Ben Hardister about a Sergeant Sandlin wanting to see him, Hardister rumbled, "You mean you're going to go over there and see somebody you don't even know? I'm not going to let you!"

Hardister rushed Owen to the office of Wesley Gardner in Napa, telling Owen that Gardner had FBI training and had solved a number of murders when he was with the sheriff's department. After listening to the story, Gardner offered the same counsel: "You couldn't identify him and you're going to walk over there with two threats? No sir!"

Hardister and Gardner, who was also now serving as a volunteer bodyguard, decided that Owen should stay at the Hardister ranch, which happened to be adjacent to George Davis'. The next morning Owen and Hardister drove over to the Davis ranch, interrupting the lawyer's breakfast. After hearing the story, Davis took charge. He phoned the Hyatt House but was told no Sergeant Sandlin was registered. Owen was glad he had taken the advice of

Hardister and Gardner. "Man, I could have walked in there and got plugged," he said, "or a fellow come along and pose as an officer and got me in a car and said, 'Well, let's go in and see the sheriff or the policemen here,' and dumped me in the bay or something.

" 'Maybe this is just the hand of God!' " Owen quoted Hardister.

Davis began a flurry of telephone calls. The Los Angeles Police Department (LAPD) confirmed that a Sergeant Lyle Sandlin had scheduled the trip, but they had decided to interview Owen when he returned to the Los Angeles area. But the officer with whom Davis talked didn't take the threats against Owen and his family seriously. "Oh, I'm sure they'll be all right," he said soothingly. "Just a misunderstanding."

This was when Davis tried to reach us, then called the Associated Press.

But the melodrama was not over. On Monday morning Owen rode into San Francisco with Davis. As he alighted from the car, Owen said, a Cadillac pulled up "with a heavy-set Italian-looking man with a cigar in his mouth and a hat on, and he pulled over and said, 'Say, was that George T. Davis who's car you just got out of?' " Owen muttered "Who's car?" and scurried inside the nearest building. And later that day when he was driving with Hardister on a country road, a car kept pulling in front of them and slowing down, and the man in the passenger seat kept looking back. When Owen tried to jot down the license number, the car sped away.

Owen's convoluted narrative finally was at an end. Turner posed some preliminary questions. "They wanted to meet you at eleven o'clock that night? Election night?" Owen nodded affirmatively. "And where did they want you to meet them?" Off of Catalina Street, Owen explained, "at the same place that I let the little fellow out the day before to see somebody that worked in a kitchen." For some reason Owen was reluctant to name the Ambassador Hotel. Turner elicited that the spot was in fact the rear entrance closest to the Embassy Room, where RFK was shot.

"Were they very insistent that you try and make it that night?" Turner asked.

"Yes, yes. That's when I was offered the hundred-dollar bill.

Give 'em a receipt and they'd have the balance of the money if I would be there and have the horse in the horse trailer, see?"

"At eleven o'clock?"

"At eleven o'clock with the horse. And then I was to pick up my money and take the horse where he wanted it."

Sirhan *did* have four $100 bills on him when arrested, Turner remembered. "In other words, the hundred dollars was an enticement for you to break your engagement in Oxnard?"

"Yeah, that's right. It looked like it. I feel that it was a come-on now. I do in the bottom of my heart."

Turner sensed that Owen was becoming a bit peeved at the persistent questioning, and he signed off the tape. It was three-fifteen in the afternoon. The LAPD had called Davis to advise that they would be delayed until the following morning, so Hardister took Owen back up to his ranch for safekeeping.

Turner entered Davis' office and closed the door. "George," he said, "there's an incredible chain of coincidence here. You call me in. Owen knows Eugene Bradley, who was indicted by Garrison. I have worked with Garrison . . ." Davis cocked his head as Turner posed the obvious question: "How well do you know Owen?"

"I've known him for thirty years," Davis said. "And I'm inclined to believe what he says."

THE LOS ANGELES LAW ENFORCEMENT CONTINGENT ARRIVED ON schedule the following morning, and Davis and Turner took them up on the private elevator to the conference room where Owen was waiting. Lieutenant Manuel Pena of the LAPD had the blocky build of a football guard, Turner thought, while Sergeant Enrique Hernandez resembled a tackle. They dwarfed a third man, Deputy District Attorney David M. Fitts, who soon would be named Sirhan's co-prosecutor.

The trio questioned Owen alone, but after two hours, during which they tried to break down his story, he held fast. The slender, youngish Fitts then instructed Pena and Hernandez to take Owen over to the San Francisco Police Department and use their polygraph instrument. Hernandez was a qualified operator.

In his polygraph report (which we did not see until much later), Hernandez stated that Owen "resisted the control test," but his responses indicated that he was "a suitable subject for testing." Hernandez was predisposed to try to prove that Owen was fabricating the story, while Owen vehemently insisted that it was true. The detective flatly told Owen that he had flunked the test, moralizing, "You're a preacher, a man of God supposedly. What does the Bible say about lying?"*

"Psalms, 120 and 2. 'Deliver my soul from deceitful lips and a lying tongue,' " the preacher responded by rote.

Hernandez lectured Owen on quoting from the Bible on the one hand and lying to the police on the other. Owen stuck to his story. The detective countered, "You failed to identify Sirhan in ten photos," shoving a mug shot at Owen that he allegedly had selected at SUS headquarters two weeks before. "That's not Sirhan."

"I—listen, I might be wrong. It might not be the guy. Maybe I picked up someone else. I don't know . . . If I saw him face to face, or heard his voice or something, then I'd come out and make a definite statement. I don't know. It looks like him to me."

But Hernandez persisted, telling Owen that he had lied when he said he had no arrest record. The preacher rose to his feet and raised his arms skyward imploringly. "Get me out of here, please, God! God, please! Please, God, listen! Please, God!"

"Try to calm yourself."

"O God, help me!" Owen cried out. "God help me. I'm not goin' to do it. I'm goin' to have a nervous breakdown, pret' near."

Hernandez handled Owen as a teacher handles an unruly child. Did Owen want to tell George Davis that he was lying or did he want Hernandez to do it? Owen sputtered incoherently. "Just wait here," the detective said, leaving the room. He phoned Davis and told him that his client had abused the truth so badly that he "blew the box." Owen had concocted the story, he said, and that was the end of it as far as the police were concerned.

While Hernandez was on the phone Owen soliloquized, "No! I'll tell you, George, what you ought to do. You're not going to

* Robert Blair Kaiser, "*R.F.K. Must Die!*" (New York: Dutton & Co., 1970), pp. 156–57.

get away with anything like this, George. Come on, George! No! No! I won't, George! They're doing everything to break me. No!" The hidden tape recorder in the polygraph room kept recording as Owen's voice trailed off to a mutter.

On his return to Davis' office Owen indignantly recounted the polygraph interrogation to Hardister, Gardner and Turner. Contrary to the taped version, he claimed that Hernandez had confided to him that the instrument indicated that he was being truthful. But then the detective would later report that Owen couldn't have picked up Sirhan on June 3 because "we've accounted for his activities for days beforehand." Hernandez insisted that there had been no conspiracy, citing the fact that the police "went through eighteen witnesses on the polka-dot-dress girl" who reportedly had been seen with Sirhan at the hotel as proof of how exhaustive the investigation had been.* The detective even disclosed that the police had dusted Owen's truck for fingerprints, but he neglected to say what the results were.

Owen said that Hernandez had accused him of "quibbling over questions" and not giving straight yes or no answers. The detective contended that the fact that Sirhan had been in the United States for thirteen years—which Owen quoted the hitchhiker as mentioning—was in the newspapers, implying that Owen had pieced together scraps of published material to manufacture his story.

At the end Hernandez tried to mollify Owen by conceding he might have made an "honest mistake" in identifying Sirhan, but warned him not to say anything on the subject to anyone because there was a court order that witnesses must remain silent. He advised Owen not even to talk to the FBI because "it wasn't necessary."

But the preacher saw no saving grace in his police inquisitors. "They walked in there [San Francisco police headquarters] and you'd think they were from Cuba," he said. "They looked like they were Al Capone's henchmen. I hear them down the hall. They're phonin' around for dates and phonin' the topless places, and phonin' the best places to eat and tryin' to get some guy to get dates

---

* A number of witnesses at the Ambassador Hotel reported seeing Sirhan with a girl wearing a polka-dot dress prior to the shooting.

for 'em. Yes, out for a fling and a good time, and they let me set there for an extree forty-five minutes 'til they got their reservation and was assured there would be some gals for 'em, and they'd see some of the new topless places. Yeah, they were up on their expense accounts."

PENA AND HERNANDEZ BEGAN MOPPING UP THE ANNOYING LOOSE ends of the Owen story on Friday, July 5, by reinterviewing Mrs. Mary Sirhan, mother of the accused assassin. They had first talked to her on Tuesday, which presumably was why they delayed their trip to San Francisco. One of the problems with writing off Owen's account was the fact that when arrested, Sirhan had, in addition to $6 and some change, four $100 bills in his pocket. Where did the long-unemployed young man get that amount of hard cash? And why was he carrying it? The policemen must have recognized one possible answer: that $300 of it was to pay Owen for the horse when he delivered it to the Ambassador Hotel.

A 21-page SUS summary report titled JERRY OWEN INVESTIGA-TION, which we obtained some time later,* revealed that in the initial interview Pena and Hernandez asked Mrs. Sirhan about a $2,000 insurance settlement that Sirhan had received a few weeks before the assassination. According to the report, she "recalled that Sirhan asked for $300 a day or two before the shooting. She said that she believed that Sirhan had spent most of the remainder from the $1000 he gave her from the insurance settlement. She thought that he had given some of the money to Adel [a brother]. Adel Sirhan was present during the interview, and he stated at one point, 'I think Sirhan wanted the $300 to buy a horse with.' "

Adel Sirhan's unsolicited information squared perfectly with the part of Owen's story that Sirhan had agreed to buy his horse for

* The SUS report was released to Christian by the Los Angeles County Clerk's office shortly after Sirhan's 1969 trial. Most of the court exhibits and investigative material had been routinely placed with the Clerk's office for storage. Although the SUS report was not supposed to be available to the public, the office of LAPD Detective Chief Robert Houghton apparently got its wires crossed and authorized release of a copy to Christian. (See Appendix.)

$300. Pena and Hernandez were armed with this when they grilled Owen in San Francisco, yet they acted as if they didn't believe a word of his story. It was not something that Owen could have picked out of the newspapers, but the policemen never asked a single question.

Pena and Hernandez seemed to have this nagging little problem very much in mind when they revisited Mary Sirhan. Where had her son been on June 3? As best as she could recall, he drove her to work at eight o'clock, but he was not at home when she returned at one. "However, there was evidence that he had just taken a shower and there was a warm cup of coffee," the SUS men reported in the best tradition of detective fiction. "Sirhan was gone most of the afternoon, but she noticed that he was watching television at 4:30 P.M." He did not leave the house again that day, Mrs. Sirhan said. "At least from the time of 4:30 P.M.," the report concluded, "Mrs. Sirhan's statement contradict's Owen's statement."

This was an overly simplistic conclusion, and SUS should have known better. What mother can recall what her son did on an uneventful day a month previously? Pena and Hernandez, perhaps with this in mind, prevailed upon Mrs. Sirhan to question her son about that day when she visited him in jail. She reported back that he said "he did not know Owen, had never seen him nor had he ever ridden in his pickup truck. He also denied that he had attempted to purchase a palomino horse."

The SUS report contained several contradictions and inconsistencies in Owen's story. For example, when he reported to the University Division of the LAPD on June 5, Owen said that on June 3 he "left his residence in Santa Ana en route to the Coliseum Hotel," where he "spoke with the manager of the coffee shop, John Bert Morris [sic], and Rip O'Reilly, a heavyweight boxer. Morris and Owen discussed the purchase of some boxing equipment from the United Sporting Goods Store." But in the version he later told Turner in San Francisco (a copy of which was subsequently furnished to SUS), he said that he was about to go directly to Oxnard when the phone rang and he was notified that boxing equipment he had ordered at United was ready. As a result he detoured through Los Angeles to pick it up. And he claimed that he had not contacted Bert Morse, an "oldtime fight manager who had Baby Armendez back in the '30s," until on his way home from Oxnard on June 5.

Perhaps the most glaring discrepancy stemmed from an SUS interview of "Rip" O'Reilly. The boxer advised that "on June 3, 1968 Owen called him at about 10:30 A.M. and invited him to attend a Saints and Sinners Club that night. At 6:30 P.M. Owen picked up O'Reilly at the Coliseum Hotel, and they drove to the meeting on Fairfax Avenue. Owen was driving a dark-colored pickup truck with a horse trailer attached. A horse was in the trailer. They remained at the meeting until 11:30 P.M., and Owen took O'Reilly back to the hotel." This statement contradicted Owen's story that he decided to remain in Los Angeles and attend the Saints and Sinners affair to kill time only after picking up Sirhan that afternoon and making a deal on the horse. And it clashed with Owen's version that he fetched a trailer and three ponies from Oxnard on June 5.

Apparently SUS didn't take seriously the implications of O'Reilly's account—that Owen had brought the trailer and horse with him to Los Angeles, that he never went to Oxnard the night of the RFK shooting, and might have been outside the Ambassador Hotel when the Senator was shot.

"TAKE THIS HOME AND PLAY IT," TURNER TOLD CHRISTIAN, HANDing him the tape recording of Owen telling his story. "Make notes as you go along."

By the time Turner got over to Christian's apartment that evening he had already found a number of discrepancies in the Owen story, which he noted on a yellow legal pad. First of all, Owen said that he was ready to leave his Santa Ana home on June 3 for Oxnard, but the speaking engagement was not until the night of June 4 and Oxnard was less than a hundred miles away. Then there was the incident in which the two men who had climbed onto his truck jumped off at a stoplight and began talking familiarly with a man and girl on the corner—the same couple who were with Sirhan at the Sunset Boulevard rendezvous that night and appeared to be a part of the implicit conspiracy. But Christian noted that Sirhan couldn't possibly have known what route Owen would take or that the light would be red when he arrived at the stoplight. And Owen said that he was going to Oxnard to pick up the horse and trailer, but slipped when he mentioned that Maxie Rosenbloom "looked at the truck and horse and laughed at Owen driving that rig right in the heart of Hollywood."

The list went on and on. Turner agreed that Owen had spun a web of fiction around elements of the truth—such as somehow being acquainted with Sirhan. But why? Owen obviously had a bent for self-promotion, but in this case he had shied away from publicity. He had quietly reported the story to the police, seeking and getting an assurance of anonymity. Instead of trying to capitalize on the polka-dot-dress-girl (conspiracy) angle that was getting heavy play in the media—the "dirty blonde" girl of his story certainly fit her description—he ran to his attorney looking for protection. It was Davis' idea to break the story in the Associated Press to provide that protection, but even then Owen insisted that his name not be used. As a result, we ruled out the possibility of a publicity stunt.

After wrestling with the problem for several days, we tried to reach George Davis to find out if he had any ideas. His secretary said that he had abruptly canceled his entire appointment schedule to go to his ranch to "meet with some business associates," among whom were Owen, Hardister and Gardner. The urgent conference stretched into five days. When Davis failed to call us back, Christian asked Peter Hitchcock to intervene. "I guess they want to talk to you about the Owen thing," Hitchcock told Davis after locating him at the ranch. "Well, you know some things take precedence and other things come later," Davis asserted, "and that's a subject that comes later as far as I'm concerned. You know, I'm not really lying awake nights worrying about whether Owen gets shot. That's basically his problem."

It was clear that Davis was ducking any further discussion of the situation. Did he now, after being closeted with Owen for five days, know more about what was behind the hitchhiker story than when he was frantically dialing the state's top law enforcement officers seeking protection? We had felt that Owen's concern for his safety was genuine, but we now began to wonder.

Owen might have been telling the essential truth despite the flaws in his story and his failure to pass the polygraph test. In his excitement he could have inadvertently garbled details, and we knew that the outcome of the polygraph test depended more on the objectivity and skill of the operator than on the instrument itself. Hernandez seemingly had arrived in San Francisco with his mind made up.

At this point we knew little about Owen's curious background —only that George Davis had vouched for him as a friend of thirty years' standing. And we were unaware that the LAPD's cavalier dismissal of the hitchhiker story as a publicity stunt was part of a pattern that had begun the moment RFK was shot.

4

Tinting Sirhan Red

WITHIN HOURS OF THE SHOOTING, A CAMPAIGN WAS UNDER way to paint Sirhan a deep Red. The chief brush-wielder was Sam Yorty, the cocky bantam-rooster mayor of Los Angeles. Yorty had a reputation for sounding off on practically every issue. During the height of the Vietnam war he made two "inspection trips" to Saigon and returned with hawkish pronouncements on the necessity to increase the American military commitment. Wags dubbed Los Angeles the only city with its own foreign policy.

The Kennedy brothers had long been near the top of Yorty's enemies list. In 1960, despite his nominal Democratic affiliation, Yorty had endorsed Richard Nixon over JFK, and in 1965 he had clashed with RFK during a Senate hearing. In 1968 he was again in Nixon's corner.

Ironically, Christian had been a kind of unofficial campaign adviser to Yorty in 1966, called in by a former colleague of friend Paul Smith. Christian didn't know that Yorty was such a hard-line right-winger when he agreed to advise him; however, he soon found out how deep ran the waters of political intrigue when he learned that the so-called Maverick Mayor had a double strategy. He intended to win, if he could, in the Democratic primary against incumbent Edmund G. "Pat" Brown, father of Jerry Brown. But in case he didn't win, he was mounting a mud-slinging and Red-baiting campaign that he hoped would alienate conservative Democrats from Brown during the November election. In fact, Yorty held five secret strategy meetings with the Republican standard-bearer, Ronald Reagan, to divide the Democrats from within. The plan worked. After Brown barely disposed of Yorty in the primary, he was battered by a vicious assault from the right in the general election and was handily beaten by Reagan.*

During the midmorning of June 5, 1968, as Robert Kennedy lay comatose in the hospital, Yorty appeared before network television cameras with Chief of Police Thomas Reddin, resplendent in his gold-braided uniform, sitting solemnly by his side and nodding in approbation. He revealed that according to a "reliable police informant," a car traceable to suspect Sirhan had been seen several times parked in front of the W. E. B. DuBois Clubs, a leftist young-people's group. The implication was that the man responsible for Kennedy's shooting was a left-wing radical.

What Yorty neglected to point out was that the DuBois Clubs were moribund and had vacated that address over a year before. One of Sirhan's brothers owned the car and played in the band at an Arabian night club a couple of doors away. Sirhan used the car frequently because his beat-up De Soto was forever breaking

---

* In 1972 Yorty announced that he was a candidate for President and campaigned in New Hampshire. He even garnered the endorsement of publisher William Loeb, noted for his radical right leanings. But Yorty was so soundly thrashed he must have wondered if anyone outside of Los Angeles had heard of him. Shortly thereafter, Yorty denounced the Democratic party, turned Republican, and (again) backed Richard Nixon.

down, and visited his brother at the Hollywood Boulevard location on many occasions.

Following the television appearance, Yorty showed up at the field command post set up in the LAPD's Rampart Division, not far from the Ambassador Hotel. The mayor began sorting through material the police had just brought in from a warrantless search of Sirhan's room in the family residence in Pasadena. His attention centered on some Rosicrucian literature—Sirhan had recently applied for membership in that mystical society—and a pair of spiral notebooks filled with repetitive and often disjointed handwriting that indicated strong occult affinities.

As Yorty left the police station he was cornered by several members of the press. "What can you tell us about Sirhan Sirhan?" one asked.

"Well," the mayor replied, "he was a member of numerous Communist organizations, including the Rosicrucians."

"The Rosicrucians aren't a Communist organization," a newsman corrected. In fact, it would turn out that Sirhan had never been affiliated with any Communist-oriented group.

"It appears," Yorty amended, "that Sirhan Sirhan was a sort of loner who harbored Communist inclinations, favored Communists of all types. He said the U.S. must fall. Indicated that RFK must be assassinated before June 5, 1968." Yorty had excerpted passages from the spiral notebooks, but at this point no one had verified that they were actually written by the man in custody. (There would remain a question of their authorship even after Sirhan was tried and convicted in 1969.)

Evidential niceties didn't faze the lawyer-mayor. Returning before the television cameras, Yorty brandished the notebooks and flipped though pages, reading off entries that he thought sounded Communistic. "He does a lot of writing, pro-Communist and anti-capitalist, anti-United States," he commented.* No one in the vast television audience could fail to get the message that Sirhan had been inspired to his deed by his Communist sympathies and occult dabblings.

State Attorney General Thomas C. Lynch phoned Yorty to

---

* San Francisco *Examiner* (June 6, 1968).

register concern that his televised statements "referred to evidence that would have to be ruled upon by the court," and prominent local lawyers upbraided him for, as one put it, "your lack of understanding of the fundamentals of American justice." But the irrepressible Yorty would not be muzzled. He held another press conference, at which he dwelt at length on the notebooks and their "timetable" to kill Kennedy. Sirhan, he said, was "inflamed by contacts with the Communist Party and contacts with Communist-dominated or infiltrated organizations."*

Both Yorty and Reddin went to great pains to convey that RFK's assassination had virtually been his own fault. Why? Because, they insisted, the presidential aspirant had allegedly told the LAPD that he wanted no police protection during his visits to Los Angeles. Thus, they said, no members of the LAPD had been present at the Ambassador Hotel at the time of the shooting.

Apparently none of the newsmen present gave any thought to the laws pertaining to the LAPD's responsibility for "public safety" and "crowd control" that should have applied to the gathering that night. (The hotel housed no fewer than three major political candidates, RFK, Senator Alan Cranston and Max Rafferty; their supporters covered the spectrum from extreme left to far right— the makings of potential spontaneous turmoil and violence.) It was also strange that no one in the RFK campaign entourage could recall anyone, RFK included, having called off LAPD protection. But no one stepped forth to challenge the contentions of the Yorty-Reddin press conference. The impression that prevailed was that RFK had somehow managed to orally sign his own death warrant.

Watching Yorty in action, Christian nodded knowingly at his display of demagoguery. "He may shoot from the lip," Christian said, "but there is *always* a motive behind it." That was one thing Christian knew from the 1966 campaign.

WHILE YORTY WAS HOLDING FORTH DOWNTOWN ON THE MORNING of June 5, a group calling itself American United called a press conference in Westwood, near the UCLA campus. American

---

* Associated Press (June 7, 1968).

United was the two-man show of John Steinbacher, a John Birch Society propagandist and part-time reporter for the Anaheim *Bulletin* in Orange County, and Anthony J. Hilder, a firebrand activist. Both were protégés of the well-known anti-Semite Myron J. Fagan, a leader of the Hollywood blacklisting clique during the McCarthy era.*

In fact, Hilder and a gaggle of followers had been at the Ambassador Hotel the previous night trying to race-bait RFK by handing out buttons and pamphlets depicting him and black Congressman Adam Clayton Powell, Jr., of New York on the same ticket. After the shooting the Hilder group created considerable confusion by alleging that the assailant was a Eugene McCarthy supporter.

Steinbacher and Hilder had prepared a press kit crammed with their prolific output of ultraright polemics. The year before, Steinbacher had published a turgid volume called *It Comes Up Murder*† that expounded the conspiracy theory of history. According to the theory, a vast international plot to control the world began in Bavaria in 1776 when Professor Adam Weishaupt organized, in Steinbacher's words, "the secret and evil cult of the Illuminati in order to wage Satan's war against Christian civilization." Weishaupt's acorn grew into a mighty oak of conspiracy, its branches numbering the Rothschild international banking family, the Rockefellers, Freemasonry, the Zionist movement and mystical societies such as the Rosicrucians and Theosophists. Through an alchemy of the most diabolical sort, the theory went, the elements of the Illuminati coalesced into the modern "international Communist conspiracy," which also manifested itself in such power centers as the United Nations, the Council on Foreign Relations and the Rockefeller Foundation, and such influential leaders as Franklin D. Roosevelt, Joseph Stalin, Charles de Gaulle and J. William Fulbright.‡

* Authors' interview with Anthony J. Hilder, 1970.

† Los Angeles: Impact Publishers, 1967.

‡ This list was recently expanded to include the Trilateral Commission—whose membership includes former Secretary of State Henry Kissinger and President Jimmy Carter.

"The success of the Illuminati," Steinbacher wrote, "lay in enlisting the services of dupes, and by encouraging the fantasies of honest visionaries or the schemes of fanatics, by flattering the vanity of the ambitious, and by playing upon the passion for wealth and power. It was in this way that the Illuminati were able to secure the services of countless thousands."

In *It Comes Up Murder* Steinbacher contended that "assassinations within the borders of the United States are carried out by the conspirators," and prophesied: "We can look forward to more strange deaths." (One grisly album cover depicted Nelson Rockefeller at the moment of his own assassination, as bullets shatter his skull and a look of terror comes on his face.) *

In early April the American United group sent a large contingent of congressmen a packet of anti-Semitic propaganda in the form of a long-playing album tagged "The ILLUMINATI-CFR (Council on Foreign Relations) . . . the MOST SHOCKING . . . REVELATORY EXPOSE of the 'IN CROWD' which has, UNTIL NOW, controlled the course of the MODERN WORLD . . . and is now attempting to bring about WORLD CURRENCY, WORLD GOVERNMENT, and WORLD CONTROL . . . The POLICIES of THIS GOVERNMENT have reached the point of INSANITY." The covering letter included the notation that records had been sent to every senator "except Morse, Fulbright, Church, Hartke, and the Brothers Kennedy . . . and the Brothers Rockefeller." The slogan emblazoned on the American United stationery warned:

---

* During a taped telephone interview on May 3, 1970, Hilder told Christian: "I *predicted* Bobby Kennedy would be shot . . . then he was shot. I *predicted* [Dr. Martin Luther] King would be shot . . . and *he* was shot! . . . Right now they have to have another killing . . . preferably a so-called Conservative . . . maybe Nixon . . . But it would be wonderful to have one-two-three [Kennedy] brothers."

Christian interviewed Steinbacher via phone on the same day. His words were equally disconcerting: "JFK was on to the thing [the alleged "Illuminati Conspiracy"], and he was about to blow the whistle [just before the President was killed. Sirhan was a lot like Oswald, *very* much so, *very* similar. They *definitely* were just patsies . . .] Ted Kennedy better not run. He would be next."

"OUR COUNTRY CAN NEVER GO RIGHT BY GOING LEFT!"* Thus, the main political leaders in America had been alerted to the "ILLUMINATI" threat to the survival of the nation. It was a name that would surface again—soon.

With RFK struck down, Steinbacher and Hilder were ready to claim that their timely prophecy had been fulfilled—that the senator was yet another victim of the "Illuminati-Communist conspiracy," which this time used Sirhan as a pawn. It just so happened that the Sirhan notebooks, which Sam Yorty was at that very moment inspecting (and which would remain out of the public domain until after the trial), contained repeated references to "Illuminati," as well as the entry "Master Kuthumi" (an apparently phonetic spelling of "Master Koot Hoomi"), a Tibetan mystic from whom Madame Helena Petrovna Blavatsky, the founder of the Theosophical Society, was said to receive ethereal guidance.

Not one member of the press showed up. Most were acquainted with the far-out ideology of Steinbacher and Hilder, and besides, were chasing down the main story and covering Yorty's press conferences. Undaunted, the pair appeared on talk shows to spread the word that the Illuminati were behind the shooting.† In jail, Sirhan added fuel to the fire by requesting *The Secret Doctrine*, by

* Letter signed by Anthony J. Hilder, April 7, 1968; mailed from 1141 North Highland Avenue, Hollywood, Calif. 90038.

Foundation researcher Walter Carrithers informed us in 1971 that American United once used the address P.O. Box 285, Woodland Hills, Calif. on some of its ILLUMINATI record albums. This is the same address on the letterhead of EUGENE BRADLEY DEFENSE FUND, an ad hoc group of right-wing preachers raising money to defend him against the charges levied by DA Jim Garrison in the JFK assassination case. One of the signators of a fund-raising letter sent out in July, 1968, was Orange County evangelist Dr. Bob Wells. In his 1968 interview with Jerry Owen, Turner asked if the preacher knew Wells: "Very well. He don't live far from me. Know him well." Did Owen know of the Bradley-Wells tie-in? "I think Bradley was to speak for him once."

† One appearance was on KHJ-TV's *Tempo* program, with right-winger Robert K. Dornan hosting (June 19, 1968). In 1976 Dornan was elected to Congress in the most costly congressional campaign in history. His main political target: the Trilateral Commission and its alleged "liberal" policies.

Madame Blavatsky, and *Talks at the Feet of the Master*, by C. W. Leadbeater, a theosophy follower, from his home library. Coupled with Yorty's disclosure of Sirhan's membership in the Rosicrucians, the pieces of an "Illuminati Conspiracy" were falling into place. "This is an Illuminist killing!" Steinbacher declaimed.

The Illuminati theme was soon picked up in the national media. Supplied with Steinbacher-Hilder "expertise," Walter Winchell devoted a column to it, and *Time* magazine ran a photograph of the late Madame Blavatsky with its story. Truman Capote, appearing on the *Tonight* show on NBC, ventured that Sirhan might have been hypnoprogrammed, and that Madame Blavatsky had shown "how you could undermine the morale of a country and create a vacuum for revolution by systematically assassinating a series of prominent leaders."

Capote was repeating a gross canard, originated by Steinbacher and Hilder, that Madame Blavatsky had authored a "secret manual" for assassination. Actually, she had pointed out in her writings how evil-minded men could employ assassination to subvert a nation. She was no Dragon Lady, but a pioneer in what is now called ESP, and her followers are the gentlest of people. They believe that God is present in all things, and advance the universal brotherhood of man. But to the radical right, such philosophies are occult-bred heresies.*

AT SEVEN-FIFTEEN ON THE EVENING AFTER THE RFK SHOOTING, a compact man with goggle eyeglasses marched into LAPD headquarters with four companions. He gave his name as Major Jose Antonio Duarte, and said he and his men were "freedom fighters against Fidel Castro." A Cuban exile, Duarte reported that on May 21 he had attended a leftist meeting because he knew that support for Castro was on the agenda. When he rose to speak out, he said, a small olive-skinned young man angrily accused him of

---

* For a convincing, thorough refutation of charges against Madame Blavatsky and the Theosophists, see *The Hall of Magic Mirrors*, by Victor A. Endersby (Fresno: The Blavatsky Foundation, 1969).

being a CIA agent, and they got into a shoving match. The young man was Sirhan Sirhan.

Duarte tried to unload his story on the news media, but it was ignored. Then, on June 11, the Anaheim *Bulletin* headlined: PRO-CASTRO LINK TO RFK SLAYING. The article, written by Duarte's political associate John Steinbacher, recounted the Cuban's putative encounter with Sirhan. Steinbacher arranged radio appearances for Duarte,* and in an instant paperback book, *Senator Robert Francis Kennedy: The Man, the Mysticism, the Murder,†* summed up: "Mayor Sam Yorty of Los Angeles has already brought out the pro-Communist inclinations of Sirhan, but it was left to Major Jose Duarte, the Cuban anti-Communist, to link Sirhan with the riots and unrest in our nation, today."

In time the LAPD discredited Duarte's identification of Sirhan by producing a look-alike Iranian student who had been at the leftist meeting and recalled being involved in the altercation. However, the entire scenario struck us as all too familiar. In August 1963 Lee Harvey Oswald was accosted by an anti-Castro exile while handing out pro-Castro literature on the streets of New Orleans. Shortly after the scuffle Oswald was invited to participate in a radio debate on the subject. In the evening of the day John Kennedy was shot, taped excerpts were broadcast nationally and Oswald was heard by millions proclaiming, "I am a Marxist!"

Both the debate and the assassination-evening airing of the excerpts were arranged by Edward S. Butler, who headed a right-wing propaganda outfit in New Orleans called the Information Council of the Americas. By 1968 Butler had moved to Los Angeles, where he carried on with financial aid from Patrick J. Frawley, Jr., chief executive officer of the Schick Safety Razor Company. For years Frawley generously supported hard-line conservatives such as Ronald Reagan, Barry Goldwater and Sam Yorty. Frawley and Yorty belonged to the American Security Council, an embodiment of the military-industrial complex that lobbied for a bigger military establishment and ran a political blacklist service

---

* Authors' interviews with Steinbacher and Hilder, spring 1970.
† Los Angeles: Impact Publishers, July 1968.

for its large corporation clients. Anthony Hilder also claimed to have the backing of Frawley.* And Butler was present when Steinbacher and Hilder held their unattended press conference.

Thus a right-wing clique colored the facts and conjured up visions of a sinister occult cabal to depict Sirhan as the pawn of an international plot. As the Anaheim *Bulletin* rhetorically asked in an editorial: "Are foreign influences at work to conquer this country? Is a hidden plot progressing to eliminate the Liberal leadership of the country and throw the movement completely into control of Communist agents?"

It was a bit mind-boggling to think of liberal leaders being knocked off by the radical left rather than the radical right, but the general theme that Sirhan had somehow been influenced by Communism stuck in the public mind. One effect of this popular impression was to permit the LAPD to suppress evidence leading in the opposite direction.†

* Hilder also claimed the backing of well-known conservative funder Henry Salvatori, in a telephone call to attorney Barbara Warner Blehr on July 27, 1971. (Salvatori was one of the principal financiers of both Sam Yorty and Ronald Reagan.)

† The LAPD is more blatantly right-wing than any other major force in the country. At the time of the RFK shooting the Fire and Police Research Association, dominated by and openly affiliated with ultraconservative groups, waged effective propaganda and lobbying campaigns. John Rousselot, then the national public relations director of the John Birch Society, claimed that some two thousand Los Angeles County law enforcement officers, including not only the LAPD but the District Attorney's staff and Sheriff's Department, were members of the Birch Society. Alan Cranston, now the senior U.S. Senator from California, found it hard "to suppress a shudder" when he heard the claim. "Whether two thousand or two hundred," Cranston said, "that frankly disturbs me more than all the reports of Minutemen training in the hills with rifles and bazookas."

5

The Cover-up

BUT THE ALLEGATIONS LEVELED BY YORTY AND STEINBACHER and Hilder also presented the LAPD with a major headache. As Chief of Detectives Robert A. Houghton, who was in overall charge of SUS, has observed in his book *Special Unit Senator*, the widespread belief that Sirhan had Communist connections and acted with premeditation raised the specter of conspiracy. So did the reports of a polka-dot-dress girl with Sirhan, and rumors that he was tied in with an Arab extremist group contemplating the assassination.*

* Houghton is alluding to a report received by SUS that an affiliate of the Arab terrorist organization El Fatah had Sirhan under control. According to Houghton, SUS learned that El Fatah had not become active in the United States until three months after the RFK shooting.

"We were faced with a crime that would be examined everywhere in the world," Houghton wrote. "There had never been one like it in Los Angeles history. Already it was under the public magnifying glass." Houghton could envision Kennedy haters and lovers, skeptical Americans, police critics and partisans of the FBI wanting to seize upon the LAPD's slightest miscalculation. Most of all he seemed haunted by a fear that the assassination "buffs" were lurking in ambush. "There were the clever people, as usual," he went on, "standing by to profit by the cry of conspiracy, hooking their theories to journalistic wagons before the Arlington soil was tamped. Sooner or later—sooner, probably—they would all come running from everywhere to demand, 'What really happened?' "*

Houghton's disparagement of those with differing views as crass opportunists was singularly inappropriate, since he himself contracted for a book exploiting his inside position while on the public payroll. But the bitterness of his attack on the critics as journalistic ghouls raises the question of how he, in the very early stages of the RFK investigation, could be so sure there was no conspiracy.

For SUS, from the inception of its probe, seemed to direct its energies at quashing evidence indicating a conspiracy while accepting uncritically information which pointed to Sirhan as a lone assassin. Because homicide is a violation of state laws, the LAPD assumed primary jurisdiction over the investigation. The FBI possessed a parallel jurisdiction under the civil rights statutes and federal legislation enacted after Dallas regarding violence against the President or a candidate for federal office. But from the start the LAPD made it clear that the FBI would be playing second fiddle. "They elbowed us out of it right away," Roger J. LaJeunesse, the senior FBI agent on the case, has said.†

Upon arriving at his office on the morning of the shooting, LaJeunesse was told that President Johnson had ordered the Bureau into the investigation and that he was to take charge. He left immediately for the "Glass House," the LAPD's Parker Center headquarters, arriving by nine-thirty at the office of Chief Houghton. Houghton appeared somewhat surprised that LaJeunesse was there,

---

* *Special Unit Senator* (New York: Random House, 1970), pp. 95–96.
† Authors' interviews with Roger LaJeunesse.

since he had talked to local FBI chief Wesley G. Grapp earlier, before the President's order arrived, and was assured that the FBI would not become involved.

Houghton expressed keen interest in the projected scope and nature of the Bureau's inquiry. He even proposed that two of his top men accompany the FBI agents on their rounds because, he said, he was planning on writing a manual about what local departments could learn from the FBI, and this would be a model case. The chief repeatedly insisted that the investigation was a "local matter" and that his men could handle it without day-to-day assistance from the FBI. LaJeunesse was somewhat disquieted by Houghton's uncharacteristic possessiveness. In his long experience with the LAPD, there had never been a "withholding" problem.*

LaJeunesse paid a visit to a special squad of detectives, isolated on the top floor of Parker Center, who were setting up an investigation office. It was later to become SUS. He noticed that an old acquaintance from his days on the bank-robbery detail, Lieutenant Manny Pena, was very much in charge.

Within days the LAPD announced that the elite squad called Special Unit Senator had been formed to handle the investigation. According to Houghton, it was entirely his idea to create SUS, "a unit completely detached from any other organizational branch of the Los Angeles Police Department." He tapped Chief of Homicide Detectives Hugh Brown, with whom he had worked for fifteen years, to head SUS, telling Brown that if there was a "great conspiracy" linking the RFK murder with those of JFK and Martin Luther King, Jr., it had better be unveiled because their work would be subject to "much fine-comb study."†

Houghton assertedly gave Brown free rein in electing the personnel for SUS—with one exception. He specifically designated Manny Pena, who was put in a position to control the daily flow and direction of the investigation. And his decision on *all* matters

---

* LaJeunesse, who had known Houghton previously, is certain that this meeting took place on the morning of June 5. However, Houghton stated in *Special Unit Senator* that he was camping in Yosemite Park at the time of the shooting and did not return to Los Angeles until two days later.

† Houghton, *op. cit.*, pp. 101–2.

was final. Working under Pena on what was called the Background/ Conspiracy team assigned to dig into Sirhan's past and the possibility of conspiracy was Sergeant Enrique "Hank" Hernandez. As a polygraph operator, Hernandez questioned the witnesses whose accounts indicated a plot. In each instance, as we have seen with Jerry Owen, Hernandez would get them to alter their stories, or if they refused, shredded their credibility with his polygraph interpretations.

The choice of Lieutenant Manuel Pena for the key slot in SUS was a curious one. Among members of the force and the Mexican-American community, Pena was a living legend—reputedly he had killed eleven suspects "in the line of duty," more than any other officer in the history of the department. In *Special Unit Senator* Houghton described him as a "stocky, intense, proud man of Mexican-American descent" with twenty-two years of experience under his belt at the time. Houghton boasted that Pena had commanded detective divisions, supervised a bank-robbery squad, and "spoke French and Spanish, and had connections with various intelligence agencies in several countries."*

What we did not know at the time that Pena and Hernandez interrogated Jerry Owen was that both had long-standing connections with the CIA. Our first clue about Pena came months later when a faded newspaper article came to our attention. On November 13, 1967, more than six months before the RFK slaying, the San Fernando Valley *Times* had reported Pena's formal retirement from the LAPD. A surprise testimonial dinner was held in his honor at the Sportsmen's Lodge, with LAPD Chief Thomas Reddin prominent among the law enforcement fraternity in attendance. It was "a rousing and emotion packed" affair, the article said, and then quoted Reddin: " 'I have known Manny for many years. I would not have missed being here for anything.' "

The article revealed: "Pena retired from the police force to advance his career. He has accepted a position with the Agency for International Development Office of the State Department. As a public safety advisor, he will train and advise foreign police forces in investigative and administrative matters. After nine weeks

* *Ibid.*, pp. 102–3.

of training and orientation, he will be assigned to his post, possibly a Latin American country, judging by the fact that he speaks Spanish fluently."

It is an open secret that the Office of Public Safety of the Agency for International Development (AID) has long served as a cover for the CIA's clandestine program of supplying advisers and instructors for national police and intelligence services in Southeast Asia and Latin America engaged in anti-Communist operations. In 1968 California Chief Deputy Attorney General Charles A. O'Brien informed us that this ultrasecret CIA unit was known to insiders as the "Department of Dirty Tricks," and that one of its specialties was teaching foreign "intelligence apparats" the techniques of assassination.

FBI agent Roger LaJeunesse, whom Turner had known years before in the Bureau, confided that Pena had left the LAPD for a "special training unit" at a CIA base in Virginia. In fact, said LaJeunesse, Pena's departure in November 1967 had not been a one-shot deal—the detective had done CIA special assignments for a decade, mostly under AID cover. On some of these assignments, in Central and South America, he worked with CIA operative Dan A. Mitrione, a former Indiana chief of police.* Further confirmation of Pena's CIA role came from his brother, a high school teacher, who casually mentioned to television newsman Stan Bohrman how proud Manny was of his services for the CIA over the years.

Reporter Fernando Faura, whose by-line appeared on the newspaper story of the farewell banquet, recounted that in April

---

* In the summer of 1970 Mitrione and an AID associate named Claude L. Fly were abducted by Uruguayan Tupamaros guerrillas. Press reports identified Mitrione as a "U.S. police advisor" to the military junta ruling Uruguay; his assignment was said to be the "special training" of militia personnel in "counterrevolutionary" tactics. The Tupamaros were more pejorative in their version of Mitrione's expertise: in a note pinned to his body after they shot and killed him, they accused him of being a "CIA killer" and "teacher of horrible tortures" whose atrocities against the revolutionaries could not remain unpublished. Fly was released unharmed. The affair was made into a 1972 motion picture, State of Siege, featuring Yves Montand as Mitrione.

1968, only five months after Pena's departure, he was sauntering along a corridor in Parker Center when he spotted a vaguely familiar figure. The square face and fireplug frame seemed to belong to Manny Pena, but now he sported an expensive dark-blue suit, a black handlebar mustache and heavy horn-rimmed glasses.

"Manny?" Faura probed.

The figure stopped and looked sheepish as the reporter approached with hand extended.

"Hey, Manny, I damn near didn't recognize you with that disguise!"

The detective was not amused. Faura asked what he was doing back in Los Angeles. Pena explained that the AID job wasn't quite what he had expected, so he quit and resumed his duties with the LAPD.

Pena's stints with the CIA were hardly unique. For example, Hugh C. McDonald, who was Chief of Detectives for the Los Angeles County Sheriff's Department before retiring in 1967, recently revealed in a book* that for many years he had gone on detached duty with the CIA as a contract agent, primarily in operations in conjunction with White Russian émigré elements in Europe. And according to Morton Kondracke of the Chicago Sun-Times, "a high-ranking former official of the spy agency said in an interview that he remembered some Chicago policemen attending training sessions at the CIA's super-secret facility at Camp Peary, near Williamsburg, Va., either in late 1967 or early 1968." The Agency itself conceded that "briefings" were given to "less than 50" policemen from "about a dozen departments."†

And we learned much later that Pena's SUS sidekick, Sergeant Hank Hernandez, who was promoted to lieutenant in recognition of his status in the special unit, also had CIA connections. Now retired from the force, he boasts in a résumé offering his services as a private investigator that in 1963 he played a key role in "Unified Police Command" training for the CIA in Latin America. He functioned under the usual cover of AID's Office of Public

* *Appointment in Dallas* (New York: Hugh C. McDonald Publishing Corp., 1975). McDonald talks about his CIA role throughout the book.
† Chicago *Sun-Times* (February 8, 1973).

Safety, and even received a medal from the Venezuelan government, then concerned with Fidel Castro's "exportation" of the Cuban revolution.

In retrospect it seems odd that two policemen who doubled as CIA agents occupied key positions in SUS, where they were able to seal off avenues that led in the direction of conspiracy. One of those avenues was the trail of "the girl in the polka-dot dress."

VETERAN LAPD SERGEANT PAUL SHARAGA WAS CRUISING IN THE vicinity of the Ambassador Hotel at 12:23 A.M. on June 5 when an "ambulance shooting" call crackled over his radio. In half a minute he wheeled his patrol car into the large parking lot at the rear of the hotel. People were running in all directions. An older couple hurried up to Sharaga. As he recalled it, "They related that they were outside one of the doors to the Embassy Room when a young couple in their early twenties came rushing out. This couple seemed to be in a state of glee, shouting 'We shot him! We shot him! We killed him!' The woman stated that she asked the young lady, 'Who did you shoot?' or 'Who was shot?,' and the young lady replied, 'Kennedy! We shot him. We killed him!'

"The only description I could get from this older couple was that the suspects were in their early twenties. The woman was wearing a polka-dot dress. Neither of the couple could furnish any additional information—they were quite hysterical and it was difficult for them to talk."

Sharaga said he jotted down the information on his note pad—he thinks the couple might have been named Bernstein—and immediately radioed a Code One (emergency) from his car. "I informed communications that I was setting up a command post in the area, and requested that they broadcast the description of the suspects as given to me." An All Points Bulletin went on the air at once advising all units to be on the lookout for the "two suspects."*

This was the debut of the famous polka-dot-dress girl. Although

* Art Kevin's taped interview with Sharaga, KMPC radio, Los Angeles, December 20, 1974.

the LAPD would later claim that she never existed, there were a number of others who reported sighting her that night.

The first was Sirhan himself. In a post-conviction interview in early 1969, Sirhan told NBC correspondent Jack Perkins that the girl materialized in mid-evening at the Ambassador Hotel as he was looking for a cup of coffee. He found a coffee urn, and a pretty girl was there. Perkins asked, "All right, after you poured coffee for the girl, then what happened?" Sirhan replied, "Then, ah . . . I don't remember much what happened after that."*

Possibly the first person to spot them together that evening was Lonny L. Worthey, who had come to the hotel with his wife and a friend for the anticipated Kennedy victory celebration. Unable to get into the Embassy Room, they went to another room on the ground floor that had been set up for campaign workers. An FBI interview report states:

> At about 10:00 P.M., when going to the bar to get a Coke for his wife, [Worthey] accidentally bumped into an individual at the end of this bar. After seeing newspaper photographs of SIRHAN SIRHAN, he believes the individual he bumped into was SIRHAN SIRHAN. WORTHEY apologized for bumping into this person to which this individual made no reply. A few minutes later WORTHEY observed a female standing along side this individual, but he did not observe them talking to each other.†

Kennedy supporter Booker Griffin, head of the Los Angeles chapter of the Negro Industrial and Economic Union, arrived at the hotel about ten-fifteen and found that he could not get into the Embassy Room without a pass. So he, like Worthey, contented himself with waiting in the other room. There he saw the small, shabbily dressed man he later identified as Sirhan. With him was a slightly taller girl with an upswept hairdo and a white dress that had designs of another color, possibly polka dots. Griffin told police

---

* Aired on NBC May 22, 1969.

† Interview June 7, 1968: unpaginated in FBI Summary Report by Special Agent Amedee O. Richards, Jr., August 1, 1969. Many of the interviews in this report, including Worthey's, remained classified until 1976, when they were released as the result of a Freedom of Information Act request.

that he thought "the two people seemed out of place . . . because everyone else but these two were celebrating the apparent Kennedy victory."

Upon obtaining a press pass from Kennedy aide Pierre Salinger, whom he knew, Griffin went to the temporary press headquarters in the Colonial Room, which was adjacent to the Embassy Room, where RFK was due to speak. It was now after eleven. Griffin noticed Sirhan and the girl standing in the corridor between the two rooms that led to the pantry where Kennedy subsequently was shot. With them was a casually dressed man, muscular and taller than six feet. Shortly before the shooting, Griffin saw Sirhan again and remarked to a friend, "There's a guy I've been seeing all evening and for some reason we don't seem to take to each other."

When the shots rang out, Griffin saw the same girl and the tall man dash out of the pantry and down the corridor. Griffin shouted, "They're getting away." Then he ran into the pantry and helped overpower Sirhan. Still bothered by the girl's escape, he ran out into the rear parking lot to try to find her, but she had vanished.*

Just before Kennedy entered the Embassy Room for his speech, campaign worker Susanne Locke noticed a girl "wearing a white shift with blue polka dots" standing between the stage and the main door. According to an FBI report, Locke "observed that the girl was not wearing a yellow press badge and thought this to be very unusual, since it was necessary to have such a badge to gain entry into the Embassy Room." As Locke recalled, "The girl was expressionless and seemed somewhat out of place where she was standing. She was a Caucasian in her early twenties, well proportioned, with long brown hair pulled back and tied behind her head. Her hair appeared to be dried out, similar in appearance to the hair of a girl who does a lot of swimming."†

Cathy Sue Fulmer, who had come to the hotel with a boy-friend and "gate crashed" the Embassy Room, advised the FBI that as Kennedy began his speech she was close to the stage and

* Interview at the LAPD Rampart Division, June 5, 1968, by Officers W. M. Rathburn and R. R. Phillips.

† Interview June 7, 1968; pp. 404–5 in FBI Summary Report, *op. cit.*

"standing near her was an individual she described as short male Mexican, about 20 years of age, whom she recognized from newspaper photographs as SIRHAN SIRHAN."*

How Sirhan and the polka-dot-dress girl gained entry to the restricted Embassy Room is answered by the testimony of twenty-year-old Sandra Serrano, a "Youth for Kennedy" volunteer. At about eleven-thirty Serrano bought a vodka and orange juice at a temporary bar set up in the southwest corner of the room. It was hot and crowded inside, so she stepped out a door that led onto a platform with metal steps leading to the ground—an emergency exit. She sat on a step about halfway down and sipped the drink. In two or three minutes a woman and two men climbed the stairs and brushed past her. "Excuse us," the woman said. As Serrano afterward described her to the FBI, the woman was

a white female, 23 to 27 years of age, 5'6" tall, medium build, 125 pounds. She had dark brown hair, ear length (bouffant style) and wore a white voile cloth dress with black quarter inch polka dots. The dots were about 1½ to 2" apart. This dress had three-quarter length sleeves, a bib collar with a small black bow and was A-lined. (SERRANO said she took special note of the dress, since she had a friend with one just like it.) This woman wore black shoes and no purse SERRANO said this woman did not wear glasses and had a "funny nose" which she described as a "BOB HOPE" type. [One of the men was] white male (Latin extraction), 5'5" tall, 21 to 23 years, olive complexion, black hair, long—straight, hanging over his forehead and needed a haircut. He wore dark pants, light shirt, and a gold or yellow cardigan type sweater and had nothing in his hands. [The other was] white male (Mexican-American), about 23 years of age, 5'3" tall, curly, bushy hair and wore light colored clothes. She said after seeing the picture of SIRHAN SIRHAN in the newspaper, she felt certain this was the same person she saw go up the stairs with this woman.†

Kennedy field worker Darnell Johnson spotted a girl answering the same description in the pantry off the Embassy Room only moments before the shooting. Johnson told the FBI that after RFK

* Interview June 8, 1968; unpaginated, *ibid.*
† Interview June 8, 1978; *ibid.*, pp. 464–67.

finished his speech and walked off the rear of the stage platform, he "walked around the platform to the narrow space in the serving area where the shooting took place and got there before KENNEDY." Sirhan was already there, among a group of four others that included a

white female wearing a white dress, with 25¢ size polka dots; the dress was fitted, not a miniskirt but was above the knees; was not a loose shift but was fashionable for the time. She was 23–25 years of age, tall, 5'8", medium build, well built, 145 pounds, long light brown hair, carrying an all white sweater or jacket, pretty full face, stubby heel shoes in the fashion of the time.

The others in the group were men, one over six feet tall in a light-blue washable sports coat and tie with "blond hair parted over on the left side with the right side long and hanging toward his face like a surfer haircut, outdoor type." The remaining two were neatly dressed in jackets and ties. Johnson could not tell whether any or all of these people knew each other or just happened to be together."*

A teen-age Kennedy fan who hoped to get close to her idol by slipping through the pantry recalled this group in vaguer terms. Robin Karen Casden told the FBI that instants before the shooting she saw someone who might have been Sirhan, as well as "several men in suits in the kitchen area [sic] and one or two women."†

Part-time waiter and college student Thomas Vincent DiPierro, the son of an Ambassador maître d', shook hands with Kennedy as he entered the pantry. DiPierro said he stopped by the ice machine to the right of Kennedy's path in the narrow pantry and "noticed there was a girl and the accused person standing on what is—what we call a tray stacker, where we had all the trays." Testifying on June 7, 1968, before the grand jury that indicted Sirhan, he explained that the tray stacker was just beyond the ice machine, to the right of Kennedy's path to the temporary press room. The

* Interview June 7, 1968; *ibid.*, pp. 406–9.
† Interview June 8, 1968; *ibid.*, pp. 432–34.

darkly handsome DiPierro said that the only reason he noticed Sirhan was that "there was a very good-looking girl next to him. That was the only reason I looked over there. I looked at the girl and I noticed him." Sirhan was "grabbing onto the tray stacker with his left hand."

"I could not see his right hand," DiPierro added. "He looked as though he was clutching his stomach, as though somebody had elbowed him." DiPierro had cause to remember the polka-dot-dress girl:

I would never forget what she looked like because she had a very good looking figure—and the dress was kind of lousy. . . . it looked like it was a white dress and it had either black or dark-purple polka dots on it. It kind of had—I don't know what they call it, but it's like a bib in the front, kind of went around like that [describing a scoop neck].

The girl had a peculiar-looking nose, and brown hair, he added. As the girl and Sirhan stood together by the tray stacker, DiPierro testified, Sirhan

looked as though he either talked to her or flirted with her, because she smiled. Together they were both smiling. As he got down, he was smiling. In fact, the minute the first two shots were fired, he still had a very sick-looking smile on his face. That's one thing—I can never forget that.

Kennedy campaign worker George Green also saw the polka-dot-dress girl. He told the FBI that he was just entering the pantry when the firing broke out, and that

once inside the kitchen door, he noticed a woman in her 20's with long blond free flowing hair in a polka dot dress and a light colored sweater and a man 5'11", thin build, black hair and in his 20's. GREEN stated that this man and woman were running with their backs toward him and they were attempting to get out of the kitchen area. GREEN stated that the reason he noticed them was that they were the only ones who seemed to be trying to get out of the kitchen area while everyone else seemed to be trying to get into the kitchen area.

Green's account was reinforced by Evan P. Freed, a press photographer, although in less explicit terms. Freed said that right after the shooting a girl and a man ran from the pantry. He thought that the girl was wearing a polka-dot dress but could not describe her further. The man was tall, thin and dark.*

The statements of Green and Freed back up Booker Griffin's report of seeing a girl and man rush from the pantry—the same girl he had seen with Sirhan on two occasions earlier.

Meanwhile Sandy Serrano was still sitting on the stairway from the emergency exit at the far side of the Embassy Room, the emptied glass in her hand. Some thirty seconds after she heard what sounded like automobile backfires,

this same woman who had gone up the stairs came running down the stairs toward her, followed by one of the men who had gone up the stairs with her. Miss SERRANO stated that as this woman ran down the stairs toward her, the woman shouted, "We shot him—we shot him!" Miss SERRANO said, "Who did you shoot?" to which this woman replied, "Senator KENNEDY!"†

Serrano's account is confirmed by the frantic report of the "Bernstein" couple to Sergeant Paul Sharaga, even to the precise language, "We shot him! We shot him!" The "Bernsteins" were within a hundred feet of the stairway where the young Kennedy volunteer was sitting.

Thus far we have traced the flight of the polka-dot-dress girl and her male companion from the pantry, diagonally across the Embassy Room, out the emergency exit, down the stairs past Serrano, past the "Bernsteins," and down a service driveway leading past the parking lot, where Sharaga would arrive in a matter of minutes.

Certainly the "dirty blonde" girl of Jerry Owen's story, as well as the three young men who appeared in his narrative, at least loosely fit the descriptions of the polka-dot-dress girl and her companions on the night of the shooting. But as Sergeant Hernandez

* Interview June 7, 1968; unpaginated, *ibid.*
† FBI interview with Serrano, *ibid.*

told Owen, in illustrating the supposed thoroughness of the investigation that determined there was no conspiracy, the police "went through eighteen witnesses on the polka dot dress girl."

AFTER PUTTING OUT THE APB FOR THE POLKA-DOT-DRESS GIRL and her male companion, Sergeant Paul Sharaga continued to man his parking-lot command post. Suddenly there was a police-radio blackout. "The thing that still has me confused," Sharaga later reflected, "—and as a police officer it shouldn't affect me that way but it sends cold chills down my spine—is that for a fifteen- or twenty-minute period we lost all radio communication. I've got it recorded in my log. There was that period when I could not communicate with another car, I could not communicate with the monitor, and I could not communicate with Communications, either on the main frequency or on Tac 1 or Tac 2 [tactical channels]."*

When the blackout ended, as inexplicably as it had begun, Communications kept broadcasting the APB at fifteen-minute intervals. At about two-thirty Detective Inspector John Powers came by the command post. "You'd never forget Powers," Sharaga said. "He had a reputation for carrying more than one gun. I think at one time he carried three or four guns." Powers wanted to know, "Who's responsible for this description of the two suspects that's going on the air?" Sharaga said that he was, and briefed Powers on the report of the "Bernstein" couple. "Let's cancel that description," Powers instructed. "We don't want to make a federal case out of it. We've got the suspect in custody."

Sharaga agreed to cancel the APB on the male suspect, since in the confusion of the moment he thought it possible that the "Bernsteins" had seen the man taken into custody, even though the description did not match. But he continued in force the APB on the polka-dot-dress girl in defiance of Powers' wishes. "He didn't

* Authors' taped telephone interview with Sharaga, May 21, 1976. In 1977 the Los Angeles District Attorney John Van de Kamp announced that there was no blackout—because the LAPD radio logs didn't show one.

have any choice," Sharaga explained. "It was either that or relieve me of my post." Nevertheless Powers had the last word, contacting Communications directly and ordering the APB discontinued.

Although the APB had not resulted in anyone's being stopped and questioned, there was no way the lid could be kept on the story. Within an hour of the shooting Sandy Serrano had been corralled by NBC newsman Sander Vanocur and thrust on live national television to tell about the girl in the polka-dot dress with a "funny nose." And Vincent DiPierro, a prime witness to the shooting, mentioned her in his testimony before the grand jury that indicted Sirhan a few days later, which was duly reported in the newspapers. It was, of course, impossible for the press to resist the angle of a well-endowed mystery woman.

THE LAPD'S CONCERN OVER THE GIRL IN THE POLKA-DOT DRESS manifested itself during an urgent meeting on Sunday morning, June 9, in Robert Houghton's office. "What have you found out so far?" Houghton asked Lieutenant Charles Hughes, head of the Rampart Division detectives who had carried the initial burden of the investigation. Hughes ticked off several aspects to the case, then brought up the polka-dot-dress girl. "Do you know about her?" he queried Houghton, who purportedly had just returned from a vacation in Yosemite National Park.

"I read it in the papers," the chief replied, "but what's the story?"

Hughes summarized Sandy Serrano's account, adding, "She's a long way from the kitchen, and she calls her mother in Iowa or some place before she tells anybody about the polka-dot-dress girl. Incidentally, she didn't tell her mother, either. She was grabbed by some TV guy, and tells her story to the world."

Hughes shook his head. "Maybe? But it looks pretty thin so far."

Inspector K. J. McCauley chimed in, "Except that one of the waiters who shook hands with Kennedy says he saw a gal in a polka-dot dress there in the kitchen. How about that?"

"Yeah, I know." Hughes shrugged. "The waiter's name is DiPierro. He places Sirhan in the kitchen, and says a pretty girl in a polka-dot dress is standing next to him. I know it. That's what's convincing the Bureau [FBI]."

Thus at least some of the police brass were skeptical about the polka-dot-dress-girl sightings from the start, even though the FBI was keeping an open mind. However, the entire police investigation was tailored to the conclusion that the girl didn't exist, beginning with the suppression of the report of Sergeant Sharaga. Sharaga told the authors that he shut down his command post shortly after noon on June 5, but not before sending a detail of officers to guard the floor of the hotel on which the Kennedy family was housed. He drove directly to the Rampart Division and dictated to the secretary of Captain Floyd Phillips a report of everything that had happened, with special emphasis on the "Bernsteins' " sighting of the polka-dot-dress girl and her companion.

When SUS was officially created about five days later, Sharaga was instructed to prepare a second report covering his command-post activities "from beginning to end." He complied, in even more thorough fashion. "I personally delivered the report to SUS one night," he said. "There was a deadline on it." Sharaga recalled a brief conversation about it with Manny Pena, whom he knew, but SUS was tight-lipped about the case. "That was a locked-door type of operation," he said. "You didn't get in there."

The meticulous Sharaga had made three copies of his report "in the event additional copies were needed." He put one in the Watch Commander's drawer at Rampart, and another in the mail box in the Sergeant's Report Room. Because he had spent so much time at home drafting the report, he kept a third copy for himself. As it turned out, this minor deviation from procedure was fortuitous.

"About two weeks later," Sharaga said, "there was something I wanted to refer to in the report, and I found the copies gone." He asked his superior, Lieutenant William C. Jordan, what happened to them, but Jordan professed not to know. "I inquired from SUS if there was some reason why they came to Rampart and disposed of the copies," he continued, "and their attitude was that they didn't even know what I was talking about." At the time Sharaga thought nothing of it, but when Houghton's book was published in 1970 and there was no mention of the command post, including the report of the "Bernsteins" about the polka-dot-dress girl, "the first questions started to form in my mind."*

Sharaga's report on the polka-dot-dress girl was vitally important, for it provided independent corroboration for Sandy Serrano's story. With the report buried, Serrano was on her own and vulnerable to persuasion. On June 10 officers from the LAPD, FBI and DA's staff took her to the Ambassador Hotel and asked her to re-create the events of election night. She was treated not as a cooperative witness but as a threat to the lone-assassin theory. FBI agent Richard C. Burris, who apparently agreed with the LAPD's position, marched her from the pantry across the Embassy Room to the stairway where she had sat, pointed out that the distance was some 170 feet, and rhetorically demanded "if she still felt she had heard the shots." The young lady stood her ground, saying "she had never heard a gunshot in her life and never claimed she had heard gunshots, but had described what she heard as six backfires, four or five of which were close together."†

Burris then confronted her with the fact that when she called her mother in Ohio after learning that Kennedy had been shot, she didn't mention seeing anyone she "felt was connected with the shooting." Serrano explained that "she always had difficulty communicating with her mother and was not able to talk to her to explain anything." Referring to the Sander Vanocur television interview over NBC, the FBI agent asked why "she had not said anything about seeing this woman and the two men go up the stairs, but only told about the woman and the man coming back down. It was pointed out to her the fact she claimed one of the men going up the stairs was SIRHAN SIRHAN was the most significant part of the incident described by her."

Burris may have been trying to influence Serrano, for at the time of the NBC interview she had not seen who had been taken into custody in the pantry. It was not until the following day, when she saw published pictures of Sirhan, that she recognized him as the third person sneaking into the Embassy Room. Serrano became

* Art Kevin's interview with Sharaga, op. cit.
† Interview June 10, 1968; FBI Summary Report, pp. 540–42.

angry, and according to Burris' report, "accused those present of lying to her and trying to trick her." She became so distraught that she had to be taken home.

The Sandy Serrano problem remained high on the SUS priority list. On June 20 Manny Pena dispatched LAPD criminalist De-Wayne Wolfer to the hotel to "prove" scientifically that she could not have heard the gunfire from the pantry. Mounting a sound-level meter on the stairway where she had sat, Wolfer had assistants fire test shots in the pantry. His meter supposedly registered no higher than one half a decibel, below the minimum that a person with sharp hearing might pick up. In his book, Robert Houghton dismissed Serrano as the victim of her own imagination:

> She obviously thought, in the furor of the moment, that she heard and saw certain things which were not physically possible or did not actually occur. It happens every day, in petty cases as well as in major crimes. People are positive they see someone who later turns out to have been miles away. They hear something which can barely be detected by the most sensitive electronic device.*

Houghton's was a specious argument, avoiding the fact that she did not claim to hear gunfire and did not identify someone who was "miles away." In an ordinary case SUS might have been able to close the book on Sandy Serrano. But as Houghton observed, this was no ordinary case:

> . . . Manny Pena knew that as long as Miss Serrano stuck to her story, no amount of independent evidence would, in itself, serve to dispel the "polka-dot-dress girl" fever, which had by now, in the press and public mind, reached a high point on the thermometer of intrigue. She alone could put that spotted ghost to rest.†

So Serrano was singled out for the special attention of Hank Hernandez. As Houghton told it, Pena asked Hernandez "what he was doing for dinner that night, and suggested he might like to take Sandra Serrano out for a SUS-bought steak." Hernandez got the message. He wined and dined the young lady but was unable to break her story. So he took her to Parker Center for a polygraph

* Houghton, *op. cit.*, p. 119.
† *Ibid.*, pp. 119–20.

test at the unseemly hour of 10:15 P.M. The polygraph is a forbidding instrument, and it must have been especially so to the twenty-year-old young lady. It shares the aura of invincibility attached to scientific gadgetry, and polygraph operators rarely miss the chance to intimidate their subjects by exaggerated claims of accuracy. Yet half a century after its invention, the instrument has yet to be accepted as meeting evidentiary standards by the courts of the land. Much depends upon the operator, not only as to his competence in interpreting the graph readings, but his independence and objectivity. Some authorities believe that the principal usefulness of the polygraph is not its ability to detect lies, but to aid the interrogator to break down his subject.

Hernandez opened his interrogation of Serrano by asking about the vodka and orange juice she had consumed, thus implying that the alcohol might have affected her faculties. The burly detective warmed up to his task. "Okay, now, we have statements here that obviously are incorrect," he declared. Having confronted Serrano with a conclusion, he gave her a way out by suggesting "you heard the kid—some kid mention something about a white dress and dots." The "kid" was Vincent DiPierro, who had given the graphic account of seeing the polka-dot-dress girl next to Sirhan in the pantry. It would have been physically impossible for Serrano to have picked up the story from DiPierro, for she had never met him until after the NBC interview. "She had on a white dress with polka dots," Serrano said on NBC, "she was light-skinned, dark hair, she had black shoes on, she has a funny nose, it was . . . I thought it was really funny, my friends tell me I'm so observant." But now, under pressure from Hernandez, Serrano was beginning to doubt her own eyes. "I don't know," she said, confused.

According to Houghton, "Miss Serrano's monitored autonomic responses to key questions indicated deception: the dress she saw had merely been white, not white with black polka dots, and as the girl ran past she had not shouted, 'We shot Senator Kennedy,' but rather, 'He shot Kennedy,' or 'They shot Kennedy.' "*

* *Ibid.*, p. 122.

HAVING GOTTEN SERRANO TO MODIFY HER STORY, HERNANDEZ moved in to try and destroy it completely. He labeled it a "pack of mistruths," and asked her when it had gotten out of hand. At the Rampart Station, she responded. "I was sitting there hearing descriptions and descriptions of these people, of these people, of these people. Oh God, no, maybe that's what I'm supposed to have seen. It messed me up, that's all; and I figured, well, they must know what they're doing."

Serrano was whipped. She was conceding the impossible, since she had told the story on television *before* being taken to Rampart with scores of other witnesses. But Hernandez interpreted her concession as mission accomplished. "Of course, we're going to have to cancel all these reports," he said. "You know that."

"I know that," the defeated young lady responded.*

The detective was overreaching—all he had proved was that he had confused Serrano badly. She hadn't recanted seeing a girl hurrying down the stairway yelling, "We shot him!," which Sergeant Sharaga's suppressed report of the "Bernsteins" tended to support. She simply had consented to say that her description of the girl was adjusted to fit that of DiPierro, an idea Hernandez first proposed.

APPARENTLY CONVINCED THAT IT HAD MANAGED TO DISCREDIT Sandy Serrano's story, SUS then turned its attention to Vincent DiPierro, the only other publicly known prime witness to the polka-dot-dress girl. On July 1, eleven days after the polygraph interrogation of Serrano, Hernandez summoned DiPierro to Parker Center for a similar session. The detective again got what he wanted.

"As a matter of fact," Hernandez summed up, "you have told me now that there was no lady that you saw standing next to Sirhan."

"That's correct."

"Okay. Now, I can appreciate what you would have been or could have been going through on that evening—"

"Yes."

* Kaiser, *op. cit.*, pp. 143–45.

"—but I think what you have told me is that you probably got this idea about a girl in a black-and-white polka-dot dress after you talked to Miss Sandra Serrano."*

Hernandez was having it both ways—Serrano got it from DiPierro, DiPierro got it from Serrano. But DiPierro's credibility had to remain intact, not only because he had testified before the grand jury but because the DA's office intended to use him as a witness at Sirhan's trial. Hernandez asked if anything else he had reported was not the truth.

"No, nothing," the young man said. "Only about the girl."

"Only about the girl?"

"Yes, sir. That good enough?" DiPierro knew what the police wanted him to say.†

However, it would be harmful if Sirhan's attorneys brought out that the girl was pure invention on cross-examination. Hernandez told DiPierro that he had described the polka-dot-dress girl "so well that in my experience I believe you were describing someone that you had seen during the night." Hernandez had a "someone" in mind—Valerie Schulte, a pretty "Kennedy Girl" from the University of California at Santa Barbara who had tagged along after the Kennedy party as they headed into the pantry. Reading about the mysterious polka-dot-dress girl, she had presented herself to the police on the possibility that someone had mistaken her.

Valerie Schulte had worn a polka-dot dress, all right, but it was bright-green with yellow polka dots. Pinned to it was a big red Kennedy button. Her hair was silky blond and her nose was not "funny" but nicely shaped. Moreover, she was hobbled by a huge leg cast from her ankle to her waist, the result of a skiing accident. And she was in back of Kennedy, not in front, as was the girl seen by DiPierro. The police had already shown her to Booker Griffin, but he took one look and said no.

But all of that didn't deter Hernandez. "When did you decide to interpose or inject [sic] this girl [Valerie Schulte] that you have described to me as being the girl that was in the kitchen?" he asked DiPierro. "It's possible that when I did that I could—I don't re-

* Houghton, *op. cit.*, p. 124.
† Kaiser, *op. cit.*, pp. 154–55.

member exactly, it could have been I saw her right after the shooting in that area," he answered. "I may have done that, too. I am not sure. There was so much confusion that night."

Actually, Hernandez had planted much of the confusion with both DiPierro and Serrano. But with that, Houghton wrote: "SUS closed the vexing case of the polka-dot-dress girl."*

SANDY SERRANO QUIT HER JOB AS A KEYPUNCH OPERATOR WITH A large insurance firm and fled back to her parents' home in Ohio, reportedly to escape further police harassment. Vincent DiPierro appeared as scheduled at the Sirhan trial, where he readily identified Valerie Schulte as the girl he had seen. The defense attorneys, themselves committed to the no-conspiracy theory, made no attempt to impeach this testimony by showing how it clashed with his grand jury testimony.

Young DiPierro evidently regretted his about-face, for on April 20, 1969, he wrote a congratulatory letter to Art Kevin, then a reporter with radio station KHJ, on a series Kevin was broadcasting on the unanswered questions in the RFK assassination. Before the series was aired, LAPD Inspector John Powers had visited Kevin and put pressure on him not to raise the question of the polka-dot-dress girl, but Kevin declined. In his letter DiPierro termed that segment "the first 'real, true' report" and lauded Kevin "on the extensive research and brilliant job of reporting a factual story." DiPierro said that since the question of the polka-dot-dress girl "concerned my character personally, I was deeply interested in hearing the facts straight for a change." He offered his assistance on "this controversial issue."

Due to the pressure of work, it was several days before Kevin could drive out to the DiPierro residence. The doorbell was answered by the senior DiPierro, a maître d' at the Ambassador Hotel, while Vincent stood in the background. Kevin thought that they "looked all shook up." The father said that the FBI had come by and explained how painstakingly the police and the FBI had reconstructed events in the pantry. Almost pleadingly, he told

* Houghton, *op. cit.*, p. 126.

Kevin to forget it, that his son's life might be in danger. When Kevin pressed on, the father blurted out, "I know who you are. You run around with those kooks Bill Turner and Mark Lane."* He shoved the door shut.

In the short interval since his polka-dot-dress girl broadcast, the FBI or someone purporting to be from the Bureau had probably gotten to the DiPierros, not only giving them a hard sell on the no-conspiracy theory but libeling the two critics Kevin happened to know. Kevin recalled that one of his colleagues, Tom Browne, had overheard FBI agents and LAPD officers discussing Turner in bitter terms. And Kevin learned that after he put the polka-dot-dress girl segment on the air despite Inspector Powers' intercession, high-level elements of the LAPD tried unsuccessfully to "get" his job.†

Art Kevin's experience was not unique among the press people who tried to force the polka-dot-dress-girl issue into the open. Reporter Fernando Faura was commissioned by *Life* bureau chief Jordan Bonfante to pursue it. He interviewed DiPierro and Sandy Serrano, and had an artist draw a composite sketch of the girl they had seen. Then Faura interviewed other witnesses, prevailing upon them to submit to polygraph tests by an operator not linked to the police. All passed. At this juncture, SUS contacted Bonfante.

After a six-hour conversation with the police, Bonfante refused to call off the investigation. But within a week, Bonfante was told by *Life* editors that the story would never see the light of print. Someone had gone over his head.

Thus the LAPD buried the girl in the polka-dot dress with a blank tombstone. On the eighth floor of Parker Center, in the old sound stage that served as SUS headquarters, there was no mourning.

* Long-time Warren Commission critic and author of *Rush to Judgment*.
† Authors' interview with Art Kevin, May 12, 1969. When Kevin aired the interview with ex-LAPD Sergeant Paul Sharaga on KMPC Radio in December 1974, Powers stormed into the studio and once again threatened to "get" the newsman's job. However, KMPC management backed Kevin completely—and the LAPD chieftain backed off.

6

Investigative File

ALTHOUGH DISAPPOINTED IN THE WAY MANNY PENA AND
Hank Hernandez summarily dropped the Jerry Owen angle,
we considered that it might have been a rather typical bureau-
cratic reaction rather than a systematic cover-up. In this case,
Sirhan Sirhan was it from ground zero, and the LAPD
apparently was not budging from that position, even though
this conclusion was wholly premature.

When we decided to launch our own investigation, we
saw no reason that we could not cooperate with SUS provided they would reciprocate. If nothing else, we wanted to
compare our tape of Owen's story with the police recording
of what he had told them at the University Station. Calling

the LAPD, we were shuffled from one office to another, then told that no one would speak with us. Christian decided to go over the heads of the police. He phoned a senior aide to Mayor Sam Yorty, Jack Brown, whom he had known well during Yorty's 1966 campaign for governor. Brown was a former Hearst political editor. He said that SUS and the DA's office had shut the door on newsmen, opening it only to hand out self-serving statements. He would ask Yorty, without going into any details, to instruct the police to get in touch with us.

Within twenty minutes Sergeant Manuel "Chick" Gutierrez of SUS was on the line. When Christian mentioned Turner's taped interview with Owen, Gutierrez asked to be furnished a copy immediately. Christian obliged. But in a phone conversation several days later, Christian proposed to Gutierrez that we work closely ("undercover") with his unit on the Owen angle. We would abide by any legitimate restrictions on the release of the story, but we wanted the journalistic inside track. There was nothing precedent-shattering in the proposal—law enforcement agencies frequently open their files to friendly journalists in return for cooperation. But Gutierrez's superiors rejected the proposal out of hand. "We've already checked that out, and Owen was not involved," Gutierrez said.

It baffled us that SUS, which had been so anxious to obtain our tape, had dismissed the Owen story as merely a publicity stunt. We decided to go one step higher. In California the Attorney General is empowered to step in when local law enforcement is lax or malfeasant. In approaching the AG's office we were in luck. The Chief Deputy Attorney General was Charles A. "Charlie" O'Brien. O'Brien was a graduate of Harvard Law School, and like a number of Harvard men, he had close political ties to the Kennedy brothers over the years. After migrating to San Francisco and opening a law practice, he soon became bored and joined the AG's staff in 1958. He rose swiftly to the chief deputy's position, although some of his colleagues felt he was too active for the job. In 1964, for example, he used karate chops learned in the Army to fend off a Hell's Angel motorcycle thug intent upon maiming a young girl participating in an antiwar demonstration. Ironically,

O'Brien had been high on Robert Kennedy's list of prospects for U.S. Attorney General after he became President.

On August 13, 1968, Christian called O'Brien at his main office in the State Building in San Francisco. The chief deputy listened to his brief presentation, then invited us over. Charlie O'Brien had a bulldog Irish face, thinning hair, an ever-present pipe and a manner of cool assurance. He let the Owen tape run non-stop through its hour-and-six minutes' duration. He listened intently, cocking his head at significant points, making notes on a legal pad. When it was over, he stared at his personal shorthand, then looked up with a wry grin. He agreed that Owen was no clown performing an ego act. He handed the tape to his secretary and asked her to make a copy and type a transcript as quickly as possible. He would run all the mentioned names and pseudonyms through the files of the California Bureau of Criminal Investigation & Identification, which was under the AG's jurisdiction, and get back to us shortly. The whole case was funny, he said. His office had made numerous attempts to monitor SUS progress on the investigation, but had been thwarted at every turn. In fact, his was the *only* law enforcement agency not invited to review the case.

About a week later O'Brien called us, his voice deadly serious. "Look out for this joker," he warned of Owen. "He's got a rap sheet that runs wall to wall. He's a dangerous man." O'Brien didn't elaborate, but we got the message. It was now more important than ever to try to find out why "The Walking Bible" talked.*

A SIGN ON THE LAWN OF THE CALVARY BAPTIST CHURCH IN Oxnard read: *A truly independent Baptist Church.* The stucco building was only slightly larger than the well-kept homes lining the residential street. It was the only church of that name listed

* At that same time O'Brien had just finished reviewing the extradition request by Louisiana law enforcement authorities for Edgar Eugene Bradley, who had been indicted for conspiracy in the assassination of John F. Kennedy. O'Brien recommended to Governor Ronald Reagan that the extradition be granted. Reagan waited until after Richard Nixon's election to the White House—then turned down the request without comment.

in the directories of this farming community nestled close to the Pacific Ocean about seventy miles northwest of Los Angeles.

Jim Rose pulled up in his gray van. We had met Rose earlier when he volunteered to help in the investigation of the John Kennedy assassination. Rose was not our man's real name; Turner and he had decided upon it when they had their first meeting at midnight in the parking lot of the Rose Bowl in Pasadena (when they began working together on the JFK assassination case for DA Jim Garrison). A one-time contract employee of the CIA—as a combat and reconnaissance pilot—the man who also sported such names as Dawes, McLeish and McNabb is somewhat of a "living legend" within intelligence circles. When we asked him to take the lead for us in the "Walking Bible" angle, he'd just landed his World War II B-26 attack bomber after having made a well-publicized bombing run on the palace of Haiti's fascistic dictator, "Papa Doc" Duvalier.

We decided early on that Rose could fill our needs perfectly, and managed to scrape together enough money to send him to Southern California to retrace Owen's steps in his hitchhiker story. Rose was checking on Owen's claim that he was unable to show up at the Ambassador Hotel with the horse on election night because he had to speak at the Calvary Baptist Church in Oxnard.

Tall, blue-eyed and clean-cut, Rose was posing as a recently discharged serviceman with strong anti-Communist convictions. As he entered the church he noticed literature of the American Council of Christian Churches, the organization Owen said he was once affiliated with. Rose talked with the pastor, a Reverend Medcalf, who said that he had only taken over the church in mid-July. For the previous six months, Medcalf said, the church was closed because his predecessor had not made a financial go of it. No, the name of the Reverend Jerry Owen rang no bell.

It appeared that if Owen had in fact gone to Oxnard that night, it wasn't to preach at the Calvary Baptist Church.

In Hollywood, Rose found other discrepancies in Owen's story. Billy Gray's Band Box on Fairfax Avenue, the night club where the preacher purportedly attended a Saints and Sinners meeting on Monday evening, had for some time been remodeled into

Temple Catering. And the "bowling alley" on Sunset Boulevard where the preacher said he met with Sirhan and his companions later that night had long since given way to the offices and studios of Golden West Broadcasters.

But "right across the street," as Owen had put it, there was a hotel called the St. Moritz. This was where Owen said he spent the night after Sirhan failed to produce the $300 for the horse on the night of June 3. The registration records confirmed that one J. C. [*sic*] Owen, giving the correct address for the preacher in Santa Ana, checked into Room 203 at midnight. It was a bathless $4 room, just as Owen had said, and there was a telephone in it, so that he could have received a call the next morning.

Finally, Rose filmed and photographed the layout of the Ambassador Hotel, whose sprawling grounds occupy a large city block. The front looks north to Wilshire Boulevard across a broad expanse of lawn. At the southwest quadrant is the rear parking lot toward which the polka-dot-dress girl and her companion were seen fleeing, and where Sergeant Sharaga set up his command post. And on the eastern side is the 7th Street cul-de-sac off Catalina Street, where Owen said he dropped off Sirhan to see "a friend in the kitchen" on Monday afternoon—the spot where he asserted he was to deliver the horse on election night.*

Rose's photographs and film revealed that the cul-de-sac was an ideal place for an escape vehicle to wait. It was dimly lit, and there was virtually no traffic at night. To reach it from the Embassy Room pantry was only a short dash through a lobby and out the doors of the Palm Court, then down a palm-fringed walk to the cul-de-sac. The total distance is approximately 240 yards.

WHILE ROSE WAS IN SOUTHERN CALIFORNIA, JERRY OWEN SURfaced in Sonoma, about forty-five miles north of San Francisco,

---

* Curiously enough, we later obtained a taped interview made by Los Angeles radio newsman John Goodman with George T. Davis, wherein the lawyer insisted that Owen had been seen at the Ambassador Hotel, *with Sirhan in his company*, on the afternoon of June 3, and that the name of that witness had been turned over to the LAPD. We could find no such police report later on.

where he was staging a nightly Bible crusade.* The engagement provided an opportunity for Rose to look over Owen's residence in Santa Ana. It turned out to be a rambling ranch-style home on the outskirts of the growing city. A decrepit barn and small corral stood in the large yard, which backed onto the dry Santa Ana River. Suddenly a girl in her late teens came out of the house and asked what he was doing.

"I'm a free-lance reporter from San Francisco," Rose improvised. "I've heard about Reverend Owen's story and . . ."

The girl smiled. "Why don't you come in and ask him yourself? He's out in his office."

Concealing his surprise, Rose accepted, wondering why the preacher had flown back from Sonoma when he was due to speak again that night. Owen exuded cordiality. He said he was sorry that he could not be quoted on the Sirhan story because of a court gag order, but nevertheless launched into a fragmented account

---

* The Sonoma crusade demonstrated again that Owen sought publicity for his ministry—but shunned it in connection with the assassination. We decided to hire NBC cameraman Ron Everslage to film the preacher in action after we heard him touting the crusade over a San Francisco radio station. Everslage told Owen that he was doing a television documentary on religion in California. Owen told his audience how television viewers would see "how God put 31,173 Bible verses in this preacher's heart." He put on a banner performance, alternating between a dulcet love motif and a thundering warning that America was going to hell in a hurry because she had forgotten God. A few days later Ben Hardister, the private detective who had helped guard Owen and was involved with the crusade, called Everslage and wanted to know when the documentary would be aired. Failing to get a satisfactory answer, Hardister hopped a plane to Los Angeles to confront personnel at the television station Everslage had named in his cover story. They, of course, knew nothing. Twice Hardister contacted Everslage again, grilling him in a manner indicating that he suspected the RFK assassination inquiry was behind it. Everslage taped Hardister's thinly veiled threats, and we gave a copy to Chief Deputy Attorney General Charles O'Brien. According to one of O'Brien's aides, the AG's office had come across Hardister's name in the course of an investigation of the paramilitary right in California two years before. Hardister left one item behind at the Everslage household, however, that intrigued us the most: it was his "personal card" not as a private dick, but as "President, The California Appaloosa Horse Racing Association." Again, the smell of horse droppings and gunpowder pointed in the direction of Sirhan.

that corresponded closely with the one he had given Turner two and a half months before.

Then, with an air of confidentiality, he identified Sirhan's hitch-hiking companion as Crispin Curiel Gonzalez, a seventeen-year-old Mexican youth whose story, with photographs, had recently appeared in the press.

It was a bizarre account. On June 17 Gonzalez had stopped at a soft-drink stand in Juarez, across the Rio Grande River opposite El Paso, Texas. The woman behind the counter bought a yellow legal pad from him for one peso. Later an El Paso man was idly leafing through the pad when he noticed an entry dated June 4 that said:

I will have to try to erase completely from my memory—before the world learns about me—that I was in on the plot to kill Robert F. Kennedy. That crazy Arab has a tremendous hate for all the Kennedys . . . easy enough to get him to take some of the money and do the job. The whole world knows it was a grand plot but, unfortunately, they do not know the whole truth.

I never knew who organized the assassination but that's not important. I know the world will never know all about it. I'll probably die soon in some part of Mexico.

The El Paso man notified Mexican police, who picked up Gonzalez for questioning. "You wait and see," the youth warned the police. "The next will be Edward Kennedy. All they have to do is wait—wait—wait for the best time. They told me the Kennedys wanted to be dictators of the United States." But Gonzalez was unwilling or unable to disclose who "they" were. He claimed that he knew Sirhan, and several days before the assassination had met with him in a library in Santa Monica to plan RFK's death.

In checking out the story, Juarez police determined that on election day Gonzalez had been in the custody of the FBI in El Paso, having been brought there from Los Angeles by immigration officials uncertain of his nationality.* Although this seemed to rule out Owen's identification of him as one of the hitchhikers, it

---

* *Alerta,* Mexico City (July 6, 1968); *Alarma,* Mexico City (July 17, 1968).

did not eliminate the possibility of a link to Owen and Sirhan. Juarez Deputy Police Chief Jose Regufio Ruvalcava was quoted in the press as saying, "There were so many factors connecting Curiel with Los Angeles that when we arrested him we decided he should be investigated thoroughly. We checked with your FBI and a spokesman there told us definitely that Curiel knew Sirhan—was a friend of his. There is no doubt that Curiel knew Sirhan—they had met a number of times at the Santa Monica library and elsewhere and had usually discussed politics." (FBI agent Roger LaJeunesse later confirmed that the two were somehow linked.) Ruvalcava added that his prisoner was intelligent and politically sophisticated, and had in fact talked about forming a political party "to replace the socialistic structure of Mexico."

On July 4 Gonzalez was found dead in his isolation cell in the Juarez jail. Ruvalcava announced that he had fashioned a noose from strips of a mattress cover, tied it to a window bar, and let himself sag and strangle. The suicide verdict was greeted with skepticism by many, considering the circumstances. The father, Crispin Curiel Gonzalez, Sr., was certain it was murder. "In the last letter we had from him," the elder Gonzalez revealed, "he hinted at a promise of big money for him—but that it was very dangerous."*

Not long afterward Robert Kaiser, a journalist acting as a defense investigator, showed Sirhan a news clip with Gonzalez's picture. "Ever see this kid before?" he asked. "No," Sirhan replied. "Who is he?" But when Kaiser mentioned that he was dead, a flicker of dismay crossed Sirhan's face. A week later Sirhan implied that he had known Gonzalez. "That kid didn't have to die. He didn't do anything," Sirhan told Kaiser. "Who would have wanted to get him out of the way?" the journalist asked. Sirhan thought for a moment, then smiled. Then he changed the subject.†

Was Gonzalez merely a tortured psychotic who had written about Kennedy's death *after* the assassination in an attempt to identify himself with the crime? Or was his legal pad the same kind of "notebook" Sirhan had kept, with its mandate that "R.F.K.

---

* *Ibid.*
† Kaiser, *op. cit.*, pp. 238 and 239n.

must die!" and its mention of large sums of money? Apparently Gonzalez had been taken into federal custody shortly before the assassination, and could not have been the youthful Mexican-looking companion of the polka-dot-dress girl. But he had been in Los Angeles, and the authorities connected him to Sirhan. And now Jerry Owen was pegging him as one of Sirhan's companions.

We felt that somewhere in the assassination jigsaw puzzle, the pathetic figure of Crispin Curiel Gonzalez was a perfect fit.

AS SEPTEMBER DREW TO AN END IT BECAME OBVIOUS THAT IF we were to pursue our investigation, one of us would have to move to Los Angeles. SUS and the FBI were trying to wind up their investigations in the face of a Sirhan trial date originally set for December 14, then postponed until after the first of the year.

Christian volunteered to make the move. Before leaving, he checked out with Charlie O'Brien. The chief deputy was unhappy at the way the LAPD was still by-passing his office and mis-representing facts. "Something or someone is manipulating that goddamn investigation," he grumbled. "We're not getting any information, and I'm going to find out why!" O'Brien disclosed that SUS and the Los Angeles DA's office had already "marked" us, and admonished Christian not to "spook" his contacts within those agencies by revealing our close link with his office.

In Los Angeles a mutual friend, Dick Livingston,* offered to arrange a meeting between Christian and Deputy DA David Fitts, who had participated with Pena and Hernandez in the San Francisco interrogation of Owen. "He's a bright, nice, open-minded guy," Livingston said. To his surprise, however, Fitts declared that he already knew Christian was in town. No, he would not meet him personally, but he would talk on the phone. The conversation was chilly. Fitts told Christian that he had carried the brunt of the questioning of Owen, and that in his opinion the preacher was "a

---

* Richard Kinkaid Livingston was the first person Christian met in Los Angeles. He was one of Kennedy brother-in-law Peter Lawford's closest friends and as a consequence had known the brothers Kennedy. Ironically, Livingston was also a good friend of another (soon-to-be) "famous" man in politics—Robert Haldeman, Richard Nixon's "chief of staff."

self-serving son-of-a-bitch" who conjured up the story for publicity's sake. Fitts said he wasn't interested in seeing or hearing anything further about Owen—that chapter was closed.

Christian phoned Jack Brown, the Yorty aide who had arranged the initial contact with SUS, on the possibility that the mayor might intervene once again. Brown set up a meeting in his office with Ronald Ellensohn, the mayor's liaison with the LAPD, sitting in. Christian played the Turner interview with Owen, and ran through some of the follow-up material. Brown and Ellensohn agreed that SUS had missed some vital clues, which could lead to severe embarrassment for the Yorty administration. They concluded that an immediate liaison between us and SUS should be negotiated, and it was left that Ellensohn would contact SUS and report back to Brown. Brown would prepare a letter of recommendation for Yorty to act upon.

It took a month for Ellensohn to complete his talks with a balky SUS, and Brown was finally able to compose the memorandum:

On October 13, Ron Ellensohn and I had a lengthy conference with Jonn Christian, a free-lance investigative reporter from San Francisco. You may recall I previously memoed you about Christian and his belief that the murder of Robert Kennedy was a conspiracy. Christian played for us a taped interview with Oliver "Jerry" Owen, an evangelist and horse trader with homes in both Orange County and the Oxnard area [sic].

The memo synopsized the hitchhiker story, mentioning that Owen had reported it to the LAPD. It continued:

Apparently acting on my previous memo to you, police contacted Christian in San Francisco and he offered to turn over his tape and other material to them. But he heard nothing further from the officers. Ellensohn checked police and learned they had spent 100 manhours investigating Christian's allegations that the assassination was an ultra right-wing plot. . . . Police dismissed Owen's statement as one of the many false stories arising around the assassination. Christian was also said by the police to be an associate of Jim Garrison, District Attorney of New Orleans, which I suppose discredited him. [Actually, it was Turner, not Christian, who had been associated with Garrison. Back in 1968, critics of the Warren Report were looked upon with disdain in establishment circles.]

Brown's memorandum concluded with the news that Christian had just "called me to say that Charles O'Brien, Chief Deputy Attorney General, has taken direct interest in the Owen case." Brown advised that if the LAPD wanted "to look any further into this matter, they can now reach Christian in the Los Angeles area." The memo was tagged with Christian's temporary address and telephone number in Beverly Hills.

Brown told Christian that he was certain that the memo, especially the part about O'Brien's interest, would prompt Yorty to pick up the phone and reopen the Owen file at SUS headquarters. But the mayor did nothing; he did not even acknowledge the memo in the usual way by initialing and returning it to Brown.

It would be eight months before we found out why.

ONE DAY EARLY IN DECEMBER WHEN TURNER VISITED LOS Angeles, we had lunch with Robert Kaiser, who had spent ten years in a Jesuit seminary, then become a *Time* correspondent covering the ecumenical conferences in Rome in the early 1960s. We had met Kaiser four months earlier when *Look* magazine, for whom he was a stringer, expressed an interest in pursuing our story. Kaiser had been assigned by *Look* to evaluate our material, and submitted such a negative report that the magazine backed off.

We didn't know at the time that Kaiser had a sharp conflict of interest. He was already busy talking to Sirhan's attorneys to obtain exclusive rights to Sirhan's own story, hoping to crack the conspiracy from inside, for Kaiser instinctively felt that the enigmatic little Palestinian was not alone. He finally negotiated a deal with chief defense attorney Grant Cooper which gave him official status as a defense investigator to boot. Thus he had exclusive access not only to Sirhan but presumably to police data as well. It was a journalist's dream for Kaiser, but it had made him a competitor of ours.

Nevertheless, we decided that we should keep in touch with him. We were anxious to find out what his marathon sessions might have extracted from Sirhan in the way of a tie to Owen.

Nothing, Kaiser said, absolutely nothing. Sirhan flatly denied knowing Owen or anything about a horse transaction. But Kaiser sensed that Sirhan might have lied to him on this score. "I've caught him lying about things that he said and did before the assassination," Kaiser said, "things that can be proven conclusively, and this tends to make me believe he might be lying about being with Jerry Owen, too. He's a smart little bastard, you know. He's been playing games with me from the very start of our sessions. I can feel it down deep. I know he's concealing the actual facts— the identities of those who put him up to it."

Kaiser sounded frustrated. Here he had the man who apparently had killed Robert Kennedy and he couldn't crack him. What did Sirhan have to gain by keeping silent, by feigning ignorance, by lying? Kaiser had argued with him that if he agreed to open up, he would not only escape the death penalty but might get off with a lighter sentence for his cooperation. And if Kaiser got the exclusive inside story, they both would end up wealthy from sales to media around the world. It was a powerful argument, but Sirhan only blinked and went on with evasive word games.

Did Sirhan fear another kind of death penalty if he talked? Or was it just possible that his mind *was* a blank? "What about hypnosis," Christian offered, having read a book or two on the subject. "You know they can screw up a guy's mind with hypnosis —blow his memory—just like they can stop you from smoking." For the rest of the luncheon we talked animatedly (if not too expertly) on the possibility that Sirhan had been hypnoprogrammed to kill—and to forget.

A FEW BLOCKS FROM THE LOS ANGELES MEMORIAL COLISEUM, built for the 1932 Olympic Games, the Coliseum Hotel stands as a fading landmark in an area that has seen better days. The high-ceilinged grill—GOOD FOOD it says simply on the window—is cooled on muggy summer days by a fan mounted on a stand.

The fan must have been whirring on the morning of June 5, 1968, as Jerry Owen parked his pickup truck and horse trailer in the rear parking lot and walked inside. He had been on his way back to Santa Ana from Oxnard, he said, when he felt hungry and decided to drop in on his old pal Bert Morse, who ran the grill. As Owen told it, Morse and a waitress, Mabel Jacobs, were present when he saw Sirhan's picture on television and the front page of the Hollywood *Citizen-News* and recognized him as the hitchhiker of two days previously. So was a fight trainer named Doug Lewis, but Owen's story downplayed his presence.

The Coliseum grill was clearly the crossroads of Owen's story, where fact and fiction met. As the New Year of 1969 began, Christian resolved to interview both Lewis and Morse.

Douglas T. Lewis was an affable, rotund black man then in his early sixties. He said that he had known Owen for years through the fight game, and recalled him arriving at the Coliseum grill before noon on the morning after the shooting and "telling us that he picked up this young man on the freeway, and he brought the young man in town." The hitchhiker was on his way to the race track, and Owen said, "Well, I'm going that way and I'll drop you off at the hotel." The hotel, Lewis clarified, was the one "where the catastrophe happened." When the waitress brought over an *EXTRA!* edition newspaper, Owen immediately recognized Sirhan's picture.

What Lewis had to say contradicted Owen in one other important respect. Owen had said that his decision to stop at the Coliseum grill was impromptu, but Lewis was insistent that he and Owen's boxer, "Irish Rip" O'Reilly, were supposed to meet Owen at the grill that morning. "Yeah, I met him over there every day to take this boy to the gymnasium," he said. The time frame encompassed the entire week before the assassination. O'Reilly was staying at the Coliseum Hotel, and as we also later discovered, was present when Owen arrived as expected.

If Lewis was correct, Owen was meeting his trainer and boxer daily at the grill before going over to the gym nearby. This would mean that he went there Monday, in contrast to his version that he only detoured through Los Angeles to pick up boxing gear at a sporting-goods store. It would mean that he went there Tuesday, in contrast to his version that after checking out of the St. Moritz Hotel in Hollywood he went directly to Oxnard. That Owen had even gone to Oxnard, much less preached at the Calvary Baptist Church, was beginning to look more and more dubious.

What Bert Morse told Christian tended to back up Lewis. Morse said that Owen had come to the grill because he had a "big clown" of a boxer staying in the Coliseum Hotel. But Morse nervously denied being present when Owen recognized Sirhan, and in fact sought to minimize his relationship with the preacher. "Oh, years ago I used to see him around the fight racket," Morse conceded. "I think he was handling fighters or around fight racketeers years ago." Was he a legitimate preacher? "All those preachers are legitimate when the dollar's there," he scoffed.

We learned later that Morse was more than a fight manager turned restaurant and saloon proprietor. In Hemet in Riverside County he owned the Morse Stock Farm, where he raised thoroughbred horses and raced them at Santa Anita, Hollywood Park and other tracks throughout the state. Two of his horses, Hemet Miss and Diamond Dip, were winning their share of purses.

Owen's own connection with the race-track crowd provided a possible answer to the enigma of how he might have met so unlikely a person as Sirhan, assuming that it wasn't as a hitchhiker. In 1965 and 1966 Sirhan, aspiring to become a jockey, had worked as an exercise boy at the Santa Anita and Hollywood Park tracks, and later in 1966 was employed as a groom at a thoroughbred ranch in Corona, not far from Hemet. It was not difficult to imagine him crossing paths with Owen somewhere among the horse fanciers.

The Reverend Jonothan Perkins, the elderly minister who Owen said accompanied him for the interview at SUS headquarters, did not appear at first glance to be a promising witness. He was a long-time friend of Owen, and for over twenty years had been personal secretary to the late Gerald L. K. Smith, the virulent anti-Semite who founded the Christian Nationalist Crusade. Perkins conducted his own ministry at the Embassy Auditorium in downtown Los Angeles, a favorite meeting place for right-wing fundamentalists. The Christian Nationalist Crusade held meetings there, as did the racist Church of Jesus Christ-Christian.* And occasionally Jerry Owen staged revival meetings there.

* The Church of Jesus Christ-Christian figured prominently in the previously mentioned investigation by the California Attorney General's office into right-wing paramilitary groups. It was led by the Reverend Wesley A. Swift

As it turned out, however, the white-maned Perkins was a gold mine of information. He related that on the morning of June 5 Owen telephoned him and asked if he could come right over to his apartment in the hotel adjacent to the Embassy Auditorium. When he arrived a few minutes later, Owen was visibly shaken. "I'm about to get mixed up in that thing," Owen said in reference to the RFK shooting. "And I don't want to get mixed up in another scandal like that."

It was the second visit from Owen in two days. Perkins revealed that on election day, June 4, Owen had dropped by and mentioned that a former exercise boy at a race track was going to buy one of his horses. Owen said that he met the young man hitchhiking the day before, and he thought that a price of $400 had been reached. The only reason that Owen was hanging around Los Angeles was to complete the sale. He had the horse trailer with him and was to meet the young man and some of his friends the same night.

"You mean he was supposed to meet Sirhan at the Ambassador the night of the election?" Christian asked.

"Oh yes, the night Kennedy was shot," Perkins confirmed.

"He was out there with his horse and trailer?"

"Well, he was here in town. He came up here. I knew about that. I wasn't with him. I talked with him the next day or so."

Christian reiterated his question about whether Owen was actually at the Ambassador Hotel on election night. As Perkins recalled it, Owen said that on election night he "went down there to meet him and to pick up this other three hundred dollars—that was the night of the assassination. He waited around there, and

---

of Lancaster, on the fringe of the Mojave Desert. According to the Attorney General's 1965 report, Swift was "a former Ku Klux Klan rifle-team instructor" and legal representative of Gerald L. K. Smith. It said that he "has purchased over a hundred concealable firearms in the past few years. Moreover, he maintains a firing range on his Kern County ranch, as well as a reported secret arsenal." The church had a paramilitary arm called the Christian Defense League. In 1976, after Swift's death, a huge buried arsenal (including ground-to-air missiles) was discovered on lands that had belonged to Swift, touching off an investigation leading to the arrest and conviction of an East Los Angeles man linked to extremist causes.

when Sirhan didn't show up, he went to a hotel here. Thought he'd stay all night, that Sirhan would very likely show up in the morning because he was very much interested in the horse. If I remember correctly, he went to some little motel in Hollywood so he wouldn't have to drive back and haul this horse trailer to Santa Ana."

Perkins said that when Owen came by about ten in the morning on June 5 he seemed genuinely frightened at the asserted chance encounter with Sirhan. "Listen," he told Perkins, "that's the fella that was gonna buy my horse. I brought the horse in here to deliver it. The other man didn't show up and so forth. I waited for him. Man alive, they was just gonna use me as a getaway, as a scapegoat. They could have gone four or five miles and shot me in a vacant lot."*

What Perkins had to say seemed enormously important, for here for the first time was a witness to whom Owen had related the hitchhiker story *before* the shooting. It was a significantly different version from what he had told Turner about going to Oxnard on election day. Owen gave Perkins the impression that he was in Los Angeles with the horse and trailer from at least late Monday through Tuesday—and that he had been waiting outside the Ambassador Hotel for Sirhan when the shooting happened.

ON JANUARY 21, 1969, CHRISTIAN PAID HIS FIRST VISIT TO THE LAPD "Glass House" at the invitation of Lieutenant Roy Keene, a polite, low-keyed man who oversaw SUS's administrative paperwork. In discussions over the phone, Keene had expressed an authentic interest in Reverend Perkins' disclosure that his fellow cleric had in fact been in the company of Sirhan on election day. Christian thought he had struck a bargain with Keene: he would let SUS listen to the taped interview of Perkins in return for being allowed a dubbed copy of the original interview of Owen at the University Station. "I can't see any reason why that can't be arranged," Keene had said.

Keene ushered Christian into the office of Captain Hugh Brown, commander of Homicide Detectives, who was serving as operational

* Taped interview with Jonothan Perkins, January 8, 1969. Perkins died in 1974.

chief of SUS. Brown, a chunky, red-faced man, wasted no time on cordialities. "Look, we've spent hundreds of hours checking out that lying bastard's phony story," he boomed in reference to Owen. "There's nothing to it, absolutely nothing!"

"Well, if that's the case, why didn't you arrest him for filing a false police report?" Christian replied.

Brown softened his tone. He said that a couple of his men had gone over to the Embassy Hotel and questioned Perkins. "He is an old man," the captain argued. "His mind is fuzzy. He's senile. He got all his dates mixed up. Anyway, he admitted to us that Owen wasn't in town on June fourth. It was June fifth or sometime after that."

Christian reached into his briefcase, withdrew the Perkins tape cassette and inserted it into his Sony recorder. The minister's steady voice filled the office, reciting how Owen had visited him twice, how Owen said he was with Sirhan both days. In no way did he sound like an addled old man. As Christian ticked off examples of Perkins' keenness of mind, Brown said, "He's just not telling the truth, that's all!"

Christian caught a glimpse of Lieutenant Manny Pena, who had been standing in an adjacent room. Brown peered into Christian's briefcase and saw two dozen other cassettes. "What're those of?" he demanded.

"You'd be surprised how many witnesses we've dug up, Captain," Christian said, "and some of their statements make Owen appear more than just your 'liar.' Now, how about letting me listen to Owen's initial statement?"

Brown was angry. "We want those tapes, now!" he ordered as he rose from his chair and started toward the briefcase. Christian felt a surge of panic—several of the tapes hadn't yet been dubbed for safekeeping. He knew Brown could seize the lot and later deny it. Snapping the briefcase shut, Christian bluffed, "Sorry, Captain, but I'm on my way to an appointment with Charlie O'Brien, and he's waiting to hear all of these tapes."

The policeman stopped in his tracks. "O'Brien? Which Charlie O'Brien?" There was only *one* Charlie O'Brien in California law enforcement, and Brown knew it. "What's he want that stuff for?" he asked.

"When your people told us to get lost last year, we had the choice of backing off or going to someone in authority who would listen," Christian explained. "And O'Brien listened."

"Well, why doesn't he call us if he's so damn curious?" Brown said.

Christian replied that the AG's people had tried to get information from SUS but had received no cooperation.

"That's a lie!" Brown exploded. "We've cooperated with every law enforcement agency on this thing from the beginning!" The captain stood up and pointed a finger menacingly at his visitor. "You know, you guys are messing around with official police business. You could find yourselves in trouble, big trouble, if you don't watch it. Just remember that, eh?" The knot in Christian's stomach mutely affirmed that he took the captain at his word.*

Roy Keene seemed embarrassed as he walked Christian to the elevator. "The captain doesn't like civilians messing around with his thing," he said. "But he does mean business, you know." Keene handed Christian his card. "Keep in touch," he suggested.

With a feeling of relief Christian walked past the uniformed policemen on duty in the "Glass House" lobby and out into the bright sunlight. He had the feeling that Keene wanted to be helpful, but Keene obviously wasn't running the show. A couple of months later Keene took early retirement to become chief of a small police department in Oregon. Christian and he had a parting phone conversation. "It's a good thing you guys can't get your hands on some of our files," Keene said. "You'd go wild!"

CHARLIE O'BRIEN WAS FURIOUS WITH CHRISTIAN WHEN WE MET with him a week later in his office in the Old State Building in Los Angeles. "Goddammit!" he yelled. "I told you not to mention

---

* Behind Brown on the top of a file drawer was a framed photograph of a group of persons astride some handsome horses. He could just make out the word "Appaloosa," but couldn't read the club or association identification that followed. He instantly wondered if this had anything to do with the organization headed by Owen's long time friend and paramilitary "bodyguard, Ben Hardister"—The California Appaloosa Horse Racing Association President.

anything about our arrangement in this thing! I was set for a meeting the next morning with Chief Reddin at ten o'clock sharp and you go and tell Brown about my interest in this thing. Well, I got a call from Reddin's office a half-hour before our meeting, calling it off. Then I check with my contact at the LAPD and find out you'd been over there popping off!"

Christian tried to explain how harrowing the session with Brown had been, and that his witness tapes might have been gone forever. O'Brien's displeasure seemed to stem as much from embarrassment that he'd been caught by the police playing games with "civilians" as with the cancellation of the meeting. Christian wasn't exactly happy with O'Brien, either. Why was he letting the LAPD put him off? If the police were cooperating, as Brown insisted, he should get all the information he wanted, Christian's visit notwithstanding. And if they weren't, he should make an issue of it.

And why was he keeping our relationship in the closet? It would not have been unprecedented for O'Brien to accredit us officially. He did it for Bill Davidson, a veteran journalist who wrote a book called *Indict and Convict* that chronicled O'Brien and his staff in action. "For six months I worked out of a desk in their office," Davidson said in the book. "I had complete access to their files and memoranda, and I personally accompanied them into the courtroom and into the field—even, on one occasion, as a 'Special Assistant to the Attorney General.' "

But there was of course an obvious difference: Davidson hadn't been bucking the official police position.

SEVERAL WEEKS LATER CHRISTIAN AGAIN CALLED THE REVEREND Perkins, who said that the police had questioned him for a second time a few days after Christian's visit with Captain Brown. Christian was just a phony and would cause him and Owen nothing but trouble, they said, warning him that he should not talk to any member of the press because witnesses were under a blanket court order to remain silent. Perkins complained that the police had tried to get him to change his story, but he had refused.

It was beginning to sound as if Captain Brown was getting

worried. If he was so sure that Owen fabricated his story, why was he sending his men around to discredit Christian and threaten an old man with a nonexistent gag order? Neither the prosecution nor the defense had any intention of calling Perkins or Owen as a witness at the trial.

7

The Quiet Trial
of Sirhan Sirhan

CAPTAIN BROWNE'S EDGINESS OVER THE PERKINS DISCLOSURES may have been heightened by the fact that the trial of Sirhan Sirhan had begun on January 13 with both sides resolved not even to hint at a conspiracy. During pre-trial hearings, the prosecution had been instructed to turn over, under discovery rules, any evidence in its possession that the defense might require. At an October 14, 1968, hearing, co-prosecutor David Fitts plunked down a tall pile of documents on the table in front of Sirhan attorney Russell Parsons. Among them were the interviews of sixty-seven persons who had seen Sirhan at the hotel, as well as fifteen who had spotted him on election morning while practice-shooting at the San Gabriel Valley

Gun Club. Although the defense had specifically requested it at the insistence of Bob Kaiser, the LAPD's file on Jerry Owen was missing. It remained squirreled away at SUS, its contents flagged in an anonymous handwriting, "No discovery."

At a press conference following the hearing, Parsons had gone along with the prosecution. "We have seen no evidence of a conspiracy," he said. The next morning the Los Angeles *Times* banner read: BOTH SIDES AGREE SIRHAN WAS ALONE.

In the interval before the trial began, Kaiser had tried to open the minds of the defense lawyers to the indications of a conspiracy but had run up against a stone wall. "Parsons simply would not talk about the evidence, let alone pursue it," Kaiser said. "We should have demanded their file on Jerry Owen." The main stumbling block apparently was entries in Sirhan's notebooks such as "Robert F. Kennedy must be assassinated before 5 June '68" and "Please pay to the order of Sirhan the amount of . . . 8000000" which, by any literal interpretation, clearly implied that Sirhan had been a hired assassin. Looking at it that way, Kaiser agreed, the lawyers were right. "What kind of a defense would it be," he rhetorically asked Christian, "to claim that your client was some kind of paid killer?"

A PROTRACTED PERIOD OF JURY EMPANELMENT WAS PUT TO USE by the defense psychiatric team to conduct additional testing of Sirhan. Its leader, Dr. Bernard Diamond of the University of California at Berkeley, had first interviewed the defendant on December 23, after the trial was originally scheduled to start. Diamond had recently won acquittal for an Air Force officer accused of mailing a bomb, by putting him under hypnosis and enabling him to recall details that he had forgotten in his normal state. He used the same tactic on Sirhan. Because the hypnotic state is one of magnified concentration—not sleep, as is commonly thought—it can be used to dredge up thoughts impossible to recollect by any other means. But hypnosis does not necessarily bring out the truth, because the subject is prone to tell the same lies and evasions he would in the normal state.

On January 11 Diamond hypnotized Sirhan, then asked a series of questions drawn up by chief defense attorney Grant Cooper. Cooper was concerned about the entries in the notebooks that suggested not only premeditation, a requisite for first-degree murder, but a contract killing. Diamond asked, "Sirhan, did anybody pay you to shoot Kennedy? Did anybody pay you to shoot Kennedy, Sirhan? Yes or no." Sirhan sighed but didn't answer. "I can't hear you," the doctor prodded.

A. No.

Q. No? No one paid you to shoot Kennedy. Did anyone know ahead of time that you were going to do it, Sirhan?

A. No.

Q. No. Did anybody from the Arabs tell you to shoot Kennedy? Any of your Arab friends? [Cooper and Diamond supported the prosecution's belief that the young Palestinian was passionately attached to the Arab cause, and theorized that he might have been motivated by Kennedy's support for Israel. No evidence exists that Sirhan belonged to any revolutionary Arab faction.]

A. No.

Q. Did the Arab government have anything to do with it, Sirhan?

A. No.

Q. Did you think this up all by yourself?

There was a five-second pause.

A. Yes.

Q. Yes. You thought this up all by yourself. Did you consult with anybody else, Sirhan?"

Another pause.

A. No.

Q. Are you the only person involved in Kennedy's shooting?

A three-second pause.

A. Yes.

Q. Yes. Nobody involved at all. Why did you shoot Kennedy?

No response. When Diamond pressed for an answer, Sirhan mumbled something about "the bombers," which the doctor interpreted as the war planes Robert Kennedy had promised to send to Israel. Diamond snapped him out of the trance, and Sirhan noticed blood trickling down his hand. "Jesus Christ!" he yelled. "What's that?" Diamond had pricked him with a safety pin after hypnotizing him and he hadn't felt it. Diamond had instructed him not to feel the pain.

Diamond apparently assigned no particular significance to the three pauses following questions about the involvement of others. But the pauses strongly pointed to what experts call "blocking," which occurs when a subject has been hypnoprogrammed to forget certain details, a process known as "artificial amnesia."

The climactic session was on February 8, when Diamond realized that Sirhan was highly susceptible to hypnotic suggestions that ran counter to his natural instincts. After "putting him under," Diamond suggested that he climb the bars of his cell and act like a monkey. Sirhan complied, even swinging upside down ape-style. Afterward Diamond played back a tape of the session.

"Ohhh, it frightens me, Doc." Sirhan shivered. "But goddamn it, sir, killing people is different than climbing up bars."

"There's this difference, Sirhan," Diamond explained. "I couldn't force you to do something you were opposed to. But if you wanted to do it, you could do it under hypnosis. Do you know, Sirhan, if five men had wanted to stop you from climbing those bars, they couldn't have done it?"

But Diamond didn't propose that Sirhan might have been a Manchurian Candidate hypnoprogrammed to kill—that was a "crazy, crackpot theory." "I think you did it to yourself," he said, meaning that Sirhan had hypnoprogrammed himself by thinking hostile thoughts about Kennedy while in self-induced trances.*

THE PROSECUTION CASE WAS DAMNINGLY SIMPLE. A PARADE OF witnesses testified that Sirhan was caught with a smoking gun in his hand, and as the scrawlings in the notebooks attested, he committed the crime with considerable malice aforethought and premeditation. Over Cooper's objection, eight pages of the notebooks were admitted into evidence. (The most damaging page read: "May 18 9.45AM—68 My determination to eliminate R.F.K. is be-

---

* Kaiser, *op. cit.*, pp. 302–4.

coming more the more of an unshakable obsession . . . RFK must die.")

On Monday, March 3, Cooper called Sirhan to the stand. An attempt had to be made to rebut the mute testimony of the notebook pages, and Cooper's line of questioning was designed to set the stage for later psychiatric testimony.

Q. Have you heard these notebooks read?
A. Yes, sir.
Q. And you wrote these notebooks? [A prosecution handwriting examiner had already testified that Sirhan was the author.]
A. Yes, sir.
Q. And you don't deny it?
A. I don't deny it.
Q. You bought the gun?
A. Yes, sir, I did.
Q. Did you have in mind going to the Ambassador Hotel for the purpose of killing Robert F. Kennedy?
A. No, sir, I did not. That was completely forgotten from my mind. That emotion was good as long as I was writing it. Something for a time only.
Q. And did you kill him?
A. Yes, sir.

Although Sirhan had all along insisted that he had an amnesia block over the span of the shooting—he awkwardly called it "completely forgotten from my mind"—Cooper didn't pursue the point. Instead, he skipped to the question of conspiracy:

Q. Were you hired to kill Senator Kennedy?
A. No.
Q. Did any government hire you?
A. No.

With this perfunctory exploration out of the way, Cooper moved on to Sirhan's state of mind at the time.

Q. Had you been going to the races?
A. For two weeks before—almost every day.
Q. Were you betting?

A. Yes.

Q. You didn't do too good, did you? [Cooper was planting the idea that Sirhan was depressed because of consistent losses.]

A. Good and bad. I lost more than I won. I had been losing all the time before that.

The chief prosecutor was Lynn D. "Buck" Compton, the top aide to District Attorney Evelle Younger. He took over on cross-examination.

Q. What about your notebooks? You don't remember when these were written?

A. No, sir, I don't.

Q. You had a habit of doodling? [It was as if the automatic writing were no more than graffiti on a men's room wall. As we shall see, this type of writing can be indicative of a trance condition.]

A. No, sir, I don't.

Q. You had a habit of writing words or even sentences of things that were on your mind?

A. I don't know, sir. I didn't sit there and doodle intentionally.

Q. These were the things that interested you? Race horses? Girls, now and then? Poems? Sometimes you liked to write in Arabic? Jockeys' names? [Compton apparently was driving at the idea that the entries were what Sirhan might jot down in a conscious state.]

A. Yes, sir.

Q. It doesn't surprise you to find these things in your notebooks?

A. No, sir, it doesn't.

Q. Did you ever look at your notebooks at the things you wrote?

A. I guess, sir. I don't remember.

Q. You don't remember looking and thinking, "Gee whiz! Here I wrote that Kennedy must be assassinated!" and wonder why? Don't you remember that?

A. No, sir, I don't.

Q. On this envelope, see that writing? "RFK must be disposed of like his brother." Did you write that?" [Compton waved an envelope retrieved from a trash can at the Sirhan residence in Pasadena.]

A. It was my handwriting.

Q. You have no memory of ever writing that?

A. No, sir, I haven't.

Sirhan had not convinced his own defense team that he was not feigning the amnesia block, much less the prosecution and jury. On

March 21 Diamond took the stand to try to make the best of a bad situation. He testified that in his opinion Sirhan was in a trance state at the time of the shooting, citing the fact that his subject was easily hypnotizable and appeared to have been hypnotized many times in the past. Sirhan admitted, Diamond said, that he had on occasion put himself into trances by staring in a mirror. The notebooks, Diamond theorized, were the product of a series of self-induced trances in which Sirhan wrote "like a robot." On the night of the slaying, he posited, circumstances combined into a remarkable coincidence: Sirhan took the gun from his car "because he didn't want the Jews to steal it"; he met a girl and had coffee with her; he was dazed and confused by the lights, mirrors and crush of people in the hotel; he stared at a teletype machine; and people rushed at him. Involuntarily, he slipped into a psychotic, dissociated state. He cried out, "You son of a bitch!" and shot Kennedy.

Diamond was describing a surrealistic binge that he conceded sounded "absurd and preposterous." Nonetheless, he gamely summed up: "I see Sirhan as small and helpless, pitifully ill, with a demented, psychotic range, out of control of his own consciousness and his own actions, subject to bizarre, dissociated trances in some of which he programmed himself to be the instrument of assassination, and then, in an almost accidentally induced twilight state, he actually executed the crime, knowing next to nothing as to what was happening."

In other words, Sirhan was some sort of automatic assassin, a hypnotic time bomb which could go off at any time. The next day's edition of the Los Angeles *Times* headlined: SIRHAN IN TRANCE ON ASSASSINATION NIGHT, PSYCHIATRIST INSISTS.

In his final arguments, Lynn Compton derided Diamond's testimony. "Nobody knew what happened until Dr. Diamond descended on the scene. [Sirhan] did it with mirrors."

The jury deliberated for sixteen hours and forty-two minutes before returning a verdict of guilty in the first degree.

WHILE THE TRIAL WAS STILL IN PROGRESS, CHRISTIAN COMPARED notes with Bob Kaiser, who had the advantage of being inside the defense team. Kaiser was becoming increasingly addicted to the conspiracy idea. "That's the hell of it," he complained on the evening of March 23 after Diamond had testified. "It's irrelevant to both the defense and the prosecution."*

In May, after the trial was over, Christian arranged a sit-down session with Kaiser, who was now busy organizing his book "*R.F.K. Must Die!*" After about two hundred hours of interviewing Sirhan, Kaiser had not been able to extract any solid evidence of a conspiracy, but he did not see this as either an indication of no plot or as Sirhan's fault. "I'm convinced he really is suffering from some kind of amnesia in regard to some of the critical evidence against him," Kaiser said.

When Kaiser first broached the subject of Jerry Owen a couple of months before, Sirhan had flatly denied ever hearing of him, he confided. Lately, however, Sirhan had retreated a bit from that position. It came about when Kaiser threw out the possibility that on the occasions when Sirhan sat down in front of a mirror, hypnotized himself and scribbled in the notebooks, he might have been "a tool used by others." Sirhan didn't reject the notion—he simply couldn't remember anyone using hypnosis on him, let alone writing the incriminating passages. Kaiser suggested to Sirhan that he might have met someone somewhere who wanted Kennedy dead, and he ticked off the names of several known acquaintances of Sirhan. No reaction. Then he mentioned Jerry Owen. "Sirhan didn't say he didn't know Owen," Kaiser remarked. "He said that he was home on Monday, June third—raked the leaves, slept quite a bit, read the papers, and went to Corona that night."

Corona, of course, was where Sirhan had been employed in 1966 as a groom on a thoroughbred horse ranch. But this conflicted with what Mary Sirhan had told SUS: that her son was gone when she returned from work in the early afternoon of June 3, but was back watching television around four-thirty and remained home that night. However, Mrs. Sirhan had no particular reason to

---

* Christian called co-prosecutor John Howard right after the Sirhan diaries were read off in court, asking the Assistant DA if he didn't concur with our interpretation of Sirhan's having been a "programmed killer for hire." Howard indicated that there was a considerable dispute going on about this in the DA's office—although none of this difference in opinion ever surfaced in court.

remember that day and could easily have been mistaken, and Sirhan himself could have been in error or lying. As far as Kaiser was concerned, Sirhan's movements on that Monday had yet to be accounted for.

According to Kaiser, Sirhan himself had brought up the fact that Owen had failed a lie-detector test. (His mother or brothers must have passed along this LAPD contention.) "Yeah," Kaiser retorted, "but he knew more about you in that first interview with the police on June fifth than he should have."

"Bob," Sirhan replied pedantically, "I know that a person doesn't have to meet you to know all about you."

"But he had more details than he should have," Kaiser insisted.

"Well, I was home Monday."

"But later you went to Corona [some fifty miles away]?"

"Yeah," Sirhan said. "I drove out there." He had just contradicted his mother, who told SUS that she thought he had been home all evening. But he evaded saying why he went or whom he saw.

Sirhan parroted the police explanation that maybe Owen had made up the story for publicity. But then he had another thought: "Maybe he could lead to someone who was playing with my mind."

Winding him up like a toy soldier and sending him out to kill? Since he first broached the idea to Kaiser months before, Christian had become more and more persuaded that this was exactly what had happened. In his next meeting with Kaiser, Christian proposed that if Sirhan had been hypnoprogrammed, he might be deprogrammed. "When Sirhan expressed an interest, 'Do you think I could have been hypnotized?,' was he willing to discuss it at great length?" Christian asked.

"He didn't know," Kaiser replied. "We talked a couple of hours about it. He was bugged by the thought. He'd squinch up his eyes, and shake his head, and shudder and say, 'Geez! That really scares me!'"

"He could remember no circumstances whatsoever where he might have been hypnotized?" Christian asked.

"I'm not sure about that. If he was hypnotized by another, he was not willing to say who the other was, because he wouldn't want to get that person in trouble."

Christian raised the possibility that Sirhan might want to co-operate with an expert to try to unlock his mind.

"I'm kind of doubtful he wants to be deprogrammed," Kaiser offered. "He'd rather go to the gas chamber as an Arab hero than anything else. It's more noble, you see, than to have been an un-witting tool of some people who got inside his mind." But Christian discounted the "Arab hero" rationale, since Sirhan had no known involvement in Arab activism.

It was not until a meeting some months later that Kaiser con-fided to Christian that Sirhan had never trusted him because of warnings from other members of the defense team that any revela-tions about any conspiracy might wipe out what little defense he had. Of all the defense lawyers, only Emile Zola "Zeke" Berman shared Kaiser's suspicions about a conspiracy. "He knew what those diaries were saying just like I did," Kaiser said. "He tried to get his colleagues to consider the implications, but they wanted no part of it. He finally gave up."

ON MAY 16, 1969, SHORTLY AFTER THE END OF THE TRIAL, A highly irregular meeting took place in the chambers of Assistant Presiding Judge Charles A. Loring. Its purpose was to devise meth-ods to keep "cranks" away from the LAPD's investigative files that according to procedures were supposed to be deposited with the Clerk of the Court's Office in the same manner that the Warren Commission's documents were lodged in the National Archives. Participating were trial judge Herbert V. Walker, co-prosecutor David Fitts, SUS Chief Robert Houghton, and two officials from the Clerk's office. The defense lawyers had deliberately been excluded.

Houghton expressed concern about the availability to the public of files such as Owen's "which were not subject to testimony." Fitts brought up the fact that Sirhan's lawyers had asked to see the Owen file. "Most of that stuff was ordered delivered on discovery and, in one way or another, they had a lot of specific names, so they got that stuff, and let me assure you here and now that what was delivered on discovery and what was filed with the court was sealed to this extent." As Fitts explained it, the defense lawyers got only what they specifically asked for and nothing more. (That claim is disputed by the members of the defense team, who say that they asked for the LAPD file on Jerry Owen but didn't get it.) "They asked for interviews and interviews they got, but," Fitts continued, "I abstracted from the file" parts dealing with police conclusions. As for the rest of it, he said, "let it stay in the record."

But Houghton wanted to suppress it. "We had a meeting, so all of you will know," he said, "with Buck Compton and John Howard [another deputy DA] and Dave Fitts and my staff." They had discussed such "red herrings" in the case as the anti-Castro Cuban, Jose Duarte, and the preacher, Jerry Owen. Some of the material obtained by the defense on discovery was returned without reaching the press, Houghton reported, and "nobody knew it except us, the District Attorney and the FBI,"

Houghton argued that the material should only be used to rebut contentions about "the conspiracy or anything." His investigators' conclusions, he said, "are not put very tactfully as they call people liars and things like that." There was also the matter of arrest records. "As far as I'm concerned we are not going to release any of that. When we find someone has a criminal record, that is confidential information and I don't think we ought to disclose that. I don't know what you have."

Fitts did. "I am not too sure there might not be a kick-back sheet on Jerry Owen," he said.*

ON MAY 28 DISTRICT ATTORNEY EVELLE YOUNGER HANDED OUT a thirteen-page press release reviewing the Sirhan case. He disclosed that Captain Hugh Brown of SUS and his forty-seven investigators had interviewed "well in excess of 4,000 possible witnesses and others pretending to some knowledge of events." In this mass of material, the DA went on, "are the assertions of a number of individuals who have attracted the attention of the news media with respect to the possibility of a conspiracy to effect the death of Senator Kennedy."

Assuring that the allegations had been "investigated in depth"

* Transcript of official reporter Vesta Mennick.

and "discredited," Younger briefly mentioned several of the more prominent ones. There was the polka-dot-dress-girl angle, which the DA dismissed by saying that Sandy Serrano and Vincent DiPierro had changed their stories. There was the episode involving the anti-Castro Cuban Jose Duarte, which Younger said was resolved when Duarte flunked a polygraph test. There was an incident in which Sirhan's brother, Saidallah Sirhan, was shot at as he drove on the Pasadena Freeway on the early morning of July 3, but although police could not close the case, neither could they connect it with the assassination. And then there was Jerry Owen and his hitchhiker story.

Younger synopsized the story, then commented, "Although Mr. Owen professes to be a preacher of the gospel, there are a number of instances of his past conduct on the police blotters of several states that indicate a less than saintly reluctance to grasp certain opportunities which have been afforded him. The investigators have concluded that Mr. Owen concocted a bizarre tale in the expectation of some advantage from the attendant publicity."

Later that day Art Kevin gained a private interview with Younger during which he pressed for a fuller explanation of the Owen angle. "Are we to gather from the substance of your comments today that obviously the man was untruthful for whatever personal reasons he had?" Kevin prodded. Younger fidgeted with his press release, repeating excerpts from it. The two stared silently at each other.

When Kevin aired his series on the unanswered questions in the RFK case over KHJ, which had the largest listener rating of any station in the Los Angeles basin, he opened one segment by asking, "Whatever happened to the minister who claimed Sirhan and two other persons tried to dupe him into being the getaway driver after the murder?" Kevin retold the hitchhiker story, then criticized Younger and his office for their attitude and closed with a comment about the grand jury: "Even the grand jury refused to hear the minister. Grand jury foreman L. E. McKee was quoted as saying that he'd received no communication from the minister or his attorney, and furthermore that the grand jury had at that point heard as much of the Sirhan case as it intended."

Younger, apparently incensed, lifted Kevin's press privileges, but when KHJ management moved to challenge him in public, he quietly backed down.

On the same day that Younger held his press conference, the LAPD took its turn. Flanked by Hugh Brown and Acting Chief Roger Murdock (Tom Reddin had just retired to join KTLA-TV as news anchorman at $100,000 a year), Robert Houghton insisted that "there was no conspiracy whatsoever." Like Younger, Houghton ran down the major possibilities and eliminated them. "At the beginning of the investigation we did have much information from hundreds of sources," he said, "much of it highly imaginative, some of it from people with serious psychotic problems."

TOP POLICE FIND NO SIRHAN PLOT, the Los Angeles *Herald-Examiner* headlined. As Christian read the article he thought back to the angry meeting with Hugh Brown at Parker Center. What was it Brown had blurted out in a moment of frustration? Something about their having to make sure there was no conspiracy so that Younger's chances for eventually becoming governor wouldn't be jeopardized.*

* Younger's ascension toward the California governor's mansion began in earnest in 1970 when he was elected Attorney General. One of his first appointments was a new head of the Criminal Intelligence and Investigation bureau under his aegis. His choice: Robert A. Houghton.

Houghton retired as CII chief in 1976—and was appointed as a member of the 1976–77 Los Angeles County Grand Jury, at a time when the RFK case began hitting the headlines again. The grand jury refused to convene on the case during this period.

In 1978 Younger made his formal announcement about running for governor.

8

"The Walking Bible" on Television

ALTHOUGH IT SEEMED AN EXCHANGE IN FUTILITY, CHRISTIAN decided to make one last appeal to Younger and Yorty. In his letter to the DA, he sought to "sit down and compare notes" with his staff, and posed several nagging questions. "If Owen was merely seeking publicity," Christian reasoned, "as many other 'kooks' were, why didn't he approach the news media directly, as many other 'kooks' did, rather than go directly to the police, where he requested and was assured total anonymity?"

Younger wrote back that the "highly-skilled and experienced investigators" from his office, the LAPD and the FBI had failed to uncover "any credible evidence" of a conspiracy.

"There appears to be no need for any comparison between our notes and yours," he declared, but at the same time he implored Christian to turn over whatever information he had. Failure to do so, Younger sarcastically noted, would force him to conclude that "you in fact have nothing except pure speculation and a fanciful hypotheses [*sic*] upon which you seek to capitalize for monetary advantage."

Christian also wrote directly to Sam Yorty outlining the overall situation and asking for "a personal gettogether with you in total privacy, after which you can make the kind of judgment that is required in so serious a matter." A copy went to Jack Brown, the mayor's aide, who responded: "Received your communication today, and memoed my recommendation to the Mayor regarding your request for appointment. Keep the faith, baby."

But Christian heard nothing from Yorty, and Brown later said that he tried unsuccessfully to see his boss on the matter. Then, on June 11, Brown was summoned to the office of Vice Mayor Eleanor Chambers and given an ultimatum to resign or be fired. She gave no explanation.

But one came four days later on a sultry Sunday afternoon as Christian was flipping channels on his television set. Suddenly, on Channel 13, a station break faded and Mayor Yorty came on. "How do you do, ladies and gentlemen," he began. "It's a great privilege to present to you my friend, evangelist Jerry Owen, 'The Walking Bible.' Glad to see you, Jerry."

Christian watched stupefied as Owen strode into camera range and slipped a thick arm around Yorty's shoulder. "Thank you, Mayor Yorty, and I'm glad to have you here," Owen beamed. "Mayor, I know of several thousands of God-fearing people that prayed you would be elected, and I believe God answers prayer, don't you, Mayor?"

Yorty grinned sheepishly. He had just won re-election against black City Councilman Thomas Bradley after mounting a campaign that appealed to white prejudices.* "Well, I certainly do," Yorty finally agreed. "Of course, I was doing a little of that praying

* For example, Yorty claimed that Chief Tom Reddin had resigned because he was afraid that Bradley might win and the city would have an anti-police mayor.

myself, you know, along with thousands." He emitted a strained chuckle.

A grinning Owen kept up the patter. "And I'd like to ask you another question, Mayor. Don't you believe that America, the world, needs to put their faith and trust in the God of Abraham, Isaac and Jacob like never before?"

Yorty, not used to the role of straight man, hemmed and hawed. "Well, Jerry," he said, "I think that this is one of the, er, missing links that's causing so much disturbance and turmoil today, especially of young people. I think they've sort of lost their moorings, and, ah, too many have gotten away from, ah, belief, a real belief in a supreme being and a . . . a direction . . . to all the affairs of human beings."

Christian was bewildered. What was the one-time congressman, three-time mayor of Los Angeles, twice a candidate for governor of California, doing fumbling around with Owen? The question answered itself. Eight months before, Yorty had not even acknowledged Jack Brown's memorandum concerning Owen. Four days previously, Brown had been ousted when he again recommended that the Owen angle be looked into. Yorty hadn't just walked in on the television debut of *The Walking Bible*. Somehow, he and Owen were old friends.*

"Except the Lord build the house, they labor in vain that build it, and except the Lord keep the city, they waketh but in vain." Owen was now in full oratorical flush, portraying Yorty as the City of Angels' ordained guardian. The preacher clutched the "bantam mayor" around the shoulders. "How grrreat is our God," Owen warbled. "How great is His name." As he approached the end of the ancient hymn, he tailored the verse: "He rolled back the water of the mighty Red Sea, and He said, 'Mayor Yorty, keep your faith in me!' "

The camera panned to Yorty as Owen's voice clung to the last

* In his subsequent lawsuit against KCOP, Channel 13, Owen submitted several photographic exhibits showing him and Yorty in the mayor's office posing with such personages as boxer Henry Armstrong. Other exhibits contain references to Yorty's authorizing the loan to Owen of horse trailers and other city property. We were unable to determine either the duration or origins of their relationship.

note. The mayor looked a trifle embarrassed. But Owen was not through. "Do you know that fella out there?" he asked.

Yorty squinted under the bright lights in the direction Owen was gesturing. "Oh, he's an old friend of mine!"

Owen chortled. "That's 'Slapsie Maxie' Rosenbloom!" On cue, the aging fighter shuffled on stage. And there they stood, the odd couple-plus-one, gawking uneasily at one another while Christian stared incredulous at his television set.

Christian sat back to try to sort out this startling new twist. If Owen knew Yorty this well, why hadn't he simply called the mayor when he supposedly received death threats as the result of agreeing to sell Sirhan a horse? Yorty could easily have picked up the phone and instructed the LAPD to provide protection. And if Owen was having so much trouble making ends meet in June 1968 that he needed Sirhan's $400, as he himself had said, where was he now getting the kind of money an unsponsored television show cost? Most crucial of all, however—what was the mayor of the nation's third largest city doing by appearing in such a blatantly public fashion with a man his own top aide had confided was being investigated by the California Attorney General's office for possible criminal involvement in Robert Kennedy's assassination? Perhaps the strained expression on Yorty's face throughout the obvious ordeal offered an explanation of sorts: he surely didn't like being there.

A WEEK AFTER THE INAUGURAL TELECAST OF THE WALKING BIBLE show, Jonn Christian called KCOP program director Gary Waller and requested a confidential meeting with the station management. "There's someone on the air at KCOP who was involved in the Robert Kennedy assassination," Christian confided. "I'd like to come in and talk about it with your top people—in strict privacy." After a brief discussion, Waller invited his caller to come in.

Located in a modest studio at 915 North LaBrea on the south fringe of Hollywood, KCOP was the kind of chipped-paint operation common to independents struggling in the shadow of the big three networks. It was a subsidiary of Chris-Craft Industries, the pleasure-boat manufacturer that had followed the conglomerate trend of the 1960s.

Christian was ushered into an office that seemed a relative haven of luxury. It belonged to station president John Hopkins, a ruddy-faced, silver-haired man pushing sixty who spoke in nervous bursts. Waller was present at the meeting, as were two other executives and the company's general counsel, Victor F. Yacullo. There was an air of uneasiness, undoubtedly generated by the fact that the Federal Communications Commission played God over the broadcast industry, exercising the power to suspend, revoke or transfer a license should the rigid FCC codes and laws be transgressed.

Yacullo, a slight, wispy man in his mid-thirties, put on his horn-rimmed glasses and began the session by giving every indication that he would briskly dispose of the business at hand. But his summary attitude vanished as soon as the unknown visitor presented his credentials. Pulling out letters and documents from a bulging briefcase to support his statements, Christian named as local references Jesse Unruh, speaker of the California Assembly, and Unruh's political lieutenant, attorney Frank J. Burns, Jr. As a "character reference," Christian gave Charlie O'Brien.

Stressing that the information he was about to present must be held in the utmost confidence, Christian began by playing Turner's taped interview with Owen. Then he played the tape of Art Kevin's recent interview with DA Evelle Younger, commenting that Younger's "publicity stunt" explanation was hardly reasonable. Christian pointed out that there had been no publicity, and that the preacher had in fact shied away from it. So the question remained: Why would a man with a voluminous police record come forward with such a story to the police?

Christian continued that we had undertaken our own investigation to try to provide answers to that enigma and others that had cropped up. He urged the executives to keep Owen on the air in the hope that his source of funds to pay for the program could be discovered. Not long before, Christian said, Owen reportedly had complained that unspecified repercussions from the hitchhiker incident had put him in debt "more than eighteen hundred dollars." How much was he laying out for the program? Waller roughly estimated that each weekly program cost upward of $1,350, on top of which were Owen's own production and advertising costs, including display ads in *TV Guide*, television spots and newspaper ads.*

Christian quickly calculated that the preacher was committed to more than $113,000 a year, not much by Oral Roberts and Billy Graham standards but apparently far more than he previously had been able to pull out of his pocket.

The show did generate a modicum of revenues. During the premiere broadcast Owen held up a record album featuring a religious singing group that had just performed: "Everyone that will write in this week and send a free-will donation of five dollars or more to help purchase this time, we're going to send them one of these albums."

On the second broadcast Owen said, "Now Roberta, my partner, my wife, I want her to read some letters. We got so many wonderful letters and some of 'em just made tears come in our eyes. Honey, would you read this wonderful letter to our viewers right now?" Sitting at the organ console, Roberta Owen read a letter from a "sister in Christ" in Pomona who enclosed $5 and wanted Owen to send "the story of your life."

The Walking Bible would have to have taken in sufficient "love offerings," as Owen styled his appeal, to paper the walls of Winchester Cathedral to break even, and we seriously doubted that donations were pouring in at that rate. Although we didn't know it at the time, the preacher was actively planning to go national with the program with an air time budget approaching a million dollars, not including production and promotion costs. What we also didn't know at the time was that there was limited and quiet police curiosity about Owen's source of money. In the 1975 trial, KCOP president John Hopkins would testify that shortly after Christian's visit to the station, an Officer Reed of the Hollywood Station bunco-vice squad contacted him and asked if *The Walking Bible* "was a paid political program." Reed revealed that Owen's "activities were being watched" to try "to determine where the money was coming from."

---

* Case file *Owen* vs. *KCOP*, Plaintiff's Exhibit 18.

Hopkins inferred from what Reed said that he suspected it came from a tainted source.*

Upon leaving the meeting at KCOP, Christian wrote letters to Hopkins and counsel Yacullo reiterating his opposition to terminating the program, warning that such a move might lead to a lawsuit as well as "sever a valuable line of investigative pursuit." But Yacullo would testify in 1975 that "after we had concluded the meeting with Mr. Christian the intent to cancel the program and my advice to do so and the general concurrence along those lines took place that same day."

Before acting, however, Yacullo wanted to verify Owen's brushes with the law. "We were in a position," he testified, "where we would have an individual on television as a man of God, a man of the cloth, who would be portraying himself as a person of the absolute highest ethical and moral character, that under those circumstances it might be considered as being a deception of the public if, in fact, he did have a police record much less was involved in all of the various allegations which Mr. Christian at some length went through that day."

Yacullo set up a meeting with Robert Houghton, the former SUS chief, who said "that Mr. Owen did have a police record, that he was—he said—I think the words he used were 'had been involved peripherally' " in the RFK case. Houghton claimed there was a code section on privileged information that prevented him from saying more, but suggested that Yacullo contact Sirhan prosecutor Lynn Compton. Compton produced what looked like an investigative file on Owen, and although he would not let Yacullo inspect it, read off a number of items that confirmed Owen's police record.

Yacullo's meeting with Compton took place on the morning of

---

* In an interrogatory filed March 26, 1974, in his suit against KCOP, Owen maintained that he put $12,000 from the sale of the Santa Ana home, which was part of his wife's inheritance, toward the program, and "borrowed $10,000 from church friends in Northern California for additional television time." If this was true, it was still far short of his projected costs versus income. By his own count, for example, he sold only twenty-six of the record albums, for a net profit of $55.90.

July 10, 1969. That afternoon John Hopkins dictated the letter notifying Owen that his program was being canceled. Owen responded by mailing letters to his contributing viewers seeking their support.

S.O.S. EMERGENCY!! This is a hurried note to let you know we have been FORCED OFF OF TV for the time being! Just when we have begun to win many souls, and are hearing of thrilling results! Many enemies of the gospel such as atheists and communists are fighting this program, we know.

We believe we will be back on TV very soon!

Meanwhile Owen showed up at the KCOP studios attempting to buy his way back on the air. At this point he apparently assumed that the sole reason for the termination was the shoplifting arrest at Orhbach's department store, which had made him late for a scheduled taping. One of Owen's long-time sidekicks, John L. Gray, would later give testimony that when Owen confronted John Hopkins, he whipped out a roll of seven $1,000 bills and demanded, "Why won't you accept my money? What are you doing canceling my program?"

"We don't want any phony preachers on the station," Hopkins is said to have replied.

"Do you mean 'The Walking Bible' is a phony?"

Hopkins supposedly responded by not only citing the shoplifting rap but accusing Owen of burning churches and being "tied up" with the Kennedy assassination.

Hopkins' alleged accusations, coupled with purported statements made by KCOP personnel to viewers who called in to the station in response to the "S.O.S." letter gave Owen sufficient grounds to file suit, claiming that the station "published" defamations. There would be five years of preliminary sparring and delays before the case finally came to trial. In that interval we would learn much more about "The Walking Bible."

9

The Weatherly Report

WE FIRST GOT WIND OF "THE WEATHERLY REPORT," AS WE
came to call it, from Peter Noyes, then television news producer at KNXT, the Los Angeles outlet for CBS. We had been
friendly with Noyes, who shared our views on the JFK and
RFK assassinations, for some time, and he called regularly to
compare notes. "Have you guys ever run into any reports about
Sirhan being seen hanging around a horse stable in Orange
County, in Santa Ana to be exact?" he asked during a conversation in late July 1969. No, Christian said, but Santa Ana
was where Jerry Owen had lived in 1968. "Have you ever
heard the name Powers, Bill Powers, from Santa Ana?" No
again. "How close have you guys been working with Bob

Kaiser?" Noyes wanted to know. Close enough, Christian replied. Noyes obviously felt he was walking a tightrope. "Why don't you call Kaiser and ask him if he knows anything about the name Bill Powers?" he urged. "But don't tell I'm your source."

At first Kaiser acted as if the name didn't register, but when he realized we had a solid tip he opened up. While reviewing some files obtained from the LAPD by court order, he said, he came upon a confidential memorandum that had inadvertently been stuck between the pages of a report on another subject. That memorandum was so potentially explosive that he had approached Pete Noyes on the idea of having CBS fund an independent investigation. But the network had declined with only a cursory evaluation of the report's ramifications. Yes, it did concern Jerry Owen, although not by name. Kaiser guessed that Noyes had tipped us off because of our interest in the Owen angle.

Christian proposed that we conduct a joint investigation, but Kaiser said that he was so tied up with his book manuscript that he had no time to help in the interviews. We could have the contents of the memorandum, and follow it up ourselves. It was about a couple of cowboys named Bill Powers and Johnny Beckley, and a teen-ager in trouble with the law named John Chris Weatherly. Don't get too excited, he cautioned, because in the interim he had checked it out with the LAPD. At first they stalled, then told him that the follow-up reports to the memorandum were confidential and not available to outsiders. But forget it, they said, Powers and Beckley and Weatherly were not worth worrying about.

ON NEW YEAR'S EVE 1968, SEVENTEEN-YEAR-OLD JOHN CHRIS Weatherly was arrested by Los Angeles County sheriff's deputies for auto theft and forgery of a gasoline credit card. Weatherly had tried to use the card at a service station in Lakewood, a small town near the Orange County border. It was strictly a routine police case in that Lotusland of souped-up, wide-track cars where auto thievery is as common as oil derricks on the landscape.

Routine, that is, until young Weatherly suddenly switched the topic of his interrogation in the sheriff's substation from mag wheels and racing stripes to what he described as a plain Chevrolet one-ton truck that was used to transport horses. In an evident attempt to bargain his way out of trouble, Weatherly linked that truck to the Robert Kennedy assassination.

As immediately written up by Deputy F. G. Fimbres, the sheriff's report stated that Weatherly

was told by a Bill Powers m/w/37 . . . that a preacher (name unknown) that preaches in a church in Santa Ana and Sirhan Sirhan had come to Bill Powers' house at the A-Bar-T Ranch in Santa Ana and borrowed his 1967 Chevrolet 1-ton truck, blue in color, with a body used for transporting horses, to take a horse to Los Angeles for sale the day of the Kennedy murder; that when the preacher returned Sirhan was not with him, but he still had the horse, said he couldn't sell it in LA.

Weatherly told the deputies that not only Powers but a cowboy named John Beckley "said that this was true." The report continued:

Preacher and Sirhan Sirhan were seen numerous times riding horses at the A-Bar-T Stables. Subject claims that Powers will exaggerate on many things, but in this case he was certain in his own mind that Powers was not exaggerating; that the reason Powers would not give him any additional information was because he was afraid of the preacher and stated if the preacher found out they had given the press any information he had enough money to "waste" both of them.

Subject stated in his opinion he felt that the preacher wanted Senator Kennedy killed because the Senator wanted the war stopped. He felt the preacher's reasoning was that if the war was stopped the North Vietnamese would come to this country via Honolulu or Hawaii and God would get angry and cause a tidal wave.

Lt. O'Keefe and W. J. Glidden, Lakewood Station, feel that subject is sane, all points in his story regarding the theft of the credit card which he claims he stole in Buena Park and forged four or five times, check out and other parts of his story appear to be true.

Inspector Humphreys notified L. White, Homicide Bureau, who contacted LAPD, Sgt. Manuel Gutierrez of the SUS Kennedy Investigation Team; he stated they would come to Lakewood Station at 5:30 PM this date and talk to subject.

Manuel "Chick" Gutierrez was the SUS operative who had contacted us in August 1968 in response to Christian's initial overture to Yorty's office, and subsequently dismissed Owen as a crackpot. When he received the news from Lakewood, he called his SUS partner, Sergeant Dudley Varney, at home. Together they hurried to the Lakewood sheriff's substation, where they quizzed Weatherly for three hours. Gutierrez had no difficulty in identifying the preacher in Weatherly's account as Jerry Owen. The SUS pair began a follow-up investigation that was treated as a military secret; not even the FBI, which was supposed to be kept apprised of developments, knew about it.

We tracked down Weatherly on October 2, 1969, at his parents' home in Chino, a Riverside County town thirty miles east of Los Angeles. He turned out to be a soft-spoken young man raised in ranch country who had naturally gravitated to stables. His information was hearsay, he said, from Bill Powers and Johnny Beckley. At first he declined to talk. "I've been asked not to say anything by Sergeant Varney and Sergeant Gutierrez," he apologized. "They just said I shouldn't speak to anyone. The judge was, ah—that any publicity would be against the law, that I couldn't even tell anyone."

Once again SUS had tried to silence a witness. The judge's order had applied to potential trial witnesses only, and the trial had been over for six months. Weatherly's name was never on the list anyway. When we explained to Weatherly that the court order never did apply to him, he loosened up.

Johnny Beckley, he said, knew Owen "pretty well." About a week after the assassination, Beckley confided to him that he had seen Owen and Sirhan "ride up and down the Santa Ana River together quite often." (The river is bone-dry in the summer and is used as a bridle trail.) "That morning that Kennedy was assassinated, they came out and borrowed Bill's truck." Weatherly evidently didn't know that Powers had sold the truck to Owen sometime before.

Weatherly told several friends what Beckley had divulged. They suggested that he and Beckley cash in on the story by going to the press. But when he broached the idea to Beckley, the older man apparently realized the jeopardy involved and "didn't want no part of it." So, around November, Weatherly phoned the Los Angeles *Times* himself. "They thought it was a joke," he recounted. "I didn't talk to the reporter for more than two minutes." He made no further overtures to the press.

After Weatherly spilled the story to the sheriff's deputies, Beckley gave him a dressing down. "The reason John didn't want to say anything," Weatherly explained, "was because he felt this preacher had enough money to get us all knocked off." Powers, too, was upset. "Bill told Beckley that he was gonna twist my head off," Weatherly said, "but I seen Bill and he never said nothin' to me."

Gutierrez and Varney traced Beckley through an outstanding traffic warrant and hassled him roughly. "He got frustrated," Weatherly said. "They had him handcuffed at his mother's house, and they was gonna take him in." But Beckley didn't talk—he just said, "Bill Powers knows all about it. Go talk to him!"

We intended to talk to Bill Powers ourselves, but we had one final question for Weatherly: how had he fared on the stolen-car and credit-card rap?

"I wasn't even charged with a misdemeanor," he chuckled.

It would be the last time he found the situation even faintly amusing.

BEFORE WORLD WAR II, SANTA ANA WAS THE SOMNAMBULANT seat of Orange County. But the postwar boom saw bulldozers swarming like locusts, leveling acre after acre of citrus groves to make way for housing tracts and industrial parks. Space-age industries sprang up, and Disneyland, and freeways. Lured by the balmy climate and coastal beaches, immigrants flocked in from east of the Rockies and the nation's Southern tier. Despite its phenomenal growth, Orange County was hardly a melting pot—even by the mid-1960s the Jewish and black populations both amounted to less than one percent. It was an ultraconservative stronghold, a place where the John Birch Society flourished and the Santa Ana *Register* advocated private ownership of schools and the police department. "Orange County is radical in its conservatism," Republican Governor Goodwin Knight once remarked.

In early 1968 Bill Powers sold his interest in the A-Bar-T

Stables and moved a couple of miles downstream to set up his Wild Bill's Stables. Weatherly apparently had the two stables confused when he reported to the deputy sheriffs.

When Christian interviewed him on October 12, 1969, Powers initially exhibited the cowboy's characteristic suspicion of strangers. But the suspicion soon melted, and he began talking about Jerry Owen in his easy drawl. He had known Owen, who lived within walking distance up the river, for some four years through their mutual interest in horses. The preacher kept a small private stable himself, selling and trading on occasion, and often bought or borrowed bundles of hay from Powers. Powers was awed by the shifts in Owen's moods. The preacher might be a roistering good fellow one minute, then lapse into "little spells when he'd want to tell you how tough he was."

Powers thought that there was a bit of Elmer Gantry in Owen. Once when he went to the preacher's home to talk about a horse trade, he found him locked in an outhouse in the backyard. "He couldn't talk to nobody," Powers recounted. "His wife said he couldn't be bothered. He was meditatin'. And a few days later he come by my place and, boy, he was all cleaned up and really shaven and he said he fasted for three days and nights and meditated, and he said the Lord told him how to do it. And I said, 'What's that, Jerry? Make a little money?,' and he said, 'Yeah!' "

On a couple of occasions Owen hinted that Powers was sharp enough to get away with something illegal. "He told me that I was smart enough that I didn't have to fool with them horses," the cowboy recalled, "that I could do something else." Once Owen talked vaguely about a deal in which Powers would help in transporting horses around the first week in June 1968—up in the Oxnard area, he thought the preacher said. But Powers never rose to the bait.

Powers corrected Weatherly's impression that Owen and Sirhan had borrowed his late-model Chevrolet truck on election day to drive into Los Angeles. When he bought this vehicle, he sold Owen his old 1951 Chevrolet pickup that Owen had previously borrowed to haul hay. "So then a few weeks before the assassination he came down and bought the truck," Powers explained. The price was either $300 or $350, and Owen made a $50 down payment. Powers hung on to the "pink slip" proving ownership until the balance would be paid.

It never was. On or about Monday, June 3, Powers related, Owen drove into Wild Bill's Stables at the wheel of a late-model Lincoln Continental four-door sedan. When Powers brought up the money due, the preacher nodded and said he had to go to the bank. Upon returning, he fished in his pocket and pulled out a roll of $1,000 bills. "I don't know how many of them there was," the cowboy marveled, "but there was a big handful of them."

"I'll pay you for that truck," Owen said, peeling off a $1,000 bill.

"Jerry, I don't have no change for *that*," Powers replied.

"Well, I'll have to go to the bank and get one cashed and bring you back the money for the truck."

Owen drove off in his luxury car, but didn't return. "The assassination was the next day, I guess," Powers said. "I never did figure him," he continued. "He often had to borrow a bundle of hay. I don't know where he got his money, but it sure wasn't in the horse business." Could Owen have flashed a "Montana bankroll"? Christian asked, referring to a roll of $1 bills covered with a $1,000 note that con men use to impress their victims. "No, no, no," Powers insisted—he knew a Montana bankroll when he saw one. "Oh, no! I'd say there was probably twenty-five, maybe thirty of them, at least. They filled one pocket, and there were money orders, traveler's checks, something like that in the other pocket. He showed me that roll of bills a couple of times. He showed 'em to all of us there." The sight of Owen in his flashy new car had attracted several of the stable hands. Johnny Beckley was one of them.

If Powers was correct, "The Walking Bible" was walking around with a cool $25,000 to $30,000 in cash. But if he had any fear of being mugged, he wasn't relying on the Lord for his only protection. With him that afternoon were two other men, one a bulky and powerful-looking black man and the other young, small and "Mexican-lookin'." How did Owen introduce him? Christian asked. "Can't remember what his name was," Powers replied. "He said a friend of a partner, or an associate. I shook hands with . . . ah . . . him, and the nigger both." The cowboy commented on the black man's appearance: "He just shined like a diamond in a goat's ass!"

"Was Sirhan with him when he had the roll of thousand-dollar bills?"

"Ah, yeah." Powers was slightly hesitant, perhaps feeling himself slipping into deep waters. He backed off a bit by saying, "There was two guys with him."

"Did the kid get out of the pickup and walk around?" It was a rigged question, but the cowboy wasn't trapped.

"No, he was in the car," he corrected. "He just raised forward there and I shook hands with him."

Shortly after the assassination, Bill Powers told Christian, he returned from a brief trip trying to round up wild mustangs to be broken and trained when his stablehands told him, "The FBI's been looking for you." Two men identifying themselves as Bureau agents had come by in an unmarked beige Chevrolet. Concerned, Powers dialed the FBI resident agency in Riverside but was informed that there was no record there or in Los Angeles that he was being sought.

A day or so later two plain-clothes men showed up, but they said they were from the LAPD. It was a routine interview, apparently prompted by the fact that Powers was still listed as the legal owner of the pickup truck Owen had driven. The policemen mentioned that the truck had been dusted for fingerprints, and that Sirhan's had in fact been found on the glove compartment and rear window.

Then, about a week later, the first pair of detectives reappeared, driving the same Chevrolet. They announced themselves as "FBI" and flashed credentials. They told Powers that the old pickup truck had been recovered abandoned in Barstow, some 130 miles northeast of Los Angeles on the route to Las Vegas, and had been brought back to the FBI crime lab in Los Angeles for fingerprint testing. In a menacing manner they demanded to know what Powers knew about Owen and Sirhan and the RFK case. "They tried to scare me," Powers recounted. "They tried to give me a bunch of bullshit at first. They wanted to make sure I knew who they were, and that they weren't fooling around. All I told them is what they asked me. I didn't make no statements, no nothin'."

Powers said that the putative FBI men handed him a card "and told me that if anybody tried to arrest me or pick me up to phone them before I went with them, that I wasn't to get in no cars or anything like that. They told me it was for my own protection—'they' might bump me off." The cowboy was specifically instructed not even to speak to other law enforcement officers. Turning nastier, the pair intimated that they had been watching Powers, knew of his dalliance with a girl of "jailbait" age, and might have to "bust" him if he didn't "cooperate."

The "FBI agents" returned three times in the next few months. "They asked me something and I'd tell 'em if I wanted to. And if I didn't, I didn't say nothin'.

"I figured it was none of their business if that was Sirhan with Owen in the car," Powers declared. "I mean, I don't care who it was, you know. There's no use gettin' involved. Why should I care who it was, you know. There's no use gettin' involved. Why should I get involved? The only thing it might do is get me killed or something. I'll tell you the truth, I'm kinda scared."

It was the preacher who frightened Powers. "He can have you bumped off. He wouldn't just think about it—he'd do it.

"And then he'd say a little prayer."

After the assassination, Powers told Christian, Owen never returned to Wild Bill's Stables. But five months later, in November 1968, they encountered each other at the Hilton Hay Company in Santa Ana. Owen either knew or guessed that Powers had been questioned by the police, and pumped him on what he told them about "that day" at the stables. "They asked me a lot of questions," Powers replied. "But I didn't say nothin' at all."

Apparently satisfied, Owen pulled Powers off to the side and whispered confidentially about his innocence in the case. As Powers remembered it, the preacher said "well, he guessed he'd kinda got mixed up in the deal. He didn't know anything about it, but he thought they was gonna have him take Sirhan out of the country in that little truck with the horse in back. They'd never look for him back there with the horses."

IT APPEARED TO US THAT THE HILTON HAY COMPANY INCIDENT was an attempt by Owen to quell what suspicion Powers might have of him as anyone other than a victim of circumstances. Once he had established that Powers had not divulged what he saw and heard "that day" at the stables, he probably felt he owed the cowboy some kind of explanation for the roll of $1,000 bills, Sirhan's presence in the Lincoln and Sirhan's fingerprints on the pickup truck.

Had Sirhan's lawyers known about Bill Powers, the whole complexion of the trial might have changed. Powers impressed us as a straight shooter, and we didn't doubt that what he recounted was accurate to the best of his recollection. This raised the question of the supposed FBI agents who had intimidated Powers into silence. They had shown up even before the legitimate LAPD plain-clothes men checking on the ownership of the truck, and had returned several times over the months. It seemed obvious to us that the pair was determined that neither the prosecution nor defense would learn that Powers even existed.

We doubted that they were actually from the FBI. For one thing, the FBI did not have a crime lab in Los Angeles. For another, the Bureau knew nothing about the Jerry Owen angle until a month after the assassination, when George Davis contacted the San Francisco office. At that juncture the FBI, relying on the representations of SUS that the Owen story was spurious, promptly lost interest in it. We had discussed the Owen matter with Roger LaJeunesse, the FBI's top agent on the RFK case, back in May 1969; he said that Captain Brown and Manny Pena had assured him that the hitchhiker story had been gone over with a fine-tooth comb. LaJeunesse had read the SUS summary report on Owen, and while he found it too opinionated by FBI standards, he did not quarrel with its conclusions.

But at the time LaJeunesse had not mentioned Bill Powers and the incident at Wild Bill's Stables, and we now wondered if he knew about them. Christian arranged a meeting and played the tape of his interview with Powers. The agent's pugnacious face writhed in displeasure as he heard Powers' voice spill out of the recorder. SUS had never mentioned Powers or the cowboys despite an agreement for the complete exchange of information. LaJeunesse doubted that anyone from the FBI had ever interviewed Powers and Beckley. Just to make sure, he promised to check the master case index when he got back to the office.

LaJeunesse called back to report that the FBI's index was in fact negative on the cowboys. Moreover, he had phoned the Riverside resident agency and received confirmation from agent Sanford L. Blanton that Powers had called in shortly after the assassination inquiring as to who from the FBI was looking for him. LaJeunesse at first speculated that Powers and the stablehands might mistakenly have assumed that the detectives were from the FBI when they were actually from the LAPD. In fact, the description of the detective who had shoved Powers into the back seat of the beige Chevrolet and gruffly warned him of the danger of talking was very close to that of Manny Pena. But if it was the LAPD, what became of their reports? LaJeunesse conceded that it was highly peculiar that there was not even an allusion to Powers or Beckley or Weatherly in the SUS final report.

ELEVEN DAYS AFTER HE INTERVIEWED POWERS, CHRISTIAN CALLED Chick Gutierrez at the LAPD. After striking out with Johnny Beckley, Gutierrez and his SUS partner Dudley Varney had questioned Bill Powers, but the cowboy, still intimidated by the "FBI agents" and a fear of Owen, had responded only grudgingly and equivocally.

"Did you ever get any reports at all on Sirhan being seen down in Orange County with Jerry Owen?" Christian probed. The former SUS man* sounded surprised that we had gotten wind of the Weatherly Report. Although the Sirhan trial was over, the LAPD remained concerned that Charlie O'Brien might step in and reopen the case on the basis of new evidence. "I think there was some guy that said something about he'd heard of him down there," Gutierrez hedged. "Weatherly said he saw them riding down there, but we followed that up and it turned out to be nothing."

"Another crank?" Christian prodded.

"No, I think the kid just wanted some help—he was incarcerated

---

* Special Unit Senator was officially disbanded on July 25, 1969. This would be our last contact with Gutierrez. In 1972 the forty-year-old physical-fitness buff was stricken with a fatal heart attack. It was said that he had privately voiced doubts about the police conclusion.

on some other thing. He'd heard this other guy talk about Jerry
Owen, so I guess he made up the story." But Gutierrez admittedly
had no proof that Weatherly was lying. "How are you going to
disprove his story unless you put him on a polygraph?" he said.
"He was half high on weed and all that. We made a real good
follow-up and there was nothing to it."

Funny, Christian thought, the sheriff's deputies who arrested
Weatherly made no mention of marijuana in their report, and in
fact described him as normal and lucid. But SUS had a habit of
slurring witnesses whose accounts did not square with the police
version. Like Sandy Serrano. And Vincent DiPierro. And now
Dianne Lake, late of the Manson Family. At the time of Christian's
call, Gutierrez was working on the yet-unsolved Tate-LaBianca
murders that had taken place the previous August. Although there
was no evidence that the sixteen-year-old Lake, a fringe member
of the Family, was implicated in the murders, Gutierrez tried to
coerce her. "I don't know how tight you are with the Family," he
asserted. "You're probably real tight with them, but somebody's
going to go down the tubes, and somebody's going to get the pill
in the gas chamber for a whole bunch of murders which you are a
part of, or so some other people have indicated." Then Gutierrez
tossed her a life preserver: "I'm prepared to give you complete
immunity, which means that if you are straight with me, right down
the line, I'll be straight with you, and I'll guarantee that you will
walk out of that jail a free woman . . ."*

Gutierrez had absolutely no authority to guarantee immunity—
that was a decision for the DA's office, subject to ratification by
the court. In any event, Dianne Lake told Gutierrez nothing. She
was later interviewed by Inyo County sheriff's deputies, without
the threats and false promises, and they secured her cooperation to
the point where she became one of the prosecution's most valuable
witnesses. As Vincent Bugliosi commented after listening to a tape
of Gutierrez's blustering tactics, "I couldn't believe what I was
hearing."†

---

* *Helter Skelter*, by Vincent Bugliosi with Curt Gentry (New York:
Bantam edition, 1975), p. 204.

† *Ibid.*, p. 203.

FOUR DAYS AFTER TALKING TO GUTIERREZ, CHRISTIAN REACHED Captain Hugh Brown and repeated the question he had put to Gutierrez: Had Brown heard of reports that Owen and Sirhan had been seen together down in Orange County? "There was some kind of report," Brown answered, "where they were supposed to have been seen at some riding stable—which we checked out and was proven erroneous. In other words, the people couldn't identify Owen's picture or Sirhan's picture." Brown was either ignorant of the facts or dissembling: Powers and Beckley were well acquainted with Owen, and could identify him without photographs.

But Brown volunteered a fresh bit of information. Somewhere in the El Monte area (east of Los Angeles, not far from Sirhan's home) Sirhan reportedly rode horses regularly, not with Owen but with somebody else. And there was another stable where Sirhan and Owen were spotted, although not necessarily together. Brown was frustratingly vague, but in his view it didn't really matter. "Every one of those reports that came in was thoroughly checked through," he said, "and none of them proved that these guys were together any place."

ON NOVEMBER 3 CHRISTIAN PHONED CHIEF ROBERT HOUGHTON and charged that Pena and Hernandez never asked Owen, when they interrogated him in San Francisco, whether he had any kind of conspiratorial arrangement with Sirhan. "Oh yes, they did too!" he retorted. "I read the manuscript [sic]. They asked him if he ever knew, if he ever saw him. And that's certainly very pertinent!" Actually, Hernandez had simply asked Owen if the man who shot Kennedy ever offered to buy his horse, which caused the polygraph to give a strong indication of deception. But Christian pointed out that this question stayed within the framework of the hitchhiker story—which no one believed—and consequently was useless in determining if a different relationship had existed.

"Well, I think we basically agree the guy's a liar," Houghton conceded in exasperation. "Our problem was finding concrete proof leading to conspiracy. We couldn't find any."

Christian didn't bring up the Weatherly Report, for Houghton seemed intractable. In two months his book, *Special Unit Senator,* would be out, and it systematically rejected conspiracy theories, including the Jerry Owen angle.*

ON NOVEMBER 11 CHRISTIAN COMPLETED HIS TELEPHONIC ROUNDS of former SUS men by calling Sergeant Dudley Varney, Gutierrez's partner in the Weatherly Report investigation. Asked about Bill Powers, Varney was curious how we knew about the "rumor," which he contended was cooked up by a bunch of cowboys who wanted to sell it to the Los Angeles *Times* at a big price. "You understand cowboys?" he asked. "Well, they're a breed all to themselves. They talk their own language, they have their own humor. The humor will throw you. You can't understand them. They're wild!"

Varney downplayed events at Wild Bill's Stables, saying simply that the police had a report that Owen had rented a stable before the assassination for a horse he was going to sell to Sirhan. SUS uncovered no information that the report was accurate, "so it came to a dead end right there."

Christian was incredulous: "You mean if Owen hadn't rented a stall for a horse for Sirhan at that stable, then—"

"—then I wouldn't have to pursue it further, would I?"

Varney obviously had no inkling of how much we knew, or he wouldn't have expected to put off Christian with that gambit. When Christian kept plugging, Varney revealed that the source of their information was a James Clark, the "other owner" with Powers of the A-Bar-T Stables. Clark told them that he was aware of a rumor that Owen had something to do with Sirhan, but that there had been no arrangement for Sirhan to keep a horse there. Varney said

* Houghton, *op. cit.,* p. 148. Houghton described our theory: "The clergyman, the two journalists argued, feared he would be uncovered, now that Sirhan had been captured alive. So he had come to the police with his 'discrepancy-ridden' alibi, one designed to establish his 'innocent' contact with Sirhan. . . . Actually, they alleged, he was part of the 'get-away' plan, and should have been waiting with his truck and horse at the side exit of the hotel the night of June 4–5."

this indicated that Powers either was lying or was "honestly mistaken."

Could the SUS duo have been that confused? Christian wondered. It had been Weatherly who was mistaken in naming the A-Bar-T in place of Wild Bill's Stables. Apparently sensing that we knew more than he had thought at first, Varney pulled out his files, and flipping through the pages, gave a brief rundown of their interview of Powers. The cowboy said that he sold the pickup truck to Owen in May 1968, at which time the preacher was accompanied by a large Negro. Owen had at least one $1,000 bill covering what might have been a Montana bankroll, and when Powers couldn't change it, Owen gave him $100 as down payment. Nothing was recorded about Powers' mentioning a third man being in the preacher's company.

This version was a far cry from what Powers had told us. A few basic elements were there, but they were telescoped in time so that they all took place on the day Owen bought the truck. It was a Montana bankroll, not the real thing, as Powers had insisted to us. And there was no Lincoln Continental, and no "skinny man in the back seat." Of course, Powers might not have been forthcoming with Gutierrez and Varney because of their heavy-handed approach.

Varney claimed that Powers had made some conflicting statements, and that SUS had requested him to come in to headquarters to clear them up. But they canceled the request after finally locating Johnny Beckley. The way Varney told it, Beckley denied ever seeing Sirhan. Yes, he had seen Owen riding along the Santa Ana River bed many times, but not with Sirhan or anyone who resembled him.

For SUS, that perfunctory denial was sufficient to mark the Weatherly Report "closed."

10

Flying Bullets

OUR INVESTIGATION REMAINED OPEN. WE WERE STILL STUMPED as to the identity of the bulky black ex-fighter who had been in the front seat of Owen's Lincoln. Whoever he was, he was a prime witness.

Doug Lewis, the trainer of "Irish Rip" O'Reilly, had provided a possible clue when Christian interviewed him about Owen's appearances at the Coliseum Hotel. Lewis had said that he was filling in for one Johnny Gray, O'Reilly's regular trainer who supposedly was working temporarily with another boxer. From Lewis' description, Gray might be our man. But we had no idea of his current whereabouts, even though we'd been trying to locate him on general principle for several months. Anyone who knew Owen was worth talking to, we believed from the very outset.

On a hunch Christian called Owen's younger brother, Richard Owen, an instructor at Los Angeles Trade Tech College. He didn't know Gray, but he was familiar with a man named Edward E. Glenn who had claimed he was O'Reilly's co-manager with his brother and footed the bills for the fighter's stay at the Coliseum Hotel. Perhaps Glenn would know where Gray was. Glenn was president of the Midland Oil Company of Wyoming, which purportedly was exploring for oil in that state. Glenn had sold stock in the company to Richard Owen and several other instructors. When he became uneasy about his investment, Owen said, Glenn assigned him "stock" in O'Reilly as a good-faith gesture. Glenn left Los Angeles immediately after the assassination and Richard Owen had not heard from him since.

A check with Dun & Bradstreet disclosed that Midland Oil had been headquartered in Littleton, Colorado, in 1968 but had disappeared, abandoning a single wildcat well in Lusk, Wyoming. The dry-hole venture was under investigation by the Attorney General of Wyoming for possible violation of state securities laws regarding the sale of unregistered stock and fraud.*

Since Glenn appeared to have been a fast-buck operator in several states, we threw his name at FBI agent Roger LaJeunesse. "How did you get on to him?" LaJeunesse asked with an astonished look on his face. Yes, he said, the mysterious Mr. Glenn had come to the attention of the Bureau. Glenn moved in circles known to have right-wing views and underworld ties. His headquarters had been in Littleton, all right, but he frequently ranged to Los Angeles, San Diego, Phoenix, Albuquerque, Dallas, Miami, New Orleans and Chicago as well as Central and South America. His line? "Oil-equipment salesman."

"You guys know Jim Braden?" LaJeunesse asked, knowing the answer full well. "He and Glenn pal around together on occasion— from Miami to San Diego—with stops in between like Dallas and New Orleans."

* Christian telephone conversation with the Wyoming Attorney General's Office, November 1969.

Jim Braden had been detained by Dallas sheriff's deputies minutes after the assassination of John Kennedy after being found on the third floor of the Dal-Tex Building on Dealey Plaza, across the street from the building from which Lee Harvey Oswald allegedly fired at the President. Braden told the deputies that he was an "independent oil dealer" from Los Angeles and that he had walked in off the street to try to find a telephone. He was released.*

However, Turner had suspected that there was more to Jim Braden than met the eye, so in 1967, while visiting Los Angeles, he tried in vain to find him at the two addresses given on the Dallas sheriff's report. However, the report had Braden's California driver's license number scrawled on it, which led Turner to a posh Beverly Hills office building whose directory listed Braden under the Empire Oil Company. But the receptionist said that Braden traveled most of the time and only stopped by to pick up his mail.

Turner handed over his findings to Peter Noyes, the CBS producer who had excellent sources in the Los Angeles area. Noyes obtained a three-page rap sheet under FBI Number 799 431 showing that Jim Braden was one of several aliases for Eugene Hale Brading. LAPD intelligence files revealed that Brading had hung around with Mafia heavies, among them Jimmy "The Weasel" Fratiano, described as "the executioner for the Mafia on the West Coast," and the Smaldone brothers of Denver. In 1956 the LAPD tied Brading in with two California syndicate men operating the Sunbeam Oil Company in Miami, characterizing Sunbeam as "a pure front for con men schemes." Noyes found out that Brading's Empire Oil Company also had an office in New Orleans, and that Brading was in Dallas on the day of the JFK shooting with the permission of his parole officer, who reported that Brading "planned to see Lamar Hunt and other speculators while there." On the day before the assassination, Brading did see Lamar Hunt and his brother Nelson Bunker Hunt, executives of the Hunt Oil Company. The patriarch of the family, H. L. Hunt, was noted for his ultra-right activism, and Nelson Bunker Hunt helped pay for the full-page ad in the Dallas *Morning News* of November 22, 1963, that

* Warren Commission, Decker Exhibit No. 5323, Vol. 19, p. 469.

showed a picture of John Kennedy with the legend "WANTED FOR TREASON."

From what Noyes was able to learn from his law enforcement sources, Brading was a syndicate courier transporting large amounts of cash around the United States and to Europe. His home base was the luxurious La Costa Country Club north of San Diego, built with Teamsters loans and run by the Las Vegas syndicate of Moe Dalitz. Following the Robert Kennedy assassination, Noyes tipped off Robert Houghton about Brading's curious background, and Houghton dispatched "Chick" Gutierrez to La Costa to question him. Brading admitted that he had been in Los Angeles the night RFK was shot, but claimed he was at the Century Plaza Hotel, a half-hour drive from the Ambassador.* SUS was apparently satisfied with the alibi, for Houghton chalked up the matter to "historical coincidence." In *Special Unit Senator* the chief alluded to Brading by saying: "In addition to his Mafia and oil contacts, he was friendly with 'far-right' industrialists and political leaders of that [the Texas] area."†

After LaJeunesse's startling revelation, Christian put in a call to Edward Glenn's home in Colorado. Mrs. Glenn answered. "This is the Attorney General's Office," he bluffed in his most official voice. It worked. Mrs. Glenn said her husband was out of the country, probably in South America. She related that on the day Robert Kennedy was shot her husband had called from Los Angeles and told her how his new partner, Jerry Owen, had had a "brush with history" by picking up Sirhan. Several months before, Mrs. Glenn said, Owen had wanted her husband to play some role in his projected television series, but he had declined for reasons unknown to her.

Yes, she had heard of Johnny Gray. In fact, he had called frantically only a few weeks before and told her husband about a shooting scrape he and Owen had just been in. Mrs. Glenn read off Gray's unlisted number in Los Angeles. Then she volunteered

* Peter Noyes, *Legacy of Doubt* (New York: Pinnacle Books, 1973), pp. 37–38.

† Houghton, *op. cit.*, p. 158.

that Owen frightened her, especially when he went off on his religious tangents, and that she had been suspicious of his story about Sirhan from the moment she heard it.

"My husband isn't in any trouble, is he?" she asked plaintively. Without answering, Christian thanked her for her help.

WHEN CHRISTIAN MADE A PRETEXT CALL TO THE HOLLYWOOD DI-vision of the LAPD, an officer in the records section obligingly read off the report of the shooting incident involving Owen and Gray.* It stated in part that on August 14, 1969, "Owen was northbound on Vermont Canyon Road from the Griffith Park Observatory, in Owen's '65 Continental being driven by a friend. [Note that Johnny Gray's name is omitted here—a highly unlikely oversight, as we'll soon see.] They were going downhill on Vermont Canyon Road about 25 miles an hour. Suspects' vehicle approached from the opposite direction. The vehicle passed Owen's vehicle and made a U-turn and swung in behind his car. They pulled up alongside of Owen's car. Suspect #1 pointed an unknown type rifle at his moving vehicle and fired two rounds. He states there were no hits on the vehicle. The suspects car was described as a '67 or '68 Mustang, dark blue." Complainant Owen described the man who fired as being in his late twenties, tall, with a "hippie haircut." The driver was a black man with a heavy build and long hair.

The shooting incident gave Christian a handle for contacting Johnny Gray. He reached Gray on his unlisted number on November 20, 1969, again posing as an "Attorney General" deputy. Gray said that in mid-August he was standing by while Owen was making a phone call from a booth outside the Carolina Pines restaurant in Hollywood when a dark-blue Mustang with two occupants pulled up to the curb. One of them yelled, "You son of a bitch! You better keep your motherfuckin' mouth closed!" The car sped off. Gray wasn't sure whom they were yelling at or why, but he was frightened.

He and Owen hopped into Owen's Lincoln Continental and

* Report No. DR 69-589-101, written by Officer Howard Moses, August 14, 1969.

hurried to the preacher's apartment on Gramercy Place in Hollywood that he had moved into after selling the home in Santa Ana. As they were pulling into a parking space Owen cried out, "That looks like the same car that those guys were in!" The suspect car wheeled into a U-turn, and Owen yelled, "Yes, it is!" and dashed for his apartment building. The two men got out and started after him. Soon they returned to their car and sped away. Owen then returned to the Lincoln and slipped into the back seat.

Gray began to stammer at this point, and complained about having high blood pressure. Christian prompted him, "What next, Gray?"

Gray related that after a while Owen decided, "Well, take me for a ride. I gotta get all this worry and pressure off me!" Gray drove the Lincoln while Owen slumped in the back seat. At the preacher's direction he drove past the crowd entering the Hollywood Greek Theater and up into Griffith Park near the observatory. It was dusk. Suddenly the same Mustang came out from a hillside tunnel and pulled abreast of them. One of the men raised something. "I figured it was a rifle," Gray recounted. "I says, 'Duck, Reverend! I think they got a rifle!' And just about that time they passed by. *Whing! Whing!* They fired two shots right straight through the car." Only moments before, Owen had instructed Gray to "switch open" the windows, and Gray assumed the bullets went right through.

The story had an even more bizarre ending. Owen ordered Gray to rush to the Hollywood Station. Gray said that as they were sitting in a room reporting the shooting, "two shots went off by the window there. And the officers said, 'Well, it's just a couple of the boys, ah, you know, havin' some fun.' But it wasn't no fun to us, you know. This was right in the police station. Down in Hollywood! *Bang! Bang!*, you know, two bullet shots. Well, we hit the deck and I didn't know what the hell was goin' on."

Christian made a mental note of the fact that the police report had mentioned nothing about any gunshots at the station. Gray doubted that the two shooting episodes had been an innocent joke. In fact, he sensed that the entire evening's events might have been staged by the police—that the occupants of the Mustang "might have been two police officers, a colored and a white officer." Gray said he was so frightened that his blood pressure shot up to the danger level, and he had to be rushed to the hospital.

Christian broached the subject of Wild Bill's Stables in Santa Ana, and Gray remembered being there with Owen. "Were you with him there just before the assassination of Senator Kennedy, the day before?" Christian asked.

"Yeh, uh-huh," Gray acknowledged, apparently not suspecting what Christian was leading up to.

"You and Owen there in the Lincoln?"

"Yeh."

"Our report says there was a colored fellow in the front seat with him." Christian pretended that he was reading from an official report.

"That was—that was me," Gray said, his voice beginning to waver.

The boxing trainer recalled vaguely that Owen had driven down there to find out about "a trailer or horses or something." Gray was introduced to the owner of the stables but remained in the car while the business was being discussed.

"Did Owen have a big wad of money with him when you were down at the stables that day?" Christian wanted to know.

"Every time I've seen him he's got a wad," Gray said evasively.

"Where does he get that money?"

"I don't know."

"Preaching?"

"I don't know. It might have been from preachin'. Maybe he had other things, I don't know. He can be broke when he wants to be broke." Gray gave a forced laugh.

Christian sprung the loaded question: "Was there a skinny Mexican kid or anything with you that day?"

Gray haltingly said he couldn't remember; then said no.

"Are you *sure* there was nobody with you?" Christian asked with a tone of skepticism.

"I can't remember exactly," Gray said. "There might have been, but you know, I'm just sitting there, and I been to the hospital twice." He lapsed into his high-blood-pressure complaint.

After hanging up, Christian analyzed the situation. Gray had talked fairly freely about the shooting incident, but once the topic shifted to the stables he became extremely nervous and flustered. The "You son of a bitch! You better keep your motherfuckin' mouth closed!" threat hurled at Owen and Gray from the Mustang had an altogether familiar ring. It was virtually word for word the threat Owen claimed he had received twice over the phone shortly after the assassination. Gray was apparently being truthful as far as he went, but there were sensitive areas he was obviously terrified to get into.

Christian decided to make another run at him, calling on Thanksgiving Day with the excuse that he had developed new information. "Did Owen introduce you to the young man in the back seat?" Christian asked.

"No," Gray muttered. "The only one I was introduced to was the man at the stables. He didn't introduce me to the other fella." Christian permitted himself a slight smile—Gray had now let slip that there was an "other fella" in the back seat.

Well, Christian went on, the man in the back seat had been identified by other witnesses as Sirhan Sirhan. "Is that right?" Gray responded. "Well, it could have been . . . I really can't say." Gray allowed as to how Owen picked up an awful lot of different people. "I don't remember if he was Sirhan or who he was," Gray said, " 'cause I've met a lot of people with him."

Christian kept his questioning on the positive side by asking, "Did Sirhan leave the house with you and Owen that day?"

There was a pause, followed by raspy coughing. Gray moaned about another siege of high blood pressure coming on.* Christian left him to his holiday, thankful for the bountiful information.

---

* The high-blood-pressure aspect seemed to fit into the theme that either the Griffith Park attackers had deliberately missed their target(s) or fired blanks. If Gray's blood pressure was dangerously high in the first place, the sudden shock of gunfire might cause a fatal stroke or heart attack, both of which could be classified as "natural causes." The gun explosion at the Hollywood Station makes this all the more a distinct possibility—that Gray had been a witness to things that neither Owen nor the police wanted him capable of repeating. (And remember: Gray's name did *not* appear on the LAPD interview.) All this took place shortly after Christian had begun to inquire around the local boxing emporiums about the background and location of Johnny Gray (early July 1969). We knew he'd been close with Owen for some years.

SINCE THE UNEXPECTED WAS NOW BECOMING COMMONPLACE, WE took the next bit of news in stride. On August 16, two days after the shooting scene in Griffith Park, Owen reported to the Hollywood Division that his Gramercy Place apartment had been burglarized and all his records taken. This meant, he said, that he could not account for his "love offerings" income for the year 1968. The police report filed by Owen noted that the burglar had scrawled *"Remember S. S."* on the bottom of the toilet seat, which the preacher took to mean Sirhan Sirhan. When Christian relayed the news to Turner, the ex-FBI man asked, "Was the seat up or down?"

"Up," Christian replied.

"Ah ha," Turner deduced, "we have a male suspect."

Owen evidently found no humor in the latest developments. On the day after Christian's second "Attorney General" interview with Gray, Owen precipitously moved out of the Gramercy Place apartment and headed for a remote spot high up in the Sierra Nevadas. But he left behind yet another bizarre episode that we would not learn about for several months. On January 8, 1970, Christian finally reached Captain Hugh Brown after repeated attempts and asked him if he knew that Owen had been shot at. "I don't think that ever got to us," Brown replied. "I'm sure it didn't happen, or I would have known about it." Christian didn't argue.

The two renewed their argument over the police position that Owen had told the hitchhiker story to reap publicity. To try and bolster his point, Brown suddenly revealed that the preacher had also injected himself into the Tate-LaBianca murder case. He reported to the Hollywood Division that the day before the killings he picked up a hitchhiker named William Garretson—the nineteen-year-old caretaker of the Tate estate whom the police held for several days as a suspect before releasing him. Owen said that Garretson was looking for extra work as a dishwasher, and he took the young man to the Carolina Pines restaurant to introduce him to the management. (The Carolina Pines was the origin point of the Griffith Park shooting incident, which occurred five days after the Tate-LaBianca murders.)

However, Brown said the police had dismissed this latest episode as simply another publicity stunt by Owen. "He just wanted to get himself involved," Brown said. "Anything that gets a little publicity he wants to get involved with, apparently."

But Christian was not so sure. He asked Brown to name a newspaper or broadcast facility approached by Owen. He couldn't recall any names. Christian then checked every media outlet in the Los Angeles area for the pertinent period, with negative results. Once again, Owen's purpose in involving himself in still another major murder case did not seem to be "publicity."*

DURING HIS DAYS AS KHJ'S ACE NEWSCASTER, BAXTER WARD HAD a reputation not only for courage and tenacity, but an occasional touch of impulsiveness. For this reason Christian blocked out the names on the Weatherly Report and our follow-up investigation when he handed Ward a copy in the spring of 1971. Ward could be a valuable ally, but Christian didn't want a story put on the air that might jeopardize Weatherly and the cowboys.

But as fate would have it, Bob Kaiser had just joined Ward's news staff and he was able to fill in the names and details so that Ward could pick up the story and run with it. Ward began by querying the LAPD, which summarily dismissed Weatherly's story. This only made him more suspicious, so he went ahead and talked to Weatherly at his parents' home in Chino. Ward was so impressed with the young man's evident sincerity and the consistency of his story that he decided to put it on the air. He paraphrased the script, changing names and places and altering events to protect the witnesses. Afterward, Ward told us that he had hoped his "bombshell" story would force an official review of the case.

Ward broadcast the story in early August 1971. A few days

---

* In late 1975 we informed Vince Bugliosi about Owen's "involvement" in the Manson case. His reaction was instant: "I personally examined every single LAPD report in that case, including those dealing with publicity freaks and the nuts. Owen's name never appeared anywhere. If it had—especially after his involvement in the Kennedy case—you can bet I'd have found out why, fast!"

later, at approximately three o'clock in the morning on August 11, Weatherly pulled into the driveway of his parents' home. Two teen-age companions were with him, both slumped in their seats, dozing. A shot from a high-powered rifle pierced the night air. The bullet smashed through the rear window of Weatherly's 1957 sedan, exploding it into shards of flying glass. The missile narrowly missed Weatherly's head. His foot hit the accelerator, and the car crashed into a tree next to the house, its horn stuck and one headlight smashed. The three young men lay frozen, terrified that the unseen gunman would approach the car and fire again.

A shaken Baxter Ward went on the air that same evening to report the attempt on the life of a crucial witness in the RFK case. Still disguising Weatherly's identity and whereabouts, he reconstructed the incident with diagrams and photographs of the damaged vehicle. He ruled out the idea of a "scare shot"—the bullet had come too close. He pointed out that the target was "part of a small, very small group, who claim to have some knowledge of Sirhan prior to the Kennedy assassination. They knew him. That group had members who say they saw Sirhan several times with a man later identified as a possible co-conspirator. They say that co-conspirator was with Sirhan prior to the assassination."

The newsman pleaded that the shooting merited an immediate and thorough official investigation. "We would be relieved if there were nothing to it," he closed. "But we would be shocked if it were true that the links do exist, and that a man was marked for murder because he knew of the links."

Ward conveyed his concern to U.S. Attorney Robert L. Meyer, who promised to look into the matter. Meyer called in the FBI. But the Bureau subsequently phoned Ward's office with the message that it had no interest in a purely "local matter."

11
Bucking City Hall

WE HAD NOW GONE ABOUT AS FAR AS WE COULD WITH OUR own investigation. To sum up, no fewer than three cowboys were able to put Owen's relationship with Sirhan in a context different from Samaritan and hitchhiker. They had seen the two riding horses together along the Santa Ana River bed, and believed that it was Sirhan in the Lincoln on the day Owen was flaunting the thick roll of $1,000 bills. Johnny Gray had grudgingly confirmed this sighting, and obviously knew much more than he cared to admit. There were other witnesses, such as the Reverend Jonothan Perkins, who had much to tell, and other leads, such as Owen's connection with Edward Glenn, that needed exploring.

The investigation was at the stage where it should pass into the hands of a special prosecutor or grand jury with the power to subpoena witnesses and suspects, grant immunity and send its own investigative staff into the field.

We were in a quandary as to where to turn. The LAPD was stonewalling the case. The FBI door had been shut by J. Edgar Hoover himself, who took the unprecedented step, according to LaJeunesse, of ordering all the files shipped back to Washington. Not only had Sam Yorty ignored us, he turned out to be an old pal of Jerry Owen's. District Attorney Evelle Younger had made it abundantly clear that he would resist any attempt to reopen the investigation. The cover-up had become institutionalized on a national scale.

At this point W. Matthew Byrne, the U.S. Attorney in Los Angeles, entered the picture. Handsome Matt Byrne was one of the ambitious young Kennedy New Frontiersmen who would continue to rise in succeeding Administrations. In the late summer of 1969 Frank Burns, Jesse Unruh's lieutenant, had discussed the case privately with him. Byrne was interested in what we had found out, and Burns suggested that we give him a call.

"Cops?" Byrne exclaimed after Christian gave him a rundown that included the intimidation of Bill Powers by FBI imposters. He apparently sensed the same thing that Charlie O'Brien had complained about—manipulation of the investigation at a high level of the LAPD. Byrne asked for copies of what material we had that might fall under federal purview—as, for example, impersonating an agent of the FBI. He called Christian back shortly after receiving the package. He was impressed with what he had seen, he said, and wanted to arrange a meeting with us and Bob Kaiser. "But I'm not sure what I can do about it," he remarked, referring to the array of political power lined up against any reopening.

The meeting never came off. At the last minute Kaiser had to fly back to New York to meet with his editor, and time ran out on a rescheduling. President Nixon appointed Byrne to the Scranton Commission on campus violence, and, later, to the federal bench.*

---

* In 1973 Matt Byrne was the presiding judge in the Daniel Ellsberg trial. It was during the trial that he took his celebrated strolls with John

Nixon named Robert L. Meyer, a conservative Republican from a staid Los Angeles law firm, to succeed Byrne as U.S. Attorney. On the face of it, it did not look very likely that Meyer would buck the establishment by reviewing the RFK case. But through a mutual friend we put out feelers, and the feedback was positive. A discreet meeting was proposed at a residence in Beverly Hills which Charlie O'Brien would also attend. At the last minute, however, Meyer called it off, saying he was busy with other matters and would reschedule it. It never happened.

Meyer, it turned out, had already started marching to a different drumbeat from Nixon and his Attorney General, John Mitchell. The rift came to a head in 1971 when Meyer stepped in to prosecute three Los Angeles policemen involved in the fatal "mistake" shooting of two Mexican nationals after local authorities, most prominently Evelle Younger, had turned the other way. According to the Los Angeles *Times*, LAPD Chief Edward M. Davis told the Justice Department in Washington that Meyer had been overheard to say that "prosecution of cops was good for President Nixon's political future." The remark was reported to Davis by Manny Pena, by now the LAPD's liaison with Sam Yorty's City Hall.* Caught in a squeeze play by Yorty and the LAPD, Meyer was forced to resign.†

OUR LAST HOPE FOR INTERVENTION RESTED WITH THE CALIFORNIA Attorney General's office and Charlie O'Brien. In the summer of 1970 O'Brien marched into the office of his boss, Thomas C. Lynch, to announce that he had something important to discuss about the RFK assassination. Lynch, a lugubrious Irishman who had been elected to the post after years as San Francisco's DA, was the only

---

Ehrlichman during which the possibility of his being named FBI director was brought up. Byrne dismissed the charges against Ellsberg on the basis that he had been illegally wiretapped.

* Los Angeles *Times* (January 19, 1972).

† On November 14, 1972, Meyer was found dead at the wheel of his car in the parking lot of the Orange County Court House. The *Times* reported: "Friends were surprised at word of his death; they knew of no history of heart trouble."

Democrat left holding statewide office after Reagan's Republican sweep of 1966. Sixty-five and ailing, Lynch was on the verge of retirement. He had long since let it be known that he would not run again, and he had hand-picked O'Brien to run as his successor.

This morning Lynch looked more doleful than usual. He had known for some time that his chief deputy suspected malfeasance in the Kennedy case, and he had ducked a showdown in the hope the issue would fade away. Now he knew it wouldn't.

We had been keeping O'Brien posted on developments in our investigation, and he had reciprocated by telling us what he knew through his law enforcement contacts. O'Brien gave Lynch a brief status report and reminded him that the AG had the responsibility of taking over when local law enforcement is inadequate or obstructing justice. Earlier he had sent Lynch a memorandum outlining the case against the Los Angeles authorities.

"Tom," O'Brien told Lynch, "I think we should go for a special prosecutor to investigate the Kennedy case."

"Charlie," Lynch replied, "you can do anything you want after you're elected. But as long as I'm attorney general of this state, we'll make no such move."

O'Brien strenuously argued that the case should be pre-empted without delay, but Lynch was adamant. The discussion ended on an acrimonious note, with O'Brien hinting he might "go public" with the issue, and an ashen, trembling Lynch shouting that if he did, he would revoke his endorsement.*

Lynch's determination to leave office without fuss did not enhance O'Brien's election chances. O'Brien was pitted against Evelle Younger, and although it was not a motivating factor in his desire to reopen the case, he realized that it could tip the scales. If a grand jury was merely convened, it would be politically embarrassing to Younger because of his role in prosecuting Sirhan and shutting down the conspiracy angle. And if a grand jury returned indictments, Younger's whole political future—he intended to run for governor eventually—could go up in smoke.

But to simply make a campaign issue out of the assassination was a different matter, and O'Brien's brain trust counseled against

---

* Authors' interview with O'Brien, August 1971.

it. What baffled us, however, was O'Brien's reticence to exploit another whiff of scandal that had been hanging over Younger's head for some time. The central figure was a high-powered Beverly Hills attorney named Jerome Weber whose clientele numbered celebrities such as Desi Arnaz and crime-syndicate kingpins such as Frank M. "Big Frank" Matranga of San Diego. Interestingly, Weber was a past president of the Saints and Sinners Club, whose meeting Jerry Owen purportedly attended as he waited to sell Sirhan the horse. And Weber was Owen's first attorney in the suit against KCOP television.

The potential scandal revolved around Thomas E. Devins, a former parking-lot attendant who had talked a wealthy widow out of a large chunk of money and then taken her to Europe, where she disappeared (her remains were later found in the Swiss Alps). An indictment for murder was pending against Devins. Weber told him that he could quash the case through his "influence" inside the DA's office. According to grand jury testimony, Weber's asking price was $35,000, of which $25,000 would go to two top DA investigators. To demonstrate his "control" of the situation, the attorney said he would have a pesky DA investigator transferred so that his "two top investigators" could take charge. The transfer went through. Then Weber told Devins that he had arranged for senior investigator George Murphy to accompany the investigator to "control" an out-of-town interview. We considered this of more than passing interest, since Murphy and chief investigator George Stoner had been Younger's two top men on the RFK case, and had put down Owen as nothing more than an unfunny clown.

Devins paid part of the money, but then, perhaps sensing a double cross, went to the AG's office and complained of being blackmailed. O'Brien's agents hid a transmitter in his clothing and sent him in to bargain further with Weber. The attorney produced a confidential report from the DA's office to prove his connections. Devins expressed skepticism: "Have they ever failed to come through—that is, have they ever taken any bread and then that's it?" "No, no, no," Weber replied. "Never in a million years."

Weber was convicted of bribery and eventually disbarred. When he appealed the conviction, none other than Jerry Owen supplied an affidavit on his behalf. Owen claimed that he was introduced to

Devins by Weber, who said, "Curly, this is Mr. Devins. Mr. Devins, this is Curly Owen; he is a minister." Several months later Owen and Devins met on the Sunset Strip and Devins tried to get Owen to say he overheard Weber solicit the bribe "to give to somebody downtown to take care of the thing." Owen said he answered, "No, I didn't hear that." The California Supreme Court, in denying Weber's appeal, opined that "Owen's testimony was incredible" and full of "discrepancies and suspicious statements."*

The Weber case was potential dynamite, since Younger had made no move to clean house by singling out the corrupt investigators and prosecuting them. But O'Brien never detonated it, electing instead to try to outgun Younger on his strong point of law and order. A major general in the Air Force reserve, Younger was firmly identified with the Nixon Administration's hard line that was in vogue before Watergate. O'Brien lost in a photo finish—by less than one third of 1 percent of the total votes.

For the time being, at least, we had no place to turn. But in the meantime, a controversy was shaping up that would cast extreme doubt on the police position that Sirhan, and Sirhan alone, gunned down Robert F. Kennedy.

* Decision June 20, 1974, California Supreme Court, Case No. Cr. 16157.

12

Too Many Guns– Too Many Bullets

ONE MORNING IN AUGUST 1971, VETERAN CRIMINALIST WIL-liam W. Harper pulled out of the driveway of his Pasadena home on a quiet, tree-lined street within punting distance of the Rose Bowl. As he headed downtown to pick up his wife he noticed that a blue Buick seemed to be following him. He made several evasive turns, but the car kept on his tail. He could see two men in it, both wearing workmen's caps pulled down over their foreheads. Harper floored the accelerator pedal and put the family car through its paces. His pursuers gave chase. As he spun back and forth in the maze of residential streets, his car hit a deep dip. Coming out of it with the rear end bouncing high, he heard a muffled explosion from the rear and the familiar slap of a bullet striking metal.

Eluding the other car, Harper drove straight to the home of another prominent criminalist, Raymond Pinker, the retired founder of the LAPD crime lab. They examined the dent in the rear bumper and agreed that it had been caused by a slug from a high-powered gun—possibly a .45 or a .357 Magnum. Harper shuddered to think what might have happened had he not hit the dip at that moment. If the car had been running level, the shot could have gone through the rear window and struck him in the head.

The attempt on Harper's life came within days of the sniper attack on John Chris Weatherly in Chino. As in the case of Weatherly, the timing was too exquisite to ignore: Harper was scheduled to testify the next day before a grand jury investigating the handling of firearms evidence in the RFK case. Harper had set in motion the train of events leading to the grand jury probe by fathering, in 1970, what has become known as the "second gun" theory.

In over three decades as a qualified criminalist, Harper had conducted thousands of examinations for both prosecution and defense, and testified as a firearms expert in more than three hundred criminal trials around the nation. For seven years he had been a forensic science consultant to the Pasadena Police Department. His crime lab is in a detached structure in the backyard of his old brown-shingle home. It is a warren of scientific instruments, weapons mounted on the walls, blown-up photographs of footprints, tire treads and expended bullets, and shelves of criminalistics texts. A crusty septuagenarian with a dry sense of humor, Bill Harper labors under a green celluloid eyeshade like those worn by old-time city editors.

Initially, Harper had no special interest in the RFK case, but he belongs to a dwindling breed of criminalists who jealously guard the integrity of their profession. For some time he had been double-checking the work of LAPD laboratory examiner DeWayne Wolfer. Harper was skeptical about the quality of Wolfer's work. This doubt first cropped up in the 1967 trial of Jack Kirschke, a former Los Angeles deputy DA charged with the love triangle murders of his wife and another man. The cocksure Wolfer displayed blown-up photographs of bullets to the jury and declared, "No other gun in the world other than Jack Kirschke's could have killed his wife and her lover." Then he disposed of a sticky problem with an inventive explanation. A reconstruction of the crime scene conclusively showed that the victims were lying on their backs in bed when shot, but when discovered, the man's body was on the floor. Wolfer said that a post-mortem settling of body fluids caused the center of gravity to drop, rolling the body onto the floor.

It was a crucial point, for the time element involved tended to discredit alibi witnesses that placed Kirschke halfway to Las Vegas. Called by the defense, Harper and a pathologist disputed the "rolling body" theory—the pathologist sarcastically observed that the only way the body could roll off the bed was if "there was a major earthquake." Both testified that the body had to have been moved by someone after rigor mortis set in. After Kirschke was convicted, an appellate judge agreed that Wolfer had been wrong but ruled that "just as error is not the equivalent of perjury, neither is ignorance."*

Before the Sirhan trial began, Harper warned chief defense attorney Grant Cooper not to accept Wolfer's testimony at face value, but Cooper, as we have seen, adopted a strategy of not contesting the state's contention that Sirhan had acted alone. Harper even approached District Attorney Evelle Younger, an old friend and one-time Pasadena neighbor, cautioning him to "watch out" for Wolfer's handling of the evidence. But during the trial Wolfer's testimony went unchallenged—he did not even bring blown-up photographs to show the jury how he made his bullet comparisons.

After the trial and appeals, Harper decided to make his own review of Wolfer's findings. Late in 1970 he obtained permission from Sirhan's attorney to examine the evidence bullets that were stored in the County Clerk's office. Since they could not be taken out, Harper took along a portable Balliscan camera that he had helped develop. The camera takes a series of photographs of a

* Opinion of Judge George W. Dell, Los Angeles Superior Court, filed November 1, 1973, in response to habeas corpus petition.

cylindrical object rotated in front of its lens; the photographs are later blown up and used for comparison purposes.

Harper focused on two bullets that were relatively unmutilated, one from the body of Senator Kennedy and the other from injured ABC newsman William Weisel. "I can find no individual characteristics in common between these two bullets," he concluded, although warning that his findings should not be regarded as complete and definitive. Harper also compared the bullets with ones Wolfer said he had test-fired from Sirhan's gun. Again, there was no match. Harper's conclusions clashed head-on with Wolfer's trial testimony that the bullets from the victims were fired from Sirhan's gun "to the exclusion of all other weapons in the world."*

Coincidentally with Harper's findings, Wolfer was promoted to chief forensic chemist in charge of the crime lab. Appalled, Harper tried to block the promotion in the Civil Service Commission. He retained attorney Barbara Warner Blehr, who submitted a request for a hearing on Wolfer's competency by setting forth six universally accepted precepts of firearms identification and alleging that in one case (Kirschke) Wolfer violated two, and in the Sirhan case four. For example, Blehr charged that Wolfer apparently did not compare bullets from the victims with bullets test-fired from Sirhan's gun (Serial No. H53725), but with bullets from a similar but unrelated weapon (Serial No. H18602), which was destroyed a month after the testing. This "glaring error," Blehr asserted, led like a chain reaction to the four precept violations.†

Blehr's charges, which could have paved the way for a reversal of Sirhan's conviction, stunned Los Angeles officialdom. District

---

* A bullet is impressed with two types of markings and indentations by the barrel of the gun from which it is fired. One type is distinctive to the make and model of gun. The other, consisting of wear marks, scratches and other imperfections, is distinctive to the individual gun. If sufficient imperfections are present, the bullet can be positively mated to the gun.

† To prove the immutability of the precepts, Blehr attached declarations from three unimpeachable experts: Raymond H. Pinker, who founded the LAPD crime lab in 1929; Dr. LeMoyne Snyder of Paradise, California, a medical doctor and lawyer who wrote the landmark text *Homicide Investigation*; and W. Jack Cadman, chief criminalist for the Orange County crime lab. Implicit in their declarations was a deep concern over Wolfer's competence.

Attorney Joseph P. Busch, Evelle Younger's hand-picked successor, announced that his office would look into the matter and report in three weeks, but his probe actually was strung out for half a year. Police Chief Edward M. Davis immediately created an internal board of inquiry, composed of two deputy chiefs and a commander, but this was widely interpreted as no more than a public relations gesture. Any doubt about Davis' intent was dispelled shortly thereafter when he branded the allegations a vendetta and hailed Wolfer as "the top expert in the country."*

IN ADDITION TO THE FIREARMS EVIDENCE, THERE WAS EYEWITNESS testimony of the most compelling sort to reinforce the theory that more than one gun was fired.

Donald Schulman, a CBS News employee who was behind Kennedy in the pantry and whose line of vision included both Sirhan and a uniformed security guard, told radio reporter Jeff Brant moments after the shooting: "A Caucasian gentleman stepped out and fired three times, the security guard hit Kennedy all three times. Mr. Kennedy slumped to the floor. They carried him away. The security guard fired back."

Brant said, "I heard about six or seven shots in succession. Is this the security guard firing back?"

"Yes, the man who stepped out fired three times at Kennedy,

---

* Davis is noted for his verbal intemperance, and one of his favorite forums is John Birch Society meetings. He has contended that the city's "swimming-pool Communists" pose a serious threat to law and order, and resisted the hiring of minorities and gays with the crack, "I could envision myself standing on the stage on graduation day and giving a diploma to a 4-foot-11-inch transvestite moron who would kiss me instead of saluting."

A far more qualified evaluator of Wolfer than Davis was of an opposite mind. He was Marshall W. Houts, a former FBI agent, law professor, medico-legal expert and author of *Where Death Delights*, an account of the New York City Medical Examiner's office. Houts was a conservative Republican and Establishment-oriented. Yet he felt obligated to write his friend Evelle Younger a letter, dated June 26, 1971, over "blunders" committed by Wolfer. The purpose of the letter was to warn Younger, who aspired to succeed Ronald Reagan as governor, not to get "burned" by siding with Wolfer.

hit him all three times, and the security guard then fired back . . . hitting him . . ." Schulman apparently thought that the guard fired at Sirhan but accidentally hit Kennedy.

Contemporaneous accounts such as Schulman's are in legal circles considered to be the most reliable, since they are uncontaminated by other witnesses' versions and attempts by police questioners to lead the witness. Although Schulman's language is somewhat cloudy, due no doubt to the trauma of the moment, he clearly stated that both Sirhan and the uniformed guard fired multiple shots. At the time, Schulman was interviewed extensively by the LAPD, but his name was not put on the witness list. They had insisted that he was mistaken in what he saw.

But Schulman's account was consonant with other testimony before the 1968 grand jury that indicted Sirhan. Eyewitnesses uniformly recounted that Sirhan accosted Kennedy from the front, and never got closer than two to three feet from the senator before he was grabbed and wrestled to the floor.

Yet County Coroner Dr. Thomas T. Noguchi, who performed the autopsy, declared that all three of the bullets striking Kennedy entered from the *rear*, in a flight path from down to up, right to left. Moreover, powder burns around the entry wound indicated that the fatal bullet was fired at less than one inch from the head and no more than two to three inches behind the right ear.

Thus it would have been physically impossible for Sirhan to have fired the shots that struck Kennedy. Even allowing for the remote possibility that Kennedy twisted completely around—which is contrary to witnesses' accounts that he threw his arms in front of his face in a protective reaction and sagged backwards—there remained the point-blank shot. Noguchi later revealed that before he entered the grand jury room he was approached by an unnamed deputy DA who solicited him to revise the distance "from one to three inches" to one to three feet.* The coroner bravely refused to "cooperate" with this blatant attempt to suborn perjury.

Instead, an apparently suspicious Noguchi would attempt to set off an independent investigation of his own (coroner's offices call them "inquests"). Alerting Dr. Vincent P. Guinn that he would be

* Los Angeles *Herald-Examiner* (May 13, 1974).

needed to conduct Neutron Activation Analysis tests on the various victim bullets, the LA coroner immediately asked for access to these items of evidence; and he was immediately given the old shell-game treatment by both the LAPD and the DA's office, neither of which would allow Noguchi access to anything.

As the summer of 1968 wore on, not only did the LA coroner find his attempts to subject the official firearms conclusions to formal scientific review rebuffed at every turn, but suddenly he found himself the target of an insidious attack on his competency and character. The crux of these "rumors" centered on Noguchi's handling of the RFK autopsy. Word being passed around (and out) of his office was that he had "bungled" the examination of RFK's body because of his alleged propensity to "take drugs," with resultant "erratic behavior."* And before 1968 ended, Noguchi had found himself suspended from his position as Coroner of Los Angeles County, a suspension he would appeal.

In early 1969 an ex-LAPD officer, Ronnie Nathans, told Christian that he had come in contact with a government official with proof that "[DA] Evelle Younger suppressed evidence" in the RFK case. Naturally intrigued by this information, Christian made contact with the source of the alleged facts, one Dr. Donald Angus Stuart, a deputy coroner in Noguchi's office. During a subsequent session with Stuart (in early February 1969, in the middle of the Sirhan trial), Christian listened as the thick-accented (Australian) medical man implored him to act as a "cover" for "solid information" he wished to pass along to Christian's numerous news-media contacts. The "suppressed evidence" turned out to be verbalized details about Dr. Noguchi's alleged mishandling of the RFK autopsy —which, Stuart insisted, DA Younger was keeping from the public. Did it involve the concealing of anything relating to conspiracy in the case? a puzzled Christian asked. No, just the botching of the official autopsy, Stuart insisted, without saying either how it had been done or why. We dropped the subject and kept our eyes glued on the Sirhan trial.

When Noguchi was summoned to testify at the trial, his actual findings never saw the light of day. The DA's questioning of the

* Los Angeles *Times* (May 27, 1969).

coroner kept away from any conflict whatever with their shaky account of the assassination, and Sirhan's lawyer didn't help when he cut short Noguchi's answers, claiming it was "not necessary" for the coroner to go into "gory detail" about the nature and location of RFK's various wounds.

Noguchi was reinstated after the trial when, during a public hearing on the issue, his lawyer, Godfrey Isaac, pressed for a complete review of the RFK autopsy. A visibly nervous Deputy County Counsel Wartin Weekes shouted, "This is a terribly serious matter!" He strongly urged that no further discussion of the RFK case take place in public because it might trigger off "an international incident." Weekes didn't elaborate. Instead, he sheepishly stipulated that Noguchi's autopsy had been "superior,"* and the hearing was called to a close.

CORONER'S AIDE SEIZED ON PERJURY CHARGE read the headline in the Los Angeles *Herald-Examiner* on February 12, 1972. The story that followed outlined how one Donald Angus Stuart had been arrested that day and charged with perjury "stemming from testimony he gave regarding Dr. Thomas T. Noguchi." It seemed that Dr. Stuart had been discovered not to be a medical doctor at all; he'd been an impostor who had falsified all of his medical-background credentials, including his physician's license, No. 11279, "which had been assigned to a Harry Mathew Edward Lowell in 1914, according to the Illinois State Department of Registration." Suddenly our interest in "Dr." Stuart was rekindled. By this time we'd met criminalist Bill Harper and come to understand his discoveries about the "second gun" aspects of the case, and how Dr. Noguchi's findings fitted in to a T. However, it wasn't until April 15, 1976, that we got our chance to question Dr. Noguchi about the earlier events. Accompanying Dr. Robert J. Joling to the coroner's office at the close of day, Christian (posing as "Jack Cross," a Joling assistant) asked Noguchi two questions:

Q. Do you now believe that Stuart was some kind of "agent-provocateur" sent into your office to destroy you, and the RFK autopsy findings in the process?†

* *Ibid.*

† Stuart had arrived on the scene in the spring of 1968.

A. I can't be positive . . . but anything is possible.

Q. Well, do you now believe that the attempt to run you out of office in 1968–69 was directly related to your challenge of the official lone-assassin theory?

A. [Long pause, deep sigh] . . . . Yes.

One other thing: even though found guilty on all counts, Stuart never served a minute in jail or paid a fine—on the recommendations of Younger and his successor, DA Joseph Busch. Even so, the central issue lived on.

WHEN THE "SECOND GUN" CONTROVERSY SHOWED NO SIGN OF DYING, the authorities apparently felt they had to take steps not to get caught short. On July 14, 1971, investigators from the DA's office and Sergeants Phil Sartuche and Chuck Collins, formerly of SUS, secretly questioned a private security guard who had been at Kennedy's elbow when he was shot. The guard, Thane Eugene Cesar, was employed on the day shift at the Lockheed Aircraft plant in Burbank, and was moonlighting for the Ace Guard Service. The sallow-faced, black-haired security man was the only person in the crowded pantry other than Sirhan assumed to have drawn a gun (although witness Donald Schulman said he'd spotted two other revolvers, both of which he insisted had been fired).* Cesar told the DA and LAPD investigators that when he saw Sirhan fire the first shot, "I immediately ducked, and I immediately got knocked down." As he got up, he drew his gun. "Did you ever fire a shot?" he was asked. "No," he replied.

Cesar identified the gun he was carrying as a Rohm .38 caliber revolver that he had purchased especially for his guard duties. Asked if he owned any other handguns—the recovered bullets were .22 caliber—he said that he had had a .22 H & R pistol but sold it to a friend at Lockheed who retired in February 1968 and moved to Arkansas. Cesar mentioned that he had told a police sergeant about this gun when he was interviewed after the assassina-

* In late 1975, testimony and statements would be introduced at official hearings in Los Angeles Superior Court that would confirm three weapons having been drawn (and sighted) at the assassination scene.

tion. "In fact," he said, "I don't remember if I showed it to him, but I did mention that I had a gun similar to the one that was used that night."

The investigators picked up on this contradiction in Cesar's earlier statement that he had sold the gun three months *before* the assassination. Their initial concern was whether he had told any outsider about it, and Cesar said he couldn't be sure. He then backtracked, saying he couldn't have shown it to the sergeant because he had already sold it. That seemed to satisfy the investigators, who told Cesar that it wouldn't be necessary for him to take a lie-detector test.*

It didn't satisfy us, however, and on October 13, 1972, Christian reached the man to whom Cesar had sold the .22 revolver, Jim Yoder, who was living in Blue Mountain, Arkansas. Yoder said that he had been an engineer at Lockheed before retiring in the fall of 1968, and that he knew Cesar casually from the plant. Yoder was uncertain of what Cesar's specific job was, saying that he had "floating" assignments and often worked in an off-limits area which only special personnel had access to. (This was, said Yoder, the CIA-controlled U-2 spy-plane facility.) Yoder related that about a month after the assassination, Cesar showed him the revolver and he offered to buy it to use in the Ozarks after his retirement. At Yoder's request, Cesar later wrote out a receipt that read: "On the day of Sept. 6, 1968 I received $15.00 from Jim Yolder [sic]. The item involved is a H & R pistol 9 shot serial No. Y 13332. Thane E. Cesar."

Here was documentary evidence that Cesar sold the gun three months *after* the assassination.

Yoder remembered that during their post-assassination meeting, Cesar dragged out his security guard uniform, the H & R .22 and his .38 pistol, but didn't mention the RFK assassination. But Cesar "looked a little worried and he said something about going to the assistance of an officer and firing his gun. He said there might be a little problem over that."

* Statement of Thane Eugene Cesar, reporter's transcript, Room 113, Bureau of Investigation, DA's Office, 524 North Spring Street, Los Angeles, July 14, 1971, 7:30 P.M., pp. 47–48.

Had Yoder ever been interviewed by the LAPD? Yoder said that the Los Angeles police had called him approximately a year earlier (or shortly after Cesar was questioned), and he gave them essentially the same information. He specifically recalled telling the police about the receipt for the gun dated three months after the assassination. But he no longer had the gun. Around the time that the police called, his home was burglarized and the gun taken.

Once again the LAPD and DA's office had squelched information that might have pointed to a conspiracy. They knew that Cesar sold the gun after the assassination, not before, as he had contended. They knew that if Cesar had been situated to Kennedy's immediate right and rear, as he himself stated, the entry angle of the three bullets striking Kennedy was consistent with that position. They also must have known that Kennedy apparently clutched Cesar's snap-on bow tie from his neck. In the famous news photo showing the senator lying on his back on the floor, his head in a pool of blood, the shiny black tie appears next to his right hand. Cesar conceded that the tie was his and that he returned to the pantry to retrieve it. But no one ever asked him how it had been ripped from his neck.

In early 1976 Allard Lowenstein retrieved a series of assassination broadcast tapes from the Kennedy family and sent them on to West Coast researchers for review. One of those tapes (discovered by Lillian Castellano and Floyd Nelson) involved an interview made by KFWB reporter John Marshall within minutes following the shooting in the kitchen pantry of the Ambassador Hotel:

MARSHALL: I have just talked with an officer who tells me that he was at the senator's side when the shots occurred . . . Officer, can you confirm that the senator has been shot?
OFFICER: Yes, I was there holding his arm when they shot him.
Q. What happened?
A. I dunno. Gentleman standing by the lunch counter there and as he walked up the guy pulled a gun and shot at him.
Q. Was it just one man?
A. No, yeah, one man.
Q. And what sort of wound did the senator receive?
A. Well, from where I could see, it looked like he was shot in the head and the chest and the shoulder.

Q. How many shots did you hear?
A. Four.
Q. You heard four shots. Did you see anyone else hit at that time?
A. Nope.
Q. What is your name, Officer?
A. Gene Cesar.

In Cesar's 1971 interview by Los Angeles law enforcement officials, he (1) denied ever seeing Sirhan himself, only his gun-wielding hand, and (2) stated that he got knocked down and didn't see the actual shooting events after the initial shot was fired. Yet right after the shooting he tells reporter Marshall details that conflict severely with his later version. It is also curious that Cesar's contemporaneous account locates the exact number and placement of shots and wounds in RFK's body—inflicted from the rear, his own conceded position—when no such identifications were possible until doctors examined the senator at a nearby hospital some twenty minutes later.

We find two more of the interview answers equally intriguing: Cesar's reference that "they shot him" and his response "No, yeah, one man" shot RFK. This same information was available or known to Los Angeles officials from the outset.

But instead of focusing on Thane Cesar, District Attorney Joe Busch would swing the beams of his 1971 conspiracy probe onto Bill Harper and Jonn Christian.

IN EARLY AUGUST, BUSCH ANNOUNCED THAT HIS GRAND JURY IN-vestigation had yielded no evidence of a conspiracy to kill RFK, but that the probe would continue in a new direction. Busch said that "serious questions" had surfaced about the handling of the exhibits in the County Clerk's office. He intimated that the bullets Harper had examined had been "tampered with" sometime after the close of the Sirhan trial, and that employees of the Clerk's office might have been derelict in allowing "unauthorized persons" access to the exhibits which had resulted in "altered" and possibly even "switched" evidence. Although he didn't name names, it would soon become clear that his targets were Harper and Christian.

Christian received his first hint of this ominous turn when he got a tip that Bob Kaiser had been put on the DA's payroll as the house "expert" on the investigation. One of Kaiser's duties was to monitor the activities of the "buffs," as the journalist referred to critics of the official position. Coincidentally, a group of the critics held a meeting a few days before Busch's surprise announcement. Christian was there, and so was Kaiser. The discussion centered on the forthcoming testimony of Bill Harper before the grand jury. Kaiser took the position that if the bullets didn't match as Harper claimed, then they probably had been tampered with or possibly even switched by unauthorized persons. It was almost verbatim the line that Busch would soon make public.

"We all know how easy it would be to get hold of that evidence, don't we, Jonn?" Kaiser teased.

Kaiser's seemingly offhand remark took on serious significance a few days later when DA investigators William R. Burnett, Jr., and DeWitt Lightner interviewed Christian. Burnett produced a half-dozen or so slips that Christian had filled out in the County Clerk's office more than two years before when (due to crossed wires in Chief Houghton's office) he was given SUS material on Jerry Owen and copies of pages from Sirhan's notebooks. Christian, noticing that several of the slips had exhibit request numbers added (the numbers not only were in someone else's handwriting but were written with a different style pen), emphatically pronounced the additions crude forgeries. The investigators said nothing.

Christian thought back to a visit Kaiser had paid him just after he obtained the material from the County Clerk. Kaiser had seemed miffed that Christian had the documents, and wanted to know, "How'd you get your hands on those?" Putting on a conspiratorial smile, Christian replied, "I have friends on the inside, too!" Now the flippant remark was coming back to haunt him.

A week later Burnett notified Christian that a subpoena would be issued for him to testify before the grand jury. Fearful of a frame-up, Christian went into hiding and called Charlie O'Brien, who was now in private law practice in San Francisco. O'Brien instructed Christian to sit tight until he could fly down for a conference. When they met O'Brien said he had learned in the interim that the DA intended to charge Christian with stealing the original

Sirhan notebooks. It was obviously an absurd and malicious charge, because not only did Christian have the receipts for the copies he had obtained but the originals were in the custody of the California Supreme Court as it considered a Sirhan appeal. O'Brien was puzzled. "There's something else they're going to try and pin on you," he said. "Something big—but I can't find out what it is."

The nature of the "something big" gradually emerged as the grand jury's closed-door probe progressed. Once Christian had been set up for having obtained the notebook pages "illegally," he would be vulnerable to additional charges that he had bribed or duped employees of the Clerk's Office into allowing him to enter the restricted vault where the Sirhan exhibits were kept, and proceeded to "fondle" or "mutilate" or even "switch" the evidence bullets. The scenario was obviously designed to strike at the heart of the "second gun" theory. DA Busch could claim that the bullets Harper recently examined were not the same bullets or not in the same condition as the bullets examined by the LAPD's DeWayne Wolfer back in 1968.

With Christian missing, Bob Kaiser was called before the grand jury and questioned by hard-nosed Deputy DA Richard W. Hecht. Kaiser repeated Christian's remark about having "friends on the inside" who purportedly helped him gain access to the notebooks. But when Hecht leaned on the journalist, trying to get him to testify that Christian admitted stealing the pages, he balked. "As far as I'm concerned," Kaiser said to Hecht's dismay, "Christian's just a great big bullshitter!"*

Busch's shabby plot was collapsing, and Bill Harper, who appeared despite having been shot at the previous day, finished it off. The straight-talking criminalist stuck by his conclusion that the bullets didn't match, and steadfastly denied any tampering with them. When the DA was unwilling to produce the supposedly altered bullets for inspection, the grand jury had no other recourse than to refuse to return indictments. But it did save face for Busch by issuing a nitpicking criticism of the Chief Clerk's handling of

---

* From his hideout, Christian wrote the grand jury foreman a letter suggesting that O'Brien be called in his stead, which was calculated to panic the DA's office. However, no summons was issued.

the evidence.* Several months later, however, both the Superior Court and the County Chief Administrative Officer decided that the criticism was unwarranted, and scolded the grand jury and Busch for leveling it. But by this time the matter of the "second gun" was in limbo.

IT WAS NEARLY TWO YEARS AFTER BUSCH'S ABORTIVE GRAND JURY probe that former newsman Baxter Ward, who had been elected a county supervisor, called for a new investigation into the "unanswered questions" about whether the fatal bullet came from Sirhan's gun. "Someone is protecting a position or person," Ward charged. "People in authority in Los Angeles County have conspired to prevent the re-examination."†

In May 1974 Ward convened a hearing to present the "second gun" debate in a public forum for the first time. Harper was ailing and could not appear. DeWayne Wolfer refused to appear on orders from Chief Davis, and DA Busch declined on grounds that it was an "improper forum." But Coroner Thomas Noguchi testified as to the entry wounds in Kennedy's back, and the point-blank range from which the fatal bullet had been fired. And two independent firearms experts, Herbert MacDonnell, a New York professor of criminalistics, and Lowell Bradford, a well-known veteran of the California state crime lab, concurred with Harper that the Kennedy and Weisel bullets could "not be identified as coming from the same gun."

MacDonnell and Bradford proposed a straightforward resolution to the bullet controversy: set up a panel of experts to refire the Sirhan weapon, and compare the test bullets with those removed from the victims. The proposal and similar ones had been made before, but Busch and the LAPD had consistently opposed them. But now new forces were coming into play. Former Congressman

---

* At the urging of the DA's office, the grand jury allowed the transcript of the highly suspect and questionable testimony against Christian and Harper to be released to the press—an abject violation of both the legal requisites and the rights of both men. (Unless indictments are issued, grand juries never release such unverified information.)

† Associated Press story datelined Sacramento, April 4, 1974.

Allard K. Lowenstein, an RFK intimate who had led the "Dump LBJ" movement in 1968, had interviewed Busch and police officials about the evidence and come away appalled at the stonewalling and deceit he encountered;* he was stumping the country trying to get the case reopened. And the prestigious American Academy of Forensic Science, composed of the leading firearms, ballistics and pathology experts in the country, accepted the recommendation of its own panel that had studied the bullet evidence and requested that the case be reopened. As then-President of the Academy Dr. Robert J. Joling put it, "Only an independent, non-governmentally controlled body of experts can really be relied upon to let the arrows of truth come to rest wherever that may be."

Although the DA and LAPD continued to insist that only "assassination freaks" were raising questions about the shooting, Baxter Ward finally garnered enough votes from his fellow supervisors to officially request that the Superior Court order a reexamination of the firearms evidence. On September 18, 1975, Presiding Judge Robert A. Wenke complied. A seven-man panel of firearms experts was named.†

No sooner had the panel begun work than it was confronted with several baffling questions. For one, the LAPD unaccountably

---

* Lowenstein was introduced to us in mid-1973 by mutual friend Robert Vaughn (*The Man from U.N.C.L.E.*), another of RFK's closer friends. In the interview with Busch on January 8, 1974, Lowenstein was accompanied by Mayor Thomas Bradley, himself a former LAPD policeman. Lowenstein has confided to us that Busch overreacted emotionally, suggesting that he was terrified of the repeated challenges to the official stance. If that position was so unassailable, Lowenstein reasoned, why the refusal to open up the LAPD's files?

† Technically, Wenke acted on a civil suit brought by former union official Paul Schrade, who was wounded while in the pantry standing immediately behind RFK. The judge ruled that Schrade had a right to discover if others were responsible for his injuries. CBS Television News joined in the suit, which was supported by the City Council as well as the Board of Supervisors. Interestingly, the DA's office selected as its expert on the panel Alfred Biasotti of the state crime lab, who was on record as backing DeWayne Wolfer in the Jack Kirschke–case ballistics controversy. And Attorney General Evelle Younger picked Cortland Cunningham of the FBI crime lab, who had been the focal point of scientific dispute in the John Kennedy case.

could not produce the laboratory records supporting its claim that in 1968 it test-fired eight bullets from Sirhan's gun. For another, the gun's bore was heavily coated with lead, yet copper-jacketed bullets such as Sirhan allegedly fired leave a lead-free bore. The panel simply noted the leaded condition—two copper-jacketed bullets were fired to clean out the lead so that the testing could go ahead—and did not speculate on how it happened.

On election day (June 4) Sirhan had practiced rapid-shooting for about seven hours on a San Gabriel range, using unjacketed "wad cutter" target bullets which deposit lead in the bore. If this was the source of the extreme leading, he could not have fired copper-jacketed bullets of the type recovered from the victims and supposedly matched to his gun by Wolfer, for they would have cleaned out the lead. And Wolfer could not have test-fired bullets of that type to make the match, for they, too, would have had a cleaning effect.

A third mystery revolved around the Kennedy and Weisel bullets. After test-firing Sirhan's gun, the experts were startled to observe that the test bullets did not bear the microscopic indentations that appeared on the Kennedy and Weisel bullets as well as on a bullet Wolfer had introduced at the trial of Sirhan as having been test-fired from Sirhan's gun. Nor did the indentations appear on photographs that Bill Harper took with the Balliscan camera for his 1971 comparisons. But they were visible on photographs taken for Baxter Ward's 1974 hearing. The indentations could have been made with any sharp object, including the tip of a pencil. They coincided on each bullet, so that they could have been mistaken for matching marks. Whoever made them was obviously hoping to reinforce the single-assassin position.

The tampering must have been done sometime after Bill Harper's examination, which concluded that the bullets did not match.* By the time Harper made public his findings and the "second gun" controversy erupted, the bullets were in the custody of the

* The LAPD photograph of the bullet removed from RFK's back was located and subpoenaed. The 1968 photo revealed that this exhibit was in the identical condition as depicted in Harper's 1970 photos—meaning positive proof that no "tampering" or "mutilation" or "switching" had ever taken place in the County Clerk's office, as contended by DA Busch in 1971.

California Supreme Court in San Francisco. We learned from a clerk in the Exhibit Section of the Supreme Court that in July 1971 —about the time Joe Busch was announcing that he would look into the firearms discrepancies—a contingent from the DA's office, the LAPD and Attorney General Younger's office visited the Supreme Court offices and spent several hours alone examining the Sirhan gun and the evidence bullets.

The panel created by Judge Wenke found that three bullets— those from Kennedy, Weisel and a third victim, Ira Goldstein— were sufficiently undamaged by impact to permit comparison. It was determined that all came from the same model gun, an Iver Johnson like the one confiscated from Sirhan. But the model was a popular one. Judge Wenke had specifically asked the panel to determine whether a second gun was involved, and the panel's report on October 6, 1975, responded: "There is no substantive or demonstrable *evidence* that more than one gun was used to fire any of the bullets examined."

But when Wenke opened the sealed report on October 6, 1975, before a packed courtroom and read it aloud, the impact was entirely different. Somehow, the report was composed so that the sentence about the lack of "evidence to indicate that more than one gun was used" came first, and before the judge even completed reading it, reporters were dashing for the telephones. The erroneous impression that it was necessarily Sirhan's gun was flashed to the world. A typical story was headed: PANEL SAYS ONLY ONE GUN.*

Because of the erroneous reporting of the panel's true findings— especially by the Los Angeles *Times*' John Kendall—most of those who had believed that a second gun had been involved in RFK's assassination jumped off the bandwagon. In effect, the distorted

---

* Ironically, CBS, which had been a party to the suit, was one of the worst offenders in jumping the gun. When Lowell Bradford, the CBS expert on the panel, viewed the Walter Cronkite news that evening he was outraged. He stormed over to the Los Angeles news center and demanded that the record be set straight or he would "go public" with a press conference charging the network with intentional distortion. The next evening Cronkite apologized, and in a rare correction of a major news story, clarified the situation.

report of the seven experts had sounded the death knell for the reinvestigation into the assassination of RFK. But Allard Lowenstein, Paul Schrade's lawyer, was able to keep the inquiry alive. He petitioned Judge Wenke to allow cross-examination of the experts in a court of law on their findings, and the judge granted the petition.

It was all-important that the experts' findings be placed in their true *legal* perspective. Lowenstein reached Vince Bugliosi at the Ambassador Hotel in Chicago (he was in the Windy City on business) and importuned him to return to Los Angeles (earlier than scheduled) to conduct the crucially sensitive cross-examination. The former prosecutor had two reservations: (1) The firearms cross-examination was extremely complex and would require an enormous amount of time for preparation. There were literally hundreds of pages of documents to be reviewed by the cross-examiner, and because of other commitments, Bugliosi was concerned that he wouldn't be able to find the time; and (2) he felt that his involvement in the case might be misconstrued by the Establishment press in Los Angeles (especially the Los Angeles *Times*) as an attempt on his part to thrust himself into the spotlight of another major case. (The details of this political dilemma are covered in the Epilogue.)

Lowenstein responded with the truism that the assassination of a candidate for President of the United States, with its incalculable implications, was far more important than any concern Bugliosi might have about being accused of self-seeking. (Ironically, this was not unlike the argument Bugliosi had earlier used on witness Bill Powers.) The former congressman from New York had impressed the former prosecutor with the simple logic of his cause: the future of this nation is everyone's responsibility, if not the Establishment press, too.

Bugliosi resolved his first reservation himself: in the few days remaining, he would prepare his cross-examination in hotel rooms and airplanes as he crisscrossed the country attending to other commitments. By the time mid-November arrived, Bugliosi was ready, and then some.

Because Bugliosi's cross-examination of the experts involves sophisticated and highly complicated firearms testimony, which consumed several hundreds of pages of court transcript, we must necessarily condense the points he established as follows:

1. Although five of the seven experts testified under oath that it was their "belief" that three of the seven bullets recovered from the victims (one from RFK) came from Sirhan's gun, *not one* of the experts was willing to make a *positive* identification. (Positive ID is very common in criminal trials.) In a case of this magnitude, the *lack* of a positive identification is of monumental significance. (Note: This testimony literally destroyed the LAPD's DeWayne Wolfer's grand jury and trial testimony that he was "100% sure" that all seven bullets *positively* came from Sirhan's gun "to the exclusion of all other weapons in the world.")

2. All seven experts testified that it was *not* their conclusion that there was no second gun involved at the assassination scene. Their testimony was merely that based on the exhibits they had been furnished (and they never saw some that they should have), they could find no *evidence* of a second gun. (As Bugliosi would argue: "There's more than a semantic distinction involved here. In fact, there's all the difference in the world between *no evidence* of a second gun and a flat statement that *there was no second gun!* It would be like my walking down the street and saying I saw no avocados on the street. That doesn't mean that there *weren't* any avocados, only that I didn't *see* any avocados!")

3. Five of the seven experts recommended that further scientific tests (ballistics, spectrographic, etc.) be conducted. As Bugliosi pointed out to the court: "As the court knows, there is a tremendous controversy in this case as to which bullet struck which victim and, based on the uncontested position of Sirhan (at the assassination scene) whether it was physically possible for him to have fired all the recovered bullets. If *any* case ever cried out for a thorough, in depth independent ballistics examination, *this* case is it!" (A ballistics test attempts to determine the flight path a bullet follows from the moment it leaves the gun muzzle to its ultimate point of rest.)

4. Five out of the seven experts testified that they did reach a positive conclusion that three of the victim bullets had been fired from the "same gun," but they were *not* able to positively identify

Sirhan's gun as being the weapon from which the subject bullets were fired.

5. The experts *did* acknowledge that there were some "significant differences" between the striations (markings) on several of the victim bullets and those on the bullets test-fired by the panel from Sirhan's gun.

6. All seven experts testified that they were unable to determine the *number* of bullets fired at the assassination scene.

7. *All* seven experts testified that they *did not* rule out the possibility of a second gun.

Here, fortunately now memorialized in a courtroom under oath, were the true findings of the seven experts, not the flat "No Second Gun" reportings of an ill-informed press. The previous written findings of these panelists, which had been misinterpreted by the news media (with the sole exception of CBS reporter Bill Stout), and which appeared to slam the door tight forever on further inquiry, had, due to Bugliosi's deft cross-examination, been reduced to their proper import and accurate legal dimensions. Unfortunately, however, Bugliosi's effort came three months too late to eradicate the impression that had been embossed in the public's mind by a mostly unthinking mass media.

"CAN'T ANYONE ON THAT PANEL COUNT?" BILL HARPER FUMED. "They have just finished examining the ninth and tenth bullets and don't even know it!" Sirhan's revolver had held only eight bullets.

The two extra bullets that Harper was referring to in his phone call to Jonn Christian were labeled Court Exhibit 38 from the Sirhan trial: two expended slugs that the police had found on the front seat of Sirhan's old DeSoto sedan parked several blocks from the Ambassador Hotel. It had always been a source of curiosity as to why Sirhan would have retrieved the useless slugs and left them in his car. It was even doubtful that they had been fired from his gun, since they were so mutilated from impact that they could not be compared with test bullets.

Actually, the panel had discovered a clue as to the origins of the extra bullets. On their worksheets they had notated: "wood in nose" and "wood in nose & base." Wood? From where?

In the official LAPD ballistics report dated July 8, 1968, DeWayne Wolfer had stated that all eight shots in Sirhan's revolver had been fired, and all eight bullets were accounted for. Seven had physically been recovered from the bodies of six of the victims (two from Senator Kennedy, and five from the five victims who survived) at nearby hospitals, and the eighth "was lost somewhere in the ceiling interspace."

In other words, the official LAPD position was that *no bullets were found at the assassination scene*, and other than an entry and exit hole in the ceiling caused by the lost bullet, *there were no bullet holes on any of the doors or walls of the pantry.*

Therefore, if any bullet holes or bullets were observed *in addition* to those accounted for in the LAPD report, they would constitute almost unassailable evidence of a second gun having been fired, since no one claimed Sirhan fired more than eight bullets.

Yet there was evidence that more than eight bullets had been fired in the pantry. Only hours after the shooting, the Associated Press disseminated a wirephoto that was captioned "Bullet found near Kennedy shooting scene." (See official LAPD photo exhibit p. 10 depicting same scene.) It showed two LAPD officers inspecting an object imbedded in a doorjamb behind the Embassy Room stage, from which Kennedy had spoken. The door was in a direct line from the pantry. The ceiling panels, pierced by the bullet entering the interspace, had been removed by the LAPD, booked into its property division as evidence, and later destroyed by the LAPD. On August 22, 1975, Deputy Chief Daryl Gates advised during an interview on the NBC network, "The ceiling panels were destroyed, pursuant to the same destruction order that was issued for the destruction of the doorjambs, June 27, 1969." The destruction was highly premature, and completely improper, for Sirhan's attorneys had scarcely filed their appeal.*

---

* In a declaration and cover letter November 3, 1972, Sirhan's chief trial attorney, Grant B. Cooper, stated that although he had been "warned prior to the trial by Bill Harper that Wolfer could not be relied upon," he nevertheless took into consideration the eyewitness testimony and "proceeded under the assumption that Sirhan alone fired the shot or shots that killed Senator Kennedy." Cooper said that had he known then what he knew now, "my approach to his defense would have been materially altered."

One of the principal problems in attempting to re-open the investigation, although not an insurmountable one, was that the LAPD had engaged in almost wholesale destruction of the physical evidence in the case. In addition to the ceiling panels having been removed by the LAPD, booked into evidence, and destroyed, the center divider between the swinging doors, and the doorjamb on the left side received like treatment. (This is *not* the Rozzi-Wright doorjamb.)

The LAPD also destroyed the gun that they used for decibel sound tests in the Sandra Serrano affair. Also curiously missing are the left sleeves on RFK's coat and shirt.

Most suspicious of all, however, all-important LAPD scientific reports in this case were, per the LAPD spokespeople, "either lost or destroyed." These included the spectrographic report on all the victim bullets. The purpose of a spectrographic test is to determine the metallic and chemical constituency of the recovered bullet. Boxes of ammo have code numbers which refer to the origin of the bullets therein; by furnishing this code number to the manufacturer of the bullets, they can ascertain the metallic and chemical constituency (makeup) of the "batch" of lead from which the ammo came. If, for instance, a bullet recovered from a crime scene contains, among other elements, antimony, but a companion bullet from that same crime scene does not, a powerful inference can be drawn that the two bullets were not fired from the same gun.

Since the LAPD contended that all eight expended cartridges in the Sirhan gun came from the same box of ammo which was discovered in the Sirhan car, the spectrographic report could have supported their scientific case. Conversely, however, it could also have refuted it.

Commenting on the wanton destruction of evidence, Bugliosi said: "The destruction of the evidence may have been completely innocent, but it *looks* bad! And it is totally inexcusable! You do *not* destroy evidence in *any* case, particularly a case of this magnitude, which conceivably could have altered the course of American history."

With the jambs destroyed, the only alternative was to talk to the two policemen in the AP wirephoto. For seven years, the LAPD had refused to divulge the identity of the two uniformed officers.

In fact, no LAPD report ever mentioned their names. Who these two officers were became a talked-about mystery. In 1974 Allard Lowenstein had asked DA Busch who they were, but Busch put him off with the excuse that the policemen had never said that a bullet was in the hole, and the caption was in error. When Lowenstein showed Bugliosi the AP photo, which Bugliosi had never seen before, he told Lowenstein it would be an easy matter to ascertain the identity of the officers. "How?" Lowenstein asked, totally perplexed. "These two officers almost undoubtedly either came from Rampart Division, which has jurisdiction over the Ambassador Hotel, or from an immediately adjacent one—Wilshire or Metro," said Bugliosi. With the wirephoto in hand, Bugliosi made the rounds of the LAPD stations inquiring if anyone knew who the officers were. (Bugliosi is admired and respected by most workaday cops in Los Angeles.) On November 15, 1975, he hit paydirt at the Wilshire Division. A sergeant there identified them as Sergeants Robert Rozzi, at present with the Hollywood Division, and Charles Wright, at present out of the West Los Angeles Division. Both worked out of the Wilshire Division at the time of the assassination.

Bugliosi went straight to the Hollywood Division and showed Rozzi the photo. Rozzi readily identified himself as the officer aiming a flashlight at the hole in the doorjamb. Lodged in the hole, Rozzi said, in a signed statement he gave Bugliosi (see Exhibit 1), was "the base of what appeared to be a small-caliber bullet." Any doubt that the LAPD knew it was a bullet hole was dispelled by official police photograph A-94-cc (see photo insert p.10), in which Rozzi was pointing his pen at the hole while Wright was holding a crime-lab ruler showing it to be approximately eleven inches off the floor. Rozzi said that he himself did not remove the bullet, but was "pretty sure" someone else did.*

Bugliosi had some difficulty in reaching Sergeant Wright, but

---

* Because of the location of the "object" in the doorjamb, and the exit hole caused by the "lost" bullet in the ceiling interspace, it could not have been the lost bullet. Even the LAPD, which would benefit from the possibility that the object was the lost bullet, concedes that it was not.

finally talked with him by telephone the following evening. Wright unequivocally declared that a bullet had been in the hole. When Bugliosi mentioned that Rozzi was pretty sure someone had removed it, Wright replied, "There is no 'pretty sure' about it. It definitely was removed from the hole, but I do not know who did it." Wright agreed to meet Bugliosi the following evening to furnish another signed statement.

The next day Bugliosi appeared in Judge Wenke's courtroom to cross-examine firearms expert Stanton Berg. He showed Berg the wirephoto, and Berg agreed that a ballistics test should be done on the questioned bullets if this was indeed a bullet in the hole. Even though Rozzi's name had *not* been mentioned in court, when court adjourned, Bugliosi was approached by Sergeant Phil Sartuche, an SUS veteran who was monitoring the proceedings for Chief Ed Davis, and who had worked with Bugliosi as an investigating officer in the Manson case. "Vince, do you have Rozzi's statement?" Sartuche asked. When Bugliosi said yes, Sartuche wanted to see it, but the lawyer said he didn't have it with him. Sartuche dashed out the nearest exit in such a rush that his service revolver was jostled loose and fell clattering onto the floor.

The race was on. Bugliosi hurried to the West Los Angeles Division to try to get a statement from Sergeant Wright before the LAPD could get to him. "I was not quick enough," Bugliosi recounted. "When I arrived I was told Wright was on the phone. Ten minutes later he appeared holding a yellow paper in his hand. The name 'Sartuche' was written on it."

"Old Phil really works fast, doesn't he?" Bugliosi said with a smile to the uneasy officer. Wright admitted that Sartuche had just called, as had Deputy City Attorney Larry Nagen, who instructed him not to give a statement. The sergeant retreated from his positive position of the evening before, now saying that the object only looked like a bullet but since it was so long ago, he was not at all sure and he could have been mistaken. Moreover, he had merely assumed that someone had extracted the bullet.

The LAPD's obstructive tactics only heightened Bugliosi's determination. If, in fact, there was a bullet in the doorjamb, it constituted a *ninth* bullet and hence, a second gun. On December 1,

1975, he took a signed statement from Coroner Thomas Noguchi (see Exhibit 2), who had gone to the Ambassador Hotel as soon as he got word of the Kennedy shooting. Previous attempts by other interested parties to get the County Coroner to comment (let alone give a signed statement) about his observations at the crime scene had been futile. Noguchi told Bugliosi that he asked DeWayne Wolfer about any *bullet holes* at the scene, and the lab man pointed "to one hole in a ceiling panel above, and an indentation in the cement ceiling. He also pointed to several holes in the door frames of the swinging doors leading into the pantry." Noguchi continued, "I directed that photographs be taken of me pointing to these holes. I got the impression that a drill had been placed through the holes. I do not know whether or not these were bullet holes, *but I got the distinct impression from him that he suspected that the holes may have been caused by bullets.*"

One of a number of photographs of Noguchi taken that night shows him holding a ruler under two circled holes in one of the swinging-door jambs (see photo section p. 11). The holes had been circled and initialed by an LAPD officer. They are only a few inches apart, and chest-high. But the jambs were destroyed by the LAPD along with the ceiling panels, and the Rozzi-Wright jamb one year later.

Between the swinging doors was a center divider post that also had been sawed off and carted away by the LAPD, and like the ceiling panels, subsequently destroyed. Bugliosi sought out hotel personnel who might have been around the pantry as the police conducted their crime-scene search. One, the former maître d', Angelo DiPierro, had spotted a bullet in the divider post. In a signed statement he gave Bugliosi on December 1, 1975, DiPierro recounted that "many people, including the police and myself, started to look over the entire pantry area to piece together what had happened. That same morning, while we were still looking around, I observed a small-caliber bullet lodged about a quarter of an inch into the wood on the center divider of the two swinging doors. Several police officers also observed the bullet. The bullet was approximately 5 feet 8 or 9 inches from the ground. The reason I specifically recall the approximate height of the bullet location is because I remember thinking at the time that if I had entered the pantry just before the shooting, the bullet may have struck me in the forehead, because I am approximately 5 feet 11½ inches tall." If DiPierro's observation was correct, it would constitute a *tenth* bullet.

Bugliosi then located one of the waiters who was present at the assassination scene, Martin Patrusky. Patrusky had since changed jobs several times. He gave Bugliosi a signed statement on December 12, 1975, that four or five days after the assassination he and others who had been in the pantry at the time were summoned by the LAPD to appear for a video-taped reconstruction of the crime. "There were four or five plain-clothes officers present," he recalled. "The reconstruction incident took about an hour or so. Sometime during the incident, one of the officers pointed to two circled holes on the center divider of the swinging doors and told us that they had dug *two bullets* out of the center divider."*

If Patrusky was correct, it would constitute *eleven* bullets (one of the two bullets dug out of the divider most probably being the bullet DiPierro observed).

The LAPD explained away the holes in the center divider as "dents caused by food carts." Bugliosi went to the Ambassador Hotel. The general manager of the hotel told Bugliosi the food carts were still in use and had not been replaced. The lawyer went down to the pantry. He observed that there were absolutely no protrusions on the carts—they were flat on all sides—to cause the holes. Moreover, he joked, "Even if there were protrusions, which there are not, those food carts would have had to have been travel-

---

* The observations of Patrusky, DiPierro and Noguchi are validated by two independent photographers, William Meyer and R. Carleton Wilson, who arrived at the pantry at eleven o'clock in the morning on June 5. Surprised at finding no one guarding the pantry, they proceeded to take photographs. Meyer placed Xs on the doorjamb locations marked by the LAPD. Curious about the circled holes in the divider post, he pulled off the one-inch-thick facing, exposing two dents on the face of the inner stud that looked as if they had been caused by bullets impacting. The dents lined up perfectly with the holes.

ing at a speed of a hundred and fifty to two hundred miles an hour to have caused the deep holes in that center divider."

The new evidence, Bugliosi argued to Judge Wenke, justified an extension of the probe to study the number of shots fired and their flight path.

DA special counsel Thomas Kranz responded that it would be fruitless to continue the probe because most of the evidence had been destroyed. Bugliosi told Judge Wenke that since it was the police who had destroyed the evidence, Kranz's argument reminded him of "the story of the young man who murdered his father and mother and then begged the court for mercy because he was an orphan."

Moreover, Bugliosi pointed out that fortunately there still were close-up photos of the relevant bullet holes, and eyewitnesses like Rozzi and Wright were available to give sworn testimony and be cross-examined. He asked the judge to take judicial notice of the overwhelming concern of Americans about unresolved questions in all of the assassinations. "They want to know if there is a pernicious force alive in this land," he intoned, "which is threatening to destroy our representative form of government by systematically orchestrating the cutting down of those Presidents or candidates for President who espouse political philosophies antithetical to theirs."

Kranz had been commissioned by the Board of Supervisors to conduct an *independent* investigation to see if the LAPD and the DA's office were correct in their conclusions on the RFK case. Yet Kranz actually became part of the DA's office and was on their payroll. Furthermore, he and Dinko Bozanich, another deputy district attorney assigned to assist Kranz, were taking orders from their boss, District Attorney John Van De Kamp. And Van De Kamp was doing what he has proven to be very adept at—talk to different audiences different ways on the same subject. To the news media he proclaimed that he wanted to "get to the bottom of the RFK case," but in the courtroom, where it counted, his own deputies, Kranz and Bozanich, were fighting tooth and nail, at Van De Kamp's insistence, to discourage Judge Wenke from continuing the inquiry.

Kranz, not to be deterred by Bugliosi's last argument, countered to Judge Wenke that any further inquiry and testing would stretch costs beyond the $100,000 already expended. It was on this note of penury, a drop in the bucket compared with the cost of cracking the Watergate cover-up, that the proceedings ground to a halt with Judge Wenke refusing to broaden their scope. Wenke stated that he did not have "jurisdiction" to continue the hearing.

Bugliosi told Wenke that he had never been able to understand how the court had any jurisdiction to conduct this hearing in the first place. Since he had not been the Sirhan trial judge, and because Sirhan's conviction had long since been affirmed on appeal all the way up to the Supreme Court of the United States, any further inquiry or investigation would have to be by law enforcement, not a court such as his. However, Bugliosi reasoned, under the prevailing circumstances, and as the Presiding Judge of the Superior Court, Wenke already *had* assumed jurisdiction of the matter. Why terminate it at this crucial point when important evidence had been "uncovered," Bugliosi argued.

But Wenke reiterated that he simply had no power to continue the inquiry. And with that he closed the curtain on what might have been the first ray of light and hope in the case for legitimate judicial review.

On April 5, 1977, Kranz completed his "report" on the RFK case. Predictably, he found no evidence of a second gun.

Although for seven and a half years there had been considerable speculation as to the existence of extra bullets, prior to the signed statements obtained by Bugliosi there had been no substantive available evidence to support these suspicions. In the remarkable period of a few short days, the indefatigable and resourceful lawyer had come up with evidence which pointed to the existence of more than eight bullets and, therefore, a multiple-gun shooting.

Bugliosi, who is hardly a "conspiracy buff" and who is very conservative when it comes to the opinions he reaches in such serious matters, later told us: "I have no way of knowing for sure whether or not more than one gun was fired at the assassination scene. And I have formed no opinion at this point. What I will say is this: the signed statements given me perhaps can be explained away; but in the absence of a logical explanation, these statements, by simple arithmetic, add up to too many bullets and therefore, the *probability* of a second gun."*

In the spring of 1976 Bugliosi's findings as to extra bullets were starkly confirmed by documents released by the FBI under the Freedom of Information Act. They reveal that shortly after the LAPD had completed its crime-scene examination within hours of the shooting, the Ambassador Hotel's assistant manager, Franz Stalpers, led an FBI special agent and his photographer into the pantry area. The Bureau men proceeded to cover the same ground as had the LAPD. The results of their examination are contained in a report entitled "CHARTS AND PHOTOGRAPHS SHOWING LAYOUT OF AMBASSADOR HOTEL AREA WHERE SHOOTING OCCURRED," the pertinent section of which contains what the FBI designated as an "E" series of photographs (see photo insert p. 12):

E-1 View taken inside kitchen serving area [the pantry] showing doorway area leading into kitchen from the stage area. In lower right corner the photo shows two bullet holes which we circled. The portion of the panel missing also reportedly contained a bullet.
E-2 A close up view of the two bullet holes of area described above.

The corresponding photographs unmistakably show the same two holes that Dr. Noguchi was pointing to on the jamb. The FBI notation that the "portion of the panel missing also reportedly contained a bullet" obviously refers to a triangular piece of the adjoining wall panel that the LAPD already had torn off. This piece was about eighteen inches above the two bullet holes. The FBI report continues:

E-3 Close up view of the two bullet holes which is [*sic*] located in center door frame inside kitchen serving area and looking towards direction of back of stage area.

This photograph is of the center divider post of the swinging doors, where, Angelo DiPierro stated, he saw a bullet imbedded and from which Martin Patrusky was told by a police officer two bullets

---

* Interview with the authors, January 14, 1978.

were removed. The photograph shows the two circles drawn around the holes, just as depicted in the Noguchi and LAPD photographs. These were the holes that the DA's spokesman dismissed as gouges from food service carts. Finally the FBI report asserts:

E-4   Close up view of upper hinge on door leading into kitchen area from back of stage area. View shows reported location of another bullet mark which struck hinge.*

With the release of the FBI documents, the box score of extra bullets now reads:

Definite
    2 in a jamb of the swinging doors
    2 in the center divider post of the swinging doors
    1 in a jamb of the stage door (the Rozzi-Wright bullet)
    TOTAL: 5

Probable
    1 in the triangular piece of panel referred to in the FBI report
    1 that struck the hinge
    TOTAL: 2

This makes a total of between thirteen and fifteen bullets that were fired that night—five to seven more than the capacity of Sirhan's revolver, or those shots accounted for by the LAPD. Now we realized why many witnesses compared the sound to a string of firecrackers going off.

One was Los Angeles *Times* photographer Boris Yaro. "My first thought was some jerk has thrown firecrackers in here," he said. Another was RFK political lieutenant Frank Burns: "I heard a noise sounding like a string of firecrackers going off." Waiter Martin Patrusky agreed: "I immediately heard a sound like that of a firecracker. A second later I heard a series of sounds like fire-crackers." Erwin Stroll, who was wounded, and Kennedy supporter

---

* An RFK supporter named Roger Katz told Christian that he saw sparks from a bullet striking this hinge. Katz immediately reported it to the LAPD. No report of that interview can be found.

Suzanne Locke—among a good many other witnesses—used the firecracker analogy to describe what they heard: a rapid, erratic series of explosions. The badly wounded Paul Schrade likened the sound to the uneven crackling of "electrical discharge."*

One gun being fired as rapidly as possible would have produced distinct, evenly spaced shots, which is how the witnesses described Sirhan's firing pattern. But two or more guns would have given the "firecrackers" effect. We conducted a simple experiment to illustrate the point. First, we test-fired eight shots as rapidly as possible from the same model Iver Johnson .22 revolver as Sirhan's. Then we set off a string of thirteen firecrackers, again recording the sounds. Here are the results in graph form:

TIMESPAN/3 SECONDS:

0——————————————— 1——————————————— 2———————————————3

.22 REVOLVER:

1———— 2———— 3———— 4———— 5———— 6———— 7————8

FIRECRACKERS

1—— 2—— 3— 4— 5—— 6— 7———— 8—— 9—— 10———— 11—— 12————13

As the reader can see, the effect of a single revolver being rapid-fired does not at all resemble that of a string of firecrackers.

The question that arises about the multiple-gun theory is that witnesses, with one exception, did not report seeing anyone else fire a gun. (The exception was CBS News employee Donald Schulman, who, as we have seen, said "the security guard then fired back . . . hitting him.") This can be explained, however, in terms of people's normal reaction to a sudden, surprising event taking place before their eyes. The witnesses' attention would automatically have been riveted on Sirhan (according to one witness, he shouted, "Kennedy! You son of a bitch!"—then fired off a first shot). Some froze in their tracks, mesmerized by the sight. Others ducked for cover as Sirhan unloaded the chamber of his revolver with seven more shots while maître d' Karl Uecker, Frank Burns (and others) struggled to overpower him.

* FBI Summary Report, *op. cit.*, unpaginated.

In this mass confusion other gunmen could have fired unnoticed.

This leads us back to the autopsy report. All three of the bullets that hit Kennedy, including the point-blank fatal head shot, entered from the rear. Yet Sirhan was at Kennedy's front. It is possible that he completely missed his target. Witnesses said that he managed to fire no more than two shots at the oncoming senator before being pounced upon and thrown off target.

But there is an alternative explanation for this seeming inaccuracy, a clue to which lies in an object taken from Sirhan's pocket after the shooting. It was an unfired .22 bullet which, according to investigating officers, had been manually removed from a live cartridge. We had long theorized about this unexplained object of evidence and as to what significance this bullet might have. Then the 1975 hearings before Judge Wenke produced astounding physical evidence that tended to confirm our own earlier speculation that *three* guns, not one or two, had been fired at the assassination scene. Moreover, we can now logically contend that Sirhan never actually fired any bullets at all.

A VISIBLY NERVOUS DEPUTY DA DINKO BOZANICH FIRST BROUGHT up a matter relating to the unfired bullet in arguing against the granting of further scientific tests in the "second gun" theory before Judge Wenke. It was the heavily leaded condition of the bore of Sirhan's gun which posed a dilemma that opposing counsel, Vincent Bugliosi, was sure to raise. The seven firearms panelists had noticed that the bore was in such a "severely, extremely" leaded condition that they could not conduct their examination without first cleaning it out, which they did by firing two copper-jacketed "minimag" bullets through it—standard procedure in such instances. The first bullet removed the excessive lead, they noted, while the second cleaned out all traces.*

How had the leading been caused? Sirhan had spent a good part of election day at a San Gabriel Valley shooting range, rapid-firing

* One of the firearms experts later postulated that the leading might have "grown" within the gun barrel (like algae)—a theory completely beyond the comprehension of scientists in the field of metallurgy, we discovered.

hundreds of rounds of ammunition. The range master said he had used "wad cutters," an unjacketed lead bullet designed especially for target practice. Although cheaper and making a neater hole, wad cutters leave lead deposits.

Deputy DA Bozanich was stuck with the problem of why the copper-jacketed "minimag" bullets Sirhan allegedly fired in the pantry, and those purportedly "test-fired" in the Sirhan weapon by Wolfer, had not cleaned out the deposits, just as the firearms experts later cleaned them out by firing two rounds. *None* of the Wolfer-originated test-fired minimag slugs could be matched to the Sirhan weapon by *any* of the experts, raising the distinct possibility that they had been fired through a *different* weapon— possibly the one identified by Bill Harper—a gun that resided in the LAPD property room at the time of the assassination, the gun that the LAPD prematurely destroyed (HI8602) in July 1968. Bozanich had no pat answer, so he resurrected the 1971 ruse that someone had gained access to Sirhan's gun while it was in the County Clerk's office—then hand-pounded bullets through the bore.*

There is a plausible explanation, however, and it is bolstered by the presence of the bullet in Sirhan's pocket. It proposes that a hypnoprogrammed "robot of another" arrived at the crime scene firing *slugless* cartridges which served as hand-made "blanks." Witnesses who saw Sirhan fire the first shot uniformly attest that a tongue of flame was emitted from the gun's muzzle—a tongue they variously described as six inches to more than a foot in length. Firearms experts say that a regular "minimag" load (with a bullet) gives off a tongue of only an inch or so, and that one as long as the witnesses saw is characteristic of a slugless cartridge.

We can think of only one logical reason for Sirhan to fire a weapon loaded with slugless cartridges: to attract attention while at the same time not hitting the intended (actual) killer-gunman immediately behind Kennedy who administered the fatal

---

* The DA's steadfast refusal to allow the re-examination of the Sirhan weapon during the 1970–75 period suggests that the authorities were aware of the "problem" with the leading all along, and why the DA went to such extremes in trying to frame Christian and Bill Harper on the trumped-up "tampering" charges.

shot. In other words—and there are scientific tests available to verify or refute this—an unseen *"coup de grace."**

If this is what actually happened, it almost certainly follows that Sirhan was cast in the double role of decoy and fall guy—a "patsy"—which is the heart of our "Manchurian Candidate" theory. While this may sound like a plot straight out of detective fiction, the overwhelming evidence at hand indicates that it was actually acted out in real life.†

Taken as a whole, the firearms evidence alone virtually shouts conspiracy and is reason enough to reopen the investigation. As Vincent Bugliosi half jokingly chided newsmen at a press conference after the statements he received kept adding up: "Gentlemen, the time for us to keep on looking for additional bullets in this case has passed. The time has come for us to start looking for the members of the firing squad that night." The press then asked Bugliosi, "Does all this mean that Sirhan is not guilty?" Bugliosi responded, "No, not at all. Sirhan is as guilty as sin, and his conviction was a proper one. But just because Sirhan is guilty does not automatically exclude the possibility that more than one gun was fired at the assassination scene."

---

* In 1976 we advised Supervisor Baxter Ward that neutron activation analysis could be employed to establish the crux of our theory: that if slugless cartridges were fired through the Sirhan weapon at the crime scene, the lead deposits from the "wad-cutter" firings through the gun at the San Gabriel firing range earlier in the day would contain elements of both scorched and unfired gunpowder. Conversely, no such deposits would be present if the gun was fired as contended by the DA. (As of early 1978, no such tests were either conducted or proposed.)

† We presented our discoveries in the form of a White Paper to the American Academy of Forensic Sciences convention in Chicago on February 18–21, 1975. The treatise was titled *The RFK Assassination: An Evidential/ Theoretical Analysis of the Murder Scene*. However, scheduling difficulties kept it off the expert-panel agenda.

13

The Manchurian Candidate

ON A FOGGY DAY THE PALE-YELLOW WALLS OF SAN QUENTIN Prison seem to rise out of the waters of San Francisco Bay like a medieval fortress. On the morning of September 10, 1972, Turner visited the aged institution with the latest in Sirhan's series of attorneys, Roger S. Hanson of Beverly Hills. Hanson was drawing up a fresh appeal to the California Supreme Court based on William Harper's recent finding that the bullet that fatally wounded Robert Kennedy could not be matched to Sirhan's gun. Hanson had retained Harper, Christian and Turner as unpaid "investigative consultants" in what would turn out to be a futile attempt to gain a new trial.

At the gatehouse Hanson presented his attorney's identification while Turner displayed his California private investigator's license. After being searched, they were cleared into the visitors' waiting area, a high-ceilinged room with oaken benches reminiscent of an old-time railroad depot. A guard escorted the pair through a large adjacent room where prisoners in blue dungarees and denim shirts were conferring with their visitors and attorneys, then up several steps and into a screened-in cubicle. The guard shut the door behind them. Facing them was a grille, through which they could see into a similar cubicle on the other side.

Two heavily armed guards brought Sirhan into the opposite cubicle, shut the door and hovered outside. The prisoner's handcuffs were chained to a wide black leather belt. His face was ashen, due no doubt to long confinement under strict security measures. But it was unmistakably the face that had appeared in hundreds of newspapers and magazines, the face that had so dominated our efforts for the past four years. The eyes were soft and doe-brown, set under arched, bushy eyebrows.

As Sirhan began talking with Hanson about his appeal, Turner observed that he was bright, articulate and personable, not at all the cardboard cut-out that had emerged from the news coverage years before. But then, he had gone to college for a year and a half, and according to his brother Munir spoke fluent German and Russian in addition to Arabic and English. He had come to the United States intent upon majoring in political science, but somehow got the idea that he wanted to be a jockey.

When Turner asked about that night at the Ambassador Hotel, Sirhan's face took on a vague look. He remembered going to the hotel, he said, but not necessarily because Kennedy would be there. The night was still a jumble of twisted images. There was the meeting with the girl in the polka-dot dress whose name he never knew. "I met the girl and had coffee with her," he recounted. "She wanted heavy on the cream and sugar. After that I don't remember a thing until they pounced on me in that pantry."

That was it. Sirhan claimed to have no memory of any other detail that might provide a clue as to why he was there or what happened. The name Jerry Owen rang no bell, he insisted; he could remember no preacher of that description, no horse deal. And he could shed no light on the "Pay to the order of . . ." entries in the notebooks. The guards opened the door and announced that time was up. Sirhan was led away, shuffling under the restraint of the heavy chains.

As he walked out of San Quentin, Turner was more convinced than ever that Sirhan had been hypnoprogrammed to act out his role in RFK's death. He recalled a remark Sirhan had made when interviewed by NBC's Jack Perkins shortly before being whisked off to San Quentin. To Perkins' baiting, "You were planning to kill Senator Kennedy?," Sirhan replied, "Only in my mind. I did it, but I was not aware of it."

EARLY ON WE HAD TOYED WITH THE THEORY THAT SIRHAN WAS A real-life version of the automated killer in Richard Condon's novel *The Manchurian Candidate.* Truth may be stranger than fiction, but it is also sometimes more difficult to accept. This is especially the case when delving into the mysteries of the mind.

Yet we had entertained the possibility virtually from the moment RFK was shot. Christian recalled a night in the fall of 1966 when he was rummaging through the basement law library of Melvin Belli's Gold Rush era office building in San Francisco doing research on bank monopolies. He tripped over a thick, dust-covered legal packet that had carelessly been left on the floor. The hand-lettered name on it caught his eye: "Ruby, Jack."

Jack Ruby was perhaps Belli's most infamous client. His shooting of Lee Harvey Oswald in plain view of millions of television watchers (eliminating any chance that the prisoner might talk) made it an open-and-shut case—just like Sirhan's capture in the pantry. Belli put forth a defense of "psychomotor epilepsy," a form of insanity. But Ruby was convicted, and died in prison of galloping cancer.*

---

* Within hours of the shooting one of Belli's partners, Seymour Ellison, received a phone call from a senior partner in a Las Vegas law firm where he had previously worked. The firm was connected with organized-crime figures who had been stripped of their gambling casinos in Cuba by Castro and relocated in Nevada. "Sy," the Las Vegas attorney said, "one of our guys

Thumbing through the packet, Christian noticed a letter to Belli from a New York attorney named Leonard L. Steinman on the subject of hypnosis. It was dated January 21, 1964, not long before Ruby's trial began. Steinman noted that since his previous contact with Belli, he had done exhaustive research on case histories and concluded that everyone was

virtually on all fours with the picture presented not only by your client, but Oswald as well. I have an absolute and earnest conviction in me— that Jack Ruby was in fact hypno-conditioned.

You have probably never heard of "locking suggestions," Mel. This is the problem Ruby is up against—and the tragedy is that Ruby doesn't even know it.

Referring to the fact that the defense psychiatrists had attributed Ruby's "fugue or dissociated state" to psychosis, Steinman elucidated:

. . . the brain damage picture is not the result of previous concussion and physical trauma, but of hypno-conditioning, of induction by suggestion through deep hypnosis of an artificial psychosis. Unlocking of this psychosis, of establishing the identity of the hypno-conditioner, requires a dedicated hypno-therapist with an exhaustive knowledge not only of Freudian but of Pavlovian principles.

You must understand, that the question of hypnotic induction of criminal acts and behavior is one which has a long history. . . . I am thoroughly convinced of Ruby's innocence, that he was a robot of another. . . . The criminal who makes use of hypnotism has unrivaled opportunities of wiping out all traces of his action and, moreover, avoiding discovery.

I tell you, Mel, this case is insidious. The theory isn't really a second-line defense. It's what actually happened.

---

just bumped off that son of a bitch that gunned down the President. We can't move in to handle it, but there's a million bucks net for Mel if he'll take it." The lawyer stressed that his clients wanted their relationship with Ruby kept strictly confidential. Before long the lawyer called Ellison back and told him that the deal was off because they had just found out that Ruby had been in with another powerful element and his clients didn't want to get involved in any way. Belli eventually took the case on his own initiative, but he took a financial bath of staggering proportions.

The Steinman letter was very much on Christian's mind after RFK was shot. That Sirhan might have been programmed through hypnosis sounded like science fiction, but the symptoms began to crop up. CBS cameraman James D. Wilson, who was at the Ambassador when Kennedy was shot, told Turner that he and his colleagues covering the court case had observed that Sirhan seemed permanently depressed "with his mind working on the basis of separate compartments."

"I know this sounds silly," Wilson said, "but I still find no explanation for Sirhan as satisfactory as the hypothesis that he has been acting and talking under hypnosis or in posthypnotic suggestion."

Later Bob Kaiser also reserved the possibility that Sirhan was under the influence of hypnosis. In private discussions he said that he believed Sirhan's amnesia block, which could have been hypnotically induced, was genuine, and in his book he stated that although he didn't know who the programmer might have been, he "still had a feeling that somewhere in Sirhan's recent past there was a shadowy someone." And he quoted Roger LaJeunesse as saying, "The case is still open. I'm not rejecting the Manchurian Candidate aspect of it."*

The symptoms of hypnoconditioning are not easy to describe, but as our knowledge of the subject expanded we thought that we perceived them in abundance. In tracing Sirhan's movements after he arrived at the Ambassador Hotel during the early evening of June 4, 1968,† we came upon a number of indicators of the trance state. At first Sirhan roamed the cavernous hotel in a talkative and assertive mood, possibly emboldened by a Tom Collins or two. Around nine he dropped into the Venetian Room, where a celebration for Republican Senate candidate Max Rafferty was in progress—Sirhan had known the candidate's daughter in high school—and when a waiter balked at serving him a drink because of his scruffy attire, he contemptuously tossed a $20 bill at him.

Stalking out of the Rafferty affair, Sirhan engaged in a conver-

---

* Kaiser, *op. cit.*, p. 536.

† This reconstruction is made from FBI and LAPD interviews of witnesses.

sation with a stranger named Enrique Rabago, a Kennedy fan. "Are we going to win?" Rabago asked. "I think we are going to win," Sirhan replied. When Rabago remarked that Senator Eugene McCarthy was still slightly ahead in the count, Sirhan growled, "Don't worry if Senator Kennedy doesn't win. That son of a bitch is a millionaire. Even if he wins, he won't do anything for you or me or the poor people." Rabago's companion, Humphrey Cordero, didn't think Sirhan was on drugs or alcohol but merely disgusted with the social scene at the hotel.

In the ensuing hour, however, Sirhan underwent the kind of dramatic personality change that hypnosis can cause. At about ten-thirty, he was staring mutely at the clattering teletype machine in the makeshift press headquarters next to the Embassy Room. When Western Union operator Mary Grohs asked him what he wanted, he just looked blank. "I'll never forget his eyes," she said later.

His eyes were similarly striking to two men who helped overpower him in the pantry after the shooting. George Plimpton called them "dark brown and enormously peaceful," and Joseph Lahaiv thought that Sirhan looked "very tranquil" during the furious struggle. This seeming paradox can be explained by the hypnotic trance: the outwardly tranquil appearance belies a fierce inner concentration. Sirhan's determination to carry out posthypnotic commands was consistent with the fact that it took a half-dozen strong men several minutes to subdue him. As an encyclopedia describes the condition: "Supernormal feats cause no fatigue."

What puzzled us, however, was Sirhan's behavior after being taken into custody. Taken to the Rampart station, he verbally sparred for hours with his captors over such a foregone matter as his identity, and he had left his wallet containing identifying documents in his car parked three blocks from the Ambassador. He refused to discuss the shooting at all, acting as if it had never happened. Lieutenant William C. Jordan thought he might be stalling to allow confederates to get away.

What Sirhan did talk about, practically in a stream of consciousness, was the Jack Kirschke murder case. A former deputy DA, Kirschke had recently been convicted of the love triangle murder of his wife and another man. "I was hoping you'd clue me in on it," Sirhan told a deputy DA who interviewed him. "You know, brief me on it, you might say." Sirhan's preoccupation with the Kirschke case was leaked to the press, prompting Kirschke's lawyer to file a legal motion contending that his client's rights had been violated because the conviction was under appeal. Curiously enough, the lawyer had called for permission to employ hypnosis in the case, which the court summarily denied. The lawyer was none other than our former campaign chairman, George Davis.

We could only guess as to what was behind the leak. But its effect was to complete the picture begun by Yorty. Now he was a murder-minded Communist sympathizer occultist.

After being transferred to the county jail later in the morning, Sirhan was visited by the medical director, Dr. Marcus Crahan. The prisoner suddenly hunched his shoulders and shivered violently. "It's chilly!" he stammered, his face contorted.

"You're cold?" Crahan was puzzled, because the room was warm.

"Not cold," Sirhan replied.

"Not cold, what do you mean?"

"No comment."

"You mean you're having a chill?"

Still trembling, Sirhan conceded, "I have a very mild one, yes."

Here was a clue of withdrawal from the hypnotic state. It was illustrated again when Dr. Diamond, the defense psychiatrist, put Sirhan into a deep trance to try to fathom a motive. But his subject slipped into an even deeper trance, sobbing and causing the doctor considerable alarm. As Diamond snapped him out of it Sirhan began trembling, and goose bumps surfaced on his arms. "Doc, it's cold," he complained.

Sirhan also stubbornly insisted that temporary amnesias had blotted out any memory of writing the notebooks and committing the crime. Such a claim was obviously self-serving, but Sirhan continues to cling to it long after all appeals have been exhausted and such obstinance no longer serves any purpose. Dr. Diamond believed that the blackouts were real. "To a considerable degree," he had explained to the trial jury, "when a resistance is overcome through the use of hypnosis and an individual talks about something he was unable to talk about when awake, this is clinical evidence that the resistance against bringing it up in a conscious state was unconscious in itself and not an intentional withholding or an intentional lie."

But Diamond didn't attribute the amnesia blocks to locking suggestions implanted by a programmer—suggestions that would make Sirhan forget that he had been programmed and by whom. The doctor was, after all, functioning within the defense parameters that did not admit of a conspiracy. Instead Diamond postulated that Sirhan was the victim of his own self-hypnosis habit coupled with a chronic paranoid schizophrenia. The dazzling lights and mirrors and the confusion had somehow combined to throw him into a trance, one that he had inadvertently programmed himself as the notebooks with the anti-Kennedy scrawlings attest.

So Sirhan, in Diamond's opinion, was a kind of automatic assassin, dissociated, a dual personality acting on both the conscious and subconscious levels, the subconscious being in control when he fired. In his summary to the jury, Diamond said it was "an astonishing instance of mail-order hypnosis, dissociated trances and the mystical occultism of Rosicrucian mind power and black magic." But even Diamond conceded that his theory of "primitive, psychotic, voodoo thinking" having triggered Kennedy's death was "the ultimate in preposterous absurdity, too illogical even for a theater of the absurd."

AFTER HE WAS PLACED ON SAN QUENTIN'S DEATH ROW IN THE spring of 1969, Sirhan was thoroughly examined by Dr. Eduard Simson-Kallas, chief of the prison's psychological testing program. After spending a total of thirty-five hours with his subject, Simson was convinced that Sirhan was indeed a Manchurian Candidate. "He was easily influenced, had no real roots and was looking for a cause," Simson said to Christian during our first contact with him in late 1972. "The Arab-Israeli conflict could easily have been used to motivate him."

Simson didn't believe that Sirhan was sufficiently devious or mentally unbalanced to have planned the assassination on his own. "He was prepared by someone," the doctor maintained. "He was hypnotized by someone."

Simson disclosed the results of his examinations of Sirhan in a later interview with Turner on August 14, 1975, in his home in Monterey. Simson is now in the private practice of psychology and teaches abnormal psychology in the state universities at Santa Cruz and San Jose. On the walls of his study are such mementos as a gold-braided Heidelberg University fraternity cap and Haitian voodoo masks, as well as a bevy of diplomas from Stanford, Heidelberg (Ph.D. cum laude) and other prestigious universities. Staggered among them are plaques attesting to professional honors, including a fellowship in the British Royal Society of Health and the American Society for Clinical Hypnosis.

When he began examining Sirhan, Simson noted that his subject was not the ordinary murderer who spoke with great expression and detail about his crime. Although Sirhan was resigned to having shot Kennedy, he spoke as though he was "reciting from a book" and baffled Simson by his lack of details. "A psychologist always looks for details," he said. "If a person is involved in a real situation, there are details."

As he grew to trust Simson, Sirhan confided, "I don't really know what happened. I know I was there. They tell me I killed Kennedy. I don't remember exactly what I did but I know I wasn't myself. I remember there was a girl who wanted coffee. She wanted coffee with lots of cream and sugar." Pouring the coffee was the last act Sirhan could remember before being choked and pummeled by the crowd in the pantry.

If Sirhan was hypnoprogrammed, Simson pointed out, the girl might have been, by prearrangement, the triggering mechanism. "You can be programmed that if you meet a certain person or see something specific, then you go into a trance."

Sirhan himself tossed out the possibility that he might have been hypnotized. "Sometimes I go in a very deep trance so I can't even speak," he told Simson. "I do not remember what I do under hypnosis. I had to be in a trance when I shot Kennedy, as I don't remember having shot him. I *had* to be hypnotized! Christ!" Sirhan was exhibiting a common symptom of persons who have been hypnotized and programmed: they have no recollection of having been put in a trance without their cooperation.

Sirhan suggested that Simson hypnotize him to help him remember what happened. The doctor agreed, feeling he had achieved the high degree of rapport with his subject that deprogramming required. "He was extremely eager to talk to me," Simson related. "He himself wanted to find out. If I had been allowed to spend as much time with him as necessary, I would have found out something."

But Associate Warden James W. L. Park intervened, on the curious ground that Simson "appears to be making a career out of Sirhan." Park instructed the doctor to curtail his visits to conform with "the services offered other condemned prisoners."* Simson, who had worked in the prison for six years and had never been cut off before, handed in his resignation. "A medical doctor spends as much time with a patient as the disease demands," he said. "So does a psychologist."

Simson displayed equal indignation when he talked about the testimony of Dr. Diamond and other psychiatrists at the Sirhan trial, which he labeled the "psychiatric blunder of the century." He scoffed at Diamond's self-induction theory, pointing out that it is utterly impossible for a person to place himself in such a deep trance that he suffers an amnesia block. Simson allowed that insanity could cause a memory loss, but stressed that there is no such thing as "temporary insanity" and that Sirhan was perfectly sane when he arrived at the prison. "Nowhere in Sirhan's test responses was I able to find evidence that he is a 'paranoid schizophrenic' or 'psychotic' as testified to by the doctors at the trial. My findings were substantiated by the observations of the chief psychiatrist at San Quentin, Dr. D. G. Schmidt."

It was Simson's belief that Diamond and his colleagues erred by judging Sirhan under preconceptions that he was both guilty and deranged, prompting Sirhan, who resented the insanity inference, to turn distrustful and uncooperative in their examinations of him. "Sirhan told me he deliberately misled these doctors," Simson stated. "They were not in a position to unlock his mind. This could only be done by a doctor Sirhan fully trusted."

As Simson saw it, Sirhan was "the center of a drama that un-

* Memorandum from Park to Dr. D. G. Schmidt, chief psychiatrist, San Quentin Prison, September 24, 1969.

folded slowly, discrediting and embarrassing psychology and psychiatry as a profession. The drama's true center still lies very much concealed and unknown to the general public. Was Sirhan merely a double, a stand-in, sent there to attract attention? Was he at the scene to replace someone else? Did he actually kill Robert Kennedy?

"Whatever the full truth of the Robert F. Kennedy assassination, it still remains locked in Sirhan's other, still anonymous mind."*

FOR SIRHAN TO HAVE BEEN THE "ROBOT OF ANOTHER," HE WOULD have to be highly susceptible to hypnosis. Some people's psychological make-up renders them totally unresponsive to hypnotic induction, while others can be "put under" but only with difficulty. Noted Hollywood hypnotist Gil Boyne told us that hypnoprogramming is possible, provided that the programmer is highly skilled and the subject's psychological profile ideal. What was Sirhan's profile? Dr. Diamond had reported that he succumbed to hypnosis practically at a snap of the fingers, but we wanted to explore this crucial area further.

In 1971 Christian talked to Richard St. Charles, a practicing hypnotherapist who also performed on stage. In 1966 St. Charles was booked into the Bahama Inn, a Pasadena night club within walking distance of the Sirhan home. It was his habit to compile a mailing list by leaving slips of paper on the tables and urging customers to "Join the Richard St. Charles Fan Club" by writing down their names and addresses. After the performances he marked the slips of those customers who had volunteered to be hypnotized on stage.

Following the assassination St. Charles felt that Sirhan's name was vaguely familiar. He searched his file and found the name with the Pasadena address on a slip of paper made out in late 1966. "The notes that I had were that he was a very good subject," St. Charles said. "I would say from my notes that Sirhan had very definitely been hypnotized prior to the time that I hypnotized him. That is a matter of a professional being able to detect just from watching

---

* Affidavit by Dr. Simson-Kallas, March 9, 1973. The authors provided him with data from the investigative files, as did criminalist William Harper.

the subjects go under on the stage whether they have or have not been in a state of hypnosis previously."*

Corroboration of this evaluation came from Dr. Herbert Spiegel, a professor at the Columbia University College of Physicians and Surgeons in New York who ranks in the top echelon of American psychiatry and is a pre-eminent authority on hypnosis. Spiegel is a pioneer in the field of hypnotic susceptibility. He spent years developing and refining his Hypnotic Induction Profile, which grades persons from 0 to 5 by recognizing their "clinically identifiable configuration of personality traits."† Spiegel was first exposed to our file data on the "Manchurian Candidate" aspects of the RFK case in late 1973. The psychiatrist flew out to the West Coast and met privately with Jonn Christian, who gave him a thorough presentation on how we thought the hypnosis evidence fitted into the overall modus operandi.

Spiegel returned to New York and immediately went to his lawyer's office and executed an affidavit attesting to what he'd seen and heard from Christian, asking his personal counsel to lock the document away in the safe. It was to be released to the Rockefeller family—he is an intimate friend of both Nelson and David—if or when anything should happen to him.

One of the documents provided to Spiegel was the album cover from *It Comes Up Murder* that had been sent to congressmen and senators by American United's Anthony Hilder just before RFK's

* St. Charles mentioned that a friend of his, LAPD Sergeant Michael Nielsen, had been a member of SUS and had seen a manuscript by an unnamed author who established a convincing "direct connection between Sirhan Sirhan, Lee Harvey Oswald, Clay Shaw, James Earl Ray—and directly back to the preacher in Los Angeles." Ray had consulted a hypnotist during his stay in Los Angeles before he killed Dr. Martin Luther King, Jr., and a text on the subject was found in a Toronto rooming house where he resided briefly before fleeing to Europe. In 1977 Nielsen was named to head a new division within the LAPD that specializes in the use of hypnosis as "an investigative tool" for witnesses and suspects alike. Several lawyer groups and legislators protested the use of hypnosis by the LAPD in this pioneering effort by a law enforcement agency.

† Herbert Spiegel, M.D., "The Grade 5 Syndrome: The Highly Hypnotizable Person," *International Journal of Clinical and Experimental Hypnosis*, Vol. XXII, No. 4 (1974), pp. 303–19.

assassination. (This is the artist's depiction of Nelson Rockefeller at the moment an assassin's bullet is shattering his skull.) On August 28, 1974, Christian notified Spiegel that there were new signs that the Hilder-Steinbacher elements of the John Birch Society were making "familiar" noises again, and in the direction of Vice President Rockefeller too. He instantly forwarded it to the Rockefeller brothers, then wrote Christian: "After many months of reflection and tidbits of new information, your hypothesis still makes sense to me."*

The renewed warning to the Rockefellers went unheeded, however. Then, on the 4th of July, 1976, an attempt was made on Vice President Rockefeller's life by a man openly belonging to the Birch Society. The would-be assassin was tried and convicted as "a lone and unassisted assailant."

Turner visited Spiegel on March 17, 1976, at his uptown Manhattan office. The doctor had not personally examined Sirhan, but he had studied Dr. Diamond's testimony and the psychiatric reports on Sirhan, much as a physician would analyze X-rays without seeing the patient. Spiegel unequivocally designated Sirhan a Grade 5, placing him in the 5 to 10 percent of the general population who are the most susceptible to being hypnotized.

Spiegel emphatically rejected Diamond's diagnosis of Sirhan as a paranoid schizophrenic that was indispensable to his theory of automatic induction. A Grade 5 rarely becomes schizophrenic, the doctor said, and what Diamond misdiagnosed as schizophrenia was actually gross symptoms of hysteria under duress, a relatively new discovery. "It is a transient, mixed state, often of frightening appearance—even mistakenly thought to be a psychosis," Spiegel explained, noting that the back wards of mental hospitals are filled with misdiagnosed patients.

Spiegel offered to show Turner graphic evidence of how easily a Grade 5 could be hypnoprogrammed. In 1967 he had been retained by NBC television news to assist in a documentary special that was sharply critical of New Orleans District Attorney Jim Garrison's probe into the John Kennedy assassination. Garrison had

---

* Letter dated September 3, 1974.

used hypnosis on a star witness, Perry Russo, to try to expand his recollection of a meeting during which Oswald, anti-Castro pilot David Ferrie and the defendant in the case, Clay Shaw, purportedly discussed a plan to assassinate the President. NBC was attempting to demonstrate that Garrison had misused hypnosis to implant a conspiracy fiction in Russo's mind. The network had no proof, but wanted to show how it could be done.

Spiegel arranged an unrehearsed video-taped session in which the subject was a forty-year-old New York businessman of liberal political views who once, for example, had marched in a Bayard Rustin civil rights demonstration. Spiegel had predetermined that the subject was a Grade 5. The segment was narrated by NBC anchorman Frank McGee. But the network cut the segment out of the documentary before it was aired. "I suppose it was too graphic," Spiegel told Turner. "It might have frightened a lot of people."

Spiegel screened it for Turner. After a brief warm-up with the subject, Spiegel is seen achieving a quick induction. "Try to open your eyes, you can't," he tells the subject, whose eyelids quiver but remain shut. The doctor confides that there exists a Communist plot aimed at controlling television and paving the way for a takeover. "You will alert the networks to it," he instructs. Then he shifts the subject from the formal or deep trance to the posthypnotic condition where his eyes open and he appears normal.

At this point Spiegel explains to McGee that the subject is in the grip of what he terms the "compulsive triad": (1) he has no memory of having been under hypnosis; (2) he feels a compulsive need to conform to the signal given under hypnosis; and (3) he resorts to rationalizations to conform to the instructions of this signal.

Glaring accusingly at McGee, the subject launches into an "exposé" of the Communist threat to the networks. He talks about dupes in the media and how they are brainwashing the entire nation. "I have a friend in the media," he says, "but friendship should stop when the nation is in peril." Spiegel suggests the name Jack Harris at random, and the subject readily adopts the name as that of his duped friend. The rationalization has set in. McGee hands him a blank pad on which he says three names are written. The subject nods. Yes, those are the men who were at a Communist cell meeting in a theater loft over a restaurant.

Spiegel snaps his fingers 1-2-3, reinstating the formal trance. With his eyes closed the subject persists in the same argument about Communist penetration of the media. He names Harris as a ringleader. McGee argues against the subject, and as he increases the pressure of his rebuttal the subject slips into a deepening paranoiac depression.

Spiegel snaps him out of the trance. The subject can't remember a thing. Later, when the videotape is run for him, his face mirrors disbelief as he hears and sees himself sloganeering in Birch Society rhetoric. "I can't conceive of myself saying those things," he protests, "because I don't think that way."

When the video tape ended and Spiegel switched on the lights, Turner had to agree that it was all too graphic. "Tell me," Turner asked, "if you had stuck a gun in the subject's hand and instructed him to shoot McGee, what would he have done?"

"Ah," the doctor said, "the ultimate question. I'm afraid he might have shot him."

IN RICHARD CONDON'S NOVEL THE MANCHURIAN CANDIDATE, ANTIhero Raymond Shaw's captors in North Korea brainwash him and program him through hypnosis to act as a "hit man," using an ordinary deck of playing cards as his remote control. Back in the United States, when he hears the key phrase "Why don't you pass the time by playing a little solitaire?" he goes into a deep trance and starts laying out the cards until he comes to the queen of diamonds, which is "the second key" that will clear his mechanism for any assignments. Then, upon receiving instructions, he kills without any later remembrance of having done so.

Some authorities maintain that *The Manchurian Candidate* could never be more than fiction because, they claim, a person cannot be hypnoprogrammed to commit a crime he would not normally even think of committing. In *Hypnotism Comes of Age,** Bernard Wolfe and Raymond Rosenthal contend that "the hypnotized per-

* Bobbs-Merrill (Indianapolis, 1948).

son will perform only those acts which are compatible with his ego, his total personality. And this applies to crime as well as any other form of human activity." The late Dr. William Joseph Bryan, Jr., who had a hypnotherapy practice in Hollywood and was technical adviser on the filming of *The Manchurian Candidate,* declared in his book *Legal Aspects of Hypnosis*: "It is impossible by means of hypnosis to force a subject to commit an act which violates his basic moral code."*

Accordingly, Dr. Spiegel's law-abiding businessman would not have shot Frank McGee, and Sirhan, with no background as a killer, could not have been hypnoprogrammed to attack RFK. But as the annals of crime attest, a person's inherent reluctance to commit a crime can be overridden by conditioning him to believe that the act he is performing is in the interest of a high moral purpose. A civilian conscript who has never harmed a fly will kill the enemy in wartime in the interest of protecting his country and family, and hypnotic subjects can be inculcated with the same type of lofty imperative.

A classic case occurred in Denmark in 1952. Bjorn S. Nielsen and Palle Hardrup became intimate friends in a Danish prison. After their release the dominant Nielsen continued to forge the malleable Hardrup into a robot who would go into a trance at the sight or sound of a simple key—the letter *X*, representing a guardian spirit—and do Nielsen's bidding. How Nielsen gradually developed control over Hardrup was learned when Hardrup was being deprogrammed and related under hypnosis: "There is another room next door where Nielsen and I can go and talk on our own. It is there my guardian spirit usually comes and talks to me. Nielsen says that X has a task for me. I get uncomfortable at the thought because I know that the tasks he sets for me are usually unpleasant. He expects a lot of me." One of the first tasks was for Hardrup to arrange for his girl friend to submit to sexual intercourse with Nielsen.

Subsequently Nielsen directed Hardrup to rob banks in order to raise money for a new political party that would achieve the unification of all Scandinavia. In his hypnotized condition, Hardrup saw

* Charles C. Thomas Co. (Springfield, Ill., 1958).

the order as coming from the guardian spirit X and obeyed. The first robbery was successful and he turned over the loot to Nielsen. But during a second attempt he fatally shot a teller and bank officer in Copenhagen and was apprehended by the police. After being convicted and returned to prison, Hardrup was examined by Dr. Paul J. Reiter, chief of the psychiatric department of the Copenhagen Municipal Hospital. Reiter observed amnesia symptoms of a kind that led him to suspect hypnoconditioning. In Europe especially, the recognition of hypnosis became widespread after World War I, and Reiter explored the possibility that Hardrup had been subjected to programming. After nineteen tedious months, Reiter "unlocked" Hardrup's mind. As a result of his work the court absolved Hardrup, and on July 17, 1954, Bjorn Nielsen was convicted and sentenced to life imprisonment for "having planned and instigated by influence of various kinds, including suggestions of a hypnotic nature," the commission of robbery and murder by another man.*

In the Copenhagen case the overriding moral purpose was the unification of all Scandinavia, a goal Hardrup subscribed to. It was sufficient to make a murderer out of an innocuous petty criminal.

It is Dr. Spiegel's opinion that Sirhan may have acceded to participating in the RFK assassination through a suspension of his critical judgment. His psyche may have been altered to the point where Kennedy became a malevolent figure, to be feared and violently hated. "It's possible to distort and change someone's mind through hypnotic conditioning," Spiegel asserted. "It can be described as brainwashing because the mind is cleared of its old values and emotions, which are replaced by implanting other suggestions. Highly hypnotizable persons, when under the control of unscrupulous persons, are the most vulnerable."

There was virtually nothing in Sirhan's background to indicate that he normally viewed Robert Kennedy as a malevolent figure. (He was a Palestinian merely by birth, not by political conviction.) On the contrary, he had every reason to favor Kennedy. Sirhan was an immigrant, a member of a minority group and of meager means,

* Paul J. Reiter, *Antisocial or Criminal Acts and Hypnosis* (Springfield, Ill.: Charles C. Thomas Co., 1958).

1

1. Senator Robert F.
Kennedy, 1967, with friends
Marlon Brando (*left*) and
Robert Vaughn at campaign
fund-raising event.

2. Robert Kennedy with wife
Ethel (*left*) and campaign
chief Jesse Unruh (*right*)
after victory speech, June 5,
1968.

2

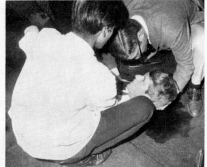

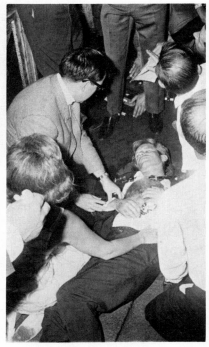

1. Gunfire erupts in the kitchen pantry. Rosey Grier (*left*) and hotel maître d' Karl Uecker (*right*) grab apparent assassin, Sirhan Bishara Sirhan.

2. Sirhan Sirhan is taken into custody by armed officers of the Los Angeles Police Department.

3. Robert Kennedy after the shooting.

4. RFK is attended by a doctor and his wife comforts him as he whispers to her, "Am I going to die?"

5. Thane Eugene Cesar (*right*) with fellow Ace Security guards moments after the shooting. Note his missing clip-on tie.

6. Robert Kennedy lies dying on the floor of the kitchen pantry of the Ambassador Hotel. Note clip-on tie near his right hand.

LOS ANGELES EVENING AND SUNDAY

HERALD EXAMINER

CLASSIFIED ADVERTISING Richmond 8-4111
All Other Calls Richmond 8-1212 or Richmond 8-4141

VOL. XCVIII   NO. 72   THURSDAY, JUNE 6, 1968   8★R   TEN CENTS

RFK IS DEAD

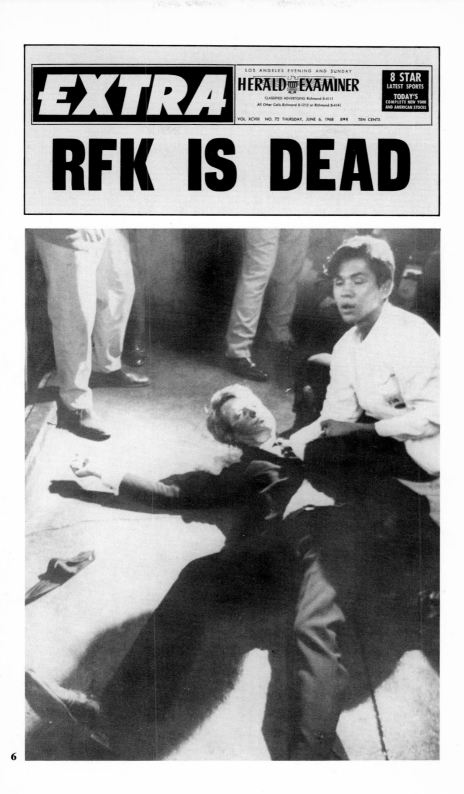

6

3

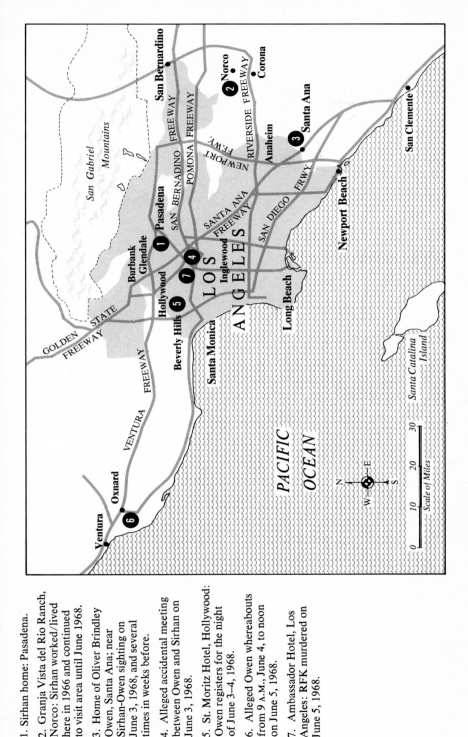

1. Sirhan home: Pasadena.

2. Granja Vista del Rio Ranch, Norco: Sirhan worked/lived here in 1966 and continued to visit area until June 1968.

3. Home of Oliver Brindley Owen, Santa Ana; near Sirhan-Owen sighting on June 3, 1968, and several times in weeks before.

4. Alleged accidental meeting between Owen and Sirhan on June 3, 1968.

5. St. Moritz Hotel, Hollywood: Owen registers for the night of June 3–4, 1968.

6. Alleged Owen whereabouts from 9 A.M., June 4, to noon on June 5, 1968.

7. Ambassador Hotel, Los Angeles: RFK murdered on June 5, 1968.

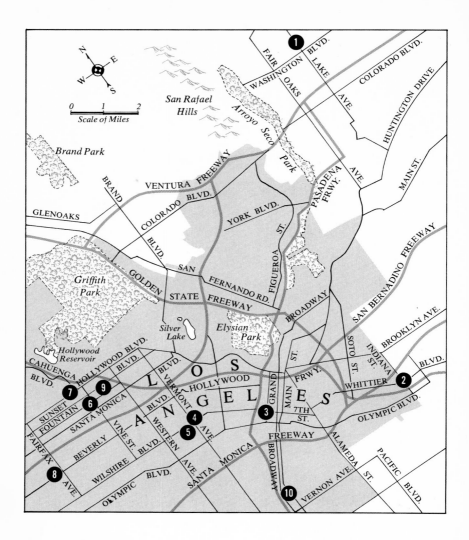

1. Sirhan family home at 696 E. Howard Street, Pasadena.

2. Beginning of Owen's alleged route through Los Angeles in his pickup truck on June 3.

3. Picks up Sirhan and friend at 7th and Grand.

4. Drops off friend with other associates at stoplight at Wilshire and Western.

5. Stops at the Ambassador Hotel at Sirhan's request "to visit a friend in the kitchen."

6. Proceeds to shoe-repair shop at Vine and Fountain in Hollywood.

7. Leaves Sirhan around 6 P.M. and goes to the Hollywood Plaza Hotel to visit "Slapsie Maxie" Rosenbloom.

8. Goes to Saints & Sinners meeting in Hollywood.

9. Meets Sirhan and associates again, then checks into the St. Moritz Hotel at midnight; meets Sirhan's associates in the early morning; then leaves for Oxnard.

10. Arrives at the Coliseum Hotel around noontime on June 5: reports to LAPD University Station to tell story at 2 P.M.

1. The corner of 7th Street and Grand Avenue, Los Angeles, where Owen allegedly first ran into Sirhan and one of his associates on June 3, 1968.
CREDIT: JIM ROSE

2. Cul-de-sac at the east entrance to the Ambassador Hotel—where Jerry Owen said that Sirhan's associates wanted him to appear with his horse and trailer at the moment of the assassination.
CREDIT: JIM ROSE

3. St. Moritz Hotel in Hollywood. Owen stayed here on the night of June 3–4 while negotiating to sell his horse to Sirhan. CREDIT: JIM ROSE

1, 2. Wild Bill's Stables, Santa Ana. Owner Bill Powers reported that Owen and Sirhan were together there just before the assassination. CREDIT: JONN CHRISTIAN

3. Stables and corrals at Owen's residence in Santa Ana, California. CREDIT: JONN CHRISTIAN

4, 5. Apparently in early 1968, Sirhan Bishara Sirhan wrote these entries in his spiral notebooks, which would later be classified by law enforcement authorities as "diaries."

6. Sirhan's final diary entries, written sixteen days before the assassination.

May 18 9.45 AM - 68

my determination to ~~determine~~ eliminate R.F.K. is becoming more the more of an unshakable obsession

please pay to the order

port wine : *port wine* *port wine*

R.F.K. must die- RFK must be killed Robert F. Kennedy must be assassinated R.F.K. must be assassinated R.F.K. must be assassinated R.F.K must be assassinated R.F.K. must be assassinated R.F.K. must be assassinated R.F.K. Must be assassinated assassinated ~~as~~ Robert F. Kennedy Robert F. Kennedy Robert F. Kennedy must be assassinated assassinated Robert F. Kennedy must be assassinated assassinated assassinated assassinated Robert F. Kennedy must be assassinated Robert F. Kennedy must be Assassinated before 5 June '68 Robert F F. Kennedy must be assassinated I have never heard please pay to the order of of of of of of of of of of of this or that HC

8 o o o o o o —– o

please pay to the order of

6

9

1. Unidentified LAPD investigators apparently pointing to bullet holes at the crime scene, June 5, 1968.
OFFICIAL LAPD PHOTO

2. LAPD criminalist Wolfer pointing toward bullet ricochet mark.
OFFICIAL LAPD PHOTO

3. LAPD officers Rozzi and Wright inspect a bullet hole discovered in a door frame in a kitchen corridor of the Ambassador Hotel in Los Angeles near where Robert Kennedy was shot. Bullet is still in the wood. CREDIT: AP WIREPHOTO

4, 5. Criminalist Wolfer attempts to demonstrate to Los Angeles County Coroner Thomas Noguchi the flight paths of bullets through RFK's jacket and body, June 8, 1968. OFFICIAL LAPD PHOTO

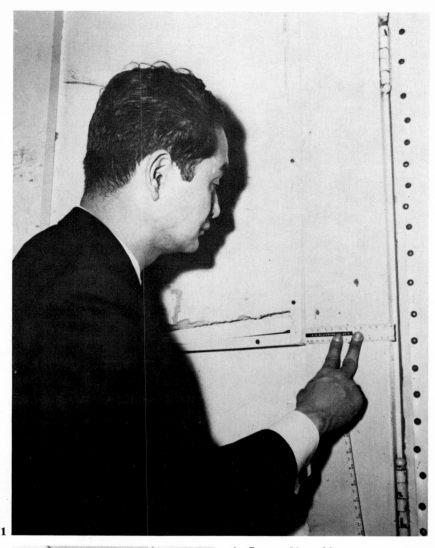

1

2

1. Coroner Noguchi measures area
near two bullet holes (circled and
initialed by LAPD officers, but
unaccounted for later on), June 5,
1968. CREDIT: LOS ANGELES COUNTY
CORONER'S OFFICE

2. Coroner Noguchi conducts his independent investigation. CREDIT: LOS
ANGELES COUNTY CORONER'S OFFICE

11

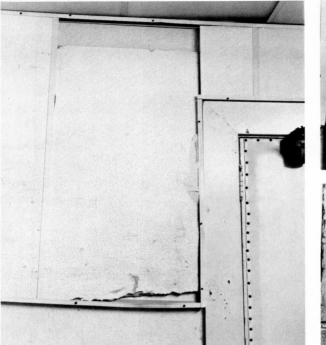

1

2

3

1. (E 1): View taken inside kitchen serving area showing doorway leading into kitchen from the stage area. The lower right corner of the photo shows two bullet holes, which are circled. The missing portion of the panel also reportedly contained a bullet.

2. (E 2): A close-up view of the two bullet holes of the area described above.

3. (E 3): Close-up view of two bullet holes located in center door frame inside kitchen serving area, and looking in the direction of back of stage area.

4. (E 4): Close-up view of upper hinge on door leading into kitchen area from back of stage area. View shows reported mark of another bullet which struck hinge.

Note: All of the above are Official FBI Photos, taken under the supervision of Special Agent Al Grenier, and verified by Special Agent William Bailey.

4

1. Sirhan diary: "Di Salvo."

2, 3, 4. Three faces of William J. Bryan, Jr., who was billed "America's Most Famous Medical Hypnotist."

1. "Concerned Citizens for Bugliosi" meeting, April 1976: Paul Le Mat (*second from left*), Jonn Christian (*fourth from left*), Vincent Bugliosi, Robert Vaughn and Joseph Gellman. Seated are Lorraine Y. S. Cradock and Jocelyn Brando. This adjunct campaign support group designed a brochure detailing Bugliosi's position on the RFK case. CREDIT: MEG GLEASON

2. Press conference conducted in Los Angeles in October 1975 by (*left to right*) Dr. Robert J. Joling, Vincent Bugliosi, Paul Schrade and Allard K. Lowenstein. New evidence of a "second gun" in the RFK case was presented. CREDIT: PAUL LE MAT

3. Authors Turner and Christian with William W. Harper in his Pasadena crime lab, June 1976. CREDIT: LORRAINE Y. S. CRADOCK

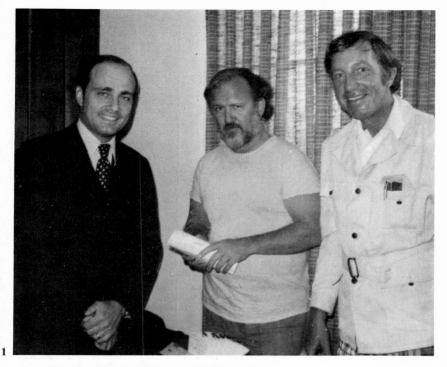

1

2

1. Vincent Bugliosi with
authors Christian and Turner,
August 1975, Beverly Hills.
CREDIT: DIANNE HULL

2. Paul Le Mat as "Big John
Milner" in *American Graffiti*
(1972). CREDIT: UNIVERSAL
STUDIOS

3. Dianne Hull with co-star
Paul Le Mat in a scene from
Aloha, Bobby and Rose
(1975). CREDIT: CINE ARTISTS,
COLUMBIA PICTURES

3

1. Rosalynn Carter with Dianne Hull during Wisconsin campaign of April 1976. CREDIT: GREG WALLING, ATLANTA, GEORGIA

2. Dianne Hull with Governor Jimmy Carter in Green Bay during Wisconsin primary tour. CREDIT: GREG WALLING, ATLANTA, GEORGIA

thus representing causes the senator championed. In his postconviction interview, NBC's Jack Perkins asked Sirhan what wish he might want granted. "I wish"—Sirhan's eyes glistened and his voice cracked—"I wish that Senator Kennedy were still alive." His hands reached up to cover a stream of tears.

Yet the Sirhan who went to the Ambassador Hotel on election night snarled that Kennedy was a millionaire who didn't give a damn for the poor. And the "automatic writing" in the notebooks reveal a Sirhan whose growing antipathy toward Kennedy culminated in a determination to get rid of him. But logic suggests that Sirhan was conditioned by someone else while in these trances. Sirhan himself had no reason to single out Kennedy from the other candidates—McCarthy, Hubert Humphrey and Richard Nixon— who also were openly in favor of aid to Israel. Yet his murderous intent was fixed on Kennedy long before the pre-election weekend when the warplanes issue arose in a debate.

Both Dr. Simson and Dr. Spiegel believe that Sirhan's latent Arab nationalism—what Spiegel terms, in his Grade 5 specifications, a personality core containing "a dynamism so fixed that it is subject to neither negotiation nor change"—was exploited to turn Sirhan against Kennedy. Once Sirhan accepted the idea that Kennedy was anti-Arab because he was pro-Israel, he would be freed from the bonds of inhibition that normally prevented him from killing. He would possess the high moral purpose that would justify eliminating Kennedy, just as Palle Hardrup had not scrupled to kill while under hypnosis in order to achieve "the unification of all Scandinavia."

FINALLY, WE TURN TO THE AMNESIA BLOCKS SIRHAN ASSERTEDLY continues to experience concerning his writing the notebooks and assaulting Robert Kennedy. Dr. Diamond thought that they were genuine, but caused by schizophrenia. However, after thorough examination of Sirhan, Dr. Simson concluded that he was not psychotic, and Dr. Spiegel agreed, contending that what appeared to be schizophrenic symptoms were actually manifestations of hysteria under duress. If Sirhan's trances were self-induced, as Dr.

Diamond felt, he should have been able to remember them. If they
were induced by another, and a locking mechanism implanted, he
would have no memory of them.

So the crucial question is whether Sirhan is telling the truth
when he says he cannot remember, as he did most recently when
Los Angeles Supervisors Baxter Ward and Kenneth Hahn visited
him in prison in May 1977. In fact, the equivalent of a lie detector
has concluded that he is telling the truth. The test was conducted
by means of a technique called Psychological Stress Evaluation.
PSE has gained wide acceptance as a substitute for the polygraph,
although the manufacturers of the PSE instrument prefer to call
it a truth detector because it can determine more positively whether
a subject is being truthful than if he is lying. They maintain that
the instrument, by "using electronic filtering and frequency dis-
crimination techniques, detects, measures and graphically displays
on a moving strip chart certain stress-related components of the
human voice," and that the stress, "induced by fear, anxiety, guilt
or conflict facilitates detection of attempted deception."*

The unique feature of the PSE instrument is that the subject
does not have to be present or even know that he is being tested—
it can analyze pre-recorded tapes. Recently the *National Enquirer*
commissioned PSE expert Charles McQuiston, a former Army
intelligence officer who helped develop the technique, to analyze the
tape recording of Jack Perkins' interview of Sirhan. The key
portions are:

SIRHAN: To me, sir, he [Kennedy] is still alive . . . I still don't believe
what has happened . . . I don't believe that he is dead. I have no
realization still that I killed him, that he is in the grave.
Analysis: Sirhan's stress level is relatively low, showing that he's telling the truth. He actually believes RFK is alive and this can only
be explained by the fact that Sirhan was under some kind of hypnotic influence.
SIRHAN: There was no American dream for me. I tried, I sincerely
tried to find a job. I had nothing, no identity, no hope.

* The PSE instrument is made by Dektor Counterintelligence and Security, Inc., Springfield, Virginia. It is used regularly by some 1,500 law
enforcement agencies in the United States and is admitted as evidence in the
courts of at least five states.

Analysis: His phrases are very indicative of hypnosis. From my days in Army intelligence, I know the words are those a skilled hypnotist would use to beat a man down, to change his thinking, to reshape his mind.

SIRHAN: I thought he was heir apparent to President Kennedy and I wish to hell he could have made it. I loved him.

Analysis: There is genuine sincerity in his statements. When Sirhan says he wished RFK could have made it, this shows me that Sirhan didn't know what he was doing—that hypnosis was governing his actions.

SIRHAN: There was a girl there.

Analysis: He's not lying. There was a girl, and, judging from the stress in his voice, he's trying to block her out of his mind. This indicates she may have played a role in the assassination. [Here again was the specter of the girl in the polka-dot dress.]

SIRHAN: I don't have the guts to do anything like that.

Analysis: He's telling the truth. There must have been some outside guiding force—hypnosis—that was responsible for him pulling the trigger.

McQuiston summed up: "Everything tells me that someone else was involved in the assassination."

Dr. John W. Heisse, Jr., president of the International Society of Stress Analysis, who has used PSE to study hundreds of persons under hypnosis, concurred with McQuiston after reviewing the PSE chart. "Sirhan kept repeating certain phrases," Heisse elaborated. "This clearly revealed he had been programmed to put himself into a trance. This is something he couldn't have learned by himself. Someone had to show him and teach him how. I believe Sirhan was brainwashed under hypnosis by the constant repetition of words like, 'You are nobody, you're nothing, the American dream is gone,' until he actually believed them. At that stage, someone implanted an idea, kill RFK, and under hypnosis the brainwashed Sirhan accepted it."*

* *National Enquirer*; also San Francisco *Examiner* (June 19, 1977).

14

Tracing
the Programmer

IF SIRHAN WAS A MANCHURIAN CANDIDATE, THERE IS LOCKED within his mind the secret of who hypnoprogrammed him and how. It can be unlocked, but only by an expert on hypnosis after painstaking search and probing. As Dr. Heinz E. Hammerschlag observed in his *Hypnotism and Crime*,* the programmer assumes that "because of his very cunning precautionary measures, his deed will not be discovered."

As we have seen in the Copenhagen case, it took Dr. Reiter nineteen months to ferret out the secrets locked in Hardrup's mind—that X was the triggering signal and that

* Published by E. Reinhardt (Munich, 1954).

there were several locking mechanisms. For example, Nielsen would instruct Hardrup under hypnosis: "As soon as I give my date of birth in court, that is, the figure 10/12/1901, you will no longer know what happened to you." Or, "As soon as I raise my hand, blow my nose, turn my head to left or right, or as soon as your name is called out you will become completely confused, you will feel faint, you will begin to shout or sing out loud, or you will say that up to now you have been lying."

Dr. Hammerschlag has described a case in Bavaria in 1934 that took even longer to unravel. A husband complained that a man had swindled his wife by posing as a doctor and giving her hypnotherapy for imagined ailments. He then pushed her into prostitution and, later, programmed her to put a gun to her husband's head and pull the trigger. Fortunately, the gun had been unloaded. The woman's mind was a blank—she had no memory of turning tricks or attempting to murder her husband. As Hammerschlag put it, "In uncovering a crime committed under hypnosis, account must be taken of the fact that the culprit has tried to suggest to his hypnotized subject loss of memory in relation to all details in the deed and the preparation for it."

The deprogrammer, after attaining a high degree of rapport with the woman, put her into deep hypnosis and had her repeat everything that came into her mind. From the spasmodic outpouring of words—similar to the automatic writing in Sirhan's notebooks—there emerged two clues: "Auto—6071" and "19-3." The former turned out to be the license number of the fake doctor's automobile, and the latter "a suggestion word for producing complete blockage of memory." The "doctor" had threatened her that "she would fall dead if she would cross the boundaries which he had set to her memory." The deprogramming took two years, but the culprit was convicted and sentenced to ten years in prison.

A more recent case occurred in 1967 in the Philippines, although it ended unsuccessfully. The National Bureau of Investigation (NBI) suspected that a man they had in custody had been hypnoprogrammed to assassinate President Ferdinand Marcos. The NBI called in a hypnotist to try to deprogram him. In his report, the hypnotist asserted that while "it is firmly accepted that a properly hypnotized subject can be made to set out a posthypnotic instruction during his normal, waking state with the use of pre-arranged key words or devices . . . the remarkable character of the zombie state in our subject is its deeply ingrained and systematic presentation, indicating a certain disturbing degree of conditioning." The subject exhibited a "deep-seated resistance due to the presence of a posthypnotic block," but the hypnotist did draw out of him that he used the name Luis Castillo and had been trained by the CIA for activities against Fidel Castro. After six months the de-programming was discontinued for political reasons and the subject deported to the United States.*

During the Napoleonic Wars, French couriers were hypnotized and given messages preceded by key words. Once they were safely through enemy lines, their contacts on the other side would repeat the key words, enabling the courier to repeat the messages. But if captured by the enemy, the hapless couriers could not remember the messages even under torture. The late Dr. G. D. Estabrooks, a pioneer in the military use of hypnosis, recounted an experiment after World War II in which a message was locked into the mind of an Army captain in Tokyo with the phrase "The moon is clear." When the unwitting captain arrived in Washington, Dr. Estabrooks spoke the phrase and the captain delivered the message he could not have remembered moments before.

There exists no clinical reason why Sirhan could not be de-programmed at this late date. In one case a woman who was put under hypnosis recalled everything she experienced in a trance thirteen years previously, although in the intervening years she had remembered nothing. To regress Sirhan hypnotically to try to find clues to the locking of his mind would require a hypnotist with whom he had attained a high degree of rapport. Dr. Simson said that he had reached such a stage and was about to begin hypnotic deprogramming sessions when he was halted by the prison ad-ministration. From his study of the case, Dr. Spiegel is convinced that he could achieve significant results in as little as three days.

But any such attempts hinge on the cooperation of the Cali-fornia authorities, and thus far it has not been forthcoming. In

* Report of Victor R. Sanchez, September 1, 1967; copy in possession of the authors.

September 1977, for example, a Los Angeles judge turned down Sirhan's request to be allowed to return to the Ambassador Hotel in the hope that his memory might be jogged. "There is no indication—psychological, medical, astrological or otherwise—that this man's memory can be refreshed." The judge, William Hogaboom, had the unfortunate luck of being put in juxtaposition, in many newspapers, with news of the CIA's MK-Ultra Mind-Control Program.* The program included a study called Operation Artichoke to determine if a person could be induced to involuntarily commit an assassination.

Returning Sirhan to the scene of the crime, however, would not have jarred a return of his capacity to recall crucial events, not if the experts are right. This still requires intensive deprogramming by medical men with the requisite training and understanding of the evidential side of the RFK assassination case.

Curiously enough, though, Sirhan's own latest lawyer, Godfrey Isaac of Beverly Hills, resisted any kind of medically supervised probing into the area of amnesia, on the grounds that too much pressure in this case might somehow jeopardize his client's parole status—which had already been set by the parole authorities in California to be 1984. How merely attempting to find out if Sirhan had been a helpless pawn in the RFK case would have been compromised by such a petition to the court was never explained by Isaac.

Then, again, neither was the strange rationale once offered by another of Sirhan's string of barristers. In early 1971 Bill Harper showed noted Hollywood lawyer Luke McKissack the evidence pointing toward an assassin other than his client. The lawyer refused to incorporate the criminalist's findings in his appeals case for Sirhan, then later insisted to newsmen that if there had been a "second gun" fired at the assassination scene, it would have been someone without any connection with Sirhan or his actions "who seized on the impulse of the moment" to fire a bullet into RFK's brain. (No newsman challenged that gem either.)

---

* See, for example, the San Francisco *Examiner* (September 2, 1977).

SPURRED BY BOB KAISER'S FEELING THAT SOMETHING IN SIRHAN'S recent past there was "a shadowy someone," we combed through our background file on Sirhan for clues. From the case histories, it appeared that the programmer would have to have had prolonged access to Sirhan in order to condition him. Even the LAPD had conceded that it was possible. In his book Chief Houghton wrote: "SUS explored the hypnotic-programming contention and was advised that it would take a series of sessions between the hypnotist and Sirhan, if, in fact, it was workable at all. No evidence of such sessions could be found; no hypnotist could be produced."*

Sirhan Sirhan had spent his early childhood in a Palestine torn by the Arab-Israeli conflict of 1948. His family belonged to a Lutheran congregation but in 1956 switched to the Greek Orthodox Church, and soon thereafter was able to migrate to America. Their immigration sponsors were a socially prominent Pasadena couple active in the Republican Party and, in time, the Nixon campaigns. (The couple had known Richard Nixon at Whittier College.)

In 1965 Sirhan took the first step toward becoming a jockey by signing on as an apprentice groom at the Hollywood Park and Santa Anita race tracks. He became friendly with a fellow groom, forty-one-year-old Walter Thomas Rathke. Rathke's main interests seem to have been fundamentalist Christianity and, paradoxically, the occult. "We had many discussions on the occult—reincarnation, karma, clairvoyance, astral projection, the human aura," Sirhan wrote us about his relationship with the older man. "But I don't remember that we ever discussed politics."

Apparently Rathke's politics corresponded with his fundamentalist beliefs. A man who knew him advised us that Rathke was "far right politically and has the general 'don't argue with 'em, knock 'em on their ass' attitude toward kid-raising, liberals and malcontents in general."†

Rathke seemingly exerted a profound influence over Sirhan. The two experimented with meditative exercises, a mild form of

---

* Houghton, *op. cit.*, pp. 149–50.

† Letters from Victor Endersby to the authors, May 28, and July 11, 1970.

hypnosis. In 1967, after Rathke moved north to the Livermore Valley near San Francisco to work at the Pleasanton Race Stables, they kept in touch. Rathke remained very much on Sirhan's mind, for in the "automatic writing" in the notebooks there appears: "Hello tom perhaps you could use the enclosed $ Sol [Sirhan's nickname at the racetracks] . . . 11 o'clock Sirhan Livermore Sirhan Sirhan Pleasanton . . . Hello Tom racetrack perhaps you could use the enclosed $ . . . Tom—Eleven Dollars—would like to come up for several days—meet me at the airport."

According to a friend of the Sirhan family, Lynne Massey Mangan, Rathke visited Sirhan in Pasadena in December 1967 and again in March 1968, on which occasion he had dinner with the family. After the assassination Mary Sirhan found a letter from Rathke that she hid from the police. "He wrote Sirhan telling him that he should stop practicing his self-hypnosis rituals with the mirror and the candles and the likes," Lynne Mangan told us, "or if he didn't he might lose control of himself and do something terrible."*

Rathke expressed this concern himself to the Theosophists in early 1968, after he had begun attending their meetings. According to Theosophist elder Victor Endersby, Rathke told a local meeting of the society shortly after the assassination that "Sirhan had been studying a course in meditation which might have had a bad effect on his psyche." When Endersby learned that Rathke was actually an "evangelistic type" who "runs some sort of spiritualistic church himself," he became suspicious of his abrupt appearance in the Theosophists' midst. The society was hardly Christian evangelist, and the spiritualists were its hereditary enemies.

Rathke came to the attention of the LAPD in early 1969 after one of Sirhan's attorneys, in his opening statements at the trial, contended that his client was in a dissociated state at the time of the shooting. The statement evidently prompted police to look for rebuttal evidence. They were curious about Sirhan's notebook entries concerning Rathke, which were followed by the exhortation "Let us do it" repeated four times. In juxaposition to these jottings appeared "Al Hilal," "Master Kuthumi," "Illuminati" and "North-

* Authors' interview with Mrs. Mangan, October 1972.

ern Valley." Al Hilal was an occult sect originating in England at the turn of the century, while Master Koot Hoomi was the Tibetan mystic from whom Madame Blavatsky, founder of the Theosophist movement, received ethereal guidance. Illuminati, of course, was the gigantic "one-world conspiracy" that was the nightmare of the ultraright. As we have seen, John Steinbacher and Anthony Hilder pointedly named the Theosophists, Rosicrucians, *et al.*, as part of the "Illuminati conspiracy" they held responsible for the JFK and RFK assassinations. "Northern Valley" was an enigma, but it was possible that it meant the Livermore Valley.

The LAPD was evidently concerned that the defense might convince the jury that Sirhan's occult practices had inadvertently compelled him to shoot Kennedy. On February 21, while the trial was in progress, SUS Sergeant Phil Sartuche flew north to the Livermore Valley and interviewed Tom Rathke. (What he learned, if anything, was not in any SUS document we were able to obtain.) While in the area, he also talked to Victor Endersby, wanting to know what connection might exist between the Theosophists and the Rosicrucians, as alleged by Steinbacher and Hilder. There was none, Endersby said. Sartuche also asked whether there were any Theosophist or Rosicrucian "meditation" or "development" practices that might have put Sirhan into a hypnotic condition. None, said Endersby. The sergeant showed Endersby a "rogues' gallery" of photographs, but none was even faintly familiar. Almost as an afterthought, Sartuche inquired about Rathke, but when Endersby offered to put him in touch with persons who could give first-hand information about Rathke's infiltration of the Theosophists, he dropped the subject.

Sartuche's line of questioning convinced Endersby that the LAPD suspected someone had tampered with Sirhan's mind, and he was equally certain that someone had set up the Theosophists to absorb the blame. We agreed. We decided to ask Sirhan himself about the "Illuminati" and "Kuthumi" entries in his notebooks. Surprisingly, he replied that he did not know "anything about the Illuminati, unless the word is attached to the name of the organization headed by Manly Palmer Hall" (it is not), and that Kuthumi "sounds familiar in occult literature." No student of Theosophy would fail to recognize Master Koot Hoomi, much less fail to spell his name correctly. Thus it seemed to us as if someone had verbally implanted these words in Sirhan's trance-susceptible mind, which produced the phonetic spelling.

In his hitchhiker story, Jerry Owen had intimated that several of Sirhan's possible co-conspirators, a swarthy man and a blond girl who negotiated for the purchase of the horse, were involved in the occult. "He had on a turtleneck sweater that was kind of an orangish-yellow color with a chain around his neck and a big, round thing that you see 'em all wearing now, even men on television," the preacher had said. "And I noticed a chain hanging around her neck with a round ornament on." Owen was clumsily describing an occult amulet with the ankh symbol, but John Steinbacher was more articulate in his book, claiming that the Illuminati were behind the RFK assassination. "Within the so-called 'peace movement' in America runs this same cabalistic and occult strain," Steinbacher wrote, "with its ANKH symbol around the necks of such celebrities as TV personality Les Crane."*

We had no direct information that Owen knew Steinbacher and Hilder, or, for that matter, that Steinbacher and Hilder had ever laid eyes on Sirhan.† But we did learn that Hilder, who had been at the Ambassador Hotel on election night passing out anti-Kennedy handbills, had acquired more than a passing interest in hypnosis. In discussing the possibility that his programmer might have discovered Sirhan at a hypnosis school or demonstration, Hollywood hypnotist Gil Boyne mentioned to Christian that he himself held a "Self-Help Institute" using hypnosis in the fall of 1967 that attracted several political extremists who might have seen some potential in Sirhan. One that Boyne named was Anthony Hilder.

Hilder signed up for instructions for himself and a girl friend, explaining that he wanted to find out the nature and effect of hypnosis on the individual. After attending several classes, they dropped out. Then, in December 1967, he came to see Boyne,

* Steinbacher, *op. cit.*, p. 19.

† There was a distant linkage of personages that trailed back to Owen, however. The admited closeness of Owen to preacher Bob Wells, his mutual link to Edgar Eugene Bradley's "Defense Fund" in the JFK conspiracy case in New Orleans, and the address of the Steinbacher-Hilder American United being used therein.

wild-eyed and agitated, muttering about something "political." He whipped out a .38 police special and two boxes of shells and offered them to the frightened Boyne as payment for arrears tuition. Hilder confided that Boyne would soon have "great need" for the weapons because an event would occur that would touch off race riots around the country. But Hilder had been quite insistent that he not be placed under hypnosis himself. He knew "big things," he said, and he didn't want them to come out.

IN THE SPRING OF 1966 SIRHAN QUIT HIS JOB AT THE RACE TRACKS because he felt he wasn't getting anywhere. Shortly thereafter he scribbled in his notebook: "I have secured a position as assistant to the manager of Corona Breeding Farm—(Dezi [sic] Arnaz's) Res Sirhan $600 per month." The farm was actually the Granja Vista del Rio Ranch near Corona, owned by a group that included Desi Arnaz, the former husband of Lucille Ball. The ranch bred and trained racing horses.

Sirhan purportedly secured the job through a Frank Donneroummas, whom he had known at the Santa Anita track and who reputedly was a relative of the ranch manager, Bert C. Altfillisch. Donneroummas' true name was Henry R. Ramistella, but he had employed the alias to hide a long rap sheet acquired in New York and Miami. Donneroummas was Sirhan's boss at the ranch, and according to co-workers, the two became quite friendly.* In one of Sirhan's notebooks was the passage: "happiness hppiness Dona Donaruma Donaruma Frank Donaruma pl please ple please pay to 5 please pay to the order of Sirhan Sirhan the amount of 5 . . ."

After the assassination the FBI interviewed one of Sirhan's co-workers, Terry Welch, who "listed Desi Arnaz, Buddy Ebsen and Dale Robertson, prominent television personalities, as horse owners who were well-acquainted with Sirhan." All three actors were prominent in Hollywood's more conservative political circles. Desi Arnaz came from a wealthy Cuban family and was a fervent opponent of Fidel Castro.

* LAPD report I-1931.

Welch pegged Sirhan as a staunch anti-Communist. "In conversations with fellow employees who were refugees from Communist countries, such as Cuba and Hungary, Sirhan always gave Welch the impression that he was very much opposed to Communism," the FBI report stated. "He indicated a strong liking for the United States and never exhibited any particular loyalty or feeling toward the country of his birth." Welch said that "the Reverend Leo Hill, Circle City Baptist Church, Ninth and Sheridan, Corona, would possibly know Sirhan inasmuch as Sirhan gave Welch a card for this church and suggested that he see Rev. Hill when he was having personal problems."* Hill's church subsequently merged with the large Riverside Baptist Church, a pillar of the fundamentalist right, and we located him there. "Sirhan attended services a couple of times," the reverend recalled. "But as far as coming to me personally, he never did that."†

It is not difficult to envision how Corona, with its mix of the horse crowd, Hollywood actors, fundamentalist religionists and political conservatives, might have been the locus where Owen's and Sirhan's paths first crossed.‡ Even though Sirhan left the ranch in December 1966—he spent the ensuing year unemployed and frequenting the Santa Anita track with Tom Rathke—Corona seems to have remained a focal point. Bob Kaiser asked him about his whereabouts on Monday, June 3. "He first denied that he was anywhere. Then, later on, he admitted that he'd gone to Corona late in the day—4 or 5 o'clock. Then, still later on, he admitted that on that occasion and other occasions he really wasn't in Corona—that Corona was on the outer periphery of his travels."

Still, it was Sirhan who had brought up Corona, which was only twenty miles upstream on the Santa Ana River from Owen's home, and the previous Saturday he had shown up at a Corona

* FBI report June 6, 1968, at Southfield, Michigan.

† Authors' interview with the Reverend Leo Hill, November 8, 1969. The Riverside Baptist Temple is listed in the "First National Directory of 'Rightist' Groups, Publications and Some Individuals in the United States," sixth edition, published by the Alert Americans Association of Los Angeles.

‡ A possible linkage might have been: Owen's close ties to Jerome Weber, the lawyer for Desi Arnaz, and Sirhan's claim to having been employed at the actor's thoroughbred-horse ranch.

pistol range. This came out at the trial when Sirhan was asked, "On June 1, do you remember you went to the range at Corona, signing in?" At first Sirhan claimed he could not remember, then acknowledged, "Yes, sir, I do. A policeman was there teaching some people, and the way he taught them to fire guns, that was the way I was taught, too." Neither prosecutor nor his defense lawyers asked the who and why behind this curious answer.

Earlier on that Saturday he was tentatively identified as a young man target-shooting in a secluded part of the Santa Ana Mountains south of Corona. A two-sentence LAPD report advised that Santa Ana insurance executive Dean Pack, who was hiking in the area with his teen-age son, "was exhibited a photograph of Sirhan" which he said "strongly resembled" the shooter, but the police dropped the matter when Pack said he "was not positive of this identification."

In an interview on December 12, 1969, Pack told Christian that the LAPD had talked to him only by telephone and thus could not have shown him a picture. But Pack related that after the assassination he thought he recognized news photos of Sirhan as the young man accompanied by another man who was six feet tall and ruddy-complexioned, with sandy hair, and a girl in her early twenties with long brunet hair.

"The main thing that struck me was how unfriendly they were," Pack recounted. "The person who looked like Sirhan didn't say a word. He just stood there and glared at me. The other fellow was the only one who would talk." They were shooting at cans set up on a hillside. "Sirhan was shooting a pistol," Pack said. "As I walked away from them, you know, you get the funny sensation that it would be possible for them to put a bullet in your back. I was relieved to get out of their sight."

Dean Pack said that he offered to take the FBI to the spot so that they could recover the bullets and shell casings and look for fingerprints on the bottles and cans the trio had handled, but the Bureau was uninterested. "I got the attitude that they had their man so why spin wheels about anything else," Pack remarked.

ALTHOUGH SIRHAN NEVER KNEW IT, HE BECAME THE STAR—AND sole actor—in a motion picture filmed after his return to the family residence in Pasadena in 1967. The 16mm color film clearly shows him roaming the streets of Pasadena, but the purpose for which it was taken remains an enigma.

The existence of the film came to light in 1969 when the manager of a Los Angeles office building was cleaning out premises vacated by private detective Earl LaFoon and found a canister labeled "Sirhan B. Sirhan—1967" that contained a reel of film. Curious, the manager ran the film on a projector, then turned it over to the FBI.* In 1975 a copy turned up in the hands of Los Angeles CBS television correspondent Bill Stout, who aired it with comments about its "strange" implications.

Shortly thereafter Jonn Christian located Earl LaFoon and found him evasive about the film. First he said it had been stolen from him, then denied having done the filming, and finally abruptly terminated the conversation by saying, "You'll have to ask the Argonaut Insurance Company about this. That's all I have to say."

The Argonaut Insurance Company was the firm that had paid Sirhan $1,705 in settlement of a workmen's compensation claim for injuries received in a fall from a horse while employed at the Corona ranch. On occasion insurance companies hire private investigators to secretly film claimants in the hope of documenting, for example, a person pretending to have a severe back injury lifting a heavy object or even playing golf. But Sirhan's injuries had been minor, and he did not claim to be disabled. There was nothing to prove by motion-picture surveillance, which undoubtedly would not have been ordered in any case because of the relatively small amount involved.

Christian decided to check with the Argonaut Insurance Company. A spokesman denied knowing anything about the film. We called on private detective Al Newman to use his inside contacts at Argonaut to see what had happened. He reported back that

* Authors' interview with United Press International photographer Michael Ellard, Los Angeles, 1976.

"their file has been destroyed."* Another trail had ended on a familiar note.

IN LATE 1967 SIRHAN INEXPLICABLY DROPPED FROM SIGHT. A VET-eran LAPD officer (who wishes to remain anonymous) told us that SUS, in tracing Sirhan's activities during the year preceding the assassination, wound up with a three-month gap in his where-abouts. A neighbor of the Sirhan family advised the FBI that Mary Sirhan became "extremely worried" when her son left home "and she did not know his whereabouts for quite some time."†

When he returned, Sirhan's interest in the occult had deepened. He haunted a Pasadena bookstore specializing in occult subjects. In March 1968 he reportedly appeared at a Theosophical Society meeting in Pasadena, although he curtly refused to identify him-self. He mailed in a membership application to the Rosicrucian Order, paying $4 dues, and in late May attended a meeting of the Pasadena lodge. These wholly tentative links with the Theosophists and Rosicrucians set the stage for the propaganda theatrics immedi-ately following the shooting, in which Mayor Sam Yorty branded the Rosicrucians a "Communist organization," and Steinbacher and Hilder implied that the Theosophists had exerted a sinister in-fluence over Sirhan. Conveniently omitted was the fact that a police search of Sirhan's car yielded a volume entitled *Healing: The Divine Art*, by Manly Palmer Hall, founder of the Philosophical Research Society (the book mysteriously disappeared from the grand jury exhibits). Hall, a man with penetrating eyes, chiseled features and a Buddha-like figure, was a master hypnotist with a practice in hypnotherapy. Some time ago he had gained consider-able publicity from hypnotic antics, on one occasion "putting under" a movie actor and convincing him he was suffocating, with the result that the actor tore apart a movie set in his frantic search for "air."

We queried Sirhan in San Quentin about Hall and his society.

---

* Memo to the authors dated October 15, 1975.
† FBI Summary Report, *op. cit.*, pp. 859–60.

He wrote back that he remembered paying several visits to the headquarters, an alabaster temple near Griffith Park. "The secretary there had a distinct foreign accent," he said (Hall's wife is German-born), "and I had to ask her to unlock the book cases for me to get the books I wanted to read in the library. I remember seeing Manly Hall himself there." Sirhan's dabbling with the occult society is, by itself, innocuous, but there is a certain irony in the fact that he was drinking from the same mystical fountain as Sam Yorty. For some two decades, the mayor had been a student of Hall, whom he regarded as his guru.

OUR QUEST FOR SIRHAN'S PROGRAMMER HAD BEEN NO MORE SUC-cessful than the search for Amelia Earhart until Dr. Herbert Spiegel gave us a lead. Anything mentioned in the presence of a subject under hypnosis is automatically etched into his mind, especially if it comes from the hypnotist. And it might flow out at any time.

This brought us back to the notebooks containing Sirhan's "automatic writing." Could he have scrawled something during a trance regression that the hypnotist had mentioned while programming him? There was a passage that stood out because it was unlike the others, having nothing to do with horses, politics, money or past acquaintances. It read: "God help me . . . please help me. Salvo Di Di Salvo Die S Salvo." The reference apparently was to Albert Di Salvo, the notorious Boston Strangler. That case had been cracked by the use of hypnotism, and the hypnotist was Dr. William Joseph Bryan, Jr., of Los Angeles. Bryan billed himself as "probably the leading expert in the world" on the use of hypnosis in criminal law, and often boasted about being called into baffling cases by law enforcement agencies, including the LAPD. The Boston Strangler case was his tour de force, and he was incessantly mentioning it.

An imposing man with a wrestler's girth, Bryan claimed he was once drummer with the Tommy Dorsey band and a commercial airplane pilot. During the Korean War he had put his hypnotic skills to use as, in his words, "chief of all medical survival training for the United States Air Force, which meant the brainwashing section."* After the war he reportedly became a CIA consultant in the Agency's experimentation with mind control and behavior modification.

Refused membership in all traditional medical societies, Bryan set up a medical and hypnotherapy practice on the Sunset Strip in Hollywood which he named the American Institute of Hypnosis. He used it as an aegis for wide-ranging symposiums on such topics as "Successful Treatments of Sexual Disorders." "I enjoy variety and I like to get to know people on a deep emotional level," he once told a magazine interviewer. "One way of getting to know people is through intercourse." In 1969 the California Board of Medical Examiners found him guilty of unprofessional conduct for sexually molesting four women patients who submitted under hypnosis.†

Despite his advocacy of sexual freedom, Bryan was a Bible-quoting fundamentalist who belonged to a fire-and-brimstone sect called the Old Roman Catholic Church, which broke away from the Vatican over a century ago.‡ Bryan claimed to be a descendant of the fiery orator William Jennings Bryan, who opposed the teaching of evolution in the celebrated Scopes "monkey trial," and he frequently was a guest preacher at fundamentalist churches in Southern California.

Only hours after the RFK shooting and before Sirhan had been identified, Bryan appeared on the Los Angeles radio program of Ray Briem (KABC) and offhandedly commented that the suspect probably acted under posthypnotic suggestion. Two years later, when Bryan appeared on another local radio program, Christian called in and asked him about his prescient analysis on the Briem show. At first Bryan hedged, then declared that he had no professional opinion because he had not personally examined Sirhan. He quickly switched the subject to the Hollywood Strangler case in which a Henry Bush was executed for murder. "He utilized self-

* Interview on KNX-FM, Los Angeles, February 12, 1972.

† Bryan was given five years' probation on the condition that he have an adult woman present whenever treating female patients.

‡ Curiously, David W. Ferrie, a prime suspect in New Orleans DA Jim Garrison's 1967 probe into the John Kennedy assassination, also belonged to this small sect. Ferrie was found dead on February 22, 1967, shortly after being interrogated.

hypnosis," Bryan asserted, noting that Bush once tried to burn off his own arm with cigarettes under self-hypnosis "to get rid of the offending part—just like the old thing in the Bible, you know: 'If the left hand offend thee, cut it off!' "

When we asked Sirhan about the Di Salvo entry in his notebook, he replied that the name was entirely foreign to him. Was it possible that Bryan had placed Sirhan in a trance state and, given his propensity to boast constantly about the Boston Strangler case, repeated Di Salvo's name over and over—thus etching it into Sirhan's subconscious? In any case, Sirhan would not remember either the circumstances of his exposure to the name or who mentioned it.

Since Bryan's ego seemed boundless, it was possible that an interview with him would produce the unexpected. It did. On June 18, 1974 Betsy Langman, a disarmingly attractive New York writer with whom we had been comparing notes, talked to Bryan in his Sunset Strip office suite on the pretext of doing a general article on hypnosis. The doctor went on at length about his standing in the field of hypnosis ("I am probably the leading expert in the world") and abilities ("I can hypnotize everybody in this office in less than five minutes"), detailed his successes with Henry Bush and Albert Di Salvo, and ventured opinions on various aspects of hypnosis. But when Langman, who had been researching the possibility of assassination through mind control, asked, "Do you feel that Sirhan could have been self-hypnotized?," his expansiveness vanished. "I'm not going to comment on that case," Bryan said curtly, "because I didn't hypnotize him." When Langman explained that she simply wanted his opinion, Bryan exploded. "You are going around trying to find some more ammunition to put out that same old crap," he said, "that people can be hypnotized into doing all these weird things." He charged out of his office, snapping, "This interview is over!"

Shaken by the angry outburst, Langman went across the street for coffee accompanied by a sympathetic secretary. Langman was in for another shock. According to the secretary, Bryan had received an emergency call from Laurel, Maryland, only minutes after George Wallace was shot. The call somehow concerned the shooting. (Governor Wallace was shot and badly injured on May 15, 1972, at

Laurel while campaigning for the presidency; his assailant was Arthur Bremer.)

In the spring of 1977 Bryan was found dead in a Las Vegas motel room, "from natural causes," the coroner said. (Curiously, this word was issued *before* the official autopsy.) Shortly thereafter we were put in contact with two Beverly Hills call girls who claim to have known Bryan intimately. They had been "servicing" him on an average of twice a week for four years, they said, and usually were present at the same time. During the last year of his life, he was deeply depressed because his paramour had run off with another man. He became strung out on drugs, and his groin and thighs were pocked with bruises from hypodermic needles. (No mention of these marks appeared on the coroner's report.)

The girls said that to relieve Bryan's depression they repeatedly titillated his enormous ego by getting him to "talk about all the famous people you've hypnotized." As if by rote Bryan would begin with his role of deprogramming Albert Di Salvo in the Boston Strangler case for F. Lee Bailey, then boast that he had hypnotized Sirhan Sirhan. The girls didn't sense anything unusual in the Sirhan angle, for Bryan had told them many times that he "worked with the LAPD" on murder cases, and they didn't know that he had absolutely no contact with Sirhan following the assassination. One of the girls thought that Bryan had mentioned James Earl Ray once, but wasn't sure. But both girls were certain of the name Sirhan Sirhan.*

The call girls also linked Bryan to the CIA. At the outset of their relationship with him, he instructed them to call an unlisted phone number at his office. If someone else answered, they were to say they were with "the Company" (an insider's term for the CIA) and they would be put through to him. According to the girls, Bryan repeatedly confided that he was not only a CIA agent but involved in "top secret projects." However, when he began

---

* In October 1977 the LAPD was awarded a $10,000 grant from the American Express Company for "pioneer work in developing hypnosis as an investigative technique." It has been established that Ray, while residing in Los Angeles immediately prior to the King assassination, did consult with a hypnotist named Xavier von Koss.

bragging about such escapades as crawling over rooftops at night in Europe, they were a bit skeptical. "We couldn't see Doc doing that kind of thing—not all three hundred pounds of him, we couldn't," one of the girls said, laughing.

Upon Bryan's death his offices were sealed off to newsmen by his estate's probate lawyer, John Miner (who had also helped prosecute Sirhan as a deputy DA). There remains the question of Bryan's claimed hypnotist-subject relationship with Sirhan, and what role his connection with the CIA might have played in it.

15
The Trial

THE LOS ANGELES SUPERIOR COURTS BUILDING PERCHES ON a slope on North Hill Street in the heart of the Civic Center complex. On the fourth floor is Judge Jack A. Crickard's courtroom. Its walls are paneled with oak squares, and a large frosted-glass ceiling panel diffuses artificial light with the effect of a skylight. The room is comfortably intimate, seating only thirty-six spectators.

Judge Crickard is one of the more anonymous components of the judicial machinery. Born in a small town in Ohio in 1920, he obtained a law degree from the University of Southern California and became a partner in a staid Glendale firm specializing in water law. In 1970 Governor Ronald Reagan appointed him to the bench. His bland, pinkish face rarely shows expression, and on the infrequent occasions when he does smile, it seems that only one side of his wide, thin-lipped mouth curls up, as if not to commit him fully to levity.

The trial of Jerry Owen versus television station KCOP began before Crickard on the late afternoon of July 2, 1975, only twenty minutes before the five-year statute of limitations governing pursuit of a lawsuit would have expired. In fact, KCOP's lawyers had been fairly certain there would be no trial—for one thing, Owen was listed as his own attorney, although it was apparent he had outside legal assistance, and for another, they could not conceive that he would want his dirty linen hung out in public.* But as the trial deadline neared and it began to look as if Owen would go through with it, KCOP offered him an out-of-court settlement of $50,000 to spare the tremendous cost of a trial. But to the station's surprise, the preacher haughtily countered with a demand for $650,000 cash plus an equal amount of free air time on KCOP. The reason for his confidence surfaced only days before the trial opened when a battery of seven lawyers from five law firms from as far away as Utah and Arizona stepped up beside him.

KCOP's trial lawyer was Michael Wayland, a short, tow-headed man whose office is lined with trophies earned in figure-skating competition with his pretty wife as a partner. Wayland's law firm (Robert Brimberry Associates), representing KCOP's insurance carrier, had assigned Wayland as an observer during the preceding three year period. He took complete charge when it began to look like a trial was imminent, some two weeks before it actually convened. At first Wayland insisted on his right to a jury, but changed his mind when he looked over the list of prospective jurors and decided that they might be susceptible to "The Walking Bible's" glib, God-invoking tongue and might not grasp the intricacies of the

---

* When Owen filed his original lawsuit on July 7, 1970, no reference whatever was made to the RFK assassination. The pleading read "Breach of Contract and Conspiracy," and it merely referred to the "starting and spreading of rumors" by the defendants. It wasn't until the lawsuit developed depositions on both sides that the RFK case became as issue—even though court records indicate that Owen knew about the alleged slander at the very outset (July 1969).

assassination issue. The attorney expected that the trial judge would be Charles Older, who had performed capably at the complex trial of the Manson Family. But at the last minute a malpractice case Crickard was scheduled to hear was settled out of court and he drew the assignment.

Neither of us were present at the trial, although both sides wanted us as witnesses. Owen had prepared subpoenas—we guessed that he wanted to question us about the material we had furnished KCOP—but Turner lived well outside the 150-mile radius that compelled his appearance. Prior to the trial Owen had offered $500 to a young assassination buff named Rusty Rhodes, who was acquainted with Christian, to serve the subpoena on him, and Rhodes had obliged. But Christian wrote the presiding judge of the Superior Courts explaining that the service was faulty and that our "file data on Owen . . . is of such a nature that it hardly belongs in any civil action." We doubted that Owen had any idea of the breadth of our knowledge about his activities, and we did not feel that a civil courtroom was the appropriate place to air them. We had seen enough intimidation, violence and disappearance of evidence over the years to justify reserving our investigative file.

For his part Mike Wayland wanted us to testify to help demonstrate that Owen himself, not KCOP, was responsible for making the hitchhiker story a public issue open to conjecture. Christian met with Wayland only four days before the trial opened, presenting him with the reasons we did not feel free to testify. He did agree, however, to assist Wayland from behind the scenes. He gave the attorney a copy of the transcript of Turner's interview with Owen in 1968 and briefed him—strictly for background—on the events at Wild Bill's Stables, the subsequent attempt on John Chris Weatherly's life and the general content of our file. After the trial began, Wayland called Christian practically every night and read pertinent portions of the "dailies"—the court reporters' hurriedly typed transcripts of the day's proceedings—to get his reaction and guidance.

The trial opened with Owen's lawyers trying to show that their client had been in the evangelistic big league until his career was ruined by the slanderous actions of the KCOP and Ohrbach's management. To this end they even subpoenaed Kathryn Kuhlman, a superstar on the Bible circuit whom Owen claimed as a close friend and co-equal in the "business," but Kuhlman's attorney successfully fought her appearance.* The first reference to the RFK assassination came when KCOP president John Hopkins was questioned by Owen attorney Arthur Evry about the June 1969 meeting between Christian and the station management.

Q. Was there a discussion of an alleged involvement of Reverend Owen in that assassination?
A. Yes.
Q. Did you understand that involvement to be criminal in the assassination?
A. Yes.

Mike Wayland objected, but Crickard overruled the objection.

An uncomfortable-looking Victor Yacullo, the KCOP counsel who had participated in the 1969 meeting, was the next witness summoned by Owen. Evry questioned him about our suspicions that *The Walking Bible* program might have been used to disguise payoff monies as contributions from a legion of viewers. "Other than Mr. Christian's allegations," Evry asked, "was there any other evidence which came to your attention to indicate that the show was being used as a method of obtaining a payoff for the Reverend Owen as a result of his being involved in the assassination of Robert Kennedy?" Yacullo shook his head; he had studiously avoided exploring the assassination aspect.

Next Owen's side put on a parade of character witnesses attesting to his ministerial goodness. Conspicuously absent was Sam Yorty, the ex-mayor who had engaged in a back-slapping session with Owen on *The Walking Bible* show. But Owen sidekick Johnny Gray took the stand, describing himself as a "boxing trainer and technical adviser" to professional fighters, among them ex-heavyweight champion George Foreman. On cross-examination during the fourth day of the trial, Wayland, armed with notes from Christian's 1969 interviews with Gray, pried an admission from Gray that for some thirty years he had been a "commissioned special officer" who performed bodyguard services for Owen around

* Ms. Kuhlman was dying of cancer at the time.

the country, which removed Gray from the "objective witness" category and raised the question of why the preacher required an armed companion. Next, Wayland brought up the 1969 shooting incident in Griffith Park.

"I don't specifically recall it," Gray mumbled, but when Wayland consulted his notes as if they were an official document, Gray's memory suddenly revived. Despite emphatic hand signals and body language from Owen, he laconically told of the two men in the blue Mustang who shot at them near the observatory, but instead of the black and white men described to Christian earlier, the assailants were "just American white boys."

After getting Gray to recount the gunfire episode at the police station, Wayland asked, "And based on that, you think that the police were trying to do away with Mr. Owen?"

"I don't know," Gray replied. "That remains open to this day. I don't know what they were doing!"

"Mr. Gray, what was your profession during the time Mr. Owen came in contact with Sirhan?" Wayland asked. Gray's mouth went sand-dry. "You wish a drink of water, sir?" the attorney inquired politely, noting that his witness seemed hypersensitive about the RFK case. He then established that Gray was living not far from the Coliseum Hotel at the time.

Q. Did you ever see Mr. Owen with Sirhan?
A. No . . . not to my recollection.
Q. Did Mr. Owen tell you what transpired on the Monday and Tuesday before Kennedy was shot?
A. Something—he told me something pertaining to that deal. He—he had a big . . . [The words hung in the air.]
Q. You had contact with him that Monday and Tuesday, is that correct?
A. Possibly.
Q. It would be very probable you did, inasmuch as you were training his fighter and living up the street from him!
A. Right. That is what I say. It is a possibility we were conferring together at that time. I can't recall explicitly.
Q. Tell me what you recall that Mr. Owen told you regarding those two days. [Owen waved his arm, but the judge ignored this attempt to coach the witness.]
A. I recall that he had a fighter by the name of Rip Reilly [sic] living

at that big hotel . . . and that he was going there and coming there or something, and he met a hitchhiker, and he gave the hitchhiker a ride.

Q. Did Mr. Owen ever identify this hitchhiker to you as Sirhan Sirhan?

A. No, he said it might have been. That is all the information I can have of that. [Gray obviously wanted to get away from this unexpected line of questioning.]

Q. That is what he told you that Monday or Tuesday *before* the assassination, is that right?

A. Yeah, right.

Q. Is that right? [the attorney wanted to make sure Gray knew what he was saying.]

A. Yes.

So the thrust of Gray's testimony was that Owen had related the hitchhiker story, including mentioning Sirhan's name, *before* the assassination. This squared with what the Reverend Perkins had told Christian, and buttressed what Bill Powers and the cowboys had reported about: a prior relationship between Owen and Sirhan. Although it was evident that Gray had been very much a part of the events of the days immediately preceding the assassination, Owen had avoided mentioning him in the versions of his story given to Turner and the LAPD. This could have been because Gray had accompanied him and Sirhan to Wild Bill's Stables.

The LAPD had learned about Gray and his close relationship with Owen, and in fact detectives had driven Gray to the Apple Valley area, on the fringe of the Mojave Desert, shortly after the assassination in a fruitless attempt to find a ranch where the preacher was said to keep horses. Gray had mentioned this to Christian in 1969, and Christian had told Wayland. Now Wayland made a tactical error. Without laying a testimonial foundation, he braced Gray with the Apple Valley trip. Evry objected, and Crickard made Wayland explain what he was driving at. Wayland said that he was engaged in a defense that Owen was somehow "involved" with the assassination, and that while he didn't want "to lay out all my cards at this point," it could be that Gray had "told something to the police which directly implicates Mr. Owen."

Crickard was seething. "Sustain the objection!" he cried. "It is not relevant!"

But Wayland forged on, asking Gray, "Have you ever been advised or admonished by any law enforcement agency not to talk about Owen's involvement in the RFK incident?"

Crickard was beside himself. "That's not relevant either!" he injected. "Sustain the objection!"

There hadn't been an objection, which gave Wayland the impression the judge was beginning to take sides. Gray was allowed to step down. But if he thought his testimonial ordeal was over, it was just beginning.

WAYLAND'S PLANNED STRATEGY WAS TO DEMONSTRATE THAT THE KCOP management, once they verified Owen's arrest record, had acted responsibly and in accordance with federal guidelines by terminating *The Walking Bible* program. But that strategy was becoming more and more snagged on the RFK assassination issue. Owen brought a parade of witnesses into court to testify that when they called the station to find out why the program had been canceled, they were told, among other things, that Owen was "involved" in the assassination.

As it turned out, Owen had solicited most if not all of these viewers to phone the station. But he hadn't stopped there, as became evident when an aging lady evangelist calling herself the Reverend Olga Graves took the stand. She produced a poor Xerox copy of a KCOP internal memorandum from counsel Yacullo to president Hopkins that summarized Christian's allegations about Owen's criminal record and connection with the assassination; crudely grafted to the bottom of it was Christian's signature over our typewritten names obviously reproduced from correspondence previously introduced. Graves testified that she had received the document in the mail approximately two weeks beforehand, and that Jonn Christian's name and address were typed on the envelope. But when asked by Wayland if she had mentioned receiving it to Owen, she said, "I did not. He asked me!"

Crickard allowed the hybrid document to be entered as a legitimate exhibit, even though the defense protested vigorously.

Grace M. Holder, the wife of a retired postal worker who had set up his own ministry, was an old friend of Owen brought in to testify about his travails at the hands of KCOP. On cross-examination it turned out that Owen had confided a great deal about Sirhan and his companions who wanted Owen to deliver a horse to the Ambassador Hotel.

Q. Mr. Owen told you that he knew who all these people were?
A. Oh, I don't know if he knew who they were.
Q. He told you that he also continues to know to this day who these people were?
A. As far as I know he said he thought he could identify them when he went and told the police about it, that it was a conspiracy, and at that time he said he thought he could identify the men if he were shown pictures or something.
Q. Mr. Owen involved himself in the Robert F. Kennedy murder by going to the police, didn't he?
A. Yes, he did.
Q. He told you he went to the police on the *night of the assassination*, didn't he? [Wayland was looking at his notes. Mrs. Holder glanced at Owen, who was vigorously shaking his head in the negative.]
A. No, wait a minute. It was that night as I recall that he was sitting in a hotel, and he saw it on television . . .

Trying to straighten her out, Wayland held up a deposition Mrs. Holder had given the previous year and read from it: " 'He went to the police and told them that at the night [*sic*] there was somebody else with him. He didn't go down to the police that night.' "

Visibly nervous, Holder explained, "The court reporter should have had in there 'at that night there was somebody else with Sirhan.' "

Q. And Mr. Owen knew who that person was?
A. Yes.
Q. Mr. Owen, in fact, continually affirmed to you that there was a conspiracy to kill Robert F. Kennedy, and has continued to affirm that to you over the years, isn't that true?
A. Yes.

Appearing on Owen's behalf, Jerome Weber was a shadow of the dapper attorney who had originally represented Owen in his suit against KCOP. "He picked up some rider, as I recall," was his vague recollection of Owen's hitchhiker story. But he did acknowledge to Wayland that he had discussed Owen's "involvement" in the Kennedy case with DA investigators George Murphy and George Stoner (the two men he had admitted bribing in the Devins murder case). "Yes, I may have," he said, "I recall I was busy with Stoner and Murphy at that time." This reinforced our suspicions that Owen had had help inside the DA's office with his "story" problems.

ON THE EIGHTH DAY OF THE TRIAL OWEN TOOK THE STAND TO testify. One of his attorneys, Walter Faber of Salt Lake City, held up Plaintiff's Exhibit 36-B, the hybrid KCOP-Christian document, and asked, "Where did you first see that document?" Owen answered that he had first seen it in a church in Modesto, California, and subsequently in churches in a host of towns around the state. Yes, he had been cut off from further preaching at the churches that received the document. Faber asked how long this "harassment" by Jonn Christian had been going on. From July 1969 to the present, the preacher replied. (This confirmed Owen's awareness of the RFK aspects prior to the original filing of his lawsuit in July 1970.)

It had caused him great mental anguish and loss of income, Owen complained. Practically sobbing, he said, "I have been shamed. I have walked in to visit at a church and set down and watched people turn around and look at me. . . . I have been to the doctor. I can bring the doctor in here. Excuse me, could I have a couple of aspirin, your Honor?"

No sooner had Owen finished this theatrical testimony than his attorneys approached the bench and demanded that Christian be brought into court—by force if necessary—to answer their questions. The matter was put off until the following morning so that college student Barbara Jean Grimes, whom Rusty Rhodes had co-opted to serve Christian with the subpoena, could appear to testify. On cross-examination Wayland got her to admit that Christian had neither acknowledged his identity nor even touched the subpoena ("I think it hit his feet," she said), raising a distinct question of whether the service was legal and proper. But Crickard ordered that a "body attachment" be issued for Christian with bail fixed at $500. "Issue that as promptly as possible," he instructed his bailiff, "and see if we can get Mr. Christian in here forthwith!"

Since the previous evening was one of the few on which he had not talked with Wayland, Christian was unaware that a warrant, highly unusual in a civil case, had been issued for his arrest. But he had already made preparations to pull up stakes because he felt a menace hanging over the trial.* On the day that it had begun, the phone rang in his apartment in the Brentwood district. It was answered by his then ladyfriend, Lorrie Cradock, a teacher at the nearby Westlake School for Girls. The caller was Jerry Owen, demanding to talk to Christian. Told that he was out, Owen turned nasty. "I know who you are," he said. "You're Christian's mistress. You work in a nursery." The blonde retorted, "Oh, yes, the flowers are lovely." Owen hung up.

When he heard about the intimidating call, Christian called Supervisor Baxter Ward and City Attorney Burt Pines to plead for protection, but both were out. He dropped a note to Ward saying: "As we both know from experience, Owen's threats have a most profound way of manifesting themselves into violence." Then he called Charlie O'Brien in San Francisco, who promised to try to contact Pines the next morning. "Why don't you pull out of that place?" O'Brien advised.

Christian took the advice, moving our files and his belongings to the home of a close friend, actor Paul Le Mat. (Le Mat of *American Graffiti* fame and his co-star in *Aloha, Bobby and Rose*, Dianne Hull, had become deeply interested in the RFK case and were attending the trial daily.) To prevent any harm to his ladyfriend, Christian put her on a plane to England to stay at her parents' home on the Isle of Wight.

One hour after Crickard had ordered the body attachment, an

---

* By this time Christian had been instrumental in getting subpoenas issued for a sizable number of police officials and their submerged documents on the Owen aspects of the case. He knew it was just a matter of time before the police figured out that it was our investigative file that was being used by the defense—and that the earlier warnings might turn into harsher reaction.

unmarked beige sedan pulled up at the Brentwood apartment that Christian had selected because it was outside the jurisdiction of the LAPD. One occupant remained at the wheel while a beefy man in a tacky sports coat and a hefty woman in a tight khaki skirt got out and asked the landlady for Jonn Christian. "Who's looking for Mr. Christian?" Marie Reno inquired. "Oh, we're just some friends," the woman lied.

Christian had returned to pick up the last of his belongings and was at that moment in a storage area, oblivious to what was going on. Apparently disbelieving the landlady's protest that Christian had moved, the man and woman went directly to his vacant apartment and searched it. "Wait a minute!" Mrs. Reno challenged. "Who are you people?" "Police!" the woman snarled, but when the landlady demanded to see their identification they ignored her. Not finding Christian in the apartment, the pair proceeded to shove open doors and peek into windows. Mrs. Reno slipped off and warned Christian, who hid as best he could. For an hour he heard the sounds of voices and tromping feet as the pair shook down every one of the twenty-four units in the building. Meanwhile two patrol cars roared up to the Westlake School for Girls, and uniformed officers searched the grounds, forced open the classroom door and riffled through the desk of his departed lady friend. They ordered the caretaker to help locate her—even though no warrant had been issued or applied to her.

Christian heard a loud and persistent banging on the locked door of his refuge, then silence. Fifteen minutes later there was the sound of rattling keys. The door opened slowly—and in slipped Paul Le Mat, Dianne Hull and Mrs. Reno, who had alerted them to what was going on. Concerned that the "police" might have begun a "stakeout," Le Mat and Christian improvised some serious theatrics of their own. Le Mat left with a plumber's helper in hand as if he had been called in to fix a plugged toilet. Then, after making sure he hadn't picked up a tail, he doubled back to the apartment and began a slow pass down the back alleyway. Christian dashed out of his lair, shuffled down the pathway like an old man, and then suddenly leaped into the moving car. Le Mat accelerated to safety as Christian took off the towel he had wrapped around his head to conceal his beard, removed the threadbare bathrobe, and rolled down his pants legs.

Christian first learned that sheriff's deputies had been authorized to bring him in when he called Wayland that night from the sanctuary of Le Mat's West Hollywood home. Wayland said that he had tried to prevent the issuance of the body attachment, but no one in the office of Presiding Judge Robert Wenke knew anything about the hand-delivered (by Paul Le Mat) letter Christian had written spelling out why he wouldn't testify. As for the trial, it was not going well and high-powered help was needed. "Do you think Vince Bugliosi would be interested in stepping in?" Wayland asked.

"You better hope so," Christian replied. "He's the only guy in the country who *might* be able to handle it."

Christian called Bugliosi and set up an appointment with him in the lawyer's Beverly Hills office on July 24, 1975. (The trial had been in progress since July 2.) Christian had met the former prosecutor for the first time in late 1972, when they had a brief chance to discuss the RFK case in mostly theoretical terms. The lawyer had no knowledge of either "The Walking Bible" or the current lawsuit aspects when the July 24th meeting (also attended by Mike Wayland) took place.

It was a pressure situation, all right. The lawsuit was scheduled to terminate by Judge Crickard's edict the following Monday, just two court days later. Christian realized that he was asking Bugliosi to undertake a "Mission Impossible," where the odds were as stacked against him as was the attitude of the court against the RFK issue. The counsel was merely being asked to assume the responsibility of establishing "The Walking Bible's" "involvement" in the assassination of Robert Kennedy, the crux of KCOP's hastily prepared defense.

Christian ended the session by giving Bugliosi a rundown on the day's events, including the heavy scene in Brentwood. "Something's very wrong here," Bugliosi said. "I never heard of a mere witness being pursued in a civil case like this. You are not a defendant, and that's the only justification for any court to turn on this kind of heat." The lawyer had heard enough of the strange events in and out of the courtroom to be intrigued with the prospect of entering the case. He would meet with Wayland the following day.

While the formalities for Bugliosi's association with the defense were being worked out, Mike Wayland got a chance to cross-examine Jerry Owen. Using the transcript of Turner's 1968 interview with Owen as a kind of road map, he led the preacher through the twists and turns of his own hitchhiker story, eliciting a number of variations on the original theme. For instance, Owen now claimed that Sirhan "showed me a hundred-dollar bill" after returning from seeing his "friend in the kitchen" of the hotel, which conflicted with his original statement that it was not until that midnight that Sirhan first tendered the $100 down payment. And the transcript showed Owen saying that Sirhan "told me that he was an exercise boy at a race track, and talked how he loved horses, and he quickly wanted to know if I had a ranch where he could get a job," but when Wayland posed these exact words to him, Owen, unaware that the lawyer was reading from a transcript, objected that they were only partially correct. "He didn't have a job at a race track," the preacher amended. "He had a job at a ranch in Corona. He needed a pickup horse where he could get a good job." It was some time before Owen realized he was being trapped by his own words, a revealing lapse for a man who claimed to recall the entire Bible. "Could I see it?" he asked, pointing at the transcript. "Not at this time," Crickard ruled.

During the cross-examination Wayland, frustrated by the judge's repeated interference on grounds of "undue consumption of time," breached his understanding with Christian by moving into the forbidden area of Bill Powers and the cowboys. He began innocuously enough, asking Owen if he had bought the pickup truck from a "Bill Parker," which the preacher readily acknowledged despite the variation on the name. But then the attorney pressed his advantage: "In truth and fact, sir, on the Monday before the assassination, on Monday the 3rd of June 1968, you were together with Mr. Sirhan at a place called Wild Bill's Stables in Santa Ana?"

"That is an untruth!" The preacher was almost shouting.

"Wild Bill's Stables in Santa Ana is just down the Santa Ana River from your more-or-less Santa Ana mini-ranch?"

"I don't know where Wild Bill's Stable is, I never heard of it before." Owen was obviously alarmed that this sensitive area had been broached.

When Wayland read the dailies to Christian over the phone that night he heard a low whistle at the other end of the line followed by a burst of expletives. The cat was out of the bag. Weatherly had already been shot at. Now Powers and the other cowboys could be in danger. Shaken by the implications of his misstep, Wayland gave Christian blanket authority to hire a bodyguard for the men.

By the next day the details of Bugliosi's entrance into the case had been settled. In his formal letter of acceptance the ex-prosecutor declared that he was aware of the "enormous implications of the case," and that when he had run for DA in 1972* "it was common knowledge that had I been elected, I intended to reopen the investigation of the Kennedy assassination. I am still of the same frame of mind." Bugliosi had taken that position after having spoken to criminalist Bill Harper.

Vincent T. Bugliosi was born August 18, 1934, in the northern Minnesota town of Hibbing, the son of Italian immigrants. His father owned a grocery store and later became a railroad conductor. In a land that wags quip has only two seasons, winter and the Fourth of July, young Bugliosi took up tennis. He edged up the ladder to become state champion, whereupon his proud father took him to Los Angeles, where the competition was hotter and the season endless. There the quick, slender youngster proved himself by winning the area high school championship, and he went off to the University of Miami on a tennis scholarship. He returned to Los Angeles and the UCLA law school, graduating in 1964 as class president.

Hired out of law school as a deputy district attorney, he wasted little time in becoming the top trial lawyer in the staff of 450. Out

* In that race Bugliosi, outspent nearly four to one, taking on an incumbent, Joseph Busch, who had the support of very nearly the entire "Establishment" of Los Angeles County, had nonetheless polled just over 50 percent of the vote on the day of the election and was overcome on absentee ballots which had been submitted two weeks earlier. Out of close to 3 million votes, Bugliosi lost by one quarter of one percent. There were those who suspected fraud in the tabulation of the absentee ballots.

of 106 felony jury trials he lost only one, which is believed to be the highest conviction rate in the history of the DA's office. The feat earned him selection as the model prosecutor in a TV series produced by Jack Webb in which he was portrayed by Robert Conrad while he served as technical adviser. Yet he was just as satisfied with those cases in which he moved for dismissal after going out into the field and digging up evidence favorable to the accused. "For far too many years the stereotyped image of the prosecutor has been either that of a right-wing, law-and-order type intent on winning convictions at any cost," he wrote in *Helter Skelter*, "or a stumbling bumbling Hamilton Burger [the fictional DA in the *Perry Mason* series], forever trying innocent people, who, fortunately, are saved at the last possible moment by the foxy maneuverings of a Perry Mason."

Harry Weiss, who has the largest criminal law practice in Los Angeles, told *Los Angeles Magazine* in November of 1972: "I've seen all the great trial lawyers of the last thirty years. None of them are in Vince's class."

Former Governor Edmund G. "Pat" Brown (the current governor's father) recommended Bugliosi as the Watergate Special Prosecutor, saying, "There is no finer and fairer prosecutor in the land than Vince Bugliosi."

However, Bugliosi's skill as trial lawyer is not limited to that of a prosecutor. Since he entered private practice, his record shows that if a defendant is fortunate enough to get him interested in his case, he is almost assured of an acquittal.

As Jonn Christian briefed Bugliosi on the contents of our investigative file, Bugliosi shaped his plan of attack. "He's the guy we have to find and get to testify," he said of Bill Powers. The same was true for Powers' former stablehands, Johnny Beckley and Chris Weatherly, whose potential testimony would tend to corroborate Powers, and perhaps plow new ground. Concurrently, Bugliosi subpoenaed LAPD records and personnel to back up the cowboys' testimony and, we hoped, shed additional light on the case.

We calculated that if the cowboys could be persuaded to testify and the police veil of secrecy ripped away, the trial might be forced to a sudden and explosive halt. Faced with probable cause to believe that a conspiracy had in fact taken place, Judge Crickard would be compelled to refer the matter to a criminal grand jury or federal prosecutive authorities.

Private detective Dan Prop located Weatherly in Chino and served him with a subpoena, but the young man promptly disappeared for the duration of the trial in the apparent belief that one brush with a bullet was more than enough. Bugliosi decided that he himself should make the overture to Powers and try to talk him into appearing voluntarily. We learned that after closing Wild Bill's Stables, Powers had moved to the tiny town of Murietta in the remote Santa Ana Mountains. Christian, Jim Rose and Paul Le Mat accompanied Bugliosi on the two-hour pre-dawn drive the next day, Saturday, playing the tapes of our 1969 interviews with the cowboy to acquaint Bugliosi with his potential testimony.

Powers wasn't home. Bugliosi was due to make his courtroom debut in the case on Monday. Unable to wait any longer, he decided to return to Beverly Hills to begin his trial preparation in what little time was left. The next day Bugliosi finally reached Powers by telephone and explained the situation.

Powers was opposed to testifying, but Bugliosi managed to convince him to come in and at least "talk it over." Punctually at seven o'clock on Monday morning Powers appeared at the attorney's office, showing the effects of a sleepless night. Bugliosi broke the ice by handing him a subpoena and telling him to tear it up if he wished. Powers responded to this candor. "My lady thinks you're a great man, and I want to help you, I really do," he said. Together they phoned Johnny Beckley at his residence in Los Alamitos and it seemed to be settled: Powers would drive down and bring his former employee back for a talk. Still, as far as his own testimony was concerned, he would have to think it over. It was nine o'clock and Bugliosi had to leave for court. He autographed a copy of *Helter Skelter* for the Powers family. The cowboy left for Murietta and some hard thinking.

16

Vincent Bugliosi's Affirmative Defense

INTRODUCED BY MIKE WAYLAND AS KCOP'S NEW ASSOCIATE counsel, Vince Bugliosi rose to address the court. "Your Honor," he led off, "as I understand it—I am just new on the case—one of the allegations by the plaintiff is that Mr. Hopkins accused Mr. Owen of somehow being involved in Senator Kennedy's assassination."

Bugliosi thought Judge Crickard looked surprised and curious that he was taking part in the trial.

"I believe then that it is an affirmative defense on our part," Bugliosi went on, "to prove the truthfulness of that charge."

The lawyer told Crickard that he had just located a "key witness" who might be able to offer relevant testimony on the issue of Owen's possible involvement in the RFK case. He asked the judge not to conclude the lawsuit that afternoon (as previously threatened) —but to put it over until the following day. The judge reluctantly consented to Bugliosi's request.

Owen and his attorneys looked stunned. Arthur Evry stammered, "Your Honor, as your Honor knows, we are caught somewhat by surprise. This is the first I have heard of any indication that there was some truth in defendant's case to the allegation that he was"—Evry paused, seemingly unable to utter the word "assassination"—"Mr. Owen was criminally involved."

Bugliosi noted the reaction of Crickard, before whom he was appearing for the first time. The judge was frowning, obviously displeased that the assassination was being made a full-blown issue in his courtroom. He was an establishment judge, Bugliosi estimated, who starts off with the idea that anything bearing the stamp of government is ipso facto valid.

That estimation was immediately put to the test. Included in the batch of subpoenas issued by the defense was one calling on the LAPD to produce all records, documents and tape recordings concerning their Owen investigation. In response, Officer Ronald L. Schaffer of the Records Identification Division showed up. After being sworn in, Schaffer declined to produce any material, saying that his superior had instructed him to invoke Section 1040 of the California Evidence Code that declares certain police records "to be considered confidential information unless ordered released to the parties by a magistrate of this state."

Wayland argued that the LAPD material was highly relevant to the defense because "an issue has been drawn" as to Owen's criminal implication in the assassination. Skirting the point, Crickard asked rhetorically, "Well, if Mr. Owen was charged with some public crime, that would be a matter of public record that is easily available to any citizen, isn't that correct? . . . So, Mr. Wayland, if you want to find out if Mr. Owen has been charged with a public crime in the State of California, all you have to do is walk over there a couple or three blocks."

The judge was sarcastically alluding to the County Clerk's office, where records of criminal filings are maintained. Bugliosi's suspicion of Crickard's blind faith in agencies of government was now confirmed.

Bugliosi observed that the LAPD claim of privilege should not be allowed unless, in the language of the code, "it would be against the public interest because there is a necessity for preserving the confidentiality of the information that outweighs the necessity for disclosure in the interests of justice." He argued that the public interest far outweighed any need for secrecy. "I think the court can take judicial notice," he said, "that the whole tone, the whole tenor in this country at this particular moment is that there is a tremendous distrust, there is a tremendous suspicion, there is a tremendous skepticism about whether or not people like Oswald and Sirhan acted alone, and many, many people, many substantial people—I am not talking about conspiracy buffs who see a conspiracy behind every tree—many, many substantial people feel that Sirhan did not act alone, that he did act in concert."

Crickard remained impassive. Bugliosi pressed on, saying that the defense was in a position to offer circumstantial evidence "which would be extremely incriminating to Mr. Owen. . . . No one is going to say that they saw Mr. Owen pull the trigger and shoot Senator Kennedy. We intend to offer evidence from which a very strong inference could be drawn that possibly Mr. Owen was a co-conspirator in this case." Bugliosi pointed out that Owen had voluntarily injected himself into the investigation by reporting the hitchhiker story to the police. "Now, all we want to do is take a look at these [LAPD] reports. Just because the LAPD concluded that Mr. Owen was not involved in the Kennedy assassination doesn't mean anything to me personally, and it shouldn't mean anything to the court. The LAPD is not the trier of fact."

Why were the police so determined to keep secret records they had deemed to be meaningless? "I have to say," Bugliosi commented, "as a prosecutor for eight years I find it extremely strange that the LAPD would not want this information at this point to be public. I find it very strange indeed. If Owen was not involved, as LAPD, I assume, has concluded, there is no conceivable reason under the moon why they shouldn't permit us to look at those records." Officer Schaffer was ordered by Crickard to fetch them immediately.

Bugliosi was understandably leery of police conclusions. As a deputy DA he had worked closely with the LAPD on major cases and was keenly aware of how inept this self-promoting agency could be. The Manson Family case, which like the Kennedy case called for a sophisticated investigation, provided numerous illustrations of police bumbling. In *Helter Skelter* Bugliosi described how a gun later determined to have been used by Manson's followers in the Tate murders was found three weeks after the crime by a citizen living not far from the scene, but the patrolman who responded to his call handled the weapon with both hands, obliterating any chance for developing fingerprints. Then the gun was filed away and forgotten in the property room of the Valley Services Division of the LAPD while headquarters carried out a nationwide search for it. It was three and a half months before the police connected the languishing gun with the case. This embarrassment was compounded by the fact that a television crew, following the same clues the police had, found bloodied clothing discarded by the killers.*

In *Helter Skelter* Bugliosi described how complacent LAPD detectives dragged their feet in the Manson case. Even after three months of police investigation the prosecution case was so evidentially weak that Bugliosi had to take charge personally; he gave the detectives a long list of overlooked leads to pursue. Hearing nothing for three more weeks, he summoned the detectives and found, to his utter dismay, that only one of the leads had been covered.† To make matters worse, there was internal rivalry between the unimaginative senior detectives assigned to the Tate investigation and their ambitious younger colleagues handling the LaBianca murders, and for a long time this intramural friction prevented the LAPD from linking the two cases. The police even failed to recognize that the inscription "Pigs" scrawled in gore at

* Bugliosi, *op. cit.*, pp. 96–97, 265, 740.
† *Ibid.*, p. 257.

both murder scenes was part of the link. And they failed to perceive Charles Manson's far-out philosophy* as a motive for what on the surface was senseless random killings. As one LAPD sleuth scoffed when a witness divulged Manson's designs, "Ah, Charlie's a madman; we're not interested in all that."†

To cap this flawed performance, Chief Edward M. Davis staged a press conference in response to public pressures to announce that the Tate-LaBianca murders were solved.‡ But there was not nearly enough backup evidence at the time to take the case to court, and the chief's premature grandstanding almost cost a successful prosecution. Yet Bugliosi sensed that Judge Crickard believed the fictional image of LAPD efficiency as portrayed in *Dragnet, Adam-12* and *The New Centurions*.

When Officer Schaffer returned with an LAPD file marked OWEN, JERRY, Judge Crickard decided that he himself would examine the investigative report to determine whether it was relevant. After a recess for this purpose he ruled that "there would be no relevant information disclosed by making the record public." Bugliosi said he was "shocked by the court's ruling on this. I am almost at a loss for words, which doesn't happen too often to me. To say that the public interest is against disclosure—"

The judge interrupted to repeat his opinion that the report was irrelevant. After further verbal sparring, the attorney began to suspect that what Crickard had read was not what the subpoena called for. Bugliosi asked to look at the index, which revealed that the report was not about Owen and the RFK case, after all.

Reading from the subpoena served on the department, Bugliosi

---

* "Helter Skelter" was Manson's term for his prediction that the blacks would rise and take over America, and practically the only whites who would survive would be those with the foresight to set up enclaves in remote areas. Manson tried to set this apocalypse in motion by killing monied whites and scrawling the word "Pigs" at the scene to suggest falsely that blacks were responsible. By his racist reckoning, the Manson Family would afterward be needed by the inferior blacks to lead the way out of chaos into a new order.

† *Ibid.*, p. 335.

‡ Davis was acting Chief of Police on the night of the RFK assassination. Headquartered at Rampart Station as "Watch Commander," he was still on duty after midnight—an unusually lengthy period for such a high-level LAPD official.

stressed that Schaffer was supposed to have brought the "entire file on plaintiff, that is, Mr. Owen, including the original tape recording and transcript of Owen's June 5, 1968, story of the Los Angeles Police Department University Station officers and including the tapes and transcripts of all other interviews made with Owen up to and including the July 3, 1968, one in San Francisco at the George T. Davis office, together with polygraph tests." That was certainly specific, but Schaffer's excuse was that he "never had the birth date of Mr. Owen."

It was as if the FBI couldn't find its Lindbergh kidnap file because it didn't have the baby's birth date. Crickard instructed Schaffer to return to headquarters with Owen's vital statistics and search for the specified material. When it was located, he was to bring it to court at once.

THAT NIGHT BUGLIOSI CALLED BILL POWERS, TRYING TO CONVINCE him to testify. But Powers was still uncertain and not at all encouraged by the fact that Johnny Beckley had vanished. Powers had gone to Beckley's residence that day as had been arranged, but found only an abandoned girl friend, who ruefully explained, "He don't want to talk about nothing." But Powers agreed once again to meet Bugliosi the first thing in the morning.

Again he showed up at seven, bleary-eyed from another restless night. For over two hours Bugliosi reasoned and cajoled, pointing out that once his testimony was in the record, any purpose in silencing him or harming his family would be gone. But it was not until the attorney waved the flag—"Don't do it for me, do it for the good of the country!"—that Powers yielded. As they were about to enter the courtroom Powers grabbed Bugliosi's arm and exacted a promise: "Be my lawyer for my estate if anything happens to me. Just make sure no shyster lawyers take everything I've put away for my son."

Powers was not put on the stand immediately, however, for Officer Schaffer had returned from his quest for the Owen material. Putting him on the stand, Bugliosi half-smiled and inquired, "You were successful?"

"No, sir, I wasn't," the policeman answered. "We looked

through all the records we could possibly go through all afternoon and we were unable to locate any such records, documents or tapes . . ."

"It is your testimony that you could find no records at the LAPD pertaining to one Jerry Owen?"

"No, sir, unless I had a DR number or something. More information possibly, like I say a DR number, an arrest booking number or something to go on."

Bugliosi frowned in disgust. Crickard said nothing. The witness was excused.

Now Bill Powers was called to the stand. Bugliosi led him through the scenes at Wild Bill's Stables: how in early 1968 Owen boarded two of his horses there; how Owen objected to Johnny Beckley's handling of his horses and threatened to bring in someone from a race track named "Sirhan" to handle them properly; how Owen, hitherto short of funds, drove up in a Lincoln Continental a day or so before the RFK shooting and flashed a thick roll of $1,000 bills; and how Powers was introduced to a young man in the back seat who bore a "likely resemblance" to Sirhan. This was Powers' skeletal story, and Bugliosi now began to expand on it to the court.

Q. This gentleman, this young gentleman who was in the back seat of Mr. Owen's Lincoln shortly before the assassination, who you testified resembled Sirhan, did you ever see that man prior to that time in Mr. Owen's home?

A. There is a possibility that I seen him there once before or maybe twice before when I was there, yes.

Q. When was that?

A. It was approximately, I would guess, ninety days before the assassination. Mr. Owen had his home for sale or wanted to sell it. Some people had a Western store there and was interested in it, and I was going to show them the home, and that's when I seen this man at Mr. Owen's house.

Q. Where was he in the house?

A. He was in the backyard.

Q. And he looked like the same individual whom you saw in the back seat of Mr. Owen's car during the thousand-dollar-bills incident?

A. That's correct.

Powers' testimony appeared to heighten Crickard's displeasure that the assassination issue had been dragged into his court, and he began to bridle at Bugliosi with increasing frequency. When the attorney asked Powers if he had ever seen the preacher with a $1,000 bill before (the answer was no), the judge interposed, "Mr. Bugliosi, we have to get to something here that bears on this case. I am going to exclude this line of questioning under Evidence Code 352, undue consumption of time." The attorney could hardly believe his ears.

BUGLIOSI: May I be heard on that?
THE COURT: Let's go to the next point.
BUGLIOSI: Well, we are talking about some things that are pretty important, your Honor, not just to this lawsuit but to Senator Kennedy's assassination.
THE COURT: They have to be relevant to this lawsuit or this isn't the place to take them up.
BUGLIOSI: May I be heard on this, your Honor? I have to state why I think it is very relevant.
THE COURT: Let's go on to the next point.

With questions about Owen's sudden prosperity cut off, Bugliosi asked Powers about the law enforcement officers who visited him following the assassination. Arthur Evry objected on grounds of relevancy, and Bugliosi asked to make an "offer of proof." Crickard hesitated, then assented, sending the witness from the courtroom.

"There is some evidence in this case," Bugliosi began, "and we will put the evidence on, which smacks of a possible cover-up. And I am not using the word cover-up because it's a word that's fashionable right now, but there are some strange things that happened in this case, and I will mention just a few of them to you.

"The most obvious thing is something that happened in this very courtroom about thirty minutes ago. An officer from the LAPD took the witness stand and testified that he could find no records on Jerry Owen over at the Los Angeles Police Department in response to a subpoena duces tecum. It is a matter of common knowledge, your Honor, that Jerry Owen was investigated by the LAPD. If the court will give us time we will present documentary evidence that he was investigated by the LAPD. A book was written by the chief detective in this case, I think the name of the book was *Special Unit Senator*, in which pages upon pages are devoted to Jerry Owen. And yet we have an officer from the LAPD taking the witness stand and searching for the records for an entire day and coming up with nothing on Jerry Owen. That's the first point."

The second point was the visit paid to Powers a day or two after the assassination by officers quizzing him about the truck he sold the preacher. It would be the first of a half-dozen interviews the police had with Powers. "They told him that it was his truck Owen was driving when he allegedly picked up Sirhan, and that Sirhan's fingerprints were found on the glove compartment and the rear window of his truck." Also, already in the trial record, Bugliosi pointed out, was Owen's testimony that when he reported his story to the University Station, the police "fingerprinted the truck and thanked me for cooperating with them." But the LAPD had never let on that fingerprints had been lifted from Owen's truck and trailer rig, let alone that they were Sirhan's. In fact, it publicly took the contradictory position that Sirhan had never been in the truck and Owen was nothing more than a "publicity seeker."

Concerning Powers, Bugliosi continued, "Now, this gentleman lives in Murietta, California, close to 100 miles from L.A., and he is a fringe witness. He did not testify before the grand jury. He did not testify at the trial. And yet law enforcement was so concerned about this man that they interrogated him six times. And the first officers that came out to see him, the ones that told him about the fingerprints, he never saw those officers again. As for the officers who came later, Bugliosi said that they told Powers they "did not want him to talk to anyone else about this case no matter who it was and to call them if anyone else came out to see him."

Bugliosi was making the point that this conduct was highly suspicious, that from his own experience he knew that law enforcement agencies ordinarily don't pay that much attention even to the star witness, much less a fringe witness. And yet here were officers going back time after time to warn Powers to keep his mouth shut. "If there was a cover-up, it's implicit in the cover-up that somebody else was involved," the attorney concluded. "And if somebody else was involved we are trying to show that maybe"—Bugliosi turned to face Owen—"maybe the gentleman seated at the counsel table now with a smile on his face, maybe it was Jerry Owen."

Bugliosi laid out the legal points establishing why Powers' testimony about the police was relevant, but Crickard would not go along with cover-up allegations. "If law enforcement people had thought that Mr. Owen was involved in any criminal activity in this connection," he admonished, "there certainly would have been some kind of prosecution within the seven years that have elapsed since that time, so—"

Bugliosi, looking incredulously at Crickard, cut in. He noted that FBI statistics showed that a substantial percentage of crimes never result in a prosecution. "The court is saying the LAPD was above board in this case and if Owen was involved he would have been prosecuted," the attorney remonstrated. Although Bugliosi had often said publicly that the LAPD was one of the least corrupt police departments in the country, he told Judge Crickard he still didn't see "how the court, sitting on the bench without the taking of *any* evidence, can categorically say that the LAPD was 100 percent above board in this case."

"I have no problem about that, Mr. Bugliosi, because that is not my job," Crickard retorted. "All I am concerned with is the civil suit of Mr. Owen against KCOP. The evidence has shown, which already has been introduced, that Mr. Compton, who was the district attorney in charge of the Sirhan investigation, knew of Mr. Owen, had checked out the story, and so far as your offer of proof in having this Mr. Powers testify to the things which you have just outlined, the objections to those things are sustained."

Crickard was referring to former Chief Deputy DA Lynn Compton, who led the prosecution of Sirhan. But Compton had not personally investigated the Owen angle—he had relied on the LAPD reports which, as we have seen, were doctored. It was a Catch-22 dilemma for Bugliosi, but Crickard's mind was made up. The question of police malfeasance was out.

Bill Powers was brought back into the courtroom. "How many times did you speak to law enforcement in this case?" Bugliosi asked him in defiance of the court's ruling. Crickard broke in,

"Mr. Bugliosi, that is exactly what we have talked about. We are not going to get into this area." With his major avenues of inquiry blocked by the judge, Bugliosi was forced to end his examination of Powers.

Arthur Evry's cross-examination was short and tame. He tested Powers' memory of some of the details of Owen's appearance at the stables driving the Lincoln, and only got him to repeat that he was not absolutely positive that it was Sirhan in the back seat.

Bugliosi asked Judge Crickard if he could cross-examine Owen. Crickard responded that he could not, because Owen had already been cross-examined by Wayland. Bugliosi said he would be satisfied to ask just "a few questions," and Crickard grudgingly consented. Bugliosi asked Owen whether he was a self-ordained minister or officially ordained.

A. I am God-ordained.
Q. Are you also called "The Walking Bible"?
A. Yes.
Q. Is that because of your memory? [The attorney was setting up a line of questioning which would show that the man with the phenomenal memory couldn't tell his hitchhiker story two times in a row without contradicting himself. But Owen would have none of it.]
A. No, not memory. It's because of the anointing of the Holy Spirit. God has given me a gift to quote the entire Bible, 31,173 verses, verbatim without looking at the Bible.
Q. . . . You have quite a memory to memorize the whole Bible, is that correct?
A. No. I flunked sandpile in kindergarten. It is a God-given gift. It is not a memory.
Q. Well, you have a gift—
A. A gift from God.
Q. Of memory?
A. Have you ever read the Bible, sir? I feel he is being sacrilegious or something. [The preacher pouted to the judge].

Bugliosi had Owen repeat his alibi for election night. No, he said, he was not at the rear entrance to the Ambassador Hotel as Sirhan had requested because he was presiding over a prayer meeting at the Calvary Baptist Church in Oxnard. The engagement had been booked several months in advance, he claimed, after he had appeared in neighboring Ventura with Maxie Rosenbloom, a former light-heavyweight champion who had embraced fundamentalist religion after retiring from the ring.* "Slapsie Maxie" Rosenbloom, who figured in one version of the hitchhiker story as the man who had enticed Owen into attending the Saints and Sinners meeting on election eve, was typical of the preacher's ecumenical choice of friends. Owen was also an old acquaintance of Paul J. "Frankie" Carbo, convicted in 1960 of an organized crime boxing extortion in Los Angeles, according to another strange exhibit Owen had entered in the suit. The exhibit was a letter from Carbo in the Marion, Illinois, federal penitentiary referring to a recent visit between the two. (Owen's choice of exhibits often seemed to be damaging to his case.)

Bugliosi, feeling very circumscribed by Crickard's imposed limitation of just a "few questions," nevertheless began a line of questioning that had been seven years too long in coming in a judicial setting:

Q. Mr. Owen, is it your belief that the man you picked up on the afternoon of June the 3rd in 1968 at 7th and Grand in downtown Los Angeles was Sirhan Sirhan; do you believe that?

A. I don't know. I don't know.

Q. Didn't you tell the police at the University Station on June the 5th, 1968, that the man you had picked up was Sirhan?

A. He looked like the picture of the man that I had in the truck, or the boy that was in the truck.

Now to "The Walking Bible's" allegedly "immaculate" memory:

Q. On the evening of June the 4th, 1968, [the night of the assassination] you spoke at the Calvary Baptist Church in Oxnard, is that correct?

A. Yes, sir.

---

* Rosenbloom retired from the ring in 1939 suffering permanent brain damage from the poundings he had taken. Like Owen, he played bit parts in movies and was type-cast as a punch-drunk fighter. In 1969 he was a partner of Owen in the R & O Boxing Stable, but shortly thereafter he entered a nursing home and died in 1976.

Q. Who invited you?

A. Mr. Compton.

Q. What's his first name?

A. *I forget.* He is the oldest delivery boy, and he is a deacon of the church. My wife has the name. She is seated outside. *I can't remember* his first name. Might be Paul. Paul Compton.

(Note: There was no Paul Compton listed in any Oxnard phone directory in 1968.)

Q. How long have you known this gentleman?

A. I only had met him about in March, I think, of 1968.

Q. Where did you meet him?

A. At a prayer meeting.

Q. In Oxnard?

A. In Oxnard.

Q. When did he invite you to this prayer meeting on the evening of June the 4th?

A. *I can't remember.* I think it was sometime in March.

Q. When did this prayer meeting start? What time in the evening?

A. 7:00 o'clock. [Owen then says both his wife and daughter were there too.]

Q. Can you give me the names of the people who were at the prayer meeting with you other than your family?

A. I can recall Mr. and Mrs. Compton, perhaps their family, and I can recall Mr. and Mrs. Rose from Ventura.

Q. Do you have a first name for the Roses?

A. I don't—*I can't recall* the first name, sir. There is others [*sic*] but *I can't recall* the others.

Q. How many people were at that prayer meeting, approximately?

A. Oh, just a handful.

Q. When you say handful, you mean five or ten?

A. No, that's an expression. There could be between—it is maybe between 5 and 18 people.

Bugliosi went for the heart of Owen's fading alibi with the kind of interrogation he was noted for:

Q. Isn't it a fact, sir, that on the evening of June the 4th, 1968, that church was shut down and hadn't been open for the previous several months?

A. That is not a fact. That's a *different* Calvary Church you are talking about.

Q. The church that *you* are talking about, can you give me an *exact* location on it?

A. *No*, but I will even take you up there and introduce you to the people.

(The court:) Can you give him an exact location?

A. I can't, your Honor. I travel so much.

(The court:) Okay.

Q. How long were the services?

A. The prayer meeting, oh, it wouldn't be over an hour.

Q. Where did you go after that?

A. I went to the home, I stayed at some people's house. *I can't recall* their name.

Q. How did you end up in their home?

A. They are friends. As an evangelist, people invite you to their home to stay. They cook for you, they give you food.

Q. You stayed at their home on the evening of June the 4th, you slept at their home?

A. Slept at their home, and from their home phoned my wife that night.

Q. You can't give me any names for these people?

A. You want to call my wife in? She will tell you.

(The court:) You don't know?

A. I can't remember thousands and thousands of people's names.

(The court:) Thank you.

Q. Do you know where the gentleman at whose home you stayed works?

A. His—*no, I don't*. I think he works for the city, and I think his wife works for one of the department stores. We'll bring my wife in, and she has them all, the names written down.

Q. Was he at the prayer meeting that night?

A. . . . *I can't remember exactly*.

Q. Could this church be located at 601 South F Street?

A. *I don't know*, sir.

Q. Does that ring a bell?

A. *I don't know*, sir.

Q. Was this church, the Calvary Baptist Church, affiliated with the American Council of Christian Churches?

A. No, it wasn't. It was independent, sir. [The sign out front of the F Street church read: "A Truly Independent Baptist Church."]

Q. Was it affiliated with the 20th Century Reformation Hour Church?

A. No, that's McIntire. No.

Q. Do you know Carl McIntire?

A. Oh, yes. I have known him for years, sir. I have held meetings in his church back here.*

Dr. Carl McIntire was the founder of the ACCC, a New Jersey preacher who feuded with the National Council of Christian Churches, the mainstream group, because of its supposed drift into liberalism. McIntire, a forceful speaker, built his rival ACCC into one of the most potent components of the religious right. His 20th Century Reformation Hour broadcast over a network of 636 small stations, and pulled in an annual gross of $3 million. McIntire zeroed in on the Roman Catholic Church, once branding it "the harlot church and bride of the anti-Christ," and when John Kennedy and Billy Graham played golf together, McIntire criticized the evangelist for associating with "persons whose fidelity to something other than the scriptures is evident."

By 1968 McIntire was embroiled in a bitter dispute with his own ACCC hierarchy, who wished to divorce themselves from his increasingly radical politics.

Q. Do you know a Reverend Medcalf?

A. No.

Q. Have you heard that name?

A. No, not to my knowledge. If I see the gentleman, I might know him.

Moving on to the incident at Wild Bill's Stables—Owen now acknowledged that he had been there, though earlier he said that he had never heard of the stables—Bugliosi got Owen to admit that he did in fact have a roll of $1,000 bills on him that day, albeit a smaller one than Powers had described.

---

* In early 1977, Christian interviewed McIntire employee Edgar Eugene Bradley, who said that neither he nor McIntire had ever known Owen under any circumstances. He also denied that the Calvary Baptist Church in Oxnard was ever associated with the ACCC.

Q. These $1,000 bills, how many did you have?

A. I think maybe at that time I had eleven or twelve because I just come back from up north with some good donations, getting ready to build up to go on television.

Q. You say donations. People gave you $1,000 bills?

A. Yes, many times, sir. I have had ten thousand dollars given to me at one time by people.

Q. In $1,000 bills?

A. I had ten $1,000 bills given to me, sir.

Bugliosi couldn't imagine bills of that denomination, which were uncommon, being dropped in the collection box of an itinerant preacher. "Do you know who these people were that gave you $1,000 bills?" he challenged. Owen seemed to sense that he was being led into a trap, and switched his story. The northern windfall had been reaped in smaller-denomination bills, and he had taken them to a bank and turned them in for ten, eleven or twelve $1,000 bills. Owen testified that he converted the smaller bills into $1,000 bills at "a Chinese bank in San Francisco."

Q. Do you have any documentary evidence to support this? Did you sign your name or anything?

A. *I don't remember.*

When Bugliosi asked him why he carried around $1,000 bills, Owen said that it expedited things. "When you go into a city to rent big auditoriums and buy television time," he explained, "they don't want out-of-state checks, but if you have the cash there you can deal." When Bugliosi raised the point that it might be more practical to deal in $100 bills, Crickard cut off the questioning as "undue consumption of time."

But Bugliosi did not let the story of a donations bonanza just before the assassination go unchallenged. Fifteen months earlier Owen had answered a compulsory interrogatory submitted by KCOP's lawyers that asked about his income. In 1965, he said, he had no income and borrowed from his wife's inheritance in the amount of $5,000. In 1966 he gave free pony rides to kids in Huntington Beach and had "No salary or income." Ditto 1967. In 1968 he "Lived off wife's tax free inheritance. Preached three weeks at Embassy Auditorium for Wings of Healing." The stint earned him $1,000 he said, not enough to file a tax return. This jibed with Powers' observation that Owen appeared chronically broke, even borrowing hay, until the sudden affluence just prior to the assassination.

Referring to the large roll of $1,000 bills that Owen admittedly displayed at the stables, Bugliosi demanded, "How come this was not declared on your income tax?"

Owen replied, "Gifts, sir. Gifts for the Lord."

Bugliosi next brought up Owen's encounter with Powers at the Hilton Hay Company in Santa Ana five months after the assassination. Owen said he vaguely remembered it. He remembered commenting about Sirhan, "Of all the thousands of millions of people in Southern California, a guy like that would have to jump in my pickup truck." But he denied having mentioned Sirhan to Powers before the assassination.

Q. Did you ever ask Mr. Powers if the police had asked him about Sirhan?
A. No, because I'm the one that told the police when they questioned me and I gave all the information.
Q. So your testimony is that you did not ask Mr. Powers?
A. I don't believe. I might have later on when I came to move when we sold the house. I might have bumped into him—yes, because he came one day and I told him if his friend bought the house I would give him a thousand dollars extra commission, and he came to the house, and I believe at my house . . . he told me the police had been there and I said—that's right, because I had to give every place I had been, names of people and so forth. I believe I did there, yes, but at my home, not at the hay place. [Owen had at least confirmed the conversations with Bill Powers.]

Bugliosi probed the threats Owen said he received because of his putative horse deal with Sirhan. As he had told the story, he had given his calling card to Sirhan's emissary in the purchase. The card was imprinted with "Shepherd of the Hills"—another of his religious trade names—and unlisted telephone number.

Q. What type of threats were these? What did the people say?

A. Whoever was phoning just said, "Are you the Shepherd of the Hills? Keep your mouth shut about the horse deal!" That's all. Hang up. Another threat was, "You want your head blown off, your family, your children? Don't go to the police."*

Q. You still have a bodyguard?

A. No. Yes, I have. God's my bodyguard, the greatest. He takes care of me. Proverbs 18 and 10, "The name of the Lord is a strong—" [Crickard interrupted, ruling the answer unresponsive.]

Under Bugliosi's questioning Owen did not deny the events Powers had testified to, but he tried to explain them away. His appearance at the stables in the Lincoln Continental was not a day or two before the assassination, but the previous March. The luxurious automobile was a gift from one of his religious flock. And the youth in the back seat was not Sirhan but Johnny Gray's son, Jackie Gray. Gray, the black ex-boxer who was sitting in the front passenger seat, had a number of sons. "He has some boys that look like they're mulattos or Creoles," Owen said. This was how Jackie Gray could have been mistaken for Sirhan.

Owen was now shifting gears so fast that he confused himself. When Bugliosi asked if he was aware that the police at the University Station "dusted the inside of the truck for fingerprints," he blurted out, "No!" One of his attorneys, David Lloyd, caught the *faux pas* and interrupted, "Objection! Asked and answered." Several days before under questioning by Wayland, Owen had testified that the police had not only dusted the truck for fingerprints but even got black powder on the horse in the trailer.

As if dictated by a seasoned Hollywood scriptwriter, the scenario was much in need of a little comic relief at this point, and Mike Wayland produced same when he called Oral K. "Buck" Weaver to the stand. Like Jerry Owen, Weaver had been a friend of heavyweight champion Max Baer for a good many years; in fact, the bearish Weaver had fought Baer in Oakland in 1929, then become good friends with him ever since 1932. Wayland asked Weaver about an incident that took place in Los Angeles in 1958,

* Owen's wife confirmed these calls.

when Baer had come into town from his home in Sacramento and Owen was with him.* Weaver recalled one aspect of the initial meeting with Owen as follows: "I am not a religious man, but Owen made a remark to me that I never forgot: 'When I get broke I hold a couple of meetings a night and I take a couple of hundred dollars off the suckers.' "

Owen looked as if he wanted to jump into the ring with Weaver. When his lawyers put him on the stand to rebut this testimony, he managed to make matters worse, and slightly hilarious; lawyer David Lloyd asked, "Do you recall who was present during the conversation [with Weaver]?" (Which took place at the Kipling Hotel in Los Angeles.)

A. Yes.
Q. Who?
A. Primo Carnera, Max Baer, I believe Humphrey Bogart and George Raft.
Q. Do you recall a comment made about evangelists taking money from suckers being made [sic]?
A. Yes.
Q. Would you relate to the court that conversation?
A. Yes, Buck Weaver came in and said that he had just seen a movie and wanted to know if I knew Elmer Gantry [sic], and I said, "That was before my time, Buck! What's it all about?"

He said, "I just saw a picture and he's attending a meeting with a lady evangelist, and Elmer Gantry was getting drunk, and this girl was trying to convert him, and they would go behind the platform and he would say, 'Now it's my turn to go out and get a few hundred dollars from those suckers out there! Watch me go get it!' "

And Buck Weaver said to me, "I'm of a different religion, Curly." And he said, "Do you do that?!"

And I says, "No, the only ones that do that, Buck, would be men that are not called of God. A real Christian wouldn't do a thing like that!"

The reality here was that Humphrey Bogart had died the year before (1957) and the Academy Award-winning motion picture

* Ironically, Christian had known Baer in 1956 when they co-hosted a broadcast that originated from the newly built Sacramento Inn.

Elmer Gantry (starring Jean Simmons and Burt Lancaster) wouldn't even be made until two years hence (1960).

"DO YOU KNOW ARTHUR BREMER'S SISTER?" BUGLIOSI ASKED OWEN. Arthur Bremer was the young man who had gunned down Alabama Governor George C. Wallace in Maryland on May 15, 1972, thus effectively removing him from the presidential race.* In fact, Bremer's elder sister had been standing by to testify for Owen —until Mike Wayland told the court that he intended to ask questions about this relationship. She was flown out of town that same night. Her name was Gail Aiken, and she had previously furnished a signed statement saying that she happened to be shopping in Ohrbach's department store when the shoplifting incident occurred. "There was a small colored lady standing near me," Aiken said, "and she stated, 'I know that man, he's "The Walking Bible" and he is on TV every Sunday, Channel 13, at 12:30.' I was curious and watched the program. . . . It astounded me how this man could quote the Bible and it was a very good program. . . . I sent in a donation for one of the records of the Gospel Lads." When the program was canceled, Aiken received one of Owen's "S.O.S." letters asking viewers to protest to KCOP. When she called the station, she reputedly was told "that Jerry Owen was a thief, an arsonist, and involved in the Sirhan Sirhan matter."

Actually, we'd discovered that Gail Aiken had known Owen for some time and undoubtedly accompanied him to the store. She had been a secretary to his college-instructor brother since 1966, and was one of his most devoted religious followers. Immediately following the Wallace shooting, Owen somehow felt compelled to report his association with Aiken in an innocent context, just as he had with Sirhan, and, again, he didn't go to the news media. However, instead of going to the police this time, he phoned newsman Baxter Ward's campaign headquarters (Ward was then running

* At the time of the shooting, the polls showed that Wallace, if he ran in the November election as an independent or third-party candidate, would siphon off enough votes from Richard Nixon to enable any top Democratic candidate to pose a serious threat.

for his supervisorial post) and excitedly insisted upon meeting with the candidate. An appointment was set for the next day, but Owen failed to show up.

Due to some five years of contact with us, Owen's name was familiar to Ward. We had informed him of the Weatherly Report and our follow-up investigation, and he had interviewed Weatherly with violent results. Quite naturally, Ward wondered what Owen wanted, but his curiosity went unsatisfied for two years. Then, on May 20, 1974, one week after his "second gun" hearing before the Board of Supervisors, Owen called again. He said he had "new evidence" in the RFK case. Ward invited him to come right over, and to the supervisor's surprise, this time he showed.

Owen settled into a padded chair in Ward's wood-paneled office in the county Administration Hall—and okayed the tape recording of this belated get-together. He was wearing a full beard —for a role in a Biblical movie, he explained.* After first insisting to Ward that he hadn't called right after the Wallace shooting, he leaned forward sheepishly and in a low voice confided, "Do you realize that the girl who worked for my brother at Trade Tech College was the sister to the fella who shot Wallace?"

"No!" Ward gasped.

". . . and she just came to me, and I helped her get an airplane ticket to go to Florida. They've been drivin' her crazy! Poor little thing. She was my brother's secretary at Trade Tech for eight years." The police and FBI had hounded her, Owen said, and she came to him "as a minister" for help. But he quickly revealed that there was more to it when he mentioned her promised return from her home in Miami to testify at his trial against KCOP and Ohrbach's.

"Unbelievable!" Ward had commented when he informed Christian about Owen's disclosure. "Owen showing up in the background of the Wallace shooting is just too much to ask of coincidence!"

Now, with Bugliosi asking him if he knew Arthur Bremer's sister, Owen suddenly tried to disown Aiken as thoroughly as he dared. "I know a Gail Aiken," he conceded. "I was told that is

---

* Owen claimed he was about to co-star in a feature motion picture with Robert Mitchum about the life of Moses—which, he said, was to be filmed in South Africa.

his sister, but I don't know Arthur Bremer and I didn't know a sister by the name of Bremer, but I know Gail Aiken who I was informed when this trial started that she had a brother that was three years old when she left him and hasn't seen him since." Owen's sworn testimony clashed with what he had told Ward—on tape.

Owen had presumably brought Aiken from Miami in the expectation that no one would identify her as Bremer's sister. But why was that connection now an embarrassment when he had volunteered it to Ward the year before? All we knew was that coincidence was being stretched to the breaking point. Two months before Owen's meeting with Ward, Bill Turner had interviewed the patriarch of the Bremer family in Milwaukee. William Bremer, Sr., was a blue-collar worker who favored Hubert Humphrey, and he seemed completely baffled by his son's act. He said that his elder daughter Gail had left home at a fairly early age, as had her brother William Bremer, Jr., who after service in the Army paratroops had settled in the Miami area.*

When Owen stepped down from the stand, he understandably looked shaken.†

---

* On August 25, 1973, William Bremer, Jr., was sentenced to eighteen months in jail and ordered to make restitution in a weight-reducing swindle in which he took $36,000 in advance fees. Bremer was represented by attorney Ellis Rubin, who had long represented CIA-sponsored anti-Castro activists and was attorney for the Miami Four (Frank Sturgis, Bernard Barker, Eugenio Martinez and Virgilio Gonzalez) in the Watergate break-in.

† In the October 1972 edition of the John Birch Society's *American Opinion*, in an article (by Arnold Stang) titled "The Communist Plot to Kill George Wallace," it was related that the FBI had interviewed Earl S. Nunnery, "boss of the Milwaukee station of Chesapeake & Ohio Ferry" where Arthur Bremer was (according to Nunnery) seen with a mystery man just before he shot Governor Wallace. The description intrigued us instantly: "With him was an older man over six feet tall . . . He was well-dressed, and he seemed to be the boss of whatever he and Bremer were involved in. Nunnery characterized the mystery man as a 'former athlete and political science teacher, who flopped at both.' " The Bircher identified a left-winger named Dennis Kushman as the mystery man, who had been found murdered in Canada under mysterious circumstances shortly after the alleged encounter with Arthur Bremer.

During the pretrial depositions, whenever Owen would mention Ms. Aiken's name he would stay away from the Bremer tie-in completely. But

There was one other exchange between Owen and Ward at that curious 1974 session that bears repeating here. It dealt with Sirhan's alleged intentions vis-à-vis the attempt to get Owen to appear with trailered horse outside the Ambassador Hotel just before the shooting began. "Was it his hope to get out in the horse van?" probed the supervisor. Owen's response was intriguing indeed:

I don't know! Wh-why would he want a horse there at eleven? I don't know. And all I know from what I've had people tell me that . . . Mr. Kennedy was s'posed to make his appearance at eleven [true], and he was late and he didn't make it until after midnight. Now . . . if I take you out and show you where he . . . wanted me to park . . . See, you come out of the kitchen and out by [a parking lot]. He could jump right in a horse trailer and tell me to drive. . . . Who's gonna stop an old farmer with a horse trailer?

Ward played Owen's game and whispered an encouraging "Yeah" as the peripatetic preacher opened up further.

I have a walk-in trailer. He could open the door and walk in. He could jump right in these beside a horse . . . and maybe have me deliver it out in the country—and BOOM! Put a bullet in me, and there they'd find the horses in the trailer. . . .

Bugliosi recalled Bill Powers to rebut portions of Owen's testimony. The first point was Owen's contention that the incident in which he flashed the roll of $1,000 bills took place in March, not June.

Q. Are you sure it was June of '68 or could it have been March?
A. There is no way at all that it could have been March because I know for a fact, I was going to Big Bear [a mountain resort northeast of Los Angeles] with horses when school got out and school gets out sometime in there, and I was going to take horses up there when

---

he did say that he had once contacted her at the Milwaukee YWCA in 1969, which meant she had gone "home" after leaving "at an early age." Was it possible that she failed to make contact with *anyone* in her family?

this happened, and so I know it wasn't in March. I mean I know for a fact that it definitely was not.

Q. Is there any other reason you feel it took place very shortly before the assassination?

A. I bought a new Chevrolet truck from Guarantee Chevrolet, and that was one reason I got rid of this other truck [that was sold to Owen]. And I remember at the time I was putting the stock rack on the truck to start transporting horses to Big Bear, so I know it was right in that time. It wasn't March, definitely not, and I can say that and be positive.*

Now Bugliosi attacked Owen's testimony that the person in his car during the $1,000-bill incident was not Sirhan, but the son of Johnny Gray, a black man.

Q. This young man in the back seat of Mr. Owen's Lincoln whom you testified earlier resembled Sirhan, did he have any Negroid features whatsoever?

A. No.

Q. Do you feel positive about that?

A. I feel very positive about it, yes.

Q. Could he have been part black?

A. I would say no, definitely not.

When Bugliosi asked, "The roll of $1,000 bills, could they have been as few as 10 or 11 or 12?" Powers replied, "No. I would guess there would be maybe twice that many."

After a mild cross-examination by Owen's lawyers that broke no new ground, Powers was dismissed. Bugliosi was pleased with Powers' testimony. He had sized up his witness as a plainly honest, retiring man who had no wish to insert himself into the limelight, and was sure this impression had come across on the stand.

BUGLIOSI'S NEXT WITNESS WAS LAPD COMMANDER FRANK J. Beeson, a cool-eyed detective who might have stepped out of the

---

* Powers annually supplied riding horses for the Big Bear resort in the San Gabriel Mountains. The season did not begin until the public schools closed for vacation—the first week in June.

Dragnet series. Bugliosi had subpoenaed Beeson because he reportedly was the officer who interviewed Owen at the University Station on June 5, 1968. But when the attorney talked to him during a recess, Beeson denied any recollection of Owen, his hitchhiker story or even any incident connected with the assassination, adding that there was another Officer Beeson at the LAPD. "Okay, if you don't know anything I guess I have the wrong guy," Bugliosi said. "But I want you to know I'm going to check this out further because my records show that you took Owen's statement."*

When court had resumed, Bugliosi informed the judge of Beeson's denial. But a few minutes later Wayland tapped him on the shoulder and whispered, "Beeson's outside again. Now he remembers interviewing Owen."

On the stand, Beeson's memory continued to be foggy, an impairment he blamed on the lapse of time. Yes, he had been a lieutenant in charge of the University Division detectives on June 5, 1968, when Owen walked in with the hitchhiker story.

Q. To the best of your recollection, officer, what did Mr. Owen tell you about his involvement, if any, in the Kennedy case?
A. That he had picked up Sirhan in his truck and driven him certain places, talked to him, and specifically I don't recall at this point what the conversation was, but I—I will end it there. [The detective shrugged, as if there was nothing more to tell.]
Q. Was your conversation with him tape-recorded? [Bugliosi knew there was much more.]
A. Yes, it was.

Beeson recalled that he had seen Owen's pickup truck, although he said he couldn't remember whether a horse trailer was attached.

Q. Do you know of any effort that was made to ascertain whether Sirhan's fingerprints were found inside that truck? [It was a key question, for a positive answer would solidify an Owen-Sirhan link.]
A. I can't recall.

Beeson said that after the initial interview a follow-up session was decided upon. This in itself indicated LAPD interest in the story.

* Authors' interview with Bugliosi, October 28, 1975.

Was Owen's story corroborated by the police investigation? Bugliosi asked.

A. His story was not corroborated. In fact, in my judgment at that time, his story was fictitious.
Q. So your judgment as a lieutenant, a detective for LAPD, is that Mr. Owen had given you a false story?
A. That is true.
Q. And you reached that conclusion based on your conversations with him and the investigation you had ordered?
A. Yes.

Knowingly furnishing false information to a law enforcement agency is a violation of the California penal code, and Owen's story had cost hundreds of hours of investigative time. Yet Beeson offered no explanation as to why Owen wasn't prosecuted.

Under cross-examination by Evry, Beeson explained why the police concluded Owen's story was "fictitious." "As I recall, it was impossible for Mr. Owen to be in two places at the same time, and if you believed his story he had to be . . . The investigation would tend to indicate that if he was here, then he couldn't have been here." Beeson demonstrated by pointing in different directions.

Where? With whom? Doing what? Had the LAPD placed him at Wild Bill's Stables that day? These are questions Evry seemed afraid to ask, realizing they might only get his client in deeper trouble.

As Beeson stepped down, Bugliosi asked for a court order compelling Beeson to return the following morning with four items of evidence: the tape recording of his interview of Owen; the transcript of the interview; all information pertaining to a fingerprint examination of the truck; and the LAPD's complete report on the Owen affair. Crickard made the order when he saw that Bugliosi was not only well within his judicial rights, but fully intended to battle him to the floor on this issue.

The unexpected developments in the courtroom that day apparently had put Owen in a foul mood. When Paul Le Mat snapped his picture in the corridor during recess, Owen pounced on him and yelled, "Give me that camera! Get the sheriff!" Dragging Le Mat into the courtroom, Owen howled at the bailiff to arrest him for taking the picture. "Now, just sit down, Mr. Owen," the bailiff directed. "There's been no harm done here. There's been no violation of the court's rules." At this point Rusty Rhodes summoned Owen and his attorneys into a huddle, identified Le Mat as a friend of Christian's, and proposed that he be called to the stand and forced to tell where Christian was hiding. But Owen broke from the huddle and grabbed Le Mat, shaking him by the shoulders. "Hold this man under arrest!" he shouted. "He knows where Christian is! He's hiding him!"

Le Mat was sorely tempted to punch it out with Owen right there, and it might have been over with quickly. Despite his mild manner and steel-rimmed glasses, Le Mat was a former AAU welterweight boxing champion with lightning fists. But he restrained himself, aware of the approaching bailiff and the .38 Cobra revolver tucked in his belt for his role as a bodyguard to Bill Powers. Bugliosi was absent, but Wayland realized the danger. "Get out of here," he whispered to Le Mat. "And get Christian out of my office, now!" Le Mat complied.

FORMER SUS LEADER MANNY PENA ARRIVED AT THE COURTHOUSE after being subpoenaed by Bugliosi. We had briefed Bugliosi on his clandestine connection with the CIA, and the attorney agreed that the question of why this detective, of all the detectives on the LAPD, was picked for the key SUS position demanded an answer. Was he selected because of his CIA affiliation? What control might the CIA have exerted through him? What did SUS know about Bill Powers and the cowboys? Was it SUS that had intimidated Powers into silence? Was there a cover-up? Pena was a vital witness—if he could be opened up.

Bugliosi approached Pena in the corridor and got an idea of what to expect. "I'll be asking you on the witness stand if you've ever been associated in any fashion with the CIA," he said.

"No, I've never been associated with them," Pena asserted. "Where'd you get the idea I was?"

"Your brother told Stan Bohrman that you were proud of what you did for the CIA over the years."

"Did my brother say that?" Pena said, frowning. "He doesn't know what he's talking about."

Bugliosi decided that in view of this bit of "plausible deniability," to borrow the CIA's parlance, a little strategy was in order. Unless the judge allowed him to bear down on Pena, he would not get the answers he was seeking. Owen's lawyers had echoed their client's belief that there had been a conspiracy in the RFK case, although not one criminally involving Owen. Bugliosi called their hand. "If that's what you believe I don't want you to object to the CIA question being posed to Pena," he told the Owen lawyers before court resumed. "So let's go back in chambers and talk to the judge."

Back they trooped, informing Crickard of their agreement. "Well, I have an objection," he grumbled. "It's not relevant."

"It's extremely relevant," Bugliosi argued. "They're obviously not covering up Sirhan's involvement, so what are they covering up?"

Crickard was adamant, falling back on his "undue consumption of time" plaint.

Bugliosi flared, "Well, we're spending all this time in your chambers arguing about it when we could settle it in court."

But Crickard had the last word. "It's not relevant and I'm not going to let you go on it."

Court resumed with Manuel S. Pena raising his right hand to be sworn in. Lulling the judge, Bugliosi began with routine questions about his police career. Then he got to the "retirement" banquet in 1967, which Pena confirmed.

Q. But you continued to work at LAPD? [The bait was out.]
A. No, I went with the U.S. State Department. I went to Washington, D.C. [Bugliosi smiled indulgently. Manny Pena, diplomat.]
Q. Is that the first time you had ever been associated with the State Department?
A. Correct.
Q. Were you trained back there at the State Department at all?
A. I attended the Foreign Service Institute while I was back there. [The game of semantical dodgeball was on.]
Q. Did you ever go on assignment for the State Department?
A. Not at this time.
Q. At a later time?

A. In I believe the latter part of '69 and first part of '70, I took a trip to South America.

Crickard finally caught on to Bugliosi's ploy and instructed him to move on to a "relevant" area. "This is his background," the attorney insisted. "I want to know about his training and education."

Q. Why did you go to South America?
THE COURT: That is not relevant!
Q. Well, were you on assignment by the State Department in South America?
THE COURT: That is not relevant either. Let's get to this case.
BUGLIOSI: I want to know whether it was a vacation or anything to do—

He never got out the word "CIA." Crickard cut in again, directing Bugliosi to the Jerry Owen inquiry that the witness had supervised.

Q. Was that truck ever checked for fingerprints to ascertain whether Sirhan's prints were inside?
A. I couldn't say without going back to the files. I can't at this moment.
Q. That would have been the normal thing to do, right?
A. Normal, routine. But I can't tell you that it was without going back through the files.

According to Pena's testimony, SUS concluded that Owen was neither with Sirhan in the truck nor implicated in the assassination. But details eluded him, due, he said, to the passage of time. Bugliosi took one more stab at pinning down his covert CIA activities, asking, "Mr. Pena, throughout your law enforcement career have you ever worked directly or indirectly for the CIA?" Pena sat in stony silence. Crickard, so angered that his gavel hand trembled, loudly interjected, "That's—you don't have to answer that. That's not relevant in this case. The court discussed that with you in chambers, Mr. Bugliosi, and told you not to inquire into that area."

After a brief exchange with the judge, Bugliosi tried another tack. "You indicated earlier that you worked for the State Department," he addressed Pena. "Was this on a paid basis or was it—" Crickard burst in again, "That's not relevant, either. You don't have to answer that question."

The door was closed. Insofar as the court record was concerned, Manny Pena wore striped pants and a homburg instead of a cloak and dagger. But Bugliosi had already gotten in the back door a good portion of what Crickard had forbidden him to elicit directly. Why was an LAPD officer attending the Foreign Service Institute (a CIA Cover-Front Outfit), and on assignment to South America for "the State Department"?*

BUGLIOSI CALLED GLADYS ROBERTA OWEN, THE PLAINTIFF'S WIFE, to the stand. His purpose was to explore a new wrinkle Owen had brought into his hitchhiker story when he testified earlier: that on the night of the RFK shooting, his wife had accompanied him on the overnight preaching trip to Oxnard. He had not mentioned this in his interview with Turner, nor, so far as we could tell, to the LAPD. Putting her on the stand was a calculated risk. If she swore that she went with him to Oxnard, it would strengthen his alibi for the night of the assassination. On the other hand, it didn't seem likely that she would claim to have been with him when he supposedly picked up Sirhan and spent the night before election day in Los Angeles. The records of the St. Moritz Hotel had showed him registered as single. It was possible

* "CIA Link to L.A. Police Reported" read the headline in the January 12, 1976, edition of the Los Angeles *Herald-Examiner*. "Documents released by the Central Intelligence Agency show the Los Angeles Police Department received training by CIA personnel" during the late 1960s, the story read. "(LAPD) Chief Edward M. Davis, in a statement issued through police department spokesman Cmdr. Peter Hagen, denied any connection between the LAPD and the CIA . . . Hagen said there would be no further elaboration."

Shortly after this story appeared, Davis appeared on *The Sam Yorty Show* (on KCOP, Los Angeles) and offered, "Heck, I don't think I've ever met anyone in the CIA," again denying the LAPD-CIA link.

After retiring in January 1978, Davis announced his candidacy for governor of California.

that he had backtracked to Santa Ana to pick her up on election day before heading for Oxnard, but not very probable.

Roberta Owen, as she preferred to be called, was a matronly grayish-blond woman with a pleasant if bland personality. Bugliosi inquired politely, "You are aware that your husband has testified that on the evening of June 4th you and he were up at Oxnard?"

A. *I don't recall any particular dates, sir.* I know we spent some time in Oxnard.

Q. Was it around the time of the assassination?

A. Yes. [Owen was nodding from his coaching box.]

Q. Do you recall a prayer meeting at a church up there called the Calvary Baptist Church?

A. Yes.

Q. Do you recall where you stayed that night? [Jerry Owen had stated that it was with lay people whose name his wife might remember.]

A. Which night, sir?

Q. The night of the prayer meeting.

A. Well, we had several prayer meetings at Oxnard and several meetings over quite a period of time.

Q. You were not with your husband when he supposedly picked up a man in downtown Los Angeles who he thinks is Sirhan?

A. No, sir, I was not.

Q. Were you with him the following day, which would be June the 4th?

A. Let's see. Yes, I think so.

Q. Where did you join him? [There was a pause. Roberta Owen was in a blind alley, and she was forced to double back.]

A. No, no, he had gone up to Oxnard and returned, which would have been probably two days before I saw him.

Q. *So he went up to Oxnard by himself?*

A. *Yes.*

Roberta Owen had just put an enormous dent in her husband's shaky alibi. There was no cross-examination. Court was adjourned for the day.

COMMANDER FRANK BEESON WAS WAITING NERVOUSLY WHEN court resumed in the morning, and Bugliosi put him right on the stand. Running down the inventory of material on the Owen investigation that Crickard had instructed him to bring, Bugliosi asked, "Were you successful in getting those documents?" The policeman said no. In his search for the material he "learned that there is deployed another task force relating to the Sirhan Sirhan investigation—"

"You say another task force?" Bugliosi interrupted. "Is this another investigative task force?"

"It's probably more of a coordination task force in that there are efforts presently under way to reopen the Sirhan investigation," Beeson replied, "and that's the purpose of this task force."

Considering the LAPD's intransigence on the matter, Bugliosi posed a perfectly logical question: "Is the purpose of the task force to resist, as far as you know, the reopening of the investigation, or go along with it?" But Crickard intervened, ruling the question immaterial. Bugliosi was left to ask Beeson to produce the material he had been ordered to bring. The policeman declined. After consulting with members of the new task force, he said, he spoke with Deputy City Attorney Ward McConnell, whose office counseled the police on legal matters.

Q. What was the position given to you by the deputy city attorney, Mr. McConnell? [Bugliosi asked.]
A. That any of the files—or any information contained in those files— the divulging of that information would be strongly resisted by the city.
Q. So you were flat-out told that you would not be given these records which you were seeking?
A. That is true.
Q. Let me ask you this: Did you ascertain yesterday afternoon whether in fact these records exist?
A. I determined there is a file, and there is a file specifically on Mr. Owen.
Q. And you have been advised by counsel, the City Attorney's office, which is the counsel for the LAPD, that this file would not be turned over voluntarily in this court?
A. That is true.

Even though Beeson had defied his order, Crickard dismissed him and thanked him for coming. On that politely ludicrous note the judge allowed the LAPD's charade to pass. It had begun with Schaffer's supposed inability to find the files, continued with Pena's circumlocutions, and ended with Beeson's flat refusal to produce the files Schaffer couldn't find. Bugliosi shook his head. What did the police have to do to affront Crickard?

17
The Trances

WHEN JERRY OWEN TESTIFIED THAT THE YOUNG MAN IN THE back seat of his Lincoln was Johnny Gray's son, he set off a game of musical chairs that had his lawyers in a tizzy. At first, David Lloyd promised to bring Jackie Gray into the courtroom that afternoon. Then, after a luncheon conference, he announced that it was not Jackie Gray, after all, but someone named Charles Butler. However, when the promised witness had not been produced by the end of the day and Bugliosi raised the issue, Arthur Evry disclosed that during lunch Johnny Gray "indicated to us the person in the car was not his son, but he will testify in our rebuttal testimony as to who that person was and it was not Sirhan Sirhan."

The next morning Johnny Gray was back in the courtroom. Bugliosi and Wayland watched expectantly as Evry cautiously questioned Gray, evoking his memory of the visit to Wild Bill's Stables.

Q. Do you recall if Reverend Owen had any amount of money with him that day?
A. Well, he had a roll. That's all I can say. I didn't count it.
Q. Do you recall seeing that roll?
A. Yes.
Q. Who was present in the car with you?
A. Well, we first had Charlie Butler. He lived close by that place over there where they had the horses at.
Q. Anyone else?
A. We went by and dropped him off. And my son was with us, Jackie Gray.

Back to Jackie Gray! Bugliosi and Wayland looked at each other, incredulous. Only the previous afternoon Evry had declared that Johnny Gray would testify that it was not his son, and overnight the signals had changed.

Evry completed his brief questioning by making sure that he and Gray were talking about the same incident. Yes, Gray said, they were in Owen's Lincoln Continental. Yes, Owen "met some tall white fellow there that run the stables"—Bill Powers, No, it was not Sirhan seated behind him, it was his son Jackie. No further questions.

In beginning his cross examination, Bugliosi couldn't resist needling Gray. "Do people ever come up to your son in your presence and say, 'Gee, you are a spitting image of Sirhan Sirhan'?" Crickard interceded, ruling the question irrelevant. Bugliosi showed a picture of Sirhan to Gray and asked whether his son "resembled the man in the photograph in any fashion whatsoever." Gray said that he did "in some respects." Then Bugliosi established the fact that in 1968 Jackie Gray was only thirteen, while Sirhan was twenty-three.

Bugliosi asked, "At the age of thirteen he looked just like the man in this picture, is that what you are saying?"

"That's right, that's right." Gray seemed unnerved.

"Are you having trouble seeing that photograph?" Bugliosi's tone was sarcastic.*

The next line of questioning concerned Owen's roll of bills, which prompted Crickard to cut in again to rule that it was repetitious and unduly consumptive of time, and that in any case the passing of the money was "an extremely collateral matter." This touched off a sharp exchange:

BUGLIOSI: How is it collateral if it happens that Mr. Owen is lying about this incident? How is it collateral if Mr. Powers is to be believed that within a couple of days of the assassination, the assassin, Sirhan, is with Owen, and Owen is in possession of 25 to 30 $1,000 bills? If that is collateral, then I have to go back to law school.

THE COURT: I am not telling you to do anything.

BUGLIOSI: In effect you are. [The attorney was exasperated with Crickard's wave-of-the-hand dismissal of the heart of the defense case, but his ridicule might have provoked some judges to threaten him with contempt.]

THE COURT: You can draw any conclusion that you want.

Bugliosi was convinced that the judge thoroughly resented the assassination issue being dragged into his court. There was nothing left to pursue with Johnny Gray. He was excused.

That afternoon Christian used a private detective contact (Dan Prop) to try and obtain copies of Johnny Gray's phone records during the time he lived just down the street from the Coliseum Hotel, June 1968. The report came back short and succinct: "Pulled— cops!"

Crickard's diminution of the Sirhan connection as an "extremely collateral matter" clearly signaled to both sides that his mind was made up. There was actually no need for the plaintiff's attorneys to attempt to rebut Bill Powers' testimony further; for all intents and purposes this issue was already decided in their favor.

---

* Dianne Hull (with Paul Le Mat) had been our eyes and ears at the trial. When she conveyed this exchange, we sent her off to scour the myriad of grade and junior high schools young Gray had attended during the 1967– 69 period. She found lots of school records on him, but none had accompanying photographs. School officials could not account for the loss.

But they knew that Bugliosi intended to call Jackie Gray to the stand if they did not. "At the risk of belaboring this one point, I would like to call Jackie Gray to the stand for just a few questions," plaintiff's attorney, David Lloyd, announced.

Jackie Gray, age twenty, was a somber, mentally deficient, mulatto-appearing young man with kinky black hair; his resemblance to Sirhan seemed superficial at best. He spoke softly, almost inaudibly, in awkward phrases, and seemed extremely uncomfortable in his role as center of attraction. Under sympathetic questioning by Lloyd, he said that he had been to the Reverend Owen's home in Santa Ana many times, often as a houseguest. Yes, he recalled accompanying his father and Owen to a nearby stables in 1967 or 1968. On this occasion he sat "in the back seat on the corner" of Owen's car.

Lloyd had called Gray for the sole and limited purpose of establishing that it was he, not Sirhan, in that back seat. No further questions.

On cross-examination Bugliosi handled Jackie Gray gently in deference to his obvious slow-wittedness. The young man remembered that Owen was buying a red truck from the cowboy at the stables, but thought it was a 1967 model. (Powers' old pickup was blue.)

Q. . . . During this incident when Reverend Owen was going to buy this 1967 truck, where were you seated in Mr. Owen's car?
A. The front seat. [He had testified during direct examination that he was seated in the back seat.]
Q. Where was your father?
A. Like, he is sitting like this [indicating to his right] and I am sitting in the middle.
Q. You both are seated in the front seat?
A. Right. [Jackie was sandwiched between Owen and his father in the front seat of the Lincoln.]
Q. Was there anyone seated in the back seat?
A. No.
Q. This white cowboy from whom Mr. Owen was going to buy the truck, was he with anyone?
A. Well, only thing I know is he had on Levi's and boots.
Q. But was he with anyone?

A. He was with a lady standing outside.

Q. Did Reverend Owen have any money in his hands, any $1,000 bills?

A. Yeah. He had them rolled up.

Q. Were they $1,000 bills?

A. Number 50's.

Q. They were $50 bills?

A. Fifties and hundreds.

Q. Not thousands?

A. Not thousands.

Q. Did Reverend Owen tell you where he got this roll of money?

A. No, he did not.

Q. Did he actually buy the truck from this man?

A. Yes.

Q. The man took the money?

A. Took the money.

Q. Do you know how much he took?

A. No.

Q. Where was the truck at this time, this red truck?

A. Sitting in a lot like this, sitting like this.

Q. Was it right next to the car?

A. Yes.

It all added up. The late-model red truck parked at the stables, a lady present rather than the stablehands, Owen carrying only $50 and $100 bills, Bill Powers accepting some cash. Jackie Gray wasn't describing the incident which occurred just before the assassination when Owen was flaunting $1,000 bills and Powers couldn't make change for the balance owed on the old pickup. He most likely was talking about the day about four weeks before when Owen first bought the pickup and handed Powers $50 or so as part payment. In fact, the elder Gray had said that he was at the stables with Owen "one other time." So Jackie Gray's visit to Wild Bill's Stables was not on the day Sirhan reportedly was there.

Intuitively, Bugliosi sought to capitalize on Jackie Gray's lack of guile, asking, "Have you ever heard the name Sirhan Sirhan?" Gray nodded affirmatively at the mention of the well-known name. Then the attorney took a shot in the dark.

Q. Did you ever hear your father mention that name?

A. Yes.

Q. When?

A. Every time I ride with him he just say it.

Q. Pardon? [Bugliosi could hardly believe what he was hearing.]

A. He just mention it. It comes out of his mouth. He mentions it. He mentions it every time. Every time it comes out of his mouth, he mentions it when he riding.

Q. You say your father talks about Sirhan all the time?

A. Uh-huh. [Again the affirmative nod.]

This was incredibly heavy testimony, and Bugliosi sensed that possibly, just possibly, the disingenuous youth on the stand could blow the lid off the case. Not wishing to alert the witness to the enormity of his testimony, Bugliosi very casually asked him to explain in more detail what his father would say about Sirhan.

A. He tells me he always look like me, and say things like me and talk like me and say good things, do good things and nice things and want to do good things and want to do excellent things and stuff like that. [The words sounded as if Gray had been told that he was practically interchangeable with Sirhan.]

Q. He told you that he knows Sirhan very well, is that correct?

A. Yes.

Q. Did he tell you where he first met Sirhan?

A. Yes.

Q. Where did he tell you he first met him?

A. He tells me he meets him—

Q. Pardon?

A. He meets him through . . . [Gray hesitated. His eyes rolled in the direction of Jerry Owen, and Bugliosi didn't have to turn around to know it.]

Q. Through Mr. Owen?

A. Through Mr. Owen.

Owen blanched while his lawyers seemed stunned. Evry started to object, but Bugliosi drove on:

Q. When is the first time that your father told you he met Sirhan through Reverend Owen?

A. First time?

Q. Yes.
A. In '67.
Q. Are you sure about that?
A. Sure.
Q. Pardon? [Gray was speaking softly, matter-of-factly. Bugliosi was encouraging him to speak up.]
A. Sure. Yes. [The emphasis was picking up.]
Q. Did your father tell you where this incident took place—where Mr. Owen—
A. Yes.
Q. —introduced him to Sirhan? [There was the hum of low voices at the plaintiff's counsel table.]
A. Yes.
Q. Where?

Lloyd rose to his feet. "Your Honor," he said, "I am going to object to the rest of the testimony and impeach my own witness. I have been informed by Mr. Gray that his son is not competent to testify and would like to talk to the court in private about this."

An air of crisis hung over the courtroom. Lloyd was impeaching his *own* witness! Presumably, an attorney has done his homework and is satisfied with the competency of his witness before putting him on the stand; and he certainly knows the risks of cross-examination. "This is so much hogwash," Bugliosi said. "I can't believe this. This is their witness, called to the witness stand for a particular point. When he is blowing the lid off the case, they say he is incompetent!"

Crickard granted Lloyd's request for a conference in chambers. Reluctant to leave young Gray unattended, Bugliosi requested that since "the testimony of this witness is exceedingly incriminating to Mr. Owen, I would like to have this witness in protective custody for his own safety." Crickard instructed his bailiff to watch over Jackie Gray while they were out of the courtroom.

Up to this juncture Owen had been his usual ebullient self, back-slapping his coterie of associates in attendance and coaching his witnesses with motions of his head and hands to such an extent that Crickard had to scold him on several occasions. But now, as Bugliosi passed his table, Owen snarled, "You're in big trouble!"

Bugliosi had the court record reflect that Owen made "some type of threat to me."

Following the conference, Lloyd made a motion in open court that all of Jackie Gray's testimony be stricken and he be dismissed on grounds of incompetency. He was under a mental physician's care, Lloyd argued, was unemployed, was receiving disability compensation and was unable to recollect events accurately. Evry chimed in that he had "mental problems through the use of drugs, particularly hallucinogenic drugs," and quoted the senior Gray as saying his son's drug use had begun as early as 1968.

Crickard decided that he himself would question the witness on the point, using as a guide *Judge Jefferson's Evidence Book*, which sets forth certain criteria of mental competency. Jackie Gray told the judge that he was a ninth child, divided his time between his separated parents and had held only one job. He said he was seeing a psychiatrist who "gets me on the right track," but flatly denied using drugs.

After Crickard's quiz had gone on for half an hour, Bugliosi interposed that although young Gray was "a little slow-witted," it was evident that under the law he was capable of testifying. "If this witness is telling the truth," he told the judge, "as I tend to believe that he is, I am very, very concerned about his safety." Bugliosi noted that the noon break was coming up, and again petitioned Crickard to place Gray in protective custody "not just for himself but for this country. We have to find out what he knows." Although Evry resented the implication that "this kid is in danger," Crickard directed his bailiff to accompany the witness to lunch.

When court resumed in the afternoon, Crickard ruled that Jackie Gray was competent to testify.

Bugliosi picked up where he had left off—the place where Owen had introduced Sirhan to Johnny Gray. It was at Owen's Santa Ana home, young Gray said. He remembered because he "was leaning on the seat and [Sirhan] was giving me a quarter." Twenty-five cents to a thirteen-year-old black from Watts was something to remember.

As Bugliosi warmed up to his questioning, Lloyd interrupted to say that young Gray's psychiatrist had arrived and "will testify

that the witness has a schizoid, paranoid, psychotic personality."
Lloyd wanted the opportunity to throw this whole aberration book
at his prodigal witness right away rather than after Bugliosi
finished. Bugliosi objected on the basis that the court had already
ruled as to competency, a question a psychiatrist could not legally
determine. "Now if they want to put this psychiatrist on to re-
habilitate the position they are now in, that is a different story,"
he argued. "But to try to prevent other words from coming out of
this witness's mouth—"

Evry broke in, objecting to "the inference we are trying to take
anything out of this witness's mouth and have it not said." All they
wanted, he insisted, was to put on the psychiatrist so he could
return to his own practice. Bugliosi estimated he would finish with
Jackie Gray about two-thirty, but Crickard, trying to compromise,
said the doctor could come on a bit earlier.

Returning to Jackie Gray, Bugliosi asked, "Did you hear
Reverend Owen talk about Sirhan many times?"

A. Yes, many times. [Owen was clutching the table edges, straining
to hear what the sotto voce young man would say next.]
Q. What did you hear your father say about Sirhan?
A. Good things like schooling and going to school and stuff like that.
Buying clothes, stuff like that. Going to school.*
Q. Who was buying clothes?
A. He, for him. For him.
Q. Who was buying clothing? Who was doing the buying?
A. The Reverend.
Q. Reverend Owen was buying clothing for Sirhan?
A. Yes.
Q. . . . What were the good things that Reverend Owen said about
Sirhan?
A. Like giving him money, you know to do something for hisself and
stuff like that. [Jackie Gray glanced at Owen, apparently unaware
of the significance of what he was saying.]

* In a 1972 interview with Christian, Mrs. Mary Sirhan and her sons
Adel and Munir said that in late 1967 and early 1968 Sirhan Sirhan talked
about going back to college, and how he needed new clothes and a new car
to return with dignity.

Q. Reverend Owen used to give Sirhan money?
A. Yes.*

At this point Bugliosi flashed onto something he recalled from skimming through our raw manuscript—the theory that Sirhan was a real-life version of the Manchurian Candidate, hypnoprogrammed to kill. The attorney had been impressed with our research, but not entirely convinced. Now he thought of the queen of diamonds that had been used to plunge the novel's antihero into a trance, and decided to draw to an inside straight.

Q. Do you know what the word trance means?
A. Yes.
Q. Did you ever hear your father or Reverend Owen say anything about Sirhan being in a trance?
A. Yes. [The answer came matter-of-factly.]
Q. What did you hear them say?
A. This is in a room to hisself, in a room that he always been in, in a room that some of the things he is doing is wrong.

The language of the man-child. Bugliosi patiently sought to clarify it, remembering that Sirhan had closeted himself in a room when he put himself into a trance and did the "automatic writing."

Q. Talking about Sirhan?
A. Yes. I don't know what it is.
Q. You heard your father and Reverend Owen saying that Sirhan used to be in a room all by himself?
A. Right.
Q. Did the word "trance" come up?
A. Right.
Q. Did you ever hear them say that sometimes Sirhan would do things and not know that he did them?
A. Right.
Q. Have you ever heard of the word "hypnosis"?

* Throughout Sirhan's notebooks containing the "automatic writing" indicative of the trance state, there are such entries as "Jeeerry," expectations of large sums of money from unspecified sources and the promise of "a new Mustang" automobile.

A. Yes.

Q. Did you ever hear Reverend Owen or your father saying anything about Sirhan being under hypnosis?

A. No.

Q. But you did hear them saying that sometimes he would be in a trance?

A. Right.

Q. Did you ever hear your father or Reverend Owen say that Sirhan was involved with other people in killing Senator Kennedy?

A. No.

The talk was mostly about Sirhan in a trance. "That's all I ever heard," Jackie Gray volunteered.

Crickard suspended Gray's testimony so that the hastily summoned psychiatrist could take the stand for the plaintiff. He was Henry Gene Robinson, a former Army psychiatrist in Vietnam, now director of the Kendrin Community Mental Health Center in Los Angeles. Dr. Robinson said that young Gray was a regular patient at the clinic. The gist of his testimony was that Gray suffered from a degree of psychotic disorder and schizophrenia, displayed hostility toward those closest to him and tended to fantasize. On cross-examination Bugliosi asked Robinson what percentage of the general population of the United States was schizophrenic to some degree. His answer: Up to 25 percent. Did Gray ever say anything that had been proven to be fantasy? No, the doctor conceded, thus neutralizing his earlier testimony. Robinson's testimony was so undamaging that Bugliosi wondered if he had been told the nature of the emergency that demanded his appearance.

Upon resuming with Jackie Gray, Bugliosi administered an impromptu test of his own. Would Jackie Gray, by his answers, *adopt* whatever was contained in a question, or was he capable of independent answers?

Q. Mr. Gray, you say that your father and Reverend Owen spoke a lot of times about Sirhan, is that correct?

A. Yes.

Q. Did they talk a lot about Joe DiMaggio?

A. Yes. They mentioned him *one time*.

Q. So you heard Joe DiMaggio's name mentioned one time, is that correct?
A. Yes.
Q. Did you ever hear them talk about Marilyn Monroe?
A. No.
Q. Did you ever hear them talk about Michael Crulowitz?
A. No.

The last name was pure invention. Bugliosi was satisfied that Gray had the ability to discriminate and sort out fact from fancy.

Jackie Gray thought that Owen had mentioned Sirhan having "a good wife," but the Palestinian immigrant had never been married.

Q. You said Reverend Owen was always talking about how Sirhan was in a trance?
A. It was a trance when he would be in his room, he would sit back and think about something to do that he liked to do all the time. [Unwittingly, Gray was describing the intense concentration preparatory to slipping into a trance.]
Q. Do you know where this room was?
A. Like a room of his own.
Q. You don't know whether that was at Reverend Owen's house or someone else's house?
A. No.

Gray said that his father and Owen talked about the fact that Sirhan had been convicted of the murder of Senator Kennedy. "What did they say?" Bugliosi wanted to know.

"A few words that he was just convicted of a crime or something and he never done that before or something like that, and that's all," Gray responded.

"Did they say anything about Sirhan being in a trance at the time he killed Senator Kennedy?" the attorney asked. The answer never came. Crickard again charged "undue consumption of time." Somewhat surprised that the judge had let him go as far as he did, Bugliosi put up only a token argument.

"Well, you have had your chance to examine him, Mr. Bugliosi."

"I have, and I am very satisfied with the answers, your Honor."

But David Lloyd was distinctly displeased with the answers, and he vehemently insisted on being allowed to cross-examine Jackie Gray as an adverse witness. He launched into a pitiless exploitation of the young man's vulnerability to leading questions. "How long had the Reverend Owen been training as a boxer?" he asked.

Gray, who never said he had, responded, "A good while."

"They were boxing in Phoenix, too, weren't they?" the attorney suggested.

Bugliosi objected to the blatantly leading questions, and Crickard sustained him. But once the words had been put in his mouth, Gray swallowed them. "Have you had occasion to spar or fight with Sirhan in Phoenix?" Lloyd asked. Yes, young Gray replied, in the summer of 1972. This was not merely fantasizing, since he had often tagged along with his father, and occasionally Owen, as they worked in various gyms with various fighters. But in his eagerness to please, he seemed to be garbling people, places and times. It was like playing with word blocks, trying to make sentences out of them.

Lloyd recalled the father to the stand. It was Johnny Gray who had said it was his son in the back seat of the Lincoln, but putting Jackie Gray on the stand to verify it had backfired badly. Now the hapless father was to be used to try to destroy his son as a witness.

No sooner had Johnny Gray mounted the stand than Bugliosi protested that information about his son's testimony had been relayed to him outside the courtroom. "We have an exclusion of witnesses order here," he reminded Crickard, "and I have received word that Reverend Owen has been kind of an errand boy, running out of the courtroom telling the witness what his son was testifying to." This might have been cause for a contempt citation or mistrial, but the matter was defused when Lloyd agreed to ask only questions about the son's mental state, not his testimony. Gray stated that in the past his son had described events that turned out to be fantasies—he couldn't think of a specific example—and had used the drug LSD.*

Bugliosi's counterquestions were succinct and direct:

---

* Jackie Gray testified that he never used LSD—and no evidence was ever produced to support this contention.

Q. You are a very close personal friend of Reverend Owen?
A. Yes, I am.
Q. Have you been talking to Reverend Owen about this case?
A. Sure I have talked with him about the case.
Q. Has he ever given you any money?

Gray squirmed and glanced quickly at a glaring Owen. "Beg pardon?" he stalled. When the question was repeated, Gray mumbled, "Well, he has given me money for sometimes different transactions."

WHILE THE TRIAL WAS TAKING ITS DRAMATIC TURN, CHRISTIAN was experiencing enough drama of his own to last a lifetime. He and Paul Le Mat had stopped at Cine Artists, a motion picture production company in the Playboy Building on the Sunset Strip that had produced *Aloha, Bobby and Rose*. Christian took the opportunity to make a phone call to our then motion picture attorney Jack Schwartzman. Schwartzman was on another line, said an unusually nervous secretary. At her suggestion, Christian left his name and the Cine Artists number.

Five minutes later the phone rang. "This is the West Los Angeles Sheriff's Department calling," the caller informed the Cine Artists secretary. "We have word that there is a man named Jonn Christian in that office. We want him. Keep him there until we arrive—we're on our way up there right now."

The secretary was well aware of Christian's "fugitive" status and said there was no employee by that name, but she would check around. Putting the caller on hold, she alerted Christian to what was going on.

Christian had no intention of being taken into custody by any Los Angeles law enforcement officers. The whole case, beginning with the heavy-handed silencing of Bill Powers and ending with the roughhouse search in Brentwood a couple of days before, had been filled with lawless law enforcement. Los Angeles cops were noted for their hair-trigger guns,* and Christian could even envision

---

* In the preceding eighteen months, Los Angeles cops had killed seventy-five civilians. In many of those cases, the use of deadly force had been

himself being shot "trying to escape." Here he was, merely a potential witness in a civil suit, and the cops were hunting him with twenty-four-hour stakeouts and wiretaps as if he were one of the FBI's Ten Most Wanted men. Why?

Expecting cops to pour out of the elevators, Le Mat and Christian started down separate stairwells, but when he heard the metallic clang of footsteps above, Christian ducked into a fourth-floor office suite. It was Playboy Productions, and it so happened that one of the executives, Eddie Rissien, had talked with Christian on the phone a couple of times about a motion picture version of this book. (Le Mat managed to escape in time.)

"Don't ask too many questions right now, Eddie," Christian implored as he shook hands with Rissien, "because there are some cops in this building trying to arrest me on bullshit charges having to do with a phony subpoena in the RFK case." Rissien blinked in astonishment, but pointed to a vacant office that could be locked from the inside and out.

Christian called Wayland's office and instructed a secretary to deliver a message personally to Bugliosi at the courthouse. "Tell him that I'm trapped in Playboy's offices—they're some cops after me—and that I need him to get over here right away or call!" She called the court instead—and passed the message through Crickard's bailiff. Christian glanced out the window and saw a sheriff's patrol car come roaring up the hill to the rear of the building and slam to a halt at the rear exit. One of the two uniformed deputies that leaped out of the car and ran into the underground garage area had his service revolver in hand. Suddenly Captain Hugh Brown's warning about Christian getting into "big trouble" for "messing around" with the Homicide Commander's "thing" hit home with full impact. Bugliosi returned Christian's call about twenty minutes later. "Vince, I'm in Eddie Rissien's office at Playboy and I—" Christian's words were clipped off in mid-sentence as Bugliosi imparted his own excitement.

"Have you heard the news? We may have blown the lid off the case!"

---

criticized by the community as unwarranted, often racist and in some instances plain murder.

"*Vince!*" howled Christian futilely.

"They put Johnny Gray's kid on the stand to try and make him into a surrogate Sirhan, and he starts talking about Sirhan being at Owen's *home* clear back in '67, and about Sirhan being in *trances* and—"

"*Goddammit*, Bugliosi!" Christian screamed, "there are cops going through this joint with drawn guns . . . and I need your *help*!"

"What?!" said Bugliosi.

"What's ass! There are cops on their way up inside this goddam building, and they are *not* planning on bringing me back alive! Do you understand what I'm saying?!" Christian's voice was trembling slightly, a sign Bugliosi quickly identified as flat-out fear.

A hasty discussion of Christian's severe plight made it clear to both that Bugliosi's dispatch to the Playboy Building, some fifteen miles away, would not accomplish anything anyway. He wasn't a DA anymore, and he'd likely arrive too late to forestall whatever might have been in store for the entrapped "fugitive." Both agreed there was a more practical solution.

Christian quickly placed calls to Supervisor Baxter Ward and City Attorney Burt Pines, government officials with the power to intervene. But to no avail. Ward's deputy Robert Pratt advised him that he'd be interfering with "due process" (i.e., the warrant that had been questionably served on Christian), and Pines refused his call.

When court resumed, Crickard called the attorneys into chambers and said that it had been brought to his attention that Bugliosi had received a message from Christian. Bugliosi readily acknowledged talking on the phone with him, saying that Christian had expressed a fear for his life at the hands of the police.

Crickard seemed so dead set on having Christian brought in that Bugliosi felt compelled to give a brief lecture. "This man apparently has devoted the last several years to finding the co-conspirators, if there are any, with Sirhan," he said, "and it is not far-fetched that more than one person was involved. And if other persons are ever found and traced up the ladder, I think the guy that will be commended ultimately in Congress is a guy by the name of Jonn Christian. I think he has done a brilliant job of investigation, and his fears, I don't know whether they are justified or not, but in view of the crazy things happening in this case, they may be justified. His life is more important to him than a court subpoena. . . . He is a very elusive guy, but understandably so. We are dealing with a case where there are a lot of bullets flying around."

As offices began closing for the day in the Playboy Building, Eddie Rissien informed Christian that the patrol cars had left in a hurry (it turned out that they were mistakenly dispatched to the Playboy Club in Century City to look for Christian). However, Rissien's security officer had just told him that two plain-clothes men posing as building inspectors were still combing the building. Rissien proposed that Christian try to get out of the building while there were still witnesses around for his possible protection. The two improvised a plan of action. Rissien would play himself and escort Christian out as if he were another Playboy producer. When the elevator automatically stopped and the doors opened at the lobby, Rissien berated Christian, "I don't care what your problems are, goddammit! We've got five days to get that film finished or you will be in big—" The guard gave Rissien a cool wink as the doors slid shut and the elevator sank to the basement level. Rissien checked for cops first. The coast was clear, and Christian slipped out the exit that earlier had been blocked by the patrol car.

Christian met up with Le Mat (by prearrangement) later that night at the seaside home of Russ O'Hara, one of the better-known radio personalities in Southern California. After midnight they side-streeted their way out of Los Angeles, staying overnight (under assumed names) at the one place they were sure no police would think to look for them: Disneyland. An hour before dawn they began their circuitous trek northward, into the backroads of the Mojave Desert. By midday the thermal temperature had passed the 120° mark. Somehow, though, Los Angeles had seemed hotter for these two "fugitives."

They hid out for several days in a small fishing village (Cayucos) some 350 miles north of Los Angeles at the earthy pad of Christian's godson, Jack De Witt. Calling in to LA from a phone booth in nearby Morro Bay, Christian was told that the trial was over, that Crickard had lifted the ominous body attachment. He didn't have to ask who had won.

Intuition told them to tarry awhile longer, and to slip into Los Angeles like a pair of Rio Grande wetbacks. Their instincts weren't wrong either. Even though Crickard's order was immediately forwarded by his bailiff to the police, Christian and Le Mat remained on their still-wanted list for five more days—hardly an oversight. (We discovered this in the trial record when it was released for public view by Crickard a year later.)

18

This Conspiracy Might Ultimately Make Watergate Look Like a One-Roach Marijuana Bust

THE DEFENSE WAS UNABLE TO PUT ON ALL OF THE WITNESSES it wanted. Process servers had been unable to find a trace of the Reverend Medcalf, the ex-pastor of the Calvary Baptist Church in Oxnard who in 1968 had told our investigator Jim Rose that the church was shuttered the night Owen claimed to have preached there. Johnny Beckley and John Chris Weatherly, both of whom might have shed considerable light on the nature and extent of Owen's association with Sirhan, had fled in fright. Bill Powers still couldn't find his former stablehands Jack Brundage and Dennis Jackson, who had been present during the $1,000 bills incident at the stables. When the LAPD refused to produce its records, the defense team had subpoenaed the Weatherly Report from the sheriff's office but were told it never existed. So they had issued subpoenas for the two sheriff's deputies whose names appeared on the report as having interrogated Weatherly, but they were not locatable.

Despite the vanishing witnesses, no time for trial preparation, and law enforcement stonewalling, Bugliosi had, in four days, accomplished what a team of lawyers and investigators working for a full year could well be very proud of, establishing what we believe to be probable cause to conclude that a conspiracy and cover-up took place. In fact, Bugliosi's final argument on the morning of July 31 was more that of criminal prosecutor than civil lawyer. Bugliosi began by referring to Owen's hitchhiker story.

It is a very strange, bizarre story. It's not a likely story. Sirhan is someone determined and hell bent on murdering Senator Kennedy, yet he is roaming around the streets of Los Angeles jumping on pickup trucks, and has this Mr. Owen drop him off at the Ambassador Hotel, and tells him he is going to go visit a friend in the kitchen, where the assassination later took place.

It is just not a believable story, it just does not have the ring of truth to it, and apparently every time Mr. Owen tells the story it overflows with contradictions and inconsistencies. He can't tell the same story the same way twice, and this is the man who has this incredible memory!

Even the police said that Mr. Owen was not telling the truth, they didn't buy his story at all. . . . Assuming that he lied—and I tend to think, based on the evidence, that Reverend Owen did lie, that he did make up this story because it's not a credible story at all and the investigators did not think it was credible—the question that of course presents itself is, Why should he lie? Why would he lie?

Now, I can imagine one could argue that maybe he was just seeking publicity, and I guess you could write it off at that. That happens many, many times. I recall a very famous murder case called the Black Dahlia murder case back in the '40s, I think, in Los Angeles. And if I recall correctly, about 250 people came forward and confessed to murdering the Black Dahlia, all of whom were hopeful that their name would be on the front page of the Los Angeles *Times*.

So you could write it off if—I say *if*—Owen never knew Sirhan. You could say that he was seeking publicity, it's a phony story. But you could write it off only if Owen never knew Sirhan.

The problem is that we have testimony from the witness stand under oath that prior to the assassination, prior even to June the 3rd, 1968, Owen may very well have known Sirhan Sirhan.

Johnny Gray's son, Jackie. We'll stipulate that he is a mental defective, that he is easily confused, that he contradicts himself, that he makes outrageous statements. . . . I will stipulate to that.

But the fact remains, and we simply cannot erase this fact from the record, that he did say he heard Reverend Owen and his father talking about Sirhan many times, that Owen bought clothing for Sirhan, gave Sirhan money, and that his father frequently said that he wanted Jackie to be just like Sirhan.

And it would be nice to say, "Well, this kid's a nut, forget about it." But sometimes nuts can say things that have much more validity than some person with an I.Q. of 200.

When Jackie said Sirhan, the obvious question is: did he mean someone else? And just because he is a mental defective, we can't automatically say he meant someone else. I don't think there is any evidence or indication that Jackie Gray confuses the names of people.

I asked him if his father and Owen had talked about Joe DiMaggio, and he testified he heard them mention his name once.

I asked, "Did you ever hear them talk about Michael Crulowitz?" And he responded, "No." He never heard them talk about Michael Crulowitz. So I wasn't putting a bib on him and spoon-feeding him and having him adopt everything I said. He was able to distinguish names.

And he was *certain* about Sirhan. I would like to read just a few excerpts from his testimony.

Page 1632 of the transcript:

Q. Jackie, you say that 1967 was the first time that Reverend Owen introduced Sirhan to your father?
A. Yes.
Q. Were you present at this time?
A. Yes.
Q. Where did this take place?
A. At his place.
Q. At whose place?
A. Reverend.

Q. And where was that located.
A. Santa Ana.

In Santa Ana. He didn't say in Madagascar, he said in Santa Ana. Where did he get this notion that he met Sirhan in Santa Ana? It just happens that Owen happened to live in Santa Ana in 1967.

If someone is a nut, and they come up with a fantasy, the likelihood that this fantasy would correspond with reality is probably one out of a million. Yet we have this young boy saying things that just happen to be accurate.

Turning to page 1640:

Q. What did you hear your father say about Sirhan?
A. Good things like schooling and going to school and stuff like that, buying clothes.
Q. Who was buying clothes?
A. He, for him. For him.
Q. Who was buying clothing? Who was doing the buying?
A. The Reverend.

I'm not putting words in his mouth.

A. *The Reverend!*

Page 1642—again, we have to ascertain whether this boy just adopts and accepts anything that's put out to him, and I don't think that's the case:

Q. Did you ever hear Reverend Owen talk about Senator Kennedy? [Senator Kennedy's name is as well-known as is Sirhan's. So if he is going to adopt names he would adopt that too.]
A. No. [Why does he say no to that?]
Q. Did you ever hear your father talk about Senator Kennedy?
A. No.
 [I said, "Have you ever heard of the word hypnosis?" Answer: "Yes."]
Q. Did you ever hear Reverend Owen or your father say anything about Sirhan being under hypnosis?
A. No.

What I am trying to say is that the boy *can* distinguish, he knows names, he knows events. So he is *not* a hopeless, mental basket case, although I will concede that unfortunately the lad is obviously not too bright. I would say that of all the things that the boy said on the witness stand there is one area, your Honor, I would ask the court to focus on. One area that from my experience as a trial lawyer stands out above everything else, because it had that unmistakeable ring of truth to it.

Jackie was a person who was easily led on the witness stand. His answers were flat. They were apathetic. But in this area, his responses were different.

I want the court to ask itself whether this sounds like someone who is fantasizing, because I am convinced that it's *not* a fantasy:

Page 1599.
Q. Have you ever heard the name Sirhan Sirhan?
A. Yes.
Q. Did you ever hear your father mention that name?
A. Yes.
Q. When?
A. Every time I ride with him he just say it.
Q. Pardon?
A. He just mentions it. It comes out his mouth. He mentions it. He mentions it every time. Every time it comes out his mouth. He mentions it when he riding.

It doesn't sound like fantasy. I didn't even ask him how many times he heard about Sirhan, and he volunteers the emphasis, not a flat, phlegmatic answer; he says, "All the time. My father talks about it all the time." [Bugliosi snapped his fingers to illustrate the spontaneity of the response.]

I can say from my experience as a trial lawyer, having hundreds upon hundreds of witnesses on that witness stand, that the answer, "That's all I ever heard," that Jackie Gray volunteered, and the aspect about his father mentioning Sirhan all the time, "He talks about it all the time. It is always coming out of his mouth," just the way those answers came out, sounded to me like he is telling the truth.

I will stipulate that Jackie Gray was certainly not the best witness in the world; and if we had to rely on his testimony as being "the star witness for the prosecution," we would be in rather sad shape.

The only problem for the plaintiff is that there happened to be another individual who was *not* a mental defective, a pretty straight-shooter, a cowboy, just as sensible and rational as the day is long, Bill Powers.

Bill Powers said some rather incriminating things about Reverend Owen. Plaintiff's counsel just glossed over his testimony like it was worthless, but there are a couple of things he said that obviously are extremely important.

He testified that a month or so before the assassination, a young lad by the name of Johnny Beckley was exercising Owen's horses, and Bill Powers and Reverend Owen were present, and Reverend Owen said something to the effect, "You're not doing a good job. And I know quite a few young boys at the track, including a kid by the name of *Sirhan Sirhan*, who I might bring in here."

That man Powers, it was obvious on that witness stand, when he didn't know something he said so. Many times he said, "I believe, I think," but he said he was *absolutely positive* that Reverend Owen used the name Sirhan!

"How can you remember?" I asked him.

He said, "Number one, it was an unusual name, and number two, shortly thereafter I heard the name again in connection with the RFK assassination."

Then we have the curious incident a day or two, or maybe a week or two, before the assassination. Reverend Owen, who prior thereto, at least in Bill Powers' mind, was not a man of substantial means—he used to drive around in an old clunker worth $50 or so—all of a sudden presents himself in a Lincoln Continental, a brand new car, and he has a roll of $1,000 bills, 25 to 30 $1,000 bills; and Powers testified that there was a black man in the front seat, and it turns out that this black man actually does exist and is a friend of Reverend Owen; and he is Johnny Gray.

So we *know* that the incident at Wild Bill's Stables was not fabricated by Powers—if the court had any notions about that.

And in the back seat there was an individual who *looks* like Sirhan. Now, Powers is not trying to frame Jerry Owen. He says the young man in the back seat of Owen's Lincoln *resembled* Sirhan. If this is a guy who was coming in here just seeking publicity, he would have said, "*Unquestionably*, it *was* Sirhan!" He would have said, "Reverend Owen *told* me it was Sirhan!" But he said, "I don't know; he *resembled* Sirhan."

Then there is this other related event where Reverend Owen takes out a thousand dollar bill and offers it to Bill Powers in payment for that pickup truck. Owen says, with respect to the thousand dollar bills, that he got them up North through his ministry, apparently talking to his flock, or his sheep, or what have you, and they gave him five or ten dollar bills, and he goes to some Chinese bank in San Francisco and has them converted into $1,000 bills. I think the court can take judicial notice that you have to sign your name when you secure $1,000 bills at a bank. "Did you sign your name?" I asked him, and he said, "I don't remember."

I say that this is a cockamamy story. Anybody who would believe a story like that would believe someone who said they heard a cow speaking the Spanish language. It is *not* a believable story!

Reverend Owen got the money someplace *other* than from the anonymous Chinese bank in San Francisco!

Jackie Gray in the back seat? Bugliosi conceded that there was a vague resemblance between Jackie and Sirhan, but the problem was that "Johnny Gray's son at the time of this incident would have been 13 years old and Bill Powers said the boy in the back seat was in his 20's." That would be difficult to mistake, he said, and so would the fact that the junior Gray "certainly has some Negroid features."

Then there was the encounter at the hay company during which Owen wanted to know whether the police had asked Powers about Sirhan. "If Owen did not know that Powers had seen him with Sirhan," Bugliosi pointed out, "he would have had no reason under the moon to ask Powers that question." As Bugliosi saw it, the issue was whether Owen or Powers was to be believed.

Well, if Owen was involved, he has every reason in the world to lie. Bill Powers, your Honor, I submit has no reason at all to lie. This man is in fear of his life. He doesn't want to get involved in this case. He wants to fade into the woodwork.

Moving to a legal point, Bugliosi argued that Owen's "cock-amamy story" about picking up Sirhan hitchhiking was circum-stantial evidence of a "consciousness of guilt." Citing the California code, he declared that "the jury is instructed that if a defendant lies about something or gives inconsistent statements, et cetera, it is circumstantial evidence of a consciousness of guilt." The attorney wanted to make sure the judge considered Owen in the context of a defendant who makes false statements to cover his participation in a crime.

Bugliosi went on to say that not too long ago, anyone who uttered "conspiracy" or "CIA" was chalked off as a "conspiracy buff."

But recent revelations, your Honor, have indicated that there is a little more credibility to the word "conspiracy." If there is a conspiracy here—[he paused for emphasis] it could possibly involve people in the highest levels of our government, or people out of the government who had substantial political interests inimicable to Senator Kennedy. And if it was a conspiracy, it most likely was a conspiracy of considerable magnitude, and someone like Owen would have been a lowly operative.

It was a quantum leap from horse trailers, boxing rings and sawdust evangelism to the corridors of power and executive suites, Bugliosi granted, but Watergate began as a "third-rate burglary" confined to low-level operatives. The attorney continued:

I will say this: if we are talking about a major conspiracy, the 25 to 30 $1,000 bills that Reverend Owen suddenly and mysteriously had in his possession just prior to the assassination is really a small amount of money, because if there was a conspiracy here, we are not talking about bugging one's opposition, which basically, when we separate the wheat from the chaff, is what Watergate is all about; we are talking about a conspiracy to commit murder, a conspiracy to assassinate someone who was a major candidate for the Presidency of the United States, a conspiracy the prodigious dimensions of which would make Watergate look like a one-roach marijuana case.

Bugliosi reiterated that the case was a circumstantial one, and that it was not necessary to present

a tape recorded conversation between Owen and Sirhan in which Owen is saying, "I want you to bump off Kennedy for me." Conspiracies are proven bit by bit, speck by speck, brick by brick, until all of a sudden you have a mosaic. They are proven by circumstantial evidence. Conspiracies are conceived in shadowy recesses. They are not hatched on television in front of 5,000,000 witnesses.

In deference to the position Crickard had taken during the trial, Bugliosi agreed that the civil trial was "an inappropriate forum to get at this issue." But he argued that Owen himself had perhaps inadvertently raised it by bringing the slander charge, and that the defense had merely attempted to prove the truth of the charge. Bugliosi closed by calling attention to the pall of fear hanging over the trial.

If Owen's story is just a silly Alice In Wonderland concoction to focus some cheap attention on himself, your Honor, and Powers lied on that witness stand, how come everyone is in fear in this case? Owen, I believe, testified that people are making death threats against him, which would be compatible with the notion that he was a lowly operative in the conspiracy, and people up above are the ones making the threats.

This young lad, Johnny Beckley, flees for his life. Bill Powers has to be brought into court with a crane. Jonn Christian, no one can find him. I don't think this is typical. I have handled many murder cases, but I have never seen a case where so many people are frightened. Are these things all meaningless? Are these people all cuckoo birds? [The deadly serious expression on Bugliosi's face answered these rhetorical questions.]

Declaring that the defense had "certainly put on just as much or more evidence that Owen was involved in the assassination of RFK than that he was not involved," Bugliosi asked the court to find for the defense in the RFK aspect of the civil defamation counts. The word "involved" (KCOP had said Owen had been "involved" in Senator Robert F. Kennedy's death) didn't necessarily mean that Owen was a witting part of a criminal conspiracy—many witnesses to crimes "don't want to get involved." But there was no escaping that he was up to his ears in the case. "If going to the police on the very same day of the assassination and telling them that you picked up the assassin the previous day and drove him to the scene of the assassination—if that's not being involved in the whole assassination episode, I don't know what in the world would be."

MIKE WAYLAND'S CLOSING REMARKS MIGHT HAVE BEEN KEPT TO himself, even though his contentions were both sound and valid:

neither KCOP nor any of its employees had, in any legal sense, done anything to libel Jerry Owen; and certainly "The Walking Bible" had presented no real evidence to prove that they had.

Wayland was to be made the victim of his secret relationship with Jonn Christian, however, once it was discovered by Judge Crickard that they had been rubbing shoulders when the suspect subpoena ("body attachment") had been issued on him. In what has to be the most questionable bit of judicial exercise ever to occur in Los Angeles Superior Court annals, Crickard virtually made Wayland throw away his clients' case, by ordering him to stipulate to one item of evidence put forth by Owen: the Yacullo-to-Hopkins memorandum that carried Christian's superimposed signature and our mailing address at the bottom, which the preacher's lady evangelist pal, Olga Graves, had densely admitted (in effect) had been sent to her by Owen, not Jonn Christian, as per the return address on the envelope.

Incredibly, Crickard instructed Wayland to make amends with the plaintiff's lawyers, who instantly demanded that he concede that his client, John Hopkins, had sent this otherwise innocuous document to Christian, with the full knowledge that he would then begin circulating it through the mails and having it attached to cars parked in lots belonging to the myriad of churches Owen insisted had shunned him. Once this Kafka-like move was effected, Crickard ruled it as valid evidence that malice had been involved by defendant Hopkins; then came his ultimate *non sequitur*, his comments on the RFK aspects of the trial:

. . . The court feels that the phraseology that we spent so much time on, that plaintiff was involved in the killing of Robert Kennedy, that the use of that phrase and the reference to the word "involved" certainly had reference to the plaintiff being criminally involved, and as such was slander against the plaintiff. . . .

The memorandum from Mr. Yacullo clearly explained to the people at KCOP [*sic*] that plaintiff's contact with the RFK assassination was not believed by the police, and we have to remember that the slander took place a year after the Kennedy assassination—the Robert F. Kennedy assassination—and so KCOP had a memorandum from its attorney, Mr. Yacullo, saying that plaintiff was not involved as far as the RFK assasination was concerned. . . .

The testimony—we have certainly spent quite a bit of time on during the trial [sic]—shows that plaintiff was not involved and that his only relationship to the assassination was that he may or may not have picked up Sirhan on the day before the assassination, but it certainly is not—does not make a person criminally involved in the killing of Robert Kennedy the next day.

The frown of puzzlement and extreme concern on Vince Bugliosi's brow rivaled anything displayed during the toughest moments of the Manson Family trial as Crickard banged down his gavel for the last time.

TV OFFICIAL FOUND GUILTY OF SLANDER
SAID EVANGELIST WAS INVOLVED
IN SEN. KENNEDY'S KILLING

The accompanying story in the Los Angeles *Times* read:

KCOP television executive John Hopkins slandered Oliver B. (Jerry) Owen, known as "The Walking Bible," when he said Owen was involved in the killing of Robert Kennedy, Superior Court Judge Jack A. Crickard ruled Thursday [after the trial ended].

Crickard, who will decide later how much KCOP must pay Owen in damages, ruled at the end of the month-long trial in which veteran prosecutor Vincent Bugliosi again raised the legal specter of a conspiracy in the June 5, 1968, slaying of Sen. Kennedy here. . . .

Bugliosi said his interest in reopening the investigation would not end with the civil trial. . . . He said he believes a special prosecutor should be named to take the case again to an "independent body," perhaps the grand jury here. . . .

A few days later Crickard fixed the award at $35,000, a token amount compared with what Owen was seeking. Moreover, the judge, who had dismissed Ohrbach's as a defendant, ordered Owen to pay the store $5,000 in court costs. Obviously the preacher considered the award a judicial slap in the face, if his behavior at an August hearing before Crickard to set counsel fees and expenses is any gauge. Arthur Evry and Mike Wayland came to an agreement, but Owen protested vehemently that he should receive

$10,000 for acting as his own attorney in pre-trial proceedings, not the mere $2,000 Crickard allowed. The preacher went so far as to tell the judge that if he would award the higher amount, the difference would be donated to his favorite charity. Wayland angrily called it a "flat-out bribery attempt," but Crickard acted as if he hadn't heard it. Later, outside the courtroom, Owen and Wayland tangled again—the ex-boxer invited the slender attorney outside to fight—before Evry and two bailiffs could separate them.

SEVERAL WEEKS LATER BUGLIOSI, CHRISTIAN AND TURNER WERE reviewing the trial in the lawyer's Beverly Hills office. As far as our own investigation was concerned, the outcome of Owen versus KCOP was not all that important—the stakes were merely monetary. For seven years we had tried to get the RFK case reopened in an appropriate criminal tribunal, for there was much more to it than could be presented within the confines of a libel and slander suit. Nevertheless, the trial had been a testing ground for important parts of our investigative file and the generating of sworn testimony from some key witnesses we had discovered. And the give-and-take questioning had convinced us more than ever that we were on target. This unprecedented trial had also produced a wealth of new information that had made the conspiracy "mosaic" Bugliosi talked of become much sharper in detail. And the cover-up was laid absolutely bare.

Bugliosi was in a reflective mood on this mid-August afternoon. He was somewhat chagrined that he had had no time to prepare for the *Owen* vs. *KCOP* trial. Nonetheless, his one-minute-to-midnight entrance into the affair had produced a near-miracle.

"Who knows where we might have been able to take this case if things had been different?" he contemplated. "But there's one thing I'm absolutely sure of now: this case has to be reopened and re-examined, from top to bottom—and not by those law enforcement officials who gave us the original conclusions either."

Epilogue

"The important thing to know about assassinations is not who fired the gun, but who paid for the bullets."

—Turkish police inspector in
Eric Ambler's *A Coffin for Dimitrios*

THE GEORGETOWN DISTRICT OF WASHINGTON IS NOTED FOR ITS lively dinner parties where high government officials and celebrities mix, discussing affairs of state as casually as the weather. But in August, 1975, shortly after the *Owen* vs. *KCOP* trial, a small circle of guests at the home of attorney Lester Hyman took bites of a forbidden conversational fruit along with dessert and coffee. The subject was the evidence of conspiracy in the assassination of Robert F. Kennedy.

The touchy point was raised by Dianne Hull and Paul Le Mat, in town to attend the premiere of their latest motion picture together, *Aloha, Bobby and Rose.* Their host, a former Democratic chairman of Massachusetts, friend of all three Kennedy brothers, and chairman of the American Jewish Committee, was well aware of Hull and Le Mat's interest in the RFK case. He knew that they were close to Jonn Christian, whom he had met two years earlier at the wedding of another friend of Robert Kennedy's, actor Robert Vaughn. And he knew that while in Washington they had buttonholed members of Congress and appeared in the media to press for a reopening of the RFK investigation.

What Hyman wasn't sure of was the reaction of his other guests that evening: Senator Walter Mondale and his wife Joan. Hyman had managed Mondale's brief campaign for the 1976 Democratic

presidential nomination, but the question of assassination conspiracy never came up, as it almost never did in Washington
political circles.

The Mondales listened intently as Hull and Le Mat gave their
presentation. "If what you say is true," the senator remarked somewhat skeptically, "this would involve a cover-up of incredible
dimensions." Hyman assured him that the stonewalling facts spoke
for themselves. Joan Mondale chided her husband, reminding him
that neither of them believed that Lee Harvey Oswald alone had
shot John Kennedy. From what Hull and Le Mat had said, there
was no reason to put stock in the official verdict in the death of
Robert Kennedy.

Ironically, all of those at the table that night would figure
prominently in the campaign of a then-obscure candidate for the
presidency, Jimmy Carter. Senator Mondale, of course, was selected
by Carter as his running mate and became Vice President. Lester
Hyman introduced Carter to former Israeli Prime Minister Golda
Meir and Jewish leaders in Beverly Hills, which both helped melt
the instinctive distrust American Jews felt for a "born again"
Christian from the South and generate vital campaign backing.
And Dianne Hull and Paul Le Mat were among Carter's earliest
supporters, drumming up interest in his candidacy in the Hollywood movie colony. After Hull had introduced him at a Green
Bay, Wisconsin, primary rally, Carter hugged and kissed her and
told the crowd, "I have had many introductions in the last few
years, but that was the finest, most moving one yet."

When Jimmy Carter won we felt that there might now be an
attentive ear in the White House. We recalled that in the early
stages of his presidential bid, in an appearance on the Los Angeles
television show of satirist Mort Sahl, he had expressed a belief that
the John Kennedy case should be re-examined, if only by unlocking
the National Archives and reviewing the many classified documents
sequestered there. But it is virtually axiomatic that political action
is contingent upon public opinion being brought to bear, particularly in controversial areas. In the JFK case the polls had long
shown that an overwhelming majority of Americans disbelieved
the conclusions of the Warren Report, but this was largely the result

of scores of books and articles published over the years demonstrating why Oswald could not have acted alone and illuminating shadowy areas. There is no comparable body of literature in the Robert Kennedy assassination, and in fact this is the first major book.

So we were heartened several years ago when the Washington *Post* decided that the RFK story should be pursued. Of all newspapers it was the least likely to reject the idea of conspiracy and cover-up in high places. Through its penetrative reporting on the Watergate affair, the *Post* was instrumental in convincing the American public of what really happened—and sending Richard Nixon to his political doom. The newspaper emerged as the paragon of what journalism was all about, and raised investigative reporting to a level of esteem it hadn't enjoyed in some time. The *Post* was the place where a new look into the RFK case should start.

IN LATE 1974 LESTER HYMAN CALLED HIS FRIEND BEN BRADLEE, the *Post* editor whose perspicacity and encouragement enabled reporters Bob Woodward and Carl Bernstein to persevere in trying to pierce the Watergate cover-up. Hyman told Bradlee about us and the elements of our investigative file. He also mentioned the "second gun" controversy that was then shaping up. The editor agreed that the *Post* should look into it. He assigned the story to veteran investigative reporter Ronald Kessler.

Before leaving for Los Angeles, Kessler phoned Turner, whom he previously had consulted on a number of stories. The reporter said that he was starting from scratch, and wanted to know whom to see and what to look for.

"Do you have the green light like on the bugging series, Ron?" Turner asked. The *Post* editors had indulged Kessler almost six months of digging on that one.

"Yes," Kessler affirmed. "I'll probably have to make several trips to Los Angeles."

"Okay," Turner said, "if you want to know what didn't happen, talk to Bill Harper, the criminalist. He can tell you why the official version is wrong—why there was more than one gun. Then if you want to know what did happen, about the conspiracy, talk to Jonn Christian." Kessler took down their phone numbers as well as the names of others Turner thought he should see to get going.

We later learned, however, that Kessler spent his first few days interviewing Los Angeles law-enforcement and FBI officials, and Bob Kaiser, who by this time had become a vehement critic of the "second gun" theory. Finally he showed up at Bill Harper's Pasadena home, but the criminalist considered his questions so uneducated that he offered Kessler a copy of his affidavit in the case, which is a kind of *McGuffey's Reader* of the "second gun" hypothesis. Kessler politely declined, saying he'd be back in several days. "There'll be plenty of time for me to read it then," he said.

Kessler never interviewed Christian or examined our files. When Christian tracked him down at his hotel, wondering what had happened, he was writing away. But he could not spare the time to talk, he said, because he was about to fly back to Washington. "How much time has Bradlee allowed to develop the story?" Christian asked, now somewhat concerned. "No deadline on this one," Kessler replied. "I'll be back next week and we can go from there."

So it was with utter disbelief that we read Kessler's by-lined story, run three days later on the *Post* front page, that was head-lined: "Ballistics Expert Discounts RFK 2d-Gun Theory." Date-lined Pasadena December 18, it began: "The nationally recognized ballistics expert whose claim gave rise to a theory that Robert F. Kennedy was not killed by Sirhan Bishara Sirhan this week admitted that there is no evidence to support his contention." The story was picked up by practically every major news outlet in the country.

Bill Harper was outraged when a distressed Lester Hyman called from Washington to find out about the story. Kessler must have distorted what he said, twisted the facts. There had been more than one gun, he was sure of it, and he had hardly "admitted" there was "no evidence" to support his position. But when Hyman called Ben Bradlee to complain, he received no satisfaction. Kessler had filed his story, and that was the end of it. The *Post* was not pursuing it further. Despite persistent requests, Bradlee refused to print a correction, retraction or Harper's version.

But the newspaper whose reporting was so exemplary in the Watergate scandal was not about to go unjudged by its peers in this one. In its September 1976 issue, the prestigious *Columbia Review of Journalism* rebuked: "The *Post*'s contentious and dilatory handling of the affair is a lesson in how *not* to accomplish [fair and accurate reporting]."

FOR THE LOS ANGELES TIMES, WHOSE RULING CHANDLER FAMILY wield enormous power in Los Angeles through their paper, the assassination of Robert F. Kennedy struck close to home. The candidate had been fatally shot in one of the city's landmark hotels, the case had been investigated by the LAPD, and Sirhan had been tried and convicted by Los Angeles prosecutors. As the *Times* saw it, the local institutions of government had performed well, unlike the shambles of Dallas. So when Vince Bugliosi declared himself a candidate for district attorney in August, 1975, only weeks after the *Owen* vs. *KCOP* trial, the *Times* raised its editorial voice in opposition to the prodigal son who wanted to reopen the RFK case.

The DA vacancy was created when Joe Busch had died suddenly a month earlier, and the County Board of Supervisors was considering a list of eleven candidates for the interim appointment. In his turn before the supervisors, Bugliosi stated that if selected he would launch a tough program against organized crime, try to get vicious criminals off the streets while preventing police harassment of those exercising First Amendment rights, and prosecute industrial polluters and corporations engaged in consumer fraud (the DA's office had always trod softly in those areas because members of the very Establishment controlling Los Angeles politics were implicated).

Bugliosi also promised to take steps to get at the actual facts in the RFK case. He said that he would name a blue-ribbon scientific task force to re-examine the evidence from top to bottom. He would assemble a team of top investigators and prosecutors in the DA's office to "examine and analyze the entire investigative files" of the LAPD, and issue a public invitation for all persons having information, including law enforcement officers, to come forward under a cloak of anonymity. He would ask the supervisors to help convene a special grand jury to hear the testimony of witnesses whose evidence contradicted the lone-assassin conclusion. He would cooperate with congressional committees that might look into the case, and open a "positive line of communication" with the citizenry after the years of secrecy.

Five years earlier, one of the *Times'* front-line reporters, Dave Smith, had recommended that the newspaper commit limited resources and backing to help our investigation progress. Contact with the *Times* had been made by our original benefactor, Peter Hitchcock of San Francisco, who interceded with his close friend Otis Chandler, the publisher. Editor Bill Thomas assigned Smith to vet our files and submit a recommendation. But after Smith urged a go-ahead, nothing happened. When he persisted he was at first ignored, then belittled, and finally shunted to a minor slot.

On August 20, 1975, the *Times* editorialized: "One interpretation of all this [Bugliosi's pronouncements on the RFK case] is that Bugliosi believes he has an emotional issue that he can exploit next summer in the election for a full-term district attorney." Bugliosi fired back an indignant letter that read in part: "For you to insinuate that my personal commitment to help resolve this controversy is selfish and politically motivated, is an affront to my professional integrity. . . . It is truly unfortunate that on the Robert F. Kennedy assassination, the editors at the *Times* are apparently out of touch with this community's attitude about this issue, and totally unaware of the concerned mood of the entire country. . . ."

It was no surprise when the supervisors passed over Bugliosi and settled on a compromise candidate, bakery heir John Van De Kamp. Although he had never even prosecuted a rape or murder case, Van De Kamp had more important credentials—his family were close to the Chandler family of the *Times*. When Bugliosi contested Van De Kamp in the 1976 election, he had a high degree of name recognition through *Helter Skelter*, which had eclipsed *In Cold Blood* as the best-selling crime book of all time. But that was about all. The Establishment saw him as someone they could not control, and closed ranks behind Van De Kamp, whose war chest brimmed with money. Even Attorney General Evelle Younger, who as a Republican might have been expected to stay out of a fight

among Democrats, was so anxious to keep the lid on the RFK case
that he endorsed Van De Kamp.

The Establishment's fear of Bugliosi was so great that they even
succeeded in pressuring CBS into blacking out the entire Los
Angeles area for the airing of the TV movie based on Bugliosi's
book *Helter Skelter*.

The *Times* naturally favored Van De Kamp but exceeded the
bounds of fair play by not reporting Bugliosi's press announce-
ments and publishing critical attacks on him instead. When actor
Robert Vaughn and Jocelyn Brando, Marlon's sister, wrote a letter protesting the manner in which the *Times* "has been using its
editorial pages and reporters to attack our friend and candidate
with a brand of journalism that is below the dignity of this community," the newspaper refused to publish it. So Vaughn, remembered from *The Man from U.N.C.L.E.* and the recent television
special *Washington Behind Closed Doors*, was left to make his
point to a thousand people at a fund-raising dinner at the Hollywood Palladium. "Vince Bugliosi alone," Vaughn told his audience
in an emotional speech, "has committed himself to resolve the very
serious and disturbing questions that have arisen about the death
of my good friend, Robert Kennedy, whose murder eight years ago
in this very city surely changed the course of American history."

Van De Kamp's public position was that he was not intractable
but would have to see proof. Six weeks before the election, veteran
CBS correspondent Bill Stout plunked down on his desk a set of
FBI photographs with captions—the same photographs that showed
extra bullet holes in the hotel pantry. The DA stared at them,
unwilling or unable to answer Stout's rhetorical questions about
their significance, then called FBI Director Clarence Kelley in
Washington. Kelley said he didn't know anything about the photographs but would check. He called back to say that the FBI had
not conducted any ballistics investigation in the case, which was
a semantical dodge. Van De Kamp assured Stout that he would
look into it and let him know. Stout is still waiting.

Bugliosi predictably lost the election, but he has lost none of
his determination to resolve the RFK case. In the fall of 1976
Bugliosi, one of the most-sought-after campus speakers in the
country, appeared before a packed house at Glassboro State College

in New Jersey to talk on the Manson Family case. By this time, however, he had been the subject of a *Penthouse* magazine interview in which he discussed the "extra bullets" aspect of the Kennedy assassination, and invariably someone would ask about it. When he finished that evening, a well-dressed man approached and politely asked, "May I have a word with you in private, Mr. Bugliosi?"

He introduced himself as William A. Bailey, an assistant professor of police science at a nearby college. He said that in 1968 he was an FBI special agent assigned to the Los Angeles office, and that some four hours after the Kennedy shooting he was instructed to meticulously examine the pantry to try to reconstruct the crime. "At one point during these observations," Bailey declared in a signed statement he wrote out for Bugliosi, "I [and several other agents] noted at least two [2] small caliber bullet holes in the center post of the two doors leading from the preparation room [pantry]. There was no question in any of our minds as to the fact that these were bullet holes & were not caused by food carts or other equipment in the preparation room."

Bugliosi now had in his pocket unimpeachable evidence that the holes had been caused by extra bullets, not food carts, as the Los Angeles authorities had tried to portray. Subsequently Bugliosi and Christian have posed a number of questions to Bailey by letter, and his answers cast further doubt on the integrity of the official investigation. Among other things, the ex-FBI agent recalled seeing bullet holes in the ceiling panels (which were destroyed by the LAPD) and discussing his observations with LAPD investigators on the scene, but there was no formal exchange between the two agencies attempting to reconcile the number and location of bullets. "I recall some discussion of FBI-LAPD discrepancies in ballistics findings by agents in the L.A. Office," he said, but he could not recall the details. Bailey said that he and his fellow agents had never bought the LAPD story that the last-minute change in routing RFK into the pantry was a "fluke" of fate. And he revealed that several agents who worked on the polka-dot-dress-girl angle "personally were not satisfied that they had found 'the right' woman," but their superiors ordered the matter closed.

As for the Jerry Owen investigation, Bailey commented: "First and foremost, to 'kiss off' OWEN's story as a 'publicity stunt' is investigative suicide considering the magnitude of the R.F.K. case and the information contained in [OWEN's] interview. One does not have to be a Sherlock Holmes to deduce that if OWEN was seeking publicity he sure 'screwed up' the chance of a lifetime." In Bailey's opinion, there were "Too many stones left unturned, too many coincidences!"*

BY THE LATE SUMMER OF 1976, WORD WAS CIRCULATING THAT the U.S. House of Representatives was seriously considering re-opening the John Kennedy and Martin Luther King, Jr., cases. The congressional black caucus had been profoundly disturbed by the account of a former Memphis police officer who had been assigned to watch over King during his visit in April 1968. The officer, Detective Ed Redditt, who is black, said that he had been pulled off the assignment only hours before the civil rights leader was slain. He was summoned to headquarters, Redditt related, and informed by Chief Frank Holloman, "Ed, there's a contract out on you." Holloman introduced him to a man identified as a Secret Service agent who had learned about the "contract" and flown down from Washington. Redditt thought the whole thing sounded fishy. Why would anyone want to pay to have him killed? Why would a Secret Service agent fly down when there was a local office that could have advised him? Holloman insisted that he not return to duty, and he was taken home in a police car to be placed under guard. Just as he was stepping out of the car, the radio blared the news that King had been shot.†

---

* The Bailey affidavit is dated November 14, 1976. His answers to the Bugliosi/Christian interrogatories are dated February 4 and June 17, 1977.

† According to Memphis *Press-Scimitar* reporter Wayne Chastain, Redditt subsequently told him about a Memphis undercover policeman who had played a part in the "security stripping" of King: "He left the police department shortly after, and the word was that he went to Washington, D.C. Then a couple of years after the King slaying I ran face to face with him in downtown Memphis. He was wearing a disguise. He acted very mysterious, saying that he was now with the Central Intelligence Agency, and begged me not to blow his cover." (San Francisco *Examiner*, October 10, 1976)

Shortly after Redditt told his story, a strikingly parallel story bobbed to the surface in Los Angeles. DID RFK's ORDER SEAL HIS DEATH? the *Herald-Examiner* bannered a front-page story on August 29, 1976. "In an angry outburst eight hours before his 1968 assassination," it began, "Robert F. Kennedy ordered Los Angeles Police Department bodyguards to stop protecting him and barred them from his presence—thereby possibly sealing his death warrant, according to sources here."

The principal source was retired LAPD security specialist Marion D. Hoover, who was quoted as saying that the LAPD had assigned a "Hot-Squad" of a dozen men from a headquarters "intelligence group" to guard Kennedy. Had the senator not ordered them off, Hoover contended, "we would have had three trained men on either side of him and one out front. And, although some of us might have been shot, we could have made all the difference in the world. . . ."

This was the first we heard that the police on their own initiative had attached an intelligence "Hot-Squad" to Kennedy (RFK intimates such as Jesse Unruh and Frank Burns knew nothing about it). But Hoover had another surprise. "Parker Center veterans don't bother to conceal their disgust over a presidential candidate entering a strange room," the story said, adding a direct quote from Hoover, "with only a few sports stars and what Secret Service could get through the mob to cover him.' " The story was doubly explicit on the matter of Secret Service protection. It asserted: "The Secret Service, traveling in two cars, advised LAPD commanders that they were 'walking on eggs' and that they were worried about their man's constant exposure from point to point." And it quoted LAPD press spokesman Commander Peter Hagan as saying of Hoover's abrupt dismissal by Kennedy: "That was one of our first indications that [Kennedy] intended to waste our usefulness and depend upon his small Secret Service contingent."

At the time that RFK was shot, the Secret Service was not authorized to protect presidential candidates—it was restricted to guarding the President and Vice President and their families. It was only as a result of the RFK assassination that the law was changed to include candidates.

From what Christian could find out from *Herald-Examiner*

City Editor Jack Brown, it appeared that the story had been planted on reporter Al Stump by the police. Braced about it by Lillian Castellano, a housewife and long-time assassination-conspiracy investigator, Commander Hagan disavowed the story completely. "He's no different than most of the others in the news media," Hagan said of Stump. But Stump, who had close law enforcement contacts, stuck by his story. "I trust the police! The police wouldn't lie!" he protested to Castellano.

Castellano brought the allegations about the Secret Service to the attention of Robert E. Powis, the agent in charge in Los Angeles. Special Agent Powis replied: "Be advised that the Secret Service was not guarding Robert F. Kennedy prior to the time of the shooting. We did not have agents with him at any time during his campaigning as a Presidential candidate." Powis said that he had written the *Herald-Examiner* asking that his letter be published or a retraction made.

A few weeks later the tabloid *National Enquirer*, in its issue of October 26, 1976, ran a feature story on Marion Hoover, who was billed as "a fantastic marksman who shot to death nine criminals in his 26-year, story-book career as a cop." Hoover repeated the claim that Kennedy had canceled the police protection, and this time was backed up by former Police Chief Thomas Reddin, who was quoted: "The indisputable fact is that he told us to get lost— and he paid for that order with his life." But this time not a word was mentioned about the Secret Service.

It was a baffling episode. While it was conceivable that the LAPD floated Hoover's story to forestall charges that it had been asleep at the switch at the time of the assassination, there is no accounting for the canard that the Secret Service guarded RFK. From the strange Secret Service man who told a Memphis detective he was under a death threat to the phantom Secret Service squad at Los Angeles, it was simply a riddle piled upon an enigma.

IT HAS BEEN A DECADE NOW SINCE ROBERT F. KENNEDY WAS MURdered, yet developments continue to unfold like a newsreel: The House of Representatives forms a Select Committee on Assassinations, but, initially at least, confines it to the John Kennedy and

Martin Luther King, Jr., cases. According to an FBI report filed
by Bill Bailey, two men claiming to be police officers and wearing
KENNEDY signs on chains around their necks had approached Ambassador Hotel busboy Juan Romero *the day before the assassination* to obtain kitchen workers' white jackets. An FBI document
is released, disclosing that a wealthy Southern California rancher
who had ties to the ultraright Minutemen and detested RFK because of his support of Cesar Chavez reportedly pledged $2,000
toward a $500,000 to $750,000 Mafia contract to kill the senator
"in the event it appeared he could receive the Democratic nomination" for President. It is revealed that in 1954 the CIA began
Project Artichoke, a secret study to determine whether a person
could unwittingly be induced to commit an assassination against
his will. It is learned that in 1963, following the John Kennedy
assassination, the CIA undertook a study of the assassination
applications of RHIC-EDOM (Radio-Hypnotic Intracerebral Control—Electronic Dissolution of Memory), scientific jargon for cre-
ating a Manchurian Candidate. Sirhan's lawyer, Godfrey Isaac,
vacillates on whether he would allow his client to submit to a
deprogramming effort, thinking it might somehow jeopardize a
future release on parole.

Considering the hostility and intransigence of the Los Angeles
Establishment, it is clear that the RFK case will have to be reopened
at the federal level, either within the Justice Department or by a
special prosecutor named by the President. With this in mind Dr.
Robert Joling, who wrote the introduction to this book, sent a
letter to President Jimmy Carter on May 17, 1977, advising him
of the obstructionist tactics by Los Angeles law enforcement officials.
"For too long now," Joling wrote, speaking of the Kennedy, King
and Kennedy assassinations, "the uncertainties, half-truths, and
blatant falsehoods about these events have led to widespread frustration and a disrespect for and a lack of faith in our governmental institutions."

A belated answer came from Albert L. Hartman, chief of the
General Crimes Section of the Justice Department, who by letter
dated October 18, 1977, maintained that while discrepancies in
the case did exist, "the evidence that Sirhan Sirhan acted alone in
the assassination remains compelling."

We hope that this book will shed enough light on the conspiracy and cover-up to persuade the Carter Administration and others in a position to act that the investigation must be reopened without further delay. Accordingly, we have asked Lester Hyman to deliver two sets of the bound galley proofs to Vice President Mondale, one for himself and one for President Carter.* To discover the truth is not simply an exercise in nostalgia, it is an insurance policy for the future. As we wrote in our 1968 congressional campaign brochure in calling for a reopening of the John Kennedy case, "To do less not only is indecent but might cost us the life of a future President of John Kennedy's instincts."

It did.

And it might again.

* In addition, we arranged for sets to be delivered to Governors Jerry Brown of California and George Wallace of Alabama; Leo McCarthy, speaker of the California Assembly; Senator James Mills, president pro tem of the California Senate; Los Angeles Mayor Thomas Bradley; Yvonne Brathwaite Burke, member of the House Select Committee on Assassinations and as of this writing a 1978 candidate for California Attorney General; U.S. Attorney Andrea Ordin, Los Angeles; and Mrs. Dorothy Courtney, foreperson of the 1977–78 Los Angeles County Grand Jury.

Appendix

The following unedited transcript is from William Turner's interview with Jerry Owen, tape-recorded on July 2, 1968; the interview took place at the law offices of Owen's personal attorney, George T. Davis, at 745 Market Street in San Francisco:

JERRY OWEN: I'm not going into full details, but I am going to give the highlights of a . . . incidents that happened . . . on a Monday afternoon . . . on June the 3rd . . . in downtown Los Angeles. I have a 19 . . . 48 Chevvy pickup truck . . . half-ton . . . and on the hood . . . I have a large . . . chrome horse that stands out that . . . everybody that is a horse-lover is attracted to it/whether driving, passing on the freeway or parked . . . and I left . . . my home in Santy Ana . . . California, headed for Oxnard to bring back . . . a Shetland pony that I had . . . sold to a schoolteacher from Huntington Beach for his two little children. . . . At Oxnard I had . . . 12 Shetland ponies and a Palomina saddle horse that I was leaving a man up there ride that works on the newspaper in . . . Oxnard.

And, I received a phone call that a robe was ready for a heavyweight boxer . . . by the name of O'Reilly . . . and I went down Los Angeles, with the truck, dressed in my old clothes . . . with Levis on . . . cowboy shoes and a plaid shirt . . . and . . . parked in the parking lot, went in and picked up the boxing shoes and picked up the robe and the trunks . . . and headed for Hollywood . . . to a friend that I know that is a sh-colored shoe man, to have him put some green shamrocks on the boxing shoes and his wife, who has her place of business joining his, who . . . is one of the leading . . . sewers, to sew the name and the decorations of shamrocks on the boxing trunks . . . and her husband put the shamrocks on his shoes.

So as I came down Hill Street, I cut over and ended up over on 7th Street . . . and was stopping at the light on 7th Street and Grand, knowing that if I made a right turn I could come in to the beginning of . . . Wilshire Boulevard, which ends on Grand.

And, as I was at the light, I noticed-eh two men . . . one of them was standing on my truck, about to crawl into the backend . . . and the other put his head in the door and asked if we were/I was going towards Hollywood out Wilshire . . . and . . . without practically sayin' . . . yes or no . . . the one boy jumped in and he said "We will ride in the back." . . . so I saw no harm in that . . . and they both crawled in the back and sat in the open pickup with their backs against the back of the cab. I looked in the mirror, occasionally, and noticed the one was kind of a bushy, dark-haired fella . . . and the other'n . . . was . . . of the same complexion and I thought that they were . . . Mexicans or . . . Hindus or something . . . and . . . got the impression that they were . . . kind of on the hippy-style and . . . as we . . . stopped at lights and went out Wilshire, out to MacArthur Park, and . . . made the stop at-eh . . . I believe its-eh . . . Wilshire . . . Place, and then maybe one more light or two—it's close to Vermont and Wilshire . . . and there, as I stopped at the light, I . . . noticed the one stand up and get out and they both got out . . . the taller one . . . and talked to someone standing there/there's a bank . . . and there is some seats . . . and they were talking to someone and quickly as I glanced, I noticed one was a well-dressed fellow that wasn't a young man, he seemed to be . . . past 30, maybe 35, in that neighborhood . . . and I noticed a girl who looked like she could have been around 19, 20, 21—dressed in slacks and-eh . . . kind of straight-like hair and kind of . . . what I would call a dirty blonde.

And . . . as . . . the light was getting ready, I was wa-watching my light to turn, the smaller of the two . . . put his head in the cab and had the door handle and he started to open the door, and said "Do you mind if I ride with you on out?"

So he got in and as we crossed, he talked about the horse . . . and he told me . . . that he was an exercise boy at a racetrack, and talked how he loved horses/quickly wanted to know if I had a ranch where he could get a job . . . and . . . talking, I . . . can't remember the exact little conversation back and forth, but something to that effect . . . and

. . . he turned to me and he said "Would it be all right if I stopped . . . I have a friend in the kitchen?" . . . and as . . . pointed to the street. . . . I made a left turn off Wilshire and, if my memory is right, I believe the street is Catalina 'r Santa Catalina or something like that . . . and there was a new-like building, a white place—Texaco—a parking place, parking lot or garage-like. He left, I waited and 10 minutes had gone by . . . I . . . felt that that was the last that I was going to see him, but he did say something about he would like to buy a lead pony . . . so he could go to work at the racetrack, and I told him I had a dandy up in Oxnard, a Palomina and so forth. And I gave up of him coming back and so I started the truck up, and I was going to make a U-turn at a little intersection, whip back and hit Wilshire and go on out to Wilshire and cut across . . . into Vine Street and Hollywood.

And he came on a run . . . I noticed his tennis shoes on . . . noticed his dress—a sweatshirt. He got in and he . . . kind of, he was sorry he was a little late, and we talked about different things going out, and I asked him if he was Mexican and . . . said "No"—and-eh . . . he informed me that he was born in Jordan. Well, that struck up a little conversation because my wife and I are planning to go to . . . Jerusalem and-eh . . . take a visit there . . . and-eh . . . we talked back and forth, and it seems to me he that he said that he had been over here for 13 years or was 13 years old when he left. Spoke good English . . . and-eh . . . seemed alright. And I just thought he was a young kid in his early 20's and so forth, and. . . .

As we turned and I stopped . . . at the Hollywood Ranch Market, where I had to park . . . and I went across the street . . . took my robe in, took the shoes in . . . came back and in the conversation he told me that if I could meet him at 11 o'clock . . . on Sunset Boulevard, that he would be able to purchase this horse . . . for the sum of $300 . . . there was a little talk of 250 or something, but I told him that I would let it go for $300, I'd guarantee the horse/if it didn't work I would take it back . . . because the horse . . . is a 10 year old, comin' 11, and he has been used as a pickup horse and as a pony horse and well-broke but he's a one-man's horse.

So, by this time, now, I would say it was . . . late in the afternoon, it was before 6 o'clock . . . and-eh I only went a few blocks up to Sunset, turned right, went a few blocks, and there . . . by the old . . . I believe back in '29 or '31 or 2 it was a Warner Brothers Studio Park, and then it was turned into a skatin' rink, and now it's a bowlin' alley . . . just before you get to the bowlin' alley on the corner is a bar, and then there is another business or somethin', and then there is a sign that says-eh . . . "Topless"—and I pulled there on that side and . . . he said "At 11 o'clock tonight I'll meet you here and I'll have the money to pay for the horse." . . . and . . . then somewhere along there in the conversation I said I could kill some time by going out to Saints and Sinners on Fairfax, and the minute I said Saints and Sinners he says kind of . . . like-startled, he wanted to know if I was a Jewish, and I said No, I'm not Jewish, I'm Welsh." . . . and he said "Well, I have no use for the . . . Hebes!" . . . and-eh . . . I kind of smiled and laughed and I said "I'll be here at 11."

So, I left, and I 'mediately went up to the Plaza Hotel and . . . put the car in the parking lot, right next to the Plaza Hotel, the truck, where Slapsie Maxie, my old friend for many years, and . . . we talked, and he said "Look" he said-eh . . . to me . . . calling me by name, "Curly, you gotta be at Saints and Sinners tonight, it's the last night, we've been there for years—Billy Gray's Bandbox—they're closin', next Monday night it's going to be out at the Friar's on Beverly, and . . . this'll be the greatest meeting in all and . . . with you and Henry Armstrong being the chartered members. . . . Come on and be there!" So . . . Max come out and he says-eh-I said "I can't go, Max. I'm dressed like a hayseed."— "Ah, what's the difference, Curly?" and he looked at the truck and the horse and he laughed, he said-eh . . . seeing me drive the old '48 truck right in the heart of Hollywood.

And . . . I went to Saints and Sinners, and I had O'Reilly . . . the boxer with me, and they introduced him that night . . . and at 11 o'clock—at little after 11, in that neighborhood—I went to the appointed place . . . down by the bowling alley . . . and as I pulled over to the right . . . plenty of places to park, and as I looked I didn't see anybody, but across the street . . . was a white . . . either 1948 or 1949 . . . Chivvy, off-colored white, and it looked like it could stand a wash job . . . and-eh . . . in the front . . . was a man . . . sittin' . . . and from the lights . . . he resembled the man . . . that I has seen, in the afternoon . . . down on Vermont and Wilshire . . . and there was the girl, from the looks of her hair and that, it looked like her, and on the other side was another person that I couldn't see . . . and this little fella . . . came across the street, come up, put his head in and said "I am very sorry" he said "Here's a hundred dollar bill . . . and I was supposed to have the rest of my money . . . but I don't have it, but if you'll meet me in the morning about 8 o'clock, I'll assure you that I'll take the horse definitely." . . . So, I didn't know . . . at first, I said "Well, now, look.

I've waited and I should be up in Oxnard . . . but I'll tell you what I'll do if you really mean business and want the horse . . . I'll . . . stay in this hotel right across the street" . . . where I registered . . . and I believe when I registers it was-it-it's have to be between 11:30 and 12:15 . . . that I registered there, in the hotel . . . and I said "I'll meet you at 8 o'clock and my truck will be in the parking lot right next to it." So, I went into a bar right next to the hotel and got a sanrich, a heated sanrich, and a cup of black coffee . . . 'cause I hadn't eaten . . . and went to bed . . . and got up and . . . I was shavin' . . . because I had a little cheap room, with . . . no shower, toilet—it was $4 for the room, plus tax . . . and the telephone rang, and a fellow . . . this-eh/I/a voice . . . that I had never heard before . . . wanted to know if I was the man that had the truck in the parking lot . . . and I said "Yes." . . . and . . . I . . . came down . . . and it was close to 8 o'clock, and all I had with me was my shavin' kit, dressed in my cowboy boots, my old clothes. I went out to the truck, which was parked right close to the street. Standing at the truck was a very well-dressed man . . . with . . . a expensive-looking late-style suit. He had on . . . a turtleneck sweater that was kind of an orangish-yellow color . . . with a . . . chain around his neck and a big, round thing that you see 'em all wearing now, even, many on television and that . . . and as I looked at him, he had . . . on what seemed to be an expensive pair of alligator shoes. He had a manicure. He had-eh . . . one of those cat's eye . . . ring on his little finger . . . and he said to me, he said . . . "Joe . . . couldn't make it." he said "Take this hundred dollars . . ." and he said "If you can be tonight . . . down, on the street . . . where you left him out this afternoon—at 11 o'clock tonight— if you can be there with the horse and a trailer . . . he'll definitely take the horse!" See? And he said "Take the hundred now, and just give us/ me a receipt . . ." and in my talkin', I look over and here set the car and I recognized the girl . . . because the car was parked close to me/ the night before the car was on the opposite side of the street, and I could just see the driver and the girl, but this time . . . the fella sittin' next to the girl, and the girl was in the car, and this man . . . was the driver, because the driver's seat was empty . . . and-eh . . . we talked back and forth and I said "Look" I said "Now, I've waited tonight . . . I stayed in the hotel . . . and I was told that we would have it definitely at 11, told we'd have it this morning. I have to be in Oxnard tonight to speak at the Calvary Baptist Church . . . and I got some . . . business there . . . and I cannot be . . . down . . . on that street" . . . which is S-S . . . Catalina 'r Santa Catalina Street . . . "tonight at 11!" . . . and finally I left, and before I left, I pulled a card out of my pocket and on the card it says:

SHEPHERD OF THE HILLS

Free Pony Rides For Boys
and Girls Who Go To The
Church Of Their Choice,
Learn A Bible Verse, And
Mind Their Parents.

. . . with my . . . unlisted phone number on it . . . and my address . . . in Santy Ana. And I said "Now, if he really means business" I said "It's not much from 11 til 8 in the morning . . ." I said "I can be there, and I'll deliver the horse where he wants it delivered . . ." and with that . . . I left, see . . . and . . . went on up to Oxnard, took care of my business, and in the morning . . . I . . . went out . . . I went down and got, I think, 5 bales of hay . . . to leave for some ponies that I have there. I have a church man that feeds them . . . and got in my truck . . . hooked on my two-horse trailer, loaded in a brown and white . . . spotted mare, and I roaded/loaded in . . . a little white stallion and a black gelding, two extrees, to see . . . if I could have Orie Tucker sell them for me . . . and I needed a little extree finances. . . .

And I drove into Los Angeles—it was around noon time, it might . . . I can't be exact. I know I was hungry and I had nothin' to eat, I didn't have any breakfast, so . . . eh-I stopped at the Coliseum Hotel, which is just off the Harbor Freeway . . . on . . . Exhibition. There . . . is a man by the name of . . . Bert Morris [Morse] who is an oldtime fight . . . manager, who had Baby Aremendez-eh . . . back in the '30s . . . and I knew that he had this restaurant and sanrich bar there by the University of Southern California and the Coliseum . . . and I thought I would go in and talk to him . . . and especially about this boxer, heavy-weight boxer, and a few things. So, I pulled off the freeway and just circled the corner, went right into the parking lot behind the hotel, and there was an entrance in . . . through his bar, into his restaurant. And . . . coming through the bar, there is a television/I heard something about the rigamarole, and people watching, and about the . . . 8 shots being fired and such, but I . . . being a minister, I just went/cut through the bar and went on into the counter/set down and ordered . . . a lunch. And . . . there was the . . . girl, the hostess and cashier, and I asked for Bert and [she] said "He will be here in just a moment." . . . So, I'm listening to television blast, and I believe there was a radio or something saying that . . . "Suspect has not spoken—can't get nothin' from him . . . but fast work by the police department/they have traced the gun . . . found out the gun was sold to a lady . . . in Pasadena . . . Lady didn't want it around"—and the lady, I think, either sold it or gave it to a neighbor or someone . . . and it came along about the name, some funny name . . . and what have you, and then as I'm listening, why I hear something sayin' . . . as a . . . commentator . . . on the boy . . . liked race horses, he was an exercise boy . . . and dressed in tennis shoes and different things . . . black, bushy hair. And, I'm not paying too much of it because . . . Bert. I'm waitin' for Bert, and Bert comes along, and I'm tellin' him, he's talkin' about his horses. He has a horse called Diamond Dip, and he has one called Hemet Mis . . . talkin' about boxing and now how . . . well he is doin' with his horses and so forth . . . and I told him, I said "You oughtta come back in back" and I said "I got some . . . nice little pony stallion back here." "Boy" he said "I got a little black one out on the ranch is a teaser, is a dandy." And, we're just talkin' old times and so forth.

"And, I-ya . . . you know, I had a funny thing happen. I-(laugh) I'm gonna have to get goin' pretty quick, my wife is 'spectin' me. I started out Monday and picked up a couple of hippies, I guess, or kids, and isn't it funny, a guy shows you a hundred dollar bill, wants the horse'n stalls you in a wait-over." and blah-you just as a matter of conversation. And all of a sudden . . . a picture was flashed . . . on the television. And doin' my talkin', I'm listening to him and thinking and . . . and as I jus/sai . . . (whisper) "Hey . . . that's the guy . . . was in my truck . . ." And then the . . . "Yeah, that's the fella was in my truck!!!"

And then the waitress and the cashier, she handed me the Hollywood Citizen News, who had a picture of him in this extree on the front page. I looked at it, and I said "That's the kid . . . That's him!!" So . . . Doug Lewis, another old trainer, has some boys who train up at Jake's (Shugrue) Gym, was there . . . and I went over the whole st-ah—said "Can you beat that. That rascal" and so forth, and we got to discussing and one of 'em said "Well, man . . . maybe they wanted you there at 11 o'clock so that if this thing went the way it should have, they could have jumped in and rode away with the horse, with you, or something." I said "Well, that could be . . . I wonder . . ." . . . just talkin' back and forth . . . so . . . Doug spoke up and said "You oughtta do the right thing and take this to the police." . . . I said-eh . . . "Ah, it's no use. They've caught him single-handed. Listen, they're fayi-sayin' that after this . . . athlete has grabbed him and they got the gun, they don't need no more." And then . . . Bert spoke up and he says "I know, but have you been following this-eh Garrison investigation of other stuff and so forth? You never can tell, maybe Kennedy'll die" . . . See at this time he was unconscious. . . .

And they . . . must have talked to me for 15 minutes, and I said "Naw, I don't want to forget it. I'm a/in church work and a minister. I don't want to be bothered with it." and so forth . . . "just a coincidence." I said-eh "He sure looks like the fella." I said "I'd have to really hear his voice/I'd ner/and I'm sure if I could hear his voice I'd know definitely." Then the waitress came over, the hostess, and she said "Well" she said "I'd tell you what I'd do if I 'as you. I'd be a good citizen. I think it's your duty." . . . and all of them together. . . .

So, the next thing you know . . . the University police station is just a little ways from there . . . and I played Freshman Football at the University of Southern California . . . and the station used to be right on the campus, but they moved up on Exhibition on there between Vermont and Western. So . . . I end up going/driving the . . . trailer down there and the car . . . my ponies on the back . . . go in and talk to the men, and . . . the minute they hear it, they . . . have me drive in and leave the car in the back, and I heard them say something about taking fingerprints. They took me inside and . . . I phoned my wife and told my wife I would be detained for a while, and-eh . . . they took a recording of . . . what I am saying here . . . and . . . also had a stenographer there, who took it all . . . in shorthand. . . . And, as I . . . told them about seeing the $100, well, one of them . . . must have been listening in the other room, because the machine wasn't there, and I think the machine was behind the desk into the relay room, and one of them came in and said . . . "He sure . . . knows what he's talkin' about 'cause it was just released now that they found $400 bills . . . on this man . . . and there was nothin' about any money on him until then . . . " and I had already told them about . . . this in the early part that I was in there before they took the recording. . . . So the detectives talked about "What shall we do? Well, it's assigned downtown . . ." . . . so I left, and I—they had me there from in the afternoon, and it was about 6:30, quarter to 7 when they were finished with everything . . . and . . . I went outside and it looked like on the doors and on the side that there'd been some kind of powder or something—I didn't see them take any fingerprints, but I heard the detectives say that they should. . . .

I got in my truck and went home. And-eh, of course my wife was-eh wanted to know, and I told my wife and my daughter about what I thought . . . had happened, that this was the fella . . . that was in the truck. And, the next afternoon . . . now the police assured me, the detectives assured me, at the University Station, that . . . my name wouldn't be mentioned and nothin'd be in the paper, 'cause I told them. I said "Look what's happened to this . . . Ruby shootin' a fella and all this stuff that's goin' on. And . . . if this is/they are together, they've got my card and my telephone number, why, anything could happen." So they said this is going to be one of the most secret things/nothin's going to happen in this case like it happened in Dallas.

So, the next afternoon . . . I don't know exactly what time but it was . . . I am sure after 2 o'clock . . . eh-telephone rang and . . . somebody answered it at—home and no answer. It rang again and no answer. It was either my wife or my daughter, and . . . wasn't too long 'til it rang again and I picked the phone up and it said—eh "Are you the Shepherd? . . . the man with the horses? . . . Keep your mother-blankety-blank mouth shut about this . . . horse deal . . . or else!" I don't know wha/by that time I was startled . . . and I remember that much of it, and I remember the phone . . . hittin' fast, like they just banged it. I went out in the back . . . where the horses were and looked at the-these . . . horses, petted the dog, and I got to thinking, and I . . . I didn't want to say nothing to my wife about it . . . and that night, she told me, she said "Well, honey, they/why did you give them the card/our phone number, unlisted?" I said "Well, you know, honey, we need some money, and . . . it'll help on the . . . payment." And I said "Three hundred bucks isn't bad, and the fella shows me a hundred dollars and says that they'd have it . . ." and I said "Well, look, I can't be there at 11 o'clock tonight, but if he . . . wants the horse and he's got the money, why . . . 8 o'clock Wednesday morning, I'll deliver the horse." So she said "Well, at least, anyhow, they know where you are." and I passed it off and didn't say anything. . . .

So, that week went by . . . next weeks/well, I-I-they've got it on record. I-I can't remember the day . . . exactly on this, but they ca-I got a call fr-to come to the detective agency downtown and whoever called me said "Look you know where the place is . . ." I said "I know where the building is/I've never been in it." He says "Come to the 3rd floor, that's the detective . . . information, you stand there and . . . you be there at such and such a time and a man'll come down and just say 'Are you Owen?' and you go from there." . . .

So, as I went downtown, I got hold of Reverend Perkins—a man that's almost 80 years old—a retired Methodist minister, a very dear friend of mine. I said "Perk, come on. Come on, let's do down to the police station" and I briefed him, I said "I want you to be with me when I go in there, don't wanna go in alone. . . ." So, he went along with me and, of course, I told him, I said "Now look" I said "Perk, you believe in prayer" I said "You pray because . . ." I said to Perk "I've had one threat, I haven't told Roberta or the kids about it . . ." . . . So . . . we walked up to the 3rd floor, and a man came up . . . at the . . . time that my appointment was made, took me to the 8th floor . . . I don't remember the room number, but . . . as you walk in a large room . . . first is a-eh small narrow . . . place, about this long, maybe 20 feet long, and it's all glass, and here's a wooden counter, and as I look through I saw 5 or 6 . . . typewriters goin' and . . . saw a bunch of men around. Found out it was a special room handling this case and everything was on this case, I guess, in there—the girls and all the detectives with their stuff. And while I'm watchin' this little door, like a cupboard I thought it was, opened up and a man came out and he said "Are you-eh . . . Jerry Owen?" "Yes." He said "Well, the man that you had the 'pointment with is called away . . . and could you wait for an hour?" and I said "Well, I tell ya, I'm leavin' for Phoenix, it's important I go to Phoenix. I want to drive straight through . . . and I want to get a little sleep tonight because I got business early." Now this is in the afternoon . . . so . . . he said "Well, just a minute." I said "I'd 'preciate if we could do it right now." So, finally, he went through the door . . . and two or three minutes elapsed, another man came out . . . and handed me . . . a stack of pictures . . . with the white, like this, facing me, but they were a little narrow and longer . . . and I believe, if I remembers right, there was . . . a picture on each side, see . . . I think it was divided in the middle and the same fellow, one with a front view and the one with the side view, all had numbers on the front of 'em, see? Ah . . . so he said "You look through here and see if you can find . . . anyone that was riding . . . in your truck." So I took them, like this . . . and turned each one of them over and put it down, covered it up and I don't know how many pictures they were, they were several . . . and after going through a few, I said "This is one of the fellows . . . right here." and I laid it down and I went on through and I said "This is all I see . . ." but I says "Let's make sure now." See? So, then I . . . turn/I ask him "I-can I turn the pictures over?" and I laid them all down on this long thing on the windows and went through them and I said "This is him." See? So, he took the picture . . . and had a piece of a report sheet, like this, with a snap on it . . . and s-took this/the picture, like this, behind them, like that . . . then he said "Now" he said "I haven't had time to read the report from the University Station . . . and-eh is there anything, anything that you can remember that you didn't put in?" See? And-eh, I said to him "Ah, yes . . . I had a threat . . . the day Kennedy died . . . in the afternoon." And then

Mr. Perkins said to him, he said "Is that Sirhan Sirhan's picture that he needs?" He wouldn't say a word, see? I don't know if that's the way they do it. He said that he wouldn't comment. He said "I don't know. I'm not at liberty, I don't know." And it was covered up, see, behind. . . .

So, now we leave. Now I go to Phoenix and drive all night and return home early in the morning—my wife and I sleep until about noon . . . and . . . she goes . . . out in the back . . . to fool with the . . . we got a big backyard and an orchard and then the corrals. And she was watering the philanth-roses or somethin'. . . . The phone rings, I answer it, right by the bed. "We told you to keep your Mother 'F' mouth shut." Again, another threat-like . . . hung up fast . . . and-eh, my wife came in and-eh "Who was that?" . . . and I said "Oh, honey, just . . . somebody callin'," . . . brushed it off. . . . Now, that's on Saturday. Sunday I go to Oxnard, with my family. I come home . . . Monday goes by . . . Tuesday goes by . . . Wednesday afternoon . . . between 3:30 and 5 . . . the phone rings . . . my wife answers, calls me to the phone. "Hello, is this-eh Jerry Owen?" "Yes." "This is Sergeant . . . somebody." Now, I don't remember the name . . . this was a sergeant. "I'd like to talk to you about this case. Could you come right down?" . . . "Well" I said "you caught me . . . at the wrong time." I said "It's 106 miles to Oxnard and I . . . speak there tonight . . . and the freeway traffic is terrible, and if I leave at 5 o'clock I'm lucky to get there at-at 7:30, 2 hours and a half going-eh all the freeway practically all the way up there to Oxnard." "Ah . . . What are you doing after your s-s-speaking tonight?" "Well" I said "I'm leaving, I'm packed. I'm leavin' for the Bay, Oakland. I got 'mportant business." . . . "When will you be back from Oakland?" I said "I don't suppose I'll be back until Monday . . . 'cause I'm goin' to speak in Hayward . . . over Sunday . . ." . . . "Just a minute . . ." . . . Now a man . . . someone comes to the phone and . . . gives the name . . . of Sandlin . . . "And it happens to be that I'm going to be in the Bay District . . . Saturday. I'd 'preciate it very much if I could see you about this and have time to sit down and go over it."—"Well" I said . . . "certainly" I said "Officer Sandlin." . . . Then he turned to me and he said to me "Are you Owens . . . was an athlete around here? . . . Did you go to high school?" I said "I went to Manual Arts." He said "That's where it rings a bell." he said "I see that you are the same age as me when you were at Manual Arts . . . I was at Jefferson." So he said "I guess we played football against each other." So we reminisced a little. Now, I never saw the man. I'm just talkin' on the phone. . . .

I leave . . . go on to Oxnard . . . drive all night. I arrive Thursday morning on this . . . last week . . . which would be about the 26th or

27th, I arrive up here, and I check in a motel on Telegraph . . . I phone
. . . Ben Hardister, who is an investigator-friend that I had been at his
ranch and rode horses 'n went deer huntin' and . . . been over to George
Davis' place, and . . . first met him when he was about 16 or 17 years
old . . . which goes back to 30 or 30/maybe 30 years ago, or maybe
28 years ago, whatever it was. And-eh I phoned him, and I said "I
drove all night." He said "Well, pardner" he said "I'll pick you up
around 1:00, maybe 12:30, 1:00, 1:30." So he came over and we got
in the car and I went with him out to Richmond where he had to put
some-eh guards on a garbage place that had been threatened by the
strike, and another few things to do. And then we drove down into
Richmond and . . . saw the windows . . . that had been broke out, and
saw the furniture store that had been fired and . . . all . . . nothin' left but
the . . . debree. . . . And I said "Ben, I am so tired. I know you are busy
and I don't want to interfere. Take me back and I'm going to bed 'cause
I . . . haven't had any sleep, and I lost sleep when I went to Phoenix,
over and back . . . I'll catch up . . . I'll go to sleep now, and I'll sleep
until noon tomorry. You come at 12." So, I went right in and . . . went
to bed early in the afternoon, maybe 5 o'clock or somethin' . . . and
slept through until 10 o'clock Friday. . . . Got up . . . and . . . what I
forgot to put in there . . . was the officer . . . that I talked to . . . this
Sandlin, he told me . . . wanta know where he could contact me up in
the Bay District and I gave him "George T. Davis, 724 Market Street" I
stated that "I don't have the phone number here, but information will
give it to you . . . but here's my brother's telephone number in San
Bruno." And if I recall, the man that I talked to said "Well, I'm going
to be in Palo Alto." I said "Well, that's not too far from San Bruno . . .
and . . . sure I'll come and see you. Let me know." Now this is Wednesday afternoon. I hear no more until I phone my wife on Friday. My wife
tells me that . . . "Mr. Sandlin will be . . . at the . . . Tower . . . of Hyatt
. . . House in Palo Alto . . ." And that he was insured, she insured him
that I'd certainly be there at . . . Saturday before noon. So, on the phone,
the girl there at the switchboard just scribbled, I told her I didn't have
a pencil . . . "Would you please write this for me?" and she wrote, I
think "The Hyatt House . . ." and the message was "Be in there Friday
night—and stay Saturday and leave Sunday morning." See? So I stuck
the message in my pocket, thought no more of it . . . and went with Ben.
And then, about 4 o'clock, 3:35 or 3:30, I think we stopped at the
Athens Club, went in and sat down . . . and Ben says "Now, I'm going
to be busy from 4 to 5."—it was about quarter 'til 4 then ". . . and-eh,
do you want a paper?" And he went over and purchased a paper. And

. . . we sat down there, and he took/he gave me the front half, he took the other half. And we read it back and forth and kicked it around a little. And I didn't read the one part of it. I looked at the Sports Page and the front and Ben left. So, I picked up the paper again and . . . the second or third page I see . . . "Witnesses Disappear. . . ." I look at the fella's picture first and see his name. Then I look and see that it's the Ray thing. The fella that's over in England. And the report there in the paper states that the two witnesses in this case mysteriously disappear, the woman that owned the rooming house, or the landlady, and one of the tenants there that saw Ray . . . there and could 'dentify him with the gun, or goin' into the bathroom or somethin'—had mysteriously disappeared. Nobody knows what happened to 'em—no information from the police . . . unless to the effect that they were under protective custody. But nobody knew anything about it. . . . Then as I looked there at his picture, I got to thinkin', I said "Isn't it a funny thing? . . ." My mind drifted back to Ruby goin' in and shootin' the fella. Then I have occasionally-eh heard flashes about Garrison and witnesses dyin' or disappearin' mysteriously or somethin' happening all of a sudden. Then I really got to thinking about it. I said "Now, what? . . . If this is so. . . ." And then there was another flash, another section, a little tiny bit. If you remember, if you get that Oakland paper, it stated that the attorney on the case now had received two threats. One of them stating there was 250,000 . . . Arabians over here, se? And-eh, that he had received . . . a phone call and a written thing, see? And I said "Well, just think. They want to go after the attorney . . . wants to prosecute a man." Then I started to thinking seriously for the first time. Now I had told . . . I was told . . . by the University Division, I don't know which one, of course, when I cam in there, I believe every detective left his desk and came around, when I was standing there telling about it, see? On Wednesday, they were all bubbling over there. The head fellows, assistants and all of 'em. And I was told not to . . . say anything, not to worry, that my name wouldn't be put in the papers or anything else. Then I got to thinkin' again about giving them the card and the two phone calls . . . and I wasn't going to tell Ben Hardister a thing about it . . . and Ben came back a little after 5 and he says "Well, let's go to the ranch for the weekend." He says "Let's go up and get your car . . . park your car in the parking lot here at the Athens . . . lock'er up and come with me. . . ." So I got to thinkin' "Well, I'd better come back and tell Ben." "Ben, I'll be at your ranch tomorrow afternoon . . ." 'cause I knew about this appointment with this supposed-to-be-man Sandlin. And I got in the car with Ben. And, if Ben remembers—he's seated right here—I said "Ben I'm gonna tell tell you somethin' . . . it's like a pipe/like a pipedream or a mystery, see? It's hard to believe, but here's what happened." So I started tellin' Ben, see? I said "Ben" I said "I'm to meet a detective tomorrow over in . . . Palo Alto. . . ." Well, I saw Ben startle a little bit. He says "Now, what is it now, pardner?"—He has an expression of sayin' "pardner."—I said "Ben, now listen to this. Of all the people in the world, and the millions of people . . . that I would be drivin' . . ." I went around the bush at first. I told him "I'm drivin' an old truck, with my old clothes on, and the horse. . . ." And I tell Ben about it, give him a rundown, tell him about the two threats, tell him about this phone call. Ben's drivin', and he says "Do you know this man?" I says "Never saw him before in my life." "You can't identify him?" Ben says "You mean to tell me you are going to go over there now and see somebody you don't know who it is?" He says "I'm not gonna let ya!" That's what he said "You're not going without me!" He says "No. sir! You got (an) appointment in the morning" he says "we'll go to the ranch and we'll think this over." So, 3 or 4 times he shook his head and he said "Just think of all the millions of people. . . ." You remember this, don't you, Ben? ". . . in California, that you have to be at that time, with that truck?" But he says "I guess" he says "I guess there's a reason for everything. I don't know what it is." and he just seemed to be startled, as he shook his head, and then he told me, he says "We'll stop in Napa." he said "I got a friend here named Wes Parker . . ." I mean Wes Gardner, I'm sorry. . . . "who has been to . . . the FBI school or something about the FBI, and he's been the under-Sheriff or next to the Sheriff and a lot of experience and solved a lot of—murders and different things. Let's go just . . . get his viewpoint on it. Let's talk to him." So, we drove into the Boy's Club, where he happened to be . . . in his own office back there, and we told him the story and he told me "No, that's the worst thing you can do. You mean to tell me you don't know who Sandlin is? You never met him? You couldn't identify him . . . and you're gonna walk over there . . . with two threats? Maybe that's just the way that they're settin' it up. No sir." and Wes says "Well, I'll tell you what we'll do" he says "We'll see if the FBI agents herein town that I knew . . ."—found out that he wasn't, that he was gone. So, then, finally, he phoned the Sheriff, and I guess the Sheriff didn't know of any FBI numbers there. The next thing, we finally got, somehow, we got hold of an FBI agent in . . . Vallejo, said "All we want you to do is find out if there is a L. L. Sandlin . . . and if he is at the Hyatt House." See? "And if this is authentic. We want to know." Well, now, that was approximately between 8 and 9 o'clock . . . on . . . Friday night, we heard no word back. They knew where to contact Ben's home number . . . the information. We get up in the morning . . . and we decide to go over and see George T. Davis, who I've known since 1937, who has a ranch . . . just a little ways from Ben's ranch, in Pope Valley. George and his wife is havin' breakfast, and we sit down and laugh a little bit. Then . . . I talkin' over old times . . . I says "George" I says "Here's a funny thing happened." So I tell George . . . and I said "George, what should I do?" He says "Why, certainly" he says "Let me/we'll solve it." He went to the phone. He picked up the phone. Now here it is between 11 and 12 o'clock noon. He puts the call through to the Hyatt House for an L. L. Sandlin, in Palo Alto. We're listenin' to him there. The answer is "There is no L.L. Sandlin registered. No reservation." They know nothing about it. So I get to thinkin' "Friday night he's supposed to be there, the man tells me Saturday. Maybe it's a good thing I did tell Ben about this. Maybe it's a good thing. Man, I could have walked in there and got plugged or . . . a fellow come along and pose [as] an officer and got me in a car and said 'Well, let's go in and see the Sheriff or the policeman here . . .' and dumped me in the Bay or something." I said "Maybe this is just the hand of God!!!"

So, then George says "Alright, the next move will be I'll phone the District Attorney's office and find out who's in charge." George ran up against a stone wall. Nobody was there Saturday. They knew nothin' . . . couldn't get through to nothin' . . . and just seemed like they were stalling. So George says "I'll get hold of . . . someone else." I don't know if it was Unruh, Jessie Unruh, or something. Now, he put another call through to the Sheriff, couldn't get the/she couldn't get the Sheriff. Then, after the D.A.—no answer. Then he got Unruh . . . and we sat in George's house.

And now it's-eh now it's pushing 1 o'clock and then the next thing, the phones start ringing back and forth. He gets the-eh ("Chief of Police") Chief of Police, phones him down there. Chief of Police says "We'll check on things . . ." this and that . . . "Phone you back." Back 'nd forth it went. So, finally, in the afternoon, maybe 3 o'clock or 3:30, the Chief of Police confirms there is an L. L. Sandlin that's a Sergeant. Nobody, I guess . . . so that's that. So we find out that much. Now, in the meantime, we've heard not a thing from the F-FBI department. ("You don't know whether Sandlin was up here?") No, sir. Now, I'm g-gonna go a little farther. No, sir, we didn't know, we didn't find a thing out. They knew nothin' about it . . . 'proximately 5:30, I was watchin' the clock . . . off and on, because they was a reporters, a cameraman there waitin' 'n come in on the thing . . . and-eh at about

5:30 the phone rings and George talks and it's another policeman in the investigation department . . . that's talkin' to George and verinfyin' that L. L. Sandlin and so forth, and they want to talk to me, so George puts me on, see? And he said "Mr. Owen" he said "I can verify that you talked to L. L. Sandlin . . . Wednesday afternoon." Now Sandlin told this man it was Thursday morning he talked to me, but it wasn't, 'cause I was up here Thursday, see? "You had a conversation with him today?" So . . . I verified "Yes, you talked to him, but we decided after he made the appointment . . . that it was the wrong thing to talk to you up in Palo Alto, see? . . . that we should talk to you here." I said "Well, then, whyyy . . . din't you notify my brother, my wife, or George T. Davis?" Well, he didn't have an answer, see? I said "You phoned me to make the appointment . . ." and I says . . . hummed and hawed around, and I said "You know I've got some threats." and he says "I've read the report."

And-eh . . . I hadn't had time, I hadn't seen him, I only told him about the first threat. I haven't told him about the second threat. That morning, Saturday, after I came back from Phoenix, but I was going to tell Sandlin when I met him . . . my next interview with him, see? And I said "I've had two threats" and so forth . . . I said "I got a wife down there, two children and a grandson. How about now?" "Oh" he says "I'm sure they will be alright. Just a misunderstanding." Yes, he should have, but something, and he tried to . . . apple-polish the thing and do something to it in someway.

And, in the meantime, I didn't know that the 'sociated Repre-Press was listening on an extension in George's front room—he heard this, see?—conversation to verify I had the appointment. So, finally he said "Well, how do you feel now?" I said "Well, I'll feel a whole lot better when I find out this was Sandlin and was/wasn't somebody else." "Well" he says "I'm sure it'll be alright. Just let things go as they were . . . before . . . When you came back in town, when you come in Monday or Tuesday, come on in and see us." and so forth. And, then, the last thing he said . . . he said "Say Owen" he said "The report's here some place, ah, could I have your telephone number and your address again?" See? And with that, then George took the phone and the 'sociated press fellow, boy, that got him, he said "Boy, what kind of a . . . police force is this? Wantin' to know your telephone number . . . what/how are they handlin' things?"

So, that is the situation and from now on, why . . . eh, that's as far as I can tell you. That's it. And if Wes wants to say something or-eh if-eh Mr. Hardister wants to say anything . . . they can both confirm . . . my part here . . . of bein' in Oakland and so forth . . . and him telling me . . . not to go over and see him and takin' me . . . to-eh-his-eh . . . the man he works for, Wes here he's with, see?

("There was the car that almost ran you off the road?") Ah, well, ahmm-eh, I'll tell you this here, what happened. When George . . . I came in with . . . George Davis then, Monday morning, and at 5th and Mission, I got out of George's car to go into the Chronicle . . . and as George pulled away from the curb, there was a . . . 'bout-eh Cadillac, that's maybe a '66 or a '65 or 7 pulled up, with a heavy-set eye-talian-lookin' man with a cigar in his mouth and a hat on, and he just pulled over and said "Say" he says "Was that George T. Davis who-who's car you just got out of?" And, with that I said "Who's car?"—and scrammed inside this building. I don't know who that was. It maybe could of been somebody who wanted George, a reporter or somethin', I don't know.

And, then I'm going to let Ben tell you-eh about the car. He knows the roads and that. We had a car . . . pull up and s-s-almost stop dead in front of us a couple of times and go real slow so we couldn't pass it . . . and put his fist up. And the ki-these/one-the fellow that wasn't driving kept lookin' back, so I took a pencil in a piece of paper and started to/got the license number, and they saw me writing. They . . . disappeared. They sped on it. But, Ben can explain that to you. That was a strange thing.

So-eh, if there's any other questions you'd like to ask me now, I'll answer 'em and maybe Ben wants to say somethin', or maybe Wes does. I don't know. Is there anything else you want to ask me?

("Jerry, you say you know Edgar Eugene Bradley of North Hollywood, that you met him in Dr. (Carl) McIntyre's company?") Yes-eh-yes, I-I met him-eh. I know that-eh he was affiliated with Dr. McIntyre. And I met him at the Embassy Auditorium . . . a place where they give all kinds of lectures . . . and so forth. And I . . . two times. I shook hands with him once, and then I seen him another time.

("Do you know Dr. Bob Wells, down in Orange?") Very well. He don't live too far from me. Yes. He has a big Sunday School and church. Know him well. He started in a . . . little garage or a tent in Orange Grove, and now he's got the largest Sunday School down there. Yes, I know Bob Wells.

("Do you know of his affiliation with Bradley?") Ah . . . no, I . . . don't really. If I remember right, I think Bradley was advertised to speak for him once, or somethin.' I'm not sure. ("Right.") Am-I-na-na-am I wrong? I'm going back to memory. ("Yeah, that's right.") Well, that's it. That's he/that's right.

("Do you know a man by the name of Lorenz? Jack Lorenz or Fred Lorenz?") Ah, Jack or Fred Lorenz? You mean the man from/that's down in Mexico? ("Well, it could be. Originally there's a Fred Lorenz . . . is originally from Germany . . .") Yes, he's another/yes-eh, I . . . ("Drives a car with Texas plates . . .") Yes, yes. I-I don't know him personally, but I'm familiar with those, bein' eh myself a minister and . . . following the-eh papers and handbills. Yes, that name's familiar, but I don't know him personally. ("OK.")

("Is there any question in your mind as to this initial engagement with these two men, that you were just a random choice for them? Is there any possibility that they could have been following you . . . ?") I don't know. It's very strange how . . . that-eh . . . I would be downtown in this truck this day to do this business, and how they would get in the back, and it makes me wonder and think. I believe I've/after thinking much now, I really believe that the man . . . approximately, I would say 35, that I told you was well-dressed, he seemed to be of the same nationality, and my feeling was that . . . he was the brains back of it or something.

("Well, in other words, they hopped on your truck. You didn't invite them?") No, no. I didn't invite them. It happened so fast. As my truck was there, I could/looking at the light at the side and this/If you look at a '48 Chivvy, custom cab, it's got a round window here and a window in the back you can see. And the tallest of the two younger fellows stepped on the running board and had one foot over, and I saw him coming over, and I'm/of course I'm wonderin' what he's doin' . . . but there's nothin' in the back of the truck, see, but some old hay that's laying . . . on the thing . . . and he's half way in, and the other one takes the door, and he's got it part-open with his head. 'Are you goin' towards Hollywood, West?' See? Like this way out Wilshire, see? 'cause I was clear in the right hand turn . . . we had to turn right. My blinker's on, I'm gonna turn right, see. And before I could OK it, see, he said "We'll ride in the back." and just helped themself . . . and they got in the back and sat down . . . and they are not beside me, so nobody can harm my . . . they are in the open, in the back.

("Now, if I understand what you are saying, one of the men that jumped in the back was the same one that offered you the $100 deposit?") No, no, that's a different one. You have three men and a woman, and they was one . . . on the corner, looked like the same nationality that was standing about 4 feet from 'em, looked like he was interested in what they were sayin', but wasn't talkin' to 'em, see?

("Now, was this when the $100 deposit was offered?") No, no. This is the first meeting on a Monday afternoon. That was the first meeting. Yes, sir. ("OK—Alright.")

("Now . . . they wanted to meet you at 11 o'clock at night on Tuesday night, right?") Just wha/I made the appointment with the smallest one. When I left him out on Sunset, he said "I'll meet you here on this corner at 11 o'clock tonight and have the money to pay for your horse." . . . ("Yes, then?") He showed me no money, yet. He said he had money coming, he was going to pick up. ("But then, that was Monday?") That was Monday night. ("Then you met them Monday night at 11?") I met him-eh, just him, the others were parked. Go ahead . . . ("Right . . . and then, the point was, now, the next morning they came around where you were staying . . .") At the hotel. (". . . and they wanted to meet you at 11 o'clock that night?") Again, Tuesday night, they would have wanted to meet me at 11 o'clock. ("And where did they want you to meet them?") That . . . would be down . . . on . . . Catalina Street . . . at the same place . . . that I let the little fellow out . . . the day before the evening to see somebody that worked in a kitchen. That's all. ("Is the Ambassador Hotel at that corner?") Yes, they-no, the-at's the side street that goes down along the side of the Ambassador. ("Yeah.") There is no automobile entrance there, but if you go down about a block you'll see a little street that dead-ends to a fence and a gate that opens up, and you go through that gate that takes you into the back of the Ambassador on the side, see.

("When you said that you had a speaking engagement in Oxnard that night, you couldn't make it, right?") I couldn't make it. That's right. ("Were they very insistent that you try and make it that night?") Yes, yes. That's when I was offered to take the $100 bill, give 'em a receipt and they'd have the balance of the money if I would deliver the/be there and have the horse in the horse trailer, see? ("At 11 o'clock?") At 11 o'clock with the horse. And then I was to . . . pick my money up and take the horse where he wanted it. ("In other words, the $100 was an indicement for you to break your engagement in Oxnard?") Yeah, that's right. It looked like it. I feel that it was a come-on, now. I do, in my/bottom my heart. ("In other words, you feel that they were striving pretty hard to get you to be there at 11 o'clock?") Yes. They wanted it very, very bad.

("When you made the alternate date of the next morning, they weren't interested?") Ah, well, I-I couldn't say that. I said 'Well, look' I said 'Look, if he wants the horse at 11 o'clock and I can't be there, see, get it? ("Yeah.") 'Here's my card. Phone me tomorrow morning at 8 o'clock . . . at my home' . . . because I always phone my wife, and if they'd a-phoned at 8 and left a message, my wife would have taken the message. Then I could have brought the horse from Oxnard to wherever they wanted it, see? ("Yeah.") So I said 'Here, phone me in the morning if he wants the horse.' I said 'I've wasted . . . yesterday evening and stayed in a motel, cost me $4, see, and nothing happened, see? ("Except that they did offer you the $100?") They offered the $100. The night before the little fellow showed me the hunderd dollars, but didn't offer it to me. He said 'I got a hunderd and I didn't get all my money. I'll have it in the morning at 8 o'clock.' See? ("Yeah—and he still didn't have it?") He didn't show. The other fellow showed. ("The well-dressed fellow?") The well-dressed fellow, and the g-g-girl and another fellow in the car/she . . .

("Can you give a comprehensive description of the well-dressed (man)?") Ah, well, ala, the well-dressed fellow, I would say, hit between 165 to 175 pounds, in there. And-eh he looked of a . . . a . . . a . . . a . . . of a Latin type . . . I mean . . . ("Could he have been from the Near East, from Jordan or somewhere like that?") Yeah, yes. He-he could/he could be either-eh he could either be an Indian or a Hindu or something. He looked of that type. ("Or he could be Mexican or Cuban?") Yes, that's right, that's right. He-he wasn't American. He wasn't . . . ("He was swarthy looking?") That's right. That's right. ("What about his accent? Did he have an accent?") Very good English ("Very good English?") As good as English as the little guy. The little guy that I thought was a Mexican. That's what got me, see. I said 'Are you from Mexico?' 'No' I said 'Well, you sure speak good English.'— 'He says 'No. I'm from Jordan.' ("Yeah, OK. Now what was . . . he was about 5 (feet tall)?") I would say he was 5/for the little fellow, I would say he was around 5' 3" or 4", and weight around maybe 135, 140 pounds. ("But the well-dressed man?") Oh, no, the well-dressed fellow, I would say was about 5' 8" or 9". ("How old?") 30 . . . 'bout/ round 35. Between 30 or 40. He could have/in there. I would say 35. ("Right. What was his hair like?") He had-eh dark hair, see . . . and it was/it wasn't kinky, see? And it wasn't straight. It had kind of a like here. ("Yeah.") He didn't have any beard. He didn't have any long sideburns. I mean he was-ah/it was neatly. ("Did he have any rings or anything that you might [notice]?") Yes. He had-ah-he had a little ring, you call 'em ah-ah . . . What are they? Cat's eye? It's not a pigeon red ruby, what's the other? I been/I can't, for two days I been trying to think of the name of those rings. You know, they're kind of a gray color. Popular ring that you wear. What is the name? I-I . . . for two days I can't think of it. I say Cat's Eye. He had that ring on. That's right, go ahead. ("Shirt and tie?") No. No. He had on a yella . . . ah . . . ah yellowish-eh turtle neck. He had a round—like a chain. Now . . . wasn't a strap. It was like a link chain with a round thing hanging on it, see? ("And you had the impression his suit looked pretty good?") His suit looked like it/well it did. It had the-the late style. In fact, I'd like to have one. It had this here . . . ("Little cuffs on it?") . . . and the pockets are like this now. It's a new style suit. Mani/his nails were manicured. He was immaculate. ("Anything distinctive about him?") No-ah, not too much . . . just . . . the little conversation 'Joe couldn't make it . . . and here's $100.' But he did ask for a receipt for his hunderd, see? Now I don't know if that was to make it legal or what, but he said 'Give me the receipt for the hunderd, be there (with) the horse, you'll have the other two hunderd and that's it, see, 11 o'clock.'

(Wes Gardner: "When he showed you the $100 bill, he mentioned that he had more of these coming, didn't he?") No. This man . . . No, no, this man didn't. The little fellow did the night before. The little fellow said 'I didn't get all my money. I'm gonna have more coming, and I'll have it . . . 8 o'clock in the morning, and I got a hunderd here, but I'll have more of 'em, these. . . .' ("At 8 in the morning?") And he, and he held it, see. He didn't stick it out, but the fellow in the morning at 8 o'clock, he's not standing too far from me, and he said 'Well' he said 'Look' he said 'Ah-take this hunderd and deliver the horse tonight.' And he's/he in a/first he . . . asked 'You got a horse trailer?' See? I said 'Yes, I have a two-horse trailer.' And I told him, I said 'I'm bringing a pony down.' I was only going to bring one pony down, see, and when I come, I brought two more shetlands and they're at Orie Tucker's for sale now, see, to help me out. If he . . . ("Were they rather insistent you bring the trailer to Santa Catalina Avenue?") On that si/on that side street, see? ("At 11 o'clock on Tuesday night?") At 11 o'clock. Tuesday night at 11 o'clock. And-eh/Look, I didn't even know . . . I didn't know that there was any reception there, nothing. Because . . . I remember . . . wh-when Reegan was up, they most generally hold all their receptions at the Amba/a-at the Biltmore, downtown. That's where Reegan was. I didn't know there was a blow-out there/I didn't know anything was going on/didn't mean a thing to me. In fact, I didn't even know where the kid went when he said 'I got a friend in the kitchen' See? ("Yeah. OK.")

["This tape was cut with Jerry Owen from approximately 2 to 3:15 P.M. on July 2, 1968, in the offices of George T. Davis. Also present during this interview were Wes Gardner and Ben Hardister."]

A cassette recording of the Turner/Owen interview can be obtained by sending $10 in check or money order to: Christian/Turner, 163 Mark Twain Avenue, San Rafael, Calif. 94903.

EXHIBIT I

Statement of Robert Rozzi given to Vincent Bugliosi on November 15, 1975

On the date June 4, 1968, I was a police officer for the Los Angeles Police Department assigned to Wilshire Division. I was assigned to the morning watch and was riding a patrol car from 2330 hour (11:30 P.M.) on. Shortly after midnight, we heard over our radio that a shooting had occurred at the Ambassador Hotel. Since the hotel is adjacent to the eastern boundary of the Wilshire Division, we drove immediately to the hotel. When we first arrived, my partner (I can't remember his name) and I directed traffic at the main entrance to the parking lot, and we were instructed to write down all the license plate numbers of the vehicles leaving the parking lot. We did this for approximately two hours at which time we proceeded into the hotel and were given the job of maintaining security in the kitchen area. Among other things, we only let authorized people, such as the police and other personnel involved in the investigation, into the crime scene. This I continued to do till approximately 0800 (8 A.M.) hours, June 5, 1968. During the night, one of the investigators for the Los Angeles Police Department suggested that we look for bullets and bullet holes. I don't recall anyone finding any bullets on the floor, et cetera. However, I personally observed some small holes in a partition behind the stage. I have no way of knowing how these small holes were caused.

Sometime during the evening when we were looking for evidence, someone discovered what appeared to be a bullet a foot and a half or so from the bottom of the floor in a door jamb on the door behind the stage. I also personally observed what I believed to be a bullet in the place just mentioned. What I observed was a hole in the door jamb, and the base of what appeared to be a small caliber bullet was lodged in the hole. I was photographed pointing to this object in a Los Angeles Police Department photograph marked A-94-C.C. 68521466, where I signed my name in the upper right-hand corner: Robert Rozzi 11-15-75. In the photograph, I am pointing my pen at the object and LAPD officer Charles Wright, also of the Wilshire Division, is holding a ruler next to the object. I am also shown in a AP Wirephoto marked in the bottom right-hand corner (rhs 40745stf) 1968. In this photo, I am holding a flashlight in my left hand and Officer Wright is pointing at what appears to be the bullet with a penknife. The object which I believed to be a bullet is shown in an LAPD photograph marked

68521466 A-59-C.C. and signed in the upper left hand corner on the reverse side: Robert Rozzi 11-15-75.

I personally never removed the object from the hole, but I'm pretty sure someone else did, although I can't remember who it was.

The above statement is a true statement to the best of my recollection. This statement was given to Mr. Bugliosi by me at Hollywood Station on 11-15-75 2030 hrs.

[signed] ROBERT ROZZI

The above two-page statement was written by me and signed by Sgt. Rozzi in my presence.

[signed] VINCENT T. BUGLIOSI
November 15, 1975

EXHIBIT 2

Statement of Dr. Thomas Noguchi, Coroner of Los Angeles County, given to Vincent Bugliosi on December 1, 1975.

On the date June 11, 1968, I went to the pantry area of the Ambassador Hotel in Los Angeles to make an "at scene" investigation of the scene of the homicide. I had requested that DeWayne Wolfer of the Los Angeles Police Department be present, which he was. I asked Mr. Wolfer where he had found bullet holes at the scene. I forget what he said, but when I asked him this question, he pointed, as I recall, to one hole in a ceiling panel above, and an indentation in the cement ceiling. He also pointed to several holes in the door frames of the swinging doors leading into the pantry. I directed that photographs be taken of me pointing to these holes. I got the impression that a drill had been placed through the holes. I do not know whether or not these were bullet holes, but I got the distinct impression from him that he suspected that the holes may have been caused by bullets.

If there are discrepancies as to the number of bullets fired in the pantry or the number of bullet holes, I would recommend, as I would do in any criminal case, further studies by an impartial panel of experts to resolve this matter. There is a certain urgency in resolving this matter, because if it is not resolved now, I am afraid that there will be a continuing doubt which will be harmful to local government on a matter of national concern.

The above statement was given by me to Mr. Bugliosi freely and voluntarily and everything I have said in this statement is true to the best of my recollection.

[signed] THOMAS NOGUCHI
December 1, 1975

The above statement was written by me and signed by Dr. Thomas Noguchi in my presence at his office on December 1, 1975.

[signed] VINCENT T. BUGLIOSI

EXHIBIT 3

Statement given by Angelo DiPierro to Vincent Bugliosi on December 1, 1975

In June of 1968, I was the maître d' at the Ambassador Hotel in Los Angeles. Just past midnight on the morning of June 5, 1968, I was escorting Mrs. Ethel Kennedy towards the pantry of the hotel. Senator Kennedy was preceding us by 20 or so feet. Five or so paces before we reached the two swinging doors leading into the pantry, I heard the first shot coming from within the pantry. We proceeded towards the two swinging doors and as we reached them, the rapid fire began, so I literally pulled Mrs. Kennedy from the open doorway to take cover behind the closed doorway. (Entering the pantry from the Embassy room, the door on the left was open and the door on the right was closed.) Immediately after the shooting ended, Mrs. Kennedy and I proceeded into the pantry to see what had happened. After Senator Kennedy had been removed from the pantry, many people, including the police and myself, started to look over the entire pantry area to piece together what had happened. That same morning, while we were still looking around, I observed a small caliber bullet lodged about a quarter of an inch into the wood on the center divider of the two swinging doors. Several police officers also observed the bullet. The bullet was approximately 5 feet 8 or 9 inches from the ground. The reason I specifically recall the approximate height of the bullet location is because I remember thinking at the time that if I had entered the pantry just before the shooting, the bullet may have struck me in the forehead, because I am approximately 5 feet 11½ inches tall. It is my belief that the bullet in the hole is the same bullet that struck the forehead of Mrs. Evans who had been standing right in front of the center divider. The reason why I feel that the bullet which struck Mrs. Evans never entered her forehead and instead continued on into the center divider is that if a bullet had entered her forehead, I would have assumed she would have become unconscious, but Mrs. Evans appeared to be coherent and was not unconscious. Her only complaint was that she had been hit.

I am quite familiar with guns and bullets, having been in the Infantry for 3½ years. There is no question in my mind that this was a bullet and not a nail or any other object. The base of the bullet was round and from all indications, it appeared to be a 22 caliber bullet.

A day or so later, the center divider that contained the bullet was removed by the Los Angeles Police Department for examination. I don't know who removed the bullet or what happened to it. The hole that contained the bullet was the only new hole I observed after the shooting. Even prior to the shooting, there were a few holes from nails, et cetera on the two swinging doors.

The above two page statement was given by me to Mr. Bugliosi freely and voluntarily and everything I have said in this statement is true to the best of my recollection.

[signed] ANGELO DiPIERRO

12-1-75

The above statement was written by me and signed by Angelo DiPierro in my presence at his office in the Palladium on December 1, 1975.

[signed] VINCENT T. BUGLIOSI

EXHIBIT 4

Statement given by Martin Patrusky to Vincent Bugliosi on December 12, 1975

On the date June 5, 1968, I was a banquet waiter for the Ambassador Hotel in Los Angeles. About 20 minutes before the assassination in the pantry, I was standing by the steam table in the pantry when this fellow, who looked like a dishwasher from the kitchen, tapped me on the shoulder and asked me if Kennedy was coming back through the kitchen. I said to him "How the hell do I know. I'm not the head waiter." He walked away by the tray rack and I never paid any attention to him, though I think he stayed around the tray rack, which is next to the ice machines in the pantry.

When Senator Kennedy came into the pantry about 20 minutes later, I was standing near the center divider of the two swinging doors. Just after he entered the pantry through the swinging doors, I shook his hand. I was to his left. As Kennedy walked forward through the pantry, I moved forward with him, to his left. I stopped at the alcove which goes into the main kitchen. I stopped and watched Kennedy as he took a few more steps forward. Karl Uecker was to Kennedy's front and was guiding him through the kitchen. The man who had asked me 20 minutes earlier if Kennedy was coming back through the kitchen came out from behind the tray rack, crossed in front of Uecker and was standing against the steam table to Uecker's left. In fact, I saw him pointing his gun over Uecker's left shoulder towards Kennedy. At this time, Kennedy was leaning slightly to the left and shaking somebody's hand or reaching to shake someone's hand. I saw the man, who turned out to be Sirhan, firing at Kennedy. Kennedy's back was not facing Sirhan. Sirhan was slightly to the right front of Kennedy. I would estimate that the closest the muzzle of Sirhan's gun got to Kennedy was approximately 3 feet. After Sirhan fired the first shot, Uecker grabbed Sirhan around the neck with one hand and with his other hand he grabbed Sirhan's right wrist. But Sirhan continued to fire.

After the shooting, I was taken to the Rampart Division of the Los Angeles Police Department with several other employees of the Ambassador. We were supposedly taken there for questioning, but we were not questioned at that time. About 7 or 8 that same morning, they took us back to the Ambassador. I went down to the pantry. The police were there and they didn't want anyone inside the pantry. My boss, Angelo DiPierro, told me I could go home and I didn't have to work the lunch hour that day.

4 or 5 days or maybe a week later, the Los Angeles Police Department tried to reconstruct the scene of the crime and where everybody was standing. I and several other employees of the Hotel were present in the pantry. There were 4 or 5 plainclothes officers present. The reconstruction incident took about an hour or so. Sometime during the incident, one of the officers pointed to two circled holes on the center divider of the swinging doors and told us that they had dug two bullets out of the center divider. The two circled holes are shown in a photograph shown to me by Mr. Bugliosi marked "Exhibit JA" at the top. A man is pointing to the two circled holes. I am absolutely sure that the police told us that two bullets were dug out of these holes. I don't know the officer's name who told us this, but I remember very clearly his telling us this when they were recreating the scene, and I would be willing to testify to this under oath and under penalty of perjury.

I have read the above three page statement which I orally gave to Mr. Bugliosi freely and voluntarily and everything in the statement is true.

[signed] MARTIN PATRUSKY
12-12-75

The above statement was written by me in Martin Patrusky's presence and signed by Mr. Patrusky in my presence in my office.

[signed] VINCENT T. BUGLIOSI
12-12-75

FEDERAL BUREAU OF INVESTIGATION

Date 7/10/68

OLIVER B. OWEN, also known as Jerry and Curly, 1113 N. Mar-Les Drive, Santa Ana, California, telephone 839-0123, appeared at the FBI for interview with prior arrangements for the interview having been made through his attorney, GEORGE T. DAVIS. OWEN appeared at the office with BEN HARDISTER, a private detective and WESLEY GARDNER, a former Deputy Sheriff in Napa County. Both of these men were acting as body guards for OWEN. Prior to the interview, GARDNER advised that OWEN had been under sedation and was somewhat tired. OWEN was interviewed out of the presence of HARDISTER and GARDNER.

At the outset of the interview, OWEN was advised that he was being interviewed concerning his knowledge of an individual whom he had identified to his attorney DAVIS and the press as possibly being identical with SIRHAN B. SIRHAN and the fact that he has stated that he had received threatening calls from persons unknown.

OWEN furnished the following information:

On June 3, 1968, he was in downtown Los Angeles on business between 3:30 and 4:00 p.m. He explained that he has part interest in a fighter named RIP O'RILEY. He also is a minister and has been since 1937. He said that he has approximately fifteen ponies which he keeps at his ranch at Santa Ana and takes these horses around to shopping centers to give free rides to children to get them to come to church. He said that his church is located at Oxnard, California, and that he kept some of the ponies at his ranch in Oxnard. His purpose for being in Los Angeles on June 3, 1968 was to pick up some sporting goods for O'RILEY at the United Sporting Goods Store. He picked up a pair of boxing shoes, a white robe, some trunks and other equipment.

He had purchased his merchandise at the sporting goods store and was proceeding on Hill Street. He stopped at a stop light and two individuals approached his truck. He said he was driving a 1942 Chevrolet pick-up truck which had a large palomino horse ornament on the hood. When the two young men approached his truck, the taller of the two asked if he was going out Wilshire Boulevard and when he said that he was, this individual asked if they could ride in the back of the truck, to which OWEN agreed. He described these individuals as follows:

ON 7/8/68 IN San Francisco, California   File # SF 62-5481 & LA 56-156
BY ROBERT W. HERRINGTON and
    H. ERNEST WOODRY / rvn   Date dictated 7/10/68

NUMBER 1

Age	Early twenties
Height	5' 8" to 5' 10"
Build	Slender
Hair	Black, bushy
Complexion	Dark, appearing to be of Latin American origin
Wearing	Sandals, two-tone Mexican type jacket, possibly a vest and a chain around his neck with a medallion thereon.

NUMBER 2

Age	Early twenties
Height	5' 3"
Build	Slender
Hair	Dark, bushy
Complexion	Dark, with Latin American appearance
Wearing	Dark colored khaki levi type pants, dark gray sweatshirt and wearing tennis shoes.

They proceeded west on Wilshire Boulevard. At the intersection of Vermont and Wilshire, OWEN stopped for a traffic light and as he did so, both men got out of the truck. Number one went directly to a bus stop near where the truck stopped and greeted a man and woman. The man was about thirty to forty years of age and dark complected, possibly Mexican. The woman was dressed in slacks with long dirty blond hair, light complexion, possibly a hippie. Number two started to follow Number one but turned around and came back to the truck. He opened the door and asked to ride up front to continue toward Hollywood. When OWEN nodded approval, he climbed in the front seat. They proceeded on leaving Number one at the bus stop.

During the ride, the conversation of horses came up and Number two asked OWEN if he owned horses and he said that he did. Number two remarked that he used to work at a race track and at present needed a horse. OWEN said that he had horses for sale and offered to sell him one for $300. They talked some more about buying and selling a horse and Number two asked OWEN if he could stop for a short time so that he could see a friend who worked in a kitchen nearby where they were at the moment. OWEN said he turned off Wilshire Boulevard onto a side street, the name of which he does not know. He described the street as a deadend street that was several blocks long. He parked the truck and waited while Number two went to see his friend.

After a wait of about ten minutes, OWEN decided that Number two was not going to return so he began to turn the truck around and leave. As he was doing this, he observed Number two come through an opened gate in a fence behind which was a tall building with many rooms. OWEN said that he was later advised by a police officer of the Los Angeles Police Department, University Station, that this building was the Ambassador Hotel.

When Number two got back in the truck, OWEN again began making conversation and asked the man if he was Mexican. He told him that he was not, saying that he was from Jordan having either come from Jordan thirteen years ago or when he was thirteen years old. OWEN could not recall which he said. He said that his name was JOE and gave a surname which OWEN did not understand, but which OWEN believed sounded like ZAHARIAS. OWEN said at about this time, he was arriving at his destination, that is a shoe shop and tailor shop where he was going to leave the boxing shoes and the robe for O'RILEY to have shamrocks put on. He said that he parked the truck in the Hollywood Ranch Market's lot and took the shoes to a bootblack named SMITTY. While he was conducting this business, Number two stayed in the truck. He returned to the truck and drove a few blocks and let Number two out on the corner of Wilshire near a bowling alley and a go-go topless bar. Before he left Number two agreed to meet OWEN at 11:00 p.m. on the same corner at which time he would have the money to buy the horse.

He met the fighter O'RILEY that evening and left him shortly before 11:00 p.m. and arrived back at the agreed meeting place and observed a 1958 or 1959 Chevrolet, off-white in color, in which there were three men and a girl. OWEN believed that one of the men and the girl may have been the same couple that Number one was talking to earlier at the bus stop. He could not get a good look at the second man in the car. Number two came over to the truck and showed him a $100 bill saying he would have the rest of the money the next day early in the morning. OWEN told him he would stay overnight in Los Angeles and pointed out a hotel which was either St. Mark's or St. Martin, which would be where he would stay. He registered at this hotel as J. C. OWEN and requested the clerk give him a call at 8:00 a.m. However, he said that he was up at 7:00 a.m. and just as he was leaving the hotel he received a call from a man asking if he was the man with the pick-up and horse. OWEN acknowledged that he was and said he would meet him in a few minutes at the truck. As he was going to the truck he saw the same white car as before parked at the curb and Number one and the girl whom he saw before, were sitting in the car. The man who had been at the bus stop was standing by the truck and as OWEN approached he said "JOE could not make it." He offered OWEN a $100 bill and asked if he could bring the horse to the same location that night at which time the remainder of the money would be available. OWEN did not take the money and explained that he would not be able to deliver the horse that night because of a prior commitment that he had in Oxnard. He left the man, giving him his business card, which had his home address and an unlisted telephone number and requested that JOE call him if he was interested in the horse. OWEN then proceeded to Oxnard on business and returned to Los Angeles the morning of June 5, 1968.

OWEN said he went to the Coliseum Hotel to see a man, BERT, who owns the restaurant and bar in the hotel. He had, at this time, three ponies in his trailer, which he had obtained in Oxnard. While in the restaurant he learned of the KENNEDY shooting hearing it on television. Someone gave him a copy of the "Hollywood Citizen News," which contained a picture of SIRHAN B. SIRHAN, which he noted looked like the man he knew as JOE. He discussed this with BERT and other of his friends in the restaurant and they suggested that he go to the Los Angeles Police Department, University Station, which was nearby and tell them what had occurred. At first he said that he did not want to do this, but they convinced him that as a good citizen this would be the thing to do. That same day, he went to the Police Department and gave them the same story that he was now relating. He said that he was at the station from about 2:00 p.m. to 7:00 p.m.

On June 6, 1968, several phone calls were received at his residence which were answered by his wife and daughter and on each occasion, the person calling hung up without saying anything. When the phone rang again, OWEN said he answered it and the caller said "Keep your mother blankedy blank mouth shut about the horse deal." He believes the caller was a man but his voice was not familiar.

On June 18 or 19, 1968, OWEN received a call from the Los Angeles Police Department requesting that he come downtown to the Detective Bureau on the third floor between 1:30 and 2:30. He took another man named PERKINS with him. When he arrived, the officer on duty asked him to wait, saying that the officer who wanted to interview him was going to be a little bit late. OWEN explained to them that he was on his way to Phoenix and desired to proceed with the interview if possible. After a few minutes wait, the interview proceeded. He said he was handed a number of pictures and asked to pick out the picture of the man who looked like the one who had ridden with him in the truck. He said that after looking through the pictures, he picked out one stating that this man looked similar to the man whom he had given a ride. He recalls that PERKINS asked the officer if the picture was SIRHAN B. SIRHAN and the officer said that he could not answer this question. At the time of this interview, he told the officer that he had received a threatening call and that he would be staying in Phoenix for approximately one week.

On June 22, 1968, OWEN said that he received another call with the caller again using profanities, stating something to the effect "Keep your mother blankedy blank mouth shut or your family may be hurt." OWEN stated that no further calls or threats have been received.

UNITED STATES DEPARTMENT OF JUSTICE
FEDERAL BUREAU OF INVESTIGATION
WASHINGTON 25, D.C.

7-12-68 256 JTN

edgar hoover

DIRECTOR

The following FBI record,   NUMBER 4 261 906   is furnished FOR OFFICIAL USE ONLY

CONTRIBUTION OF FINGERPRINTS	NAME AND NUMBER	ARRESTED OR RECEIVED	CHARGE	DISPOSITION
PD, Long Beach Calif.	Oliver Jerry Owen #9303	3-28-30	investigation Robbery	Released 3-28-30
PD, Portland Oreg.	Oliver Brindley Owen, #22115	2-17-	Dis. Condt.	Hold for Fed. Auth. 2-18-45, $50 fine and 30 days.
SO Santa Ana Calif.	Oliver Brindley Owen #97548	2-19-63	fug Arson & Conspiracy warr BRN 23790	holding for Costa Mesa PD
PD, Tucson Ariz.	Oliver Brindley Owen #31521-M-187727	3-22-63	Warr #23790-Arson in the first deg with intent to defraud Insurer and Conspiracy	
SO Tucson Ariz.	Oliver B. Owen #18701-M	3-22-63	arson	

Civil print from Calif St Bu #S-31697 was identified with this record and returned to contributor 9-24-59.

Civil print from St Athletic Comm Sacramento Calif #17724 was identified with this record and returned to contributor 8-27-62.

December 31, 1968

TO: Captain Hugh I. Brown
            Commander, Homicide Division

FROM: Lieutenant E. Hernandez
            S.U.S. Homicide

SUBJECT: Polygraph Examination of Jerry Owen

POLYGRAPH EXAMINATION

Jerry Owen was administered a polygraph examination in the polygraph facilities of the San Francisco Police Department on July 3, 1968. The examiner was Lt. E. Hernandez who utilized a three-channel Stoelting instrumentation.

The purpose of the examination was to determine if Owen was being truthful when he stated that he had picked up Sirhan and an unknown male companion in the downtown area of Los Angeles on Monday, June 3, 1968. Owen stated that he had picked up Sirhan and his companion at 7th and Grand Streets and then drove them to different locations in the Hollywood area.

Owen was advised that the purpose of the examination was to determine whether he honestly believed that he had ever seen or talked with Sirhan Sirhan in person. He was given the opportunity to discuss the matter regarding the polygraph examination with his attorney, George Davis, and to ask questions concerning the testing techniques and the procedures to be followed during the course of the examination. The instrument and its functions were explained to Owen in detail.

During the course of the control test which had been administered to determine whether Owen was a suitable subject capable of being examined instrumentally, the examiner encountered some difficulty. Owen was resisting and being uncooperative. Instead of answering questions with one word, either yes or no as instructed, he was qualifying every answer in narrative form. Owen explained that he had asked the Bible to deliver him from deceitful lips, and he had to explain his answers in detail because he had to give an account to God.

Upon conclusion of the control test, it was determined that although Owen, who is a highly emotional individual, was being uncooperative, he was emitting physiological tracings capable of evaluation.

Owen was asked a total of 25 questions of which 9 were key questions relative to the issues under investigation. His responses to the following relevant questions strongly indicated that Owen was answering untruthfully.

Q. Is everything that you have told me this morning about that hitch-hiker true?
A. Yes.
Q. Do you honestly believe that you have talked to the man that is accused of shooting Kennedy?
A. Yes.
Q. When you told George Davis that you had talked to the man that shot Kennedy, were you telling him the truth?
A. Yes.
Q. Did the man that shot Kennedy offer to buy your horse at any time?
A. Yes.

These deceptive responses were also found in his answers to the following questions that had no bearing on the issue under investigation:

Q. Between the ages of 50 and 54, do you remember telling a lie to anyone?
A. No.
Q. During the last three years of your life, do you remember lying to a police officer about something serious?
A. No.
Q. Are you a married man?
A. Yes.

Based on the physiological tracings and his responses at points where crucial questions were asked, it is my opinion that Jerry Owen was being untruthful during the course of the examination. In my opinion he cannot honestly say that he picked up, talked to or saw Sirhan Sirhan on June 3, 1968. Mr. Owen was informed of the results of the examination, and he proceeded to expound in lengthy dissertation saying in essence that maybe he had picked up someone else. He said, "I don't know; I don't know; it may not have been him, but if I had saw him face to face or heard his voice or something, then I would. I'd come out and make a definite statement. I don't know." He said that he had only mentioned that the person to whom he had given a ride looked like the picture of the man he had seen on television and accused of shooting Senator Kennedy. Owen was again informed that due to his responses, it was the opinion of the examiner that he was being untruthful, even to the point that his statements regarding threatening phone calls were contradictory.

The examination was concluded at 3:15 p.m. Subsequent to this exam, George Davis was informed of the results of the test in the presence of Owen.

JERRY OWEN INVESTIGATION

Oliver Brindley Owen, aka Jerry Owen, was an ex-prize fighter turned minister who became involved in an intricate and contradictory series of events which allegedly involved Sirhan and Jerry Owen and the attempted purchase of a horse by Sirhan. The falsehood of Owen's allegation was clearly established through a separate and independent investigation.

Essentially Owen claimed that on Monday, June 3, 1968, at approximately 3:00 p.m., he picked up two hitchhikers in downtown Los Angeles and gave them a ride to the Hollywood-Wilshire area. Owen identified one of the hitchhikers as Sirhan who rode in the cab of his truck during part of the ride. Sirhan allegedly offered to buy a horse from Owen, who had a palomino for sale. The purchase was to be made at 11:00 p.m. that night at a location in Hollywood. Owen and Sirhan then allegedly met at this location at 11:00 p.m., and Sirhan asked Owen if he could wait until the next day when he would have the necessary money. Owen registered at a local hotel for the night.

The next morning, June 4, he was met by a man in a flashy suit and a blond girl who told him that Sirhan did not have the money for the horse but that he wanted Owen to meet him again at 11:00 p.m. that night. The man offered to give him some money as part payment on the horse. The man also told Owen that there was something happening at the Ambassador Hotel that night and that Sirhan would not have the money until then. Owen told the man that he could not meet Sirhan because of an appointment in Oxnard. Owen gave the man a business card and offered to bring the horse to Los Angeles the next day.

Owen allegedly went to Oxnard, California, and remained there the night of June 4. He returned to Los Angeles at approximately 12:30 p.m. on the 5th and learned of the assassination. After allegedly recognizing a picture of Sirhan in a newspaper, he went to University Station where he made his statement to the Department.

During the ensuing months, investigators sought to conclusively establish the truth regarding Owen's allegation. On the surface his statements were not self-incriminating, and Owen presented himself as a volunteer witness who was interested in assisting the police. Essentially investigators needed only to establish the falsity of Owen's statements to refute his allegation or to verify the truth of his statements and use Owen as a material witness. All evidence seemed to indicate that Sirhan was not with Owen on the 3rd. It was necessary, however, for investigators to determine Owen's reasons for fabricating the incident or whether he was honestly mistaken.

A complication developed early in the investigation when Jerry Owen became wary about the investigation of his allegation. Owen allegedly received a threatening phone call on June 6, 1968, telling him to remain quiet regarding his horse deal with Sirhan. Owen moved to the San Francisco area where he remained for several months. During that time his allegation became publicized and Owen engaged an attorney, George T. Davis, to represent him.

A polygraph examination was arranged for Owen on July 3, 1968, at the San Francisco Police Department. His attorney, Davis, was present during the test. Owen's responses to key questions indicated that he was being untruthful. When told of the results of the test, Owen made a lengthy statement which indicated that he was unsure of his original statement.

Investigators subsequently interviewed Mrs. Mary Sirhan and Adel Sirhan, who attempted to assist investigators in determining the truth of Owen's allegations. After a visit to Sirhan at the Hall of Justice, Mrs. Sirhan told investigators that Sirhan had denied knowing anything about Jerry Owen or the purchase of a horse.

At this point in the investigation, there had been three separate accounts of the occurrence given by Owen. The number of inconsistencies which appeared between the accounts and the results of the polygraph, coupled with Sirhan's denial of knowing Owen, led investigators to the conclusion that Owen was lying. It remained for investigators to determine why and to firmly refute Owen's statements with factual information and physical evidence.

In early August 1968, Jonn G. Christian, a magazine writer, and William Turner, an ex-F.B.I. agent turned free lance writer, entered into the Owen investigation. Christian contacted this Department offering his assistance, and he suggested that he would like to be deputized to work with the Department. Christian had a taped account of Owen's story. He told investigators that he believed Sirhan and Owen were together on June 4 and that they conspired to assassinate Kennedy. Christian further alleged that Owen was involved in Sirhan's escape plans and after the aborted escape, Owen was trying to establish an alibi with his horse-selling story.

Christian subsequently wrote a letter to this Department which outlined his reasons for believing that Owen was involved in the assassination. Christian, by enumerating various conflicts in Owen's accounts of the incident, hypothesized that Owen's reasons for lying were that he was involved in the conspiracy and seeking a means to avoid association with Sirhan. Christian subsequently sought to establish a link in Owen's background with Dr. Carl MacIntyre, a minister whose name had been linked through the Garrison investigation with the assassination of President John F. Kennedy.

Investigators, attacking the inconsistencies in Owen's accounts, also concluded that he was lying; however, there was no evidence to indicate that Owen was involved with an extremist group or with Sirhan. The following is an account of the investigation into the allegation of Jerry Owen.

INITIAL STATEMENT OF JERRY OWEN

Jerry Owen went to University Station on June 5, 1968, at approximately 3:00 p.m. He gave the following account regarding a contact that he believed that he had had with Sirhan Sirhan: On June 3, 1968, Owen left his residence in Santa Ana en route to the Coliseum Hotel, 457 West Santa Barbara, Los Angeles. He spoke with the manager of the hotel coffee shop, John Bert Morris, and Rip O'Reilly, a heavyweight boxer. Morris and Owen discussed the purchase of some boxing equipment from the United Sporting Goods Store, 901 South Hill Street, Los Angeles. At approximately 3:00 p.m. Owen purchased one pair of boxing shoes at United Sporting Goods and proceeded to Lester's Shoe Repair, 1263 North Vine Street, to have green shamrocks monogrammed on the shoes.

En route to Hollywood, while stopped at a traffic light at 7th and Grand Streets, two males requested a ride. The two men jumped into the rear of his truck with Owen's permission. Both men were described as Mexican or Latin, in their early twenties, with long hair and wearing old clothing. One hitchhiker was tall and slim and the other three or four inches shorter. At Wilshire and Western the taller man alighted from Owen's truck and greeted four other young adults standing on the corner. One of them was a male in his thirties with a large build wearing a flashy suit; a female Caucasian with dirty blond hair and two other young males were with the older man. The shorter hitchhiker whom Owen subsequently identified as Sirhan asked if he could sit in the cab of the truck.

After moving into the cab, the man asked Owen if he would stop for a few minutes at the "big hotel" while he visited a friend who worked in the kitchen. The hotel was later identified as the Ambassador Hotel. The man returned to Owen's truck ten minutes later and asked if Owen would take him to Hollywood. En route they had a conversation, and the man told Owen that he was an exercise boy at the racetrack. After Owen told him that he had a palomino horse which he was to sell for $250 in Oxnard, the man expressed a desire to buy the horse after receiving some money later that evening. Owen agreed to meet him that night at 11:00 p.m. near a bowling alley on Sunset Boulevard.

The young man remained in Owen's truck while he delivered the shoes to be monogrammed. Owen recalled that the young man also discussed nationalities, and he said that he had been raised in Jordan. He also expressed his opposition to Jews.

At 11:00 p.m. Owen went to the bowling alley and found the young man with the blond female and the well-dressed male he had seen at Wilshire and Western that afternoon. They had a 1957, 1958 or 1959 off-white, hard top Chevrolet. The young man displayed a $100 bill and told Owen he could not pay for the horse at that time. He asked Owen to meet him the next morning, and he mentioned that something was happening at the hotel. Because the deal appeared certain to Owen, he registered at the St. Moritz Hotel, 5849 Sunset Boulevard for the night.

At 8:00 a.m. on the 4th, Owen received a phone call from a man who said he was calling for Joe Sahara. He then went to the parking lot of the St. Moritz Hotel where he was met by the blond woman and the man who was wearing the flashy suit. The man told Owen that the young man could not get the money until that night, and they asked Owen if he could get the young man a job at a ranch. Owen gave them a business card and told them he would be back in Los Angeles the next day. Owen then went to Oxnard where he remained until 12:30 p.m. on the 5th.

When Owen returned to the Coliseum Hotel on June 5 at 3:00 p.m., he recognized a picture of Sirhan in the Hollywood Citizen News as being the young man who offered to purchase the horse from him. He related the incident to a waitress at the hotel coffee shop who suggested that he report it to the police. Owen then went to University Station. Owen subsequently told investigators that he believed that Sirhan was planning to use his truck to escape from the assassination.

INVESTIGATION OF OWEN'S STATEMENT

Owen was reinterviewed on June 18 at Parker Center and added some details to his original account. He said that Sirhan spoke with a slight Mexican accent and that he mentioned that he might sell his home and go to the Holy Land. He told investigators of a telephone conversation which he received approximately a week before. The person sounded like a male Negro and he stated to Owen, "You mother fucker, forget about the horse deal and keep your mouth closed." At this point in the investigation, it was assumed that Owen was being truthful; however, the investigation into the details of Owen's statements had not been completed.

On June 27, Owen was contacted at his home to set up an interview. Owen refused, stating that he was going to San Francisco. When the investigators suggested a meeting in Palo Alto, Owen said, "No," but suggested that they meet at the residence of Owen's brother in San Bruno. On June 29 the scheduled interview was canceled by the Department when investigators decided to wait for Owen to return to Los Angeles. Owen was not told of this decision, and he erroneously became fearful that his life was in danger. Owen's attorney, Davis, reported that Owen had been contacted by someone alleging that he was a Los Angeles policeman.

On July 1, 1968, San Francisco area papers printed an account of Owen's story about Sirhan. The articles reported that Owen was in hiding in the Napa Valley area in fear for his life. George Davis was quoted as saying that he believed that Owen was telling the truth and that he was reliable. Davis further stated that this Department had refused protection for Owen and that he would ask Attorney General Thomas Lynch for a 24-hour guard. Davis gave an account of Owen's allegation.

The article was in many ways the same as Owen's original account, with some notable contradictions and discrepancies. In his first account Owen said that the price to be paid for the horse was $250; in the newspaper account it was $300. Davis also stated that Owen first saw Sirhan's picture on television; contrary to that Owen had said that he had first seen Sirhan's picture in a newspaper. Owen told investigators that he had met one man and a blond woman at 8:00 a.m. on the 4th, but the article said that there were two men and a woman.

On July 2, 1968, Wesley Gardner, owner of the Foremost Protective Agency, notified investigators that he was representing Owen and that future calls to Owen should be channeled through Gardner.

POLYGRAPH EXAMINATION OF OWEN

Owen and Davis were contacted and the canceled interview in San Bruno was explained to their satisfaction. Due to the confusion which was developing in the Owen investigation, investigators arranged for a polygraph to be given by Lt. Hernandez to Jerry Owen at the San Francisco Police Department on July 3, 1968. George Davis was present during the examination, and Owen was explained the purpose of the test and given the opportunity to ask questions concerning the test. Owen resisted the control test; however, his responses indicated that he was a suitable subject for testing.

Owen was asked a total of 25 questions of which 9 were key questions. In response to the following relevant questions, Owen emitted answers which strongly indicated that he was being untruthful.

Q. Is everything that you told me this morning about the hitchhiker true?
A. Yes.
Q. Do you honestly believe that you have talked to the man that is accused of shooting Kennedy?
A. Yes.
Q. When you told George Davis that you had talked to the man that shot Kennedy, were you telling him the truth?
A. Yes.
Q. Did the man who shot Kennedy offer to buy your horse at any time?
A. Yes.

It was the examiner's opinion that Owen could not honestly say that he picked up, talked to or saw Sirhan on June 3, 1968. When informed of the results of the test, he made lengthy rationalizations about the occurrence. At one point he said, "I don't know; I don't know; it may not have been him, but if I had saw him face to face or heard his voice or something, then I would. I'd come out and make a definite statement. I don't know." He said that he had only mentioned that the person to whom he had given a ride looked like the picture of the man he had seen on television and accused of shooting Kennedy.

INVESTIGATION INTO DISCREPANCIES

On July 2, 1968, Mrs. Mary Sirhan was interviewed regarding the money which Sirhan received from the insurance settlement for the fall from the horse. She recalled that Sirhan asked for $300 a day or two before the shooting. She said that she believed that Sirhan had spent most of the remainder from the $1,000 he gave her from the insurance settlement. She thought that he had given some of the money to Adel. Adel Sirhan was present during the interview, and he stated at one point, "I think Sirhan wanted the $300 to buy a horse with." This was the only statement made by either Munir or Adel Sirhan regarding the money Sirhan received from the settlement

On July 5, Mrs. Sirhan was again interviewed, this time regarding Sirhan's activities on June 3, 1968. She stated that Sirhan had driven her to work at 8:00 a.m. but that he was not at home at 1:30 p.m. when she returned. However, there was evidence that he had just taken a shower and there was a warm cup on the kitchen table. Sirhan was gone most of the afternoon, but she noticed that he was watching television at 4:30 p.m. She was certain that he remained home the rest of that night. This information conflicted with Owen's allegation. At least from the time of 4:30 p.m., Mrs. Sirhan's statement contradicts Owen's statement. This would include the conversations at the Sunset Boulevard bowling alley at 4:30 p.m. and 11:00 p.m. and casts additional doubt on the events which preceded 4:30 p.m.

Mrs. Sirhan agreed to speak to Sirhan at the Hall of Justice regarding the Owen allegation. On July 15, after she had spoken to Sirhan, Mrs. Sirhan related his response. Sirhan told her that he did not know Owen, had never seen him nor had he ever ridden in his pickup truck. He also denied that he had attempted to purchase a palomino horse.

The denial by Sirhan, the statements of Mrs. Sirhan and the results of the Owen polygraph caused investigators to conclude that Owen had lied about the incident. Owen's reasons for lying could not be completely determined; however, an intensive examination of Owen's background revealed a history of involvement in questionable and illegal activities. This information tended to cast doubt on Owen's credibility.

Owen's third account of the incident, given when he was administered the polygraph, was compared with the other two accounts. Further discrepancies were noted, some of which indicated that Owen was adding details which he should have given in his first account. In addition he left out details which were in the original account.

He stated that he had purchased a robe and a pair of boxing shoes at United Sporting Goods; this was opposed to his first statement wherein he said he had purchased only a pair of boxing shoes. He also related that during the evening hours between the time he allegedly dropped off Sirhan around 6:00 p.m. and the time he met him again at 11:00 p.m., Owen stated that he had gone to the Plaza Hotel to see a friend, the ex-fighter Slapsy Maxie Rosenbloom. They then went to a Saints and Sinners meeting. This incident did not appear in Owen's first account at University Station. Further, Owen did not mention the stop at the Coliseum Hotel and Teamsters Gymnasium; instead, he said that he went directly from Santa Ana to the United Sporting Goods Store.

When shown a set of mugs, Owen could not identify Sirhan, and he chose a look-alike as the other man who rode in his truck. In addition, Owen changed the time and date on which he received the threatening phone call. The newspaper account had stated that he had received the call the evening of the 5th. During the July 3, 1968, interview Owen said that the call came between 2:00 and 5:00 p.m. on June 6.

Investigation into the alleged activities of Owen on June 3 revealed additional discrepancies in his story. Investigators determined that sales records at the United Sporting Goods Store showed no sale of a boxing robe on June 3. A pair of boxing shoes were sold on that date but not to Owen. The manager of the store, Jack Misrach, stated that he knew most of the boxing people in this area. He does not know Owen or Rip O'Reilly, the boxer. After looking at Owen's picture, Misrach did not recall seeing Owen in his store. Jesse Edwards, the salesman who sold the shoes on that date, thought Owen looked familiar but could not recall the transaction. The transaction for the shoes included several other items including gloves, headgear, shorts, jump rope and other items totaling $39.45.

Lester's Shoe Repair at 1263 North Vine Street was checked to verify Owen's statement that he had taken the shoes for monogramming. Lester Shields, the owner, stated that he had no record of when Owen brought the shoes for monogramming. Shields remembered that Owen came to his shop three times; one time that he remembered seeing Owen's truck, there was no one in it. When he picked up the shoes, two young women were with him and Rip O'Reilly was in the truck.

Dianne Scott, owner of the seamstress shop adjacent to the shoe repair shop, stated that she recalled that Owen brought a robe to be monogrammed on June 10, 1968, not June 3. He picked up the robe on June 26.

Shields estimated the dates of Owen's appearances at his shoe shop as:

Originally brought shoes into the shop	May 23–27, 1968
Picked shoes up the first time	May 25–28, 1968
Brought shoes in second time	May 27–29, 1968
Picked up shoes the final time	June 8, 1968

Investigators interviewed the persons whom Owen stated that he told of the incident who were at the Coliseum Hotel on June 5. Owen allegedly told them of the hitchhiker incident and one of them, Mabel Jacobs, a waitress, told him to tell the police.

Jacobs stated that she spoke to Owen who was in the Coliseum Hotel Coffee Shop with Rip O'Reilly on June 5. Owen pointed to a picture of Sirhan in the newspapers and told her that he was the hitchhiker that he had picked up on June 3. Owen told her that he had taken Sirhan to the Ambassador Hotel and that Sirhan expressed a desire to purchase a horse he was transporting to Oxnard. Bert Morris, the owner, stated that he was not present during Owen's relating of the incident to Jacobs. He did recall that Owen was in the coffee shop on June 5.

Rip O'Reilly, a professional boxer under contract to Owen, was interviewed. He stated that he lives at the Coliseum Hotel and that Owen came there on June 5 to see him. Owen related the incident of the hitchhiker and told him that he believed that the young man resembled Sirhan. O'Reilly, however, provided investigators with information which strongly contradicted Owen's account.

O'Reilly stated that on June 3, 1968, Owen called him at about 10:30 a.m. and invited him to attend a Saints and Sinners Club that night. At 6:30 p.m. Owen picked O'Reilly up at the Coliseum Hotel, and they drove to the meeting on Fairfax Avenue. Owen was driving a dark-colored pickup truck with a horse trailer attached. A horse was in the trailer. They remained at the meeting until 11:30 p.m., and Owen took O'Reilly back to the hotel.

On June 5, Owen came to the hotel and related to O'Reilly that he had picked up a hitchhiker on Wilshire Boulevard on June 3 and that the hitchhiker offered him $400 for his horse. Owen said that he stayed at a hotel the night of the 3rd to complete the transaction the next day. Owen told O'Reilly that he believed that Sirhan was a Mexican. O'Reilly further advised investigators that Owen had purchased the boxing shoes mentioned by Owen prior to June 3, 1968.

Investigators had established sufficient contradiction in Owen's story that they were convinced that he was lying. Owen's uncertainty at the conclusion of his polygraph in San Francisco tended to substantiate that conclusion. The only remaining aspect of the investigation was to establish Owen's reason for fabricating the story.

OWEN'S BACKGROUND

Owen was born on April 13, 1913, in Ashland, Ohio. He attended the University of Southern California where he played varsity football.

For many years he was a sparring partner for ex-heavyweight boxing champion, Max Baer.

Owen had claimed that he had been an ordained minister since 1937 and that he held a credential with the Charles M. Holder Ministry, Inc. on Colton Street in Los Angeles. During his July 3 interview in San Francisco, Owen admitted that he had not been legally ordained. He stated that he had gone into a hotel room for several days during which time he prayed. This constituted his ordainment.

Owen was arrested on suspicion of robbery in 1930 by the Long Beach Police Department but was released the same day. Over the years Owen has been involved in various suspicious and illegal activities. An analysis of the total record of Owen's police record and investigations into his activities reveal that he has been involved in several fire insurance claims involving his personal and church properties, and he has several times been involved in extra-marital and paternity investigations. His religious activities are of the rural evangelistic type with makeshift facilities. Owen has advertised himself as "The Walking Bible" and cites Ripley's "Believe it or Not" as proof that he has complete recall of the Bible. His method is that of a huckster, calling for the believing to listen to his message. Several of those interviewed likened his approach to that of a "confidence man."

His record would tend to support that description. Owen has been involved in six fires beginning in 1939 in Castro Valley, California. On several occasions he collected insurance settlements from these fires. The cases occurred in: (1) Castro Valley, 1939; (2) Crystal Lake Park, Oregon, 1945; (3) Dallas, Texas, 1946; (4) Mount Washington, Kentucy, 1947; (5) Ellicott City, Maryland, 1951; and (6) Tucson, Arizona, 1962.

Owen's $16,000 claim for the fire in Maryland was denied because of fraud. A witness observed Owen moving personal effects out of the house prior to the fire and then return them. Owen subsequently collected $6,500 when the denial was appealed.

In 1963, Owen was arrested in Costa Mesa, California, on a fugitive warrant from Tucson, Arizona, for arson with the intent to defraud an insurance company. A church, Our Little Chapel, which was owned by Owen was destroyed by fire on July 31, 1962, in Tucson. The investigation by the Tucson Police Department revealed that arson was the suspected cause of the fire. Owen was subsequently convicted of three counts of arson and sentenced to serve 8-10 years in prison. The decision was appealed and reversed on June 27, 1966.

In addition to fire claims, Owen has been involved in sex offenses over the years. In 1943, Jacqueline Banks, 16 years of age, joined Owen's gospel camp in Milwaukee, Oregon. She had met Owen when he had his "Open Door Church" in her home town of Des Moines, Iowa. Just prior to Owen obtaining a divorce from his wife in 1947, Banks became pregnant and returned to her home in Des Moines. Owen gave Banks $65 and told her that he would come to Des Moines and marry her. The child was born in November, 1947, and Owen forwarded $420 for hospital expenses. Banks later received word that Owen had gotten drunk, married a prostitute and that he would not be able to marry her. Banks had traveled off and on with Owen's touring churches for approximately seven years. (Owen stated during his polygraph that he had had a paternity suit filed against him at one time.)

On February 17, 1945, Owen was arrested for disorderly conduct in Portland, Oregon. He was found in a motel room with a female, Francis McCarty, both were nude. Owen was fined $50 and given thirty (30) days in jail; however, Owen posted an appeal bond of $250, and the case was continued indefinitely. Intelligence Division reports of Owen's activities reveal that he was reported to have been involved with women a number of times during his evangelistic tours.

Owen's highly suspicious background caused investigators to speculate that he sought to use the story about Sirhan to bring attention upon himself. His involvement in the activities described above were questionable grounds for giving credence to his ministerial goodness, and his suspicious record indicated that he was capable of concocting a story as devious as his alleged encounter with Sirhan. Investigators further speculated that Owen probably did pick up a hitchhiker in the downtown area, though not necessarily on June 3, 1968. Owen then combined a series of events which had occurred on various dates and developed his story. The small discrepancies in his stories would account for some vague familiarity that Owen had with each incident but that he would forget minor details from telling to telling.

INVOLVEMENT OF JONN G. CHRISTIAN

Three telephone calls were received by investigators from Jonn Christian, a magazine writer, one each on August 7, 9 and 11, 1968. Christian indicated that he had a tape of Jerry Owen's account and that he wished to assist the Department in its investigation. He went so far as to suggest that he and an associate, William Turner, be "deputized." Christian sought to listen to the Los Angeles Police Department tape of

Owen's account so that he could note discrepancies. It was Christian's opinion that Owen and Sirhan were together on June 4, 1968, and that Owen was to assist Sirhan with his escape. Because Sirhan had been captured, Christian believed that Owen has concocted his story to establish an innocuous reason for being with Sirhan.

Investigators sought then to establish the validity of Christian's allegation. It was believed that Owen was not involved with Sirhan in a conspiracy or that he had ever seen him. However, Christian's claim had to be disproven completely. Christian himself carried his claim to various governmental bodies to plead for their aid in investigating his allegation. His actions caused investigators deep concern as each time they would feel that the Christian claim had been satisfactorily explained to other interested parties, Christian would successfully enlist the support of another agency.

Christian mailed two extensive confidential letters to the Department outlining his "original, unique and confidential information" regarding the assassination. The material represented Christian's theory regarding the discrepancies in Owen's story. Christian also attempted to establish a link between Owen and Dr. Carl MacIntyre, the minister reportedly connected by New Orleans District Attorney James Garrison with the John F. Kennedy assassination.

Investigators were able to establish that Christian had been contacted by George Davis, Owen's attorney, who told Christian, "I think I'm broken in on the Senator Kennedy conspiracy." Davis asked Christian to handle his press releases.

William Turner, Christian's partner and an ex-F.B.I. agent turned free lance writer, had been previously associated with Davis. Turner had lost a campaign for public office in the June primaries, and Davis had been his campaign manager. In addition, Turner had been associated with the radical publication "Ramparts" and has written a book entitled "The Police Establishment."

It is anticipated that Jonn Christian and William Turner will publish or somehow publicly reveal their theory regarding Jerry Owen and Sirhan. They have consistently attempted to attach credence to their claim by enlisting the support of high ranking government officials for their claim. They will also likely as not show up in conjunction with any attempt to link the two Kennedy assassinations, an event which will definitely occur in one form or another.

On two occasions Christian admitted to investigators that his opinions regarding Owen and Sirhan were only theories. He further admitted that he was investigating the possibility of a conspiracy as a writer and that if a conspiracy did not exist between Sirhan and Owen, he did not have a story.

This investigation has gathered such information as to indicate that Jerry Owen did not know or even meet Sirhan. The remaining pieces to be inserted into the investigation are those which could not physically be obtained. This includes a direct meeting between Sirhan and Owen. Owen himself, on the advice of his attorney, has been reluctant to continue assisting investigators.

Memorandum from Los Angeles County Supervisor Baxter Ward to Fellow Supervisors

EACH SUPERVISOR

July 29, 1975

On July 16th and 18th I wrote memos to Presiding Judge Wenke, advising him that it was my intention to renew my request to the Board of Supervisors that it develop a positive position favoring refiring tests of the Sirhan gun.

I also remarked that any reexamination of the case should deal with the initial proposal by Dr. Noguchi that there be a neutron activation analysis of all of the bullets now in evidence, and that a new spectrograph analysis be taken of these same bullets or numbered fragments, as LAPD ballistics expert De Wayne Wolfer had done in preparation for the trial.

Further, I believe that a comparison microscopic examination should be made of these same materials, which is the process viewed most favorably by law enforcement.

In addition to the continuing obligation of County government to inspect its processes, there is the challenge from one of the nation's most important scientific groups, the American Academy of Forensic Sciences, that government preside over, or at least permit, a re-study of the ballistics evidence. Also, there is the current sidelight to the basic case—the testimony developing during the course of a trial, Reverend Owen vs. KCOP, now being held in Department 32 of the Superior Court. Owen told me over a year ago that he planned to bring the suit, and now it finally is in court, with its direct references to the assassination.

It was Jerry Owen who startled law enforcement authorities the day after the shooting of Senator Kennedy by appearing at a local police station to announce that he had picked up Sirhan the day before the assassination and during the course of a conversation had agreed to sell to Sirhan a horse, which was to be delivered in a trailer to a point outside the kitchen of the Ambassador Hotel at around eleven o'clock the night Senator Kennedy was shot. Owen later was discredited by LAPD and District Attorney authorities, who complained he could not either pass a lie detector test or identify Sirhan by photographs.

In the summer of 1971 as a broadcaster, I attempted unsuccessfully to contact Owen for an interview. In the spring of 1972, while I was campaigning for political office, Jerry Owen left word at my campaign

374 | Appendix

headquarters that he would like to see me the following day. The call was placed only hours after Governor Wallace had been shot. Owen did not keep the appointment the following day.

A short time after the hearing I conducted last May into the Senator Kennedy ballistics evidence, Jerry Owen called again, saying he would like to see me to disclose the full story behind the conspiracy.

He came the following day, and I obtained his permission to tape record his conversation. In my opinion, he provided no information beyond what he had stated in 1968 to the authorities and to the press. However, there was one addition: when I questioned him as to why he did not keep our appointment the day after Governor Wallace had been shot, Owen volunteered that he was personal friends with the sister of Arthur Bremmer (who had shot Governor Wallace). Owen stated that Gale Bremmer was employed by his brother here in Los Angeles for several years and had then just left Los Angeles for Florida because she was continually harrassed by the FBI.

It would be unwise to attempt to read any significance into these associations, but I must advise you now that they and other disclosures are being made during the course of the Owen/KCOP trial.

For example, during the course of a series of broadcasts in 1971, I made reference on the air to a young man who had filed a report with the Sheriff's Department in 1968 asserting that he had information about the Sirhan case. While the information was only hearsay, I was impressed that a day or so after I mentioned that Sheriff's report on the air, the young man's automobile was shot at as he returned to his home in Chino. I reported the incident the following day to the Federal authorities.

This young man's information centered on allegations that Sirhan and Jerry Owen were acquaintances well in advance of the time admitted by Owen in his June, 1968 statements to authorities.

Here again it would be improper to conclude that Jerry Owen was in any way involved in any of the incidents that are being discussed, either before or after the assassination of Senator Kennedy. Indeed, he might be simply a publicity seeker (as has been alleged by law enforcement authorities) or a person who developed associations that might be totally innocent but which troubled him to such a degree that he attempted to explain them away.

However, there is no denying that the trial which he has brought as plaintiff has reintroduced his name into the 1968 controversy.

The longstanding rumors that two key officers (Manuel Pena and Enrique Hernandez) in the LAPD special unit set up to investigate the assassination of Senator Kennedy also had backgrounds that identified them as having had either service or training with elements of the CIA, presumably will be dealt with during the trial.

I do not believe that the Board of Supervisors should attempt to look into most of the aspects in controversy about the Senator Kennedy assassination. The KCOP-TV trial or other formal hearings can bring out the bulk of the points in question.

However, as I stated in my note to Judge Wenke on July 18, the Board does have an interest in the quality of performance by County personnel who were involved in the handling or examination of ballistics materials, etc.

Therefore, I will prepare a motion which I will submit to you for your examination in advance of its presentation, that will call for the reexamination of certain physical elements now at issue in the Senator Kennedy case.

Los Angeles Police Department
EMPLOYEE'S REPORT

SUBJECT		
Kennedy - 187 P.C.		

DATE & TIME OCCURRED	LOCATION OF OCCURRENCE	DIVISION OF OCCURRENCE
6-5-68	Ambassador Hotel	Rampart Division

TO: (Rank, Name, Assignment, Division)	DATE & TIME REPORTED
Lt. D.W. Mann, O-I-C, Criminalistics Section, S.I.D.	7-8-68

DETAILS:

The weapon used in this case was an Iver Johnson, Cadet Model, .22 caliber, 8 shot revolver (2½" barrel). This weapon had eight expended shell casings in the cylinder at the time of recovery from the suspect. A trajectory study was made of the physical evidence which indicated that eight shots were fired as follows:

#1 - Bullet entered Senator Kennedy's head behind the right ear and was later recovered from the victim's head and booked as evidence.

#2 - Bullet passed through the right shoulder pad of Senator Kennedy's suit coat (never entered his body) and traveled upward striking victim Schrade in the center of his forehead. The bullet was recovered from his head and booked as evidence.

#3 - Bullet entered Senator Kennedy's right rear shoulder approximately seven inches below the top of the shoulder. This bullet was recovered by the Coroner from the 6th cervical vertebrae and booked as evidence.

#4 - Bullet entered Senator Kennedy's right rear back approximately one inch to the right of bullet #3. This bullet traveled upward and forward and exited the victim's body in the right front chest. The bullet passed through the ceiling tile, striking the second plastered ceiling and was lost somewhere in the ceiling interspace.

#5 - Bullet struck victim Goldstein in the left rear buttock. This bullet was recovered from the victim and booked as evidence.

#6 - Bullet passed through victim Goldstein's left pants leg (never entering his body) and struck the cement floor and entered victim Stroll's left leg. The bullet was later recovered and booked as evidence.

#7 - Bullet struck victim Weisel in the left abdomen and was recovered and booked.

#8 - Bullet struck the plaster ceiling and then struck victim Evans in the head. This bullet was recovered from the victim's head and booked as evidence.

A Walker's H-acid test was conducted on Senator Kennedy's suit coat in the area of the entrance wounds. This test indicated that the muzzle of the weapon was held at a distance of between one to six inches from the coat at the time of all firings.

DATE & TIME TYPED	DIVN. RPTG.	CLERK	EMPLOYEE(S) REPORTING	SER. NO.	DIVN.
7-8-68 10 a.m.	S.I.D.	mm	Officer DeWayne A.	#6727	S.I.D.
SUPERVISOR APPROVING		SERIAL NO.	Wolfer		
Lt. D.W. Mann		#2M5			

PROGRESS REPORT - CASE PREP TEAM - CASE PREPARATION FOR TRIAL		
TIME OCCURRED 7-5-68/7-18-68	LOCATION OF OCCURRENCE	DIVISION OF OCCURRENCE S.U.S. Homicide
TO: (Rank, Name, Assignment, Division) Lt. M. S. Pena, Supervisor, S.U.S. Unit		DATE & TIME REPORTED 7-18-68 4:30 pm

DETAILS

I. RECONSTRUCTION OF CRIME:

A. Evidence

Recording - A photograph album containing 8 x 10 photos of
pertinent evidence has been prepared. These photos include
photographs of pertinent autopsy photos (Wounds and angles),
bullets and fragments of money on suspect's person at time of
arrest and ammo boxes. There is also a stand-up color photo of
the suspect at the time of booking and a full face and side
view, black and white, standard mug shot of suspect.

Evaluation - An interview conference was held with DDA Fitts on
7-10-68. At this time DDA Fitts indicated the following items of
evidence would diffently be used at the trial: The gun used by
suspect, the bullets and fragments obtained from victims, the coat
of the late Senator Kennedy and items of evidence removed from
suspect's vehicle. No other items of evidence were discussed at
this meeting.

B. Lab Work

The Iver Johnson, Cadet Model .22 caliber revolver serial
#H53725, which was taken from Sirhan has been identified as
having fired the following bullets: (1) The bullet from Senator
Kennedy's 6th cervical vertebrae; (2) The bullet removed from
victim Goldstein; (3) The bullet removed from victim Weisel.
The remaining bullets are too badly damaged for comparison
purposes. The following could be determined from the remaining
four damaged bullets. (1) Bullet fragments from Senator Kennedy's
head were fired from a weapon with the same rifling specifications
as the Sirhan weapon and are "minimag" brand ammunition.
(2) Bullet fragments from victim Stroll had the same rifling
specifications as the Sirhan weapon and is "minimag" brand
ammunition. (3) Bullet fragments from victim Evans is "minimag"
brand ammunition. (4) Bullet fragments from victim Schrade is
"minimag" brand ammunition. All eight shots fired at the
Ambassador Hotel have been accounted for and all except one
bullet recovered.

Walker's H-acid tests indicated that the shots entering Senator
Kennedy's suit coat were fired at a muzzle distance of between
one to six inches.

Powder test indicate that the bullet which entered behind Senator
Kennedy's right ear was fired at a muzzle distance of approximately
one inch.

Four hundred-eighty nine (489), .22 caliber shells were examined
and none of the shells were found to have been fired from Sirhan
weapon. These shells had been picked up by Michael Soccoman at
the San Gabriel Valley Gun Club, as he collects brass. He thought
he might have picked up shells that had been fired by Sirhan.

DATE & TIME TYPED 7-18-68 7:30 pm	DIVN. RPTG. SUS Homi.	CLERK bju	EMPLOYEE(S) REPORTING Collins, C.	SER. NO. 6207	DIVN. SUS Homi
SUPERVISOR APPROVING _SPEC Exhibit 21_		SERIAL NO.	Patchett, F.	7872 "	"
			Mac Arthur, J.	4372 "	"

AFFIDAVIT

I, WILLIAM W. HARPER, being first duly sworn, depose as follows:

1. I am a resident of the State of California and for approximately thirty-seven years have lived at 615 Prospect Boulevard in Pasadena, California.

2. I am now and for thirty-five years have been engaged in the field of consulting criminalistics.

3. My formal academic background includes studies at Columbia University, University of California at Los Angeles and California Institute of Technology where I spent four years, including studies in physics and mathematics with the major portion devoted to physics research.

4. My practical experience and positions held include seven years as consulting criminalist to the Pasadena Police Department where I was in charge of the Technical Laboratory engaging in the technical phases of police training and all technical field investigations including those involving firearms. I was, during World War II, for three years in charge of technical investigation for Naval Intelligence in the 11th Naval District, located at San Diego, California.

After my release from the Navy, I entered private practice as a consulting criminalist. Extending over a period of 35 years I have handled roughly 300 cases involving firearms in homicides, suicides and accidental shootings. I have testified as a consulting criminalist in both criminal and civil litigations and for both defense and prosecution in both State and Federal Courts. I have qualified as an expert in the courts of California, Washington, Oregon, Texas, Nevada, Arizona and Utah. I am a Fellow of the American Academy of Forensic Sciences.

5. During the past seven months I have made a careful review and study of the physical circumstances of the assassination of Senator Robert F. Kennedy in Los Angeles, California. In this connection I have examined the physical evidence introduced at the trial, including the Sirhan weapon, the bullets and shell cases. I have also studied the autopsy report, the autopsy photographs, and pertinent portions of the trial testimony.

6. Based on my background and training, upon my experience as a consulting criminalist, and my studies, examination and analysis of data related to the Robert F. Kennedy assassination, I have arrived at the following findings and opinions:

A. An analysis of the physical circumstances at the scene of the assassination discloses that Senator Kennedy was fired upon from two distinct firing positions while he was walking through the kitchen pantry at the Ambassador Hotel. *Firing Position A,* the position of Sirhan, was located directly in front of the Senator, with Sirhan face-to-face with the Senator. This position is well established by more than a dozen eye-witnesses. A second firing position, *Firing Position B,* is clearly established by the autopsy report. It was located in close proximity to the Senator, immediately to his right and rear. It was from this position that 4 (four) shots were fired, three of which entered the Senator's body. One of these three shots made a fatal penetration of the Senator's brain. A fourth shot passed through the right shoulder pad of the Senator's coat. These four shots from Firing Position B all produced powder residue patterns, indicating they were fired from a distance of only a few inches. They were closely grouped within a 12 inch circle.

In marked contrast, the shots from *Firing Position A* produced no powder residue patterns on the bodies or clothing of any of the surviving victims, all of whom were walking behind the Senator. These shots were widely dispersed.

Senator Kennedy received no frontal wounds. The three wounds suffered by him were fired from behind and he had entrance wounds in the posterior portions of his body.

B. It is evident that a strong conflict exists between the eyewitness accounts and the autopsy findings. This conflict is totally irreconcilable with the hypothesis that only Sirhan's gun was involved in the assassination. The conflict can be eliminated if we consider that a second gun was being fired from *Firing Position B* concurrently with the firing of the Sirhan gun from *Firing Position A*. It is self-evident that within the brief period of the shooting (roughly 15 seconds) Sirhan could not have been in both firing positions at the same time.

No eyewitness saw Sirhan at any position other than *Firing Position A,* where he was quickly restrained by citizens present at that time and place.

C. It is my opinion that these circumstances, in conjunction with the autopsy report (without for the moment considering additional evidence), firmly establish that two guns were being fired in the kitchen pantry concurrently.

D. There is no reasonable likelihood that the shots from *Firing Position B* could have been fired by a person attempting to stop Sirhan. This is because the person shooting from *Firing Position B* was in almost direct body contact with the Senator. This person could have seen where his shots would strike the Senator, since the fatal shot was fired (muzzle) from one to three inches from the Senator's head. Had Sirhan been the intended target, the person shooting would have extended his arm beyond the Senator and fired directly at Sirhan. Furthermore, two of the shots from *Firing Position B* were steeply upward: one shot actually penetrating the ceiling overhead.

E. The police appear to have concluded that a total of eight shots were fired with seven bullets accounted for and one bullet unrecovered. This apparent conclusion fails to take into account that their evidence shows that a fourth shot from *Firing Position B* went through the right shoulder pad of the Senator's coat from back to front. This shot was fired from a distance of approximately one inch according to the testimony. It could not have been the shot which struck Victim Paul Schrade in the forehead since Schrade was behind the Senator and traveling in the same direction. The bullet producing this hole in the shoulder pad from back to front could not have returned by ricochet or otherwise to strike Schrade in the forehead. This fourth shot from *Firing Position B* would indicate 9 (nine) shots were fired, with two bullets unrecovered. This indication provides an additional basis for the contention that two guns were involved, since the Sirhan gun could have fired only 8 (eight) shots.

F. The prosecution testimony attempted to establish that the Sirhan gun, and no other, was involved in the assassination. It is a fact, however, that the only gun actually linked scientifically with the shooting is a second gun, not the Sirhan gun. The serial number of the Sirhan gun is No. H53725. The serial number of the second gun is No. H18602. It is also an Iver Johnson 22 cal. cadet. The expert testimony, based on matching the three test bullets of Exhibit 55 in a comparison microscope to three of the evidence bullets (Exhibit 47 removed from the Senator, Exhibit 52 removed from Goldstein and Exhibit 54 removed from Weisel) concluded that the three evidence bullets were fired from the same gun that fired the three test bullets of Exhibit 55. The physical evidence shows that the gun that fired the three test bullets was gun No. H18602, not the Sirhan gun. Thus, the only gun placed at the scene by scientific evidence is gun No. H18602. Sirhan's gun was taken from him by citizens at the scene. I have no information regarding the background history of gun No. H18602 nor how the police came into possession of it.

G. No test bullets recovered from the Sirhan gun are in evidence. This gun was never identified scientifically as having fired any of the bullets removed from any of the victims. Other than the apparent self-evident fact that gun No. H53725 was forcibly removed from Sirhan at the scene, it has not been connected by microscopic examinations or other scientific testing to the actual shooting.

H. The only reasonable conclusion from the evidence developed by the police, in spite of their protestations to the contrary, is that two guns were being fired in the kitchen pantry of the Ambassador Hotel at the time of the shooting of Senator Kennedy.

I. From the general circumstances of the shooting the only reasonable assumption is that the bullet removed from victim Weisel was in fact fired from the Sirhan gun. This bullet is in near perfect condition. I have, therefore, chosen it as a "test" bullet from the Sirhan gun and compared it with the bullet removed from the Senator's neck. The bullet removed from the Senator's neck, Exhibit 47, was one of those fired from *Firing Position B,* while the bullet removed from Weisel, Exhibit 54, was one of those fired from *Firing Position A,* the position of Sirhan. My examinations disclosed no individual characteristics establishing that Exhibit 47 and Exhibit 54 had been fired by the same gun. In fact, my examinations disclosed that bullet Exhibit 47 has a rifling angle approximately 23 minutes (14%) greater than the rifling angle of bullet Exhibit 54. It is, therefore, my opinion that bullets 47 and 54 could not have been fired from the same gun.

The above finding stands as independent proof that two guns were being fired concurrently in the kitchen pantry of the Ambassador Hotel at the time of the shooting.

J. The conclusions I have arrived at based upon my findings are as follows:

1. Two 22 calibre guns were involved in the assassination.

2. Senator Kennedy was killed by one of the shots fired from *Firing Position B,* fired by a second gunman.

3. The five surviving victims were wounded by Sirhan shooting from *Firing Position A.*

4. It is extremely unlikely that any of the bullets fired by the Sirhan gun ever struck the body of Senator Kennedy.

5. It is also unlikely that the shooting of the Senator could have accidentally resulted from an attempt to shoot Sirhan.

Dated: December 28, 1970.
William W. Harper
State of California
County of Los Angeles

On this 28th day of December, 1970, before me appeared, personally, WILLIAM W. HARPER, known to me to be the person whose name is subscribed to the within instrument, and acknowledged that he executed the same.

Notary Public in and for
said County and State

(*Seal*)

ON OR ABOUT JUNE 5-6, 1968 I, WILLIAM A. Bailey, employed at that time as a special AGENT of the FBI (ASSIGNED to the Los Angeles office) WAS present IN the PREPARATION ROOM of the AmBASSador Hotel Approx. 4-6 hours after the attempt ON Sen. Robt. F. kennedy's life. The PANTRY WAS referred to as the preparation ROOM

At that time I WAS assigned to interview witnesses present at the time of the shooting. I WAS also charged with the responsibility of recreating the CIRCUMSTANCES under which same took place. This necessitated a careful examination of the entire room + ITS contents.

At one point during these observations I (and several other AGENTS) noted at least TWO (2) small CALIBER Bullet holes in the CENTER POST of the two doors leading from the preparation Room. There was no question in any of our minds as to the fact that they were bullet holes + were not caused by food CARTS or other EQUIPMENT in the preparation Room.

I resigned from the FBI in JAN. 1971 and have been employed as AN ASSISTANT Professor of Police SCIENCE at Gloucester County College, Sewell, New Jersey since that time.

The Above STATEMENT IS IN MY PRINTING + WAS furnished freely + VOLUNTARILY to Mr. VINCENT BUGLIOSI ON NOV. 14, 1976 at GLASSBORO STATE College, GLASS BORO, New JERSEY.

William Bailey
Nov. 14, 1976

The following address was delivered on the night of April 29, 1976, at the Hollywood Palladium by Mr. Robert Vaughn

It is my distinct honor and pleasure to be here tonight, to pay tribute to a man whose election to the office of District Attorney of Los Angeles is more than merely a matter of the right man for that office. It is really an election that could be of the utmost importance to our entire nation—because of the one issue that Vincent Bugliosi, alone, has committed himself to resolve. I speak of the very serious and disturbing questions that have arisen about the death of my good friend, Robert F. Kennedy, whose murder eight years ago in this very city surely changed the course of American history.

For many years I was among those who felt that the questions of conspiracy in either of the Kennedy assassinations came from the minds of the unstable types, who were merely fantasizing when they spoke of mysterious goings on in both these cases. The real truth about myself was, however, that I did not want to believe that these personally painful deaths had been the result of more than single men. However, in mid-1972—in the midst of the many emerging truths about the Watergate affair—my mind and those of a good many other previously disinterested persons were suddenly jolted into the reality that there were things going on within the government of this nation that had no place in a democracy—and the thought of assassination fitting into the mould of these events suddenly was no longer unthinkable. In fact, as the months rolled by and the endless details about Watergate and the "dirty tricks" of the FBI and the CIA began to surface, I became alarmed that such might possibly have been involved in the assassination of the Kennedys, Martin Luther King, and the attempt on the life of Governor George C. Wallace.

I have no doubt that a good many of you here tonight have had this same experience. And I have no doubt at all that the vast majority of our fellow citizens across this country now share this same concern.

At this moment, in the Congress of the United States, there are two legislative measures pending that propose to re-open the investigations into all these cases. These bills are co-sponsored by Republicans and Democrats, Liberals and Conservatives and Independents alike. It is no longer a partisan debate in Washington, D. C. It is serious business by men and women we have elected to represent and protect our interests and rights—the most important of which is the ability for us to freely elect the President of our choice; and the fact of the matter is that since the re-election of Dwight D. Eisenhower in 1956 we have not had a

Presidential election that has not been altered or distorted by the assassination process.

John Kennedy was gunned down in Dallas as he prepared for re-election in 1964—and Robert Kennedy died as he moved into a most viable position in 1968. Then in 1972 Governor George Wallace was felled as he gathered an enormous number of votes—and again, bullets, not ballots, produced a twisted outcome in the Presidential race.

And here we are now in 1976, in the midst of the most turbulent of times for this nation, with no less than eight men running for the office of President. Is there any one amongst us here tonight that has not pondered the thought that maybe—just maybe—another assassination could be upon us at any time?! I think not.

That's why the election of Vincent Bugliosi at this time is an imperative. If there is some kind of sinister force loose in this country that has been systematically cutting down our finest leaders, there is only one man in this country with the proven abilities and courage to seek out the truth and bring about justice; and the Robert Kennedy assassination is where he will begin, the instant he takes the oath of office. He is my good friend, Vince Bugliosi.

Index

Hoover's FBI (Turner), 24
Hope, Bob, 5
Hopkins, John, 4, 121, 122–23, 124,
233, 236, 246, 306, 307
Houghton, Chief Robert A., 46, 61–64,
75–77, 78, 81, 82, 113, 114, 116,
123, 137, 138, 143, 169, 216
House Un-American Activities Com-
mittee, 30
Houts, Marshall W., 161
Howard, John, 111, 114
Howe, Charlie, 29
Hughes, Lieutenant Charles, 75–76
Hull, Dianne, 239, 240, 281, 309–10
Humphrey, Hubert H., xiii, xv, 209,
267
Humphreys, Inspector, 127
Hunt, H. L., 142
Hunt, Lamar, 142
Hunt, Nelson Bunker, 142
Hyman, Lester, 309, 310, 312, 321
Hypnotic Induction Profile, 203
Hypnotism Comes of Age (Wolfe and
Rosenthal), 206–7
Hypnotism and Crime (Hammerschlag),
212

Illuminati, the, 54–58, 217, 218, 219
In Cold Blood (Capote), 314
Indianapolis *News*, 7, 8
Indict and Convict (Davidson), 102
*International Journal of Clinical and
Experimental Hypnosis*, 203
International Society of Stress Analysis,
211
*Invisible Witness: The Use and Abuse
of the New Technology of Crime
Investigation* (Turner), 24
Isaac, Godfrey, 164, 215, 320
Israel, 106, 209
It Comes Up Murder (Steinbacher),
55–56, 203

Jackson, Dennis, 14, 297
Jacobs, Mabel, 96
Jerry Owen Investigation (SUS sum-
mary report), 46–48
John Birch Society, 55, 60, 129, 161,
204, 267
Johnson, Darnell, 70–71
Johnson, Lyndon B., xiii, 22, 27, 62
Joling, Dr. Robert J., xi–xii, 164–65,
172, 320

Jordan, Lieutenant William C., 76, 197
Judge Jefferson's Evidence Book, 286

KABC (radio station), 226
Kaiser, Robert Blair, 44, 81, 91, 94–95,
105, 107, 110–13, 125–26, 149–50,
152, 169, 170, 196, 216, 221, 312
Katz, Roger, 187
KCBS (radio station), 22
KCOP-TV lawsuit, 3–4, 8–18, 122, 123,
155, 230–308, 309; beginning of,
230–31; Bugliosi's affirmative defense, 246–78; Powers testimony,
10–18; RFK assassination issue,
231, 233, 238, 241, 243, 246–308,
309
Keene, Lieutenant Roy, 99
Kelley, Clarence, 315
Kendall, John, 174–75
Kendrin Community Mental Health
Center, 289
Kennedy, Senator Edward, xv, 56, 90,
309
Kennedy, John F., xi, 12, 19, 35, 51,
143, 152, 260, 309, 317; assassination of, xiv, 34, 57, 59, 63, 86,
87, 125, 204, 226; assassination
issue (campaign of 1968), 20–30;
extracurricular romances, 24–25
Kennedy, Robert F.: California primary,
26; convention nomination of, 27;
Justice Department and, 22; suspicion of JFK's death, 26–27; on
the Warren Report, 26
Kennedy (Robert F.) assassination conspiracy and cover-up: firearms evidence, 157–91; hitchhiker story,
31–50, 87, 88–94, 115, 121, 137,
219, 238, 257, 270, 298; international plot charges (and Sirhan
as the pawn), 51–60; introduction
to, xi–xii; investigative file, 84–
103; KCOP-TV lawsuit, 3–4, 8–
18, 122, 123, 155, 230–308, 309;
"Manchurian Candidate" theory,
191, 192–211; 1968 campaign and,
20–30; Owen's story, 31–50; polka-
dot-dress-girl issue, 61–83, 84, 85,
88, 92, 115, 193; second-gun controversy, 158, 162, 163, 165–91,
311, 312; Sirhan trial, 104—16;
Weatherley Report, 125–29, 149,
266, 298

ABOUT THE AUTHORS

JONN G. CHRISTIAN, a naval airman during the Korean War, was a broadcast newsman for the American Broadcasting Company until 1966, when he developed an interest in the John F. Kennedy assassination controversy. He soon discovered that the official version (The Warren Commission Report) was untenable and sought out the involvement of high-level political leaders—including Robert F. Kennedy.

WILLIAM W. TURNER, a Navy veteran of World War II, was an FBI special agent from 1951 to 1961 when he turned to journalism. He has written for magazines ranging from *Playboy* to *The Nation* and is the author of *The Police Establishment* and *Hoover's FBI*. He became involved in the assassination investigation of President Kennedy immediately after the shooting when he flew to Dallas on assignment to look into the breakdown in security.

The authors teamed up in early 1968 when Turner ran in a Democratic primary for a U.S. congressional seat on the platform that a joint Senate-House committee should be established to reinvestigate the JFK assassination. His campaign brochure read: "To do less not only is indecent but might cost us the life of a future President of John Kennedy's instincts."